CRIMES
OF WAR

Crimes of War: What the Public Should Know.
Copyright © 1999 by Crimes of War Project

Concept: Gilles Peress
Editors: Roy Gutman and David Rieff
Legal Editor: Kenneth Anderson
Consultant, Military Law: General A.P.V. Rogers
General Counsel: Ron Goldfarb
Project Manager: Peggy Lampl
Deputy Project Manager: Alan Dorsey
Design: Jeff Streeper with Brooke Hellewell
Photo Editing/Research: Sheryl A. Mendez

The text of this book is composed in Officina Sans
with the display set in Officina Sans.
Composition by 3 Dragons, Ltd.
Manufacturing by Tien Wan Press.

Library of Congress Cataloging-in-Publication Data

Crimes of war : what the public should know /
Roy Gutman and David Rieff, editors.
        p.   cm.
Includes bibiliographical references.
ISBN 0-393-04746-6—0-393-31914-8 (pbk.)
1. War crimes. I. Gutman,Roy. II. Rieff, David.
K5301.C75   1999
341.6'9—dc21

For information contact:
W.W. Norton & Company, Inc.
500 Fifth Avenue
New York, New York 10110
http:www.wwnorton.com

W.W. Norton & Company Ltd.,
10 Coptic Street
London WC1A 1PU

1 2 3 4 5 6 7 8 9 0

CRIMES OF WAR

OF WAR

WHAT THE PUBLIC SHOULD KNOW

Edited by Roy Gutman and David Rieff
Legal Editor Kenneth Anderson

W. W. NORTON & COMPANY   NEW YORK · LONDON

TABLE OF CONTENTS

PREFACE

By Roy Gutman and David Rieff

In the early 1990s, while Western leaders were still congratulating themselves over the end of communism and the fall of the Soviet empire, the security structure that helped bring about those events began to come apart. The American-led North Atlantic alliance that had for four decades effectively counterbalanced the Russian domination of eastern Europe proved incapable of dealing with a single Yugoslav despot, Slobodan Milosevic. The alliance that had confronted the prospect of nuclear apocalypse could not develop a coherent response to a small conventional conflict in southeastern Europe.

War had returned to the European continent. First in Croatia and then in Bosnia, it was being fought seemingly without respect for the rules of warfare that had been drafted in the wake of World War II and the Holocaust. These codes of conduct in war were a lesser-known element in the architecture of international security put into place after 1945. They were an effort to prevent a repetition of the worst of the abuses of World War II: the concentration camps, the mass deportations, the terror bombing. They enabled postwar governments in Europe and North America to at least assure their publics that the lessons had been learned and standards set.

It is no exaggeration to say that these codes were intended to establish, even in war, a firebreak between civilization and barbarism. The Nuremberg Tribunals of 1945 set down the principle that there were such things as crimes against humanity, systematic crimes against civilians that can occur inside a country but that might be tried anywhere else. The Genocide Convention of 1948 gave legal meaning and force to the worst crime in the lexicon. The 1949 Geneva Conventions codified and advanced the rules governing wars between States, differentiating legal conduct from illegal and criminal acts in war. Together with the two Additional Protocols of 1977, the Geneva Conventions are the central summation of the agreed rules governing the conduct of war. Scholars and humanitarian organizations, hoping to emphasize the protections under law for noncombatants, call this field international humanitarian law. Militaries prefer to speak of the laws of war, and include in that definition the issues connected with the causes of war.

In well-off Western countries, the canons of international humanitarian law took hold—once the sometimes savage colonial wars had ended. Contrast, say, the American military's conduct in Vietnam, where many of the standards of international humanitarian law were violated, with its attempt to adhere scrupulously to these norms in the Gulf War. Unfortunately, the locus of conflict shifted to the poor world, where governments and insurgent groups routinely have disregarded the legal regime. And in the immediate post–Cold War era, no major Western power felt it had any stake in Third World conflicts unless oil was involved.

Small wonder, then, that less than two years after the fall of the Berlin Wall, the structure of international humanitarian law seemed on the brink of collapse. It took a war in Europe—Croatia in 1991—to stir public interest. The war in Bosnia-Herzegovina (1992), the Rwandan genocide (1994), and Chechnya (1995) amplified the alarm bell, though it should have been sounded a good deal earlier.

Bosnia was the trigger. In the heart of "civilized" Europe, Serbian forces had set up concentration camps, deported non-Serbs in cattle cars, destroyed towns and villages, organized the systematic rape of Croat and Muslim women, and targeted civilians in the name of ethnic cleansing. The great Western alliance watched passively, and were it not for the glare of media attention as had occurred more than two decades earlier in Vietnam, and the public outcry in western Europe and North America, the savagery might have had no bounds.

In response to the public outcry, major powers sent in food and medicine and UN forces to monitor the distribution of aid, but more as an excuse to deflect public opinion than a policy response that squarely addressed the cause of a man-made disaster. Belatedly, and well after the worst crimes had occurred, major powers set up the first war crimes tribunals since Nuremberg, first for Bosnia and then in Rwanda. They did so, at least in part, in response to pressure from human rights, relief, religious, and other nongovernmental organizations and from the news media.

This, in itself, was a singular departure. Nongovernmental organizations and committed individuals can rightly claim credit for the conception, drafting, and adoption in 1948 of the UN Universal Declaration on Human Rights and the Genocide Convention, but the public historically have been bit players in curbing crimes of war. The implementation of international standards had always been up to governments, the militaries, and the Geneva-based International Committee of the Red Cross, which for over a century has helped in the drafting, oversight, and implementation of the Geneva Conventions.

No one yet knows whether the rise to prominence of nongovernmental organizations will help shift the responsibility toward a world order based on collaboration between governments, intergovernmental organizations like the United Nations, and private groups. Perhaps, on the other hand, the talk of entering an era of international law and ending the old hard edged conception of State sovereignty is overstated. Whatever structures of world politics emerge in the next century, the editors and writers of this book—lawyers, journalists, and scholars—contend that the laws of war belong to everyone. They are among the great achievements of civilization, and in this era of uncertainty and disorder, more relevant than ever.

For the time being, accountability is not the rule, but the exception, in conflict. And realistically, international humanitarian law will not take hold without the support of governments. But as public interest grows in international humanitarian law, and this once esoteric field begins to generate news, a sense of change is in the air. Whether the story concerns the sentencing for genocide of a Rwandan mayor—the first such sentence handed down since Nuremberg—the effort to send war crimes investigators to Kosovo, a Spanish prosecutor's attempt to put the former Chilean dictator Augusto Pinochet on trial for crimes against his people, or the U.S.

government decision to award a bounty of up to $5 million for the capture of indicted Bosnian war criminals, the pattern represents a radical shift.

The question now is whether the new paradigm will prove enduring, and whether the rule of law set out in international treaties can truly be made to apply to conflict. There is ample reason for skepticism. What is certain is that it will not happen without public awareness and public engagement. And without a command of the most basic facts about the laws of war, there can be neither.

The need is pressing. Wars today increasingly are fought not between armies where officers are bound by notions of honor but by fighters, many of them children, who are not soldiers in any conventional sense of the word. The goal of these conflicts is often ethnic cleansing—the forcible expulsion of the civilian population of one's enemy—not the victory of one army over another.

The principal victims of this kind of war—slaughter is often the better term for it—are civilians. As horrible as the death toll was in World War I, the millions who died were, by and large, killed on the battlefield—soldiers killed by soldiers, not civilians killed by lawless or random or planned savagery. The rough proportion of military to civilian casualties was ninety to ten. In World War II, the proportions were roughly even. Today, for every ten military casualties there are on the order of ninety civilian deaths. The reality of our era, as demonstrated in Angola, Somalia, Bosnia, Rwanda, and Chechnya, is that torture is rampant, murdering civilians commonplace, and driving the survivors from their homes often the main goal of a particular military offensive.

This book is published on the eve of the fiftieth anniversary—in August 1999—of the Geneva Conventions, with the aim of encouraging public knowledge of the principles of conduct in war. It consists of three types of articles. The heart of the law, and of this book, are the grave breaches, or serious war crimes, delineated in the four Geneva Conventions of 1949 and the First Additional Protocol of 1977. The editors sought to find a clear example of each breach, irrespective of countries or adversaries, and then asked working reporters who had been at the scene to provide a graphic case study of what they had seen. These articles are labeled, *crime*. Leading scholars in the United States and abroad contributed shorter articles on technical topics, most labeled *the law*. There are also essay-length articles by journalists or scholars on major themes, labeled *key terms*. To provide a broader overview of contemporary conflict, the editors asked reporters and one historian to take a fresh and critical look at recent conflicts and examine them in the light of the crimes of war. These ten case studies offer insights into the dynamics of crimes in nine wars (Rwanda is addressed twice from different perspectives) and can be read as a book within a book. Complementing the case studies are three experts' overviews of the applicable law: "Categories of War Crimes" by Steven Ratner, "Crimes against Humanity" by Cherif Bassiouni, and "Genocide" by Diane Orentlicher. Every article was vetted by our legal editor, Kenneth Anderson, his colleagues at American University's Washington College of Law, and by leading military law experts in the United States and Britain.

The A-to-Z format, the use of bold-face type to indicate cross-references, and the graphic design are intended to make the book easy to use, and the photographs to provide visual bookmarks, while documenting the reality behind the words. The texts recount some of the most compelling reportage of contemporary journalism. Sydney Schanberg's case study of Cambodia, Roger Cohen's article on ethnic cleansing in Bosnia, Gwynne

Roberts's account of the gassing of Kurdish civilians in Halabja and the after-math, Frank Smyth's tale of arrest in Iraq, Ed Vulliamy's account on concentration camps, and Corinne Dufka's account of child soldiers in Liberia are a few of the articles that provide the *raison d'être* for this book.

Some contributions offer unique insights into military issues for the nonmilitary. For example, Wayne Elliott's article on POWs tells reporters or anyone visiting or inspecting a POW camp what to look for. Elliott demonstrates how merely asking questions can put the spotlight on the observance or infraction of the rules, reminding commanders that the world is watching them. Hamilton DeSaussure's essay on military objectives will alert readers to the moral debate the military officer should go through before deciding what to attack and what to spare.

Crimes of War was conceived as a handbook for reporters. But just as war is too important to be left to the generals, war coverage is too important to be left uncritically to the news media. The general public, too, should know the moral and legal benchmarks contained in the law. One reason for a commonality of interest is that coverage of contemporary conflicts increasingly is available to the public without a filter or a framework or context. A second is that every close observer has a restricted field of vision.

Journalists who cover wars and humanitarian emergencies of the post-Cold War world know far better than their audiences or their critics how much they are operating in uncharted territory. Understanding what is going on in the midst of all the havoc, confusion, and disinformation is anything but simple. And almost nothing in their training prepares reporters to be able make the necessary distinctions between legal, illegal, and criminal acts. Is it a war crime under international law or a horrible, destructive, but legal act of war when one sees a hospital being shelled in Sarajevo, a humanitarian aid convoy blocked at a checkpoint on the Dagestan-Chechen border, or combat in which no prisoners are taken in Sri Lanka? Is it a legitimate sanction on the part of a State when the homes of alleged terrorists are reduced to rubble, as happens regularly in Israel, or is it a war crime? When combatants insert themselves amongst the civilian population, as was the case in Vietnam and more recently in Rwanda, does this violate the international conventions?

The best single indicator of a major war crime often is a massive displacement of civilians. But people may be fleeing for their lives from the scene of crime or the immediate threat of crimes, as in South Sudan at many points during the civil war there; or because their leaders ordered them out, but are intending to return militarily to destroy the other side, as the Serbs fleeing Croatian Slavonia did in 1991. They may be fleeing at the insistence of their political leaders, who intend to depict them as the victims of crime, as in the case of the Tajiks who fled into Afghanistan in 1993; or because they and their leaders have committed massive crimes and fear justice or retribution, as in the case of the Rwandan Hutus who fled into eastern Zaire in 1994 in the wake of the genocide. Determinations such as these are hard to make in the best of circumstances, but all the more so under deadline pressure.

Sometimes the laws of war are frustratingly counterintuitive. International humanitarian law, as the contents of this book exemplify, does not address the causes or origins of a particular war, or which side was right and which side was wrong, only the method by which it is fought. So it is entirely possible, for example, for an aggressor to stage a war of conquest in accordance with the Geneva Conventions or for a defender to commit war crimes in a legitimate war of self-defense. But the fact that the law cannot answer every question, or shield us from every moral dilemma that war occasions, does not mean it has no answers or provides no bulwark against barbarism and crime.

In any case, understanding, while always difficult, is never more so than in war when the lure of easy explanations may be hard to resist. The British journalist Lindsey Hilsum maintains that when a journalist reports that the situation on the ground is one of anarchy, or resorts to such reductive clichés as describing a particular conflict as the product of ancient ethnic or tribal hatreds, the chances are that he or she has not fully understood what was going on.

Obviously, journalists have a primary role, but they are not the only people focused on the brutality of contemporary conflict. Groups such as Human Rights Watch, Amnesty International, and the German Society for Threatened Peoples increasingly have turned their focus to violations of humanitarian law; but they cannot take on the entire responsibility of uncovering crimes of war. Watch groups have exceptional expertise and devoted staffers, but they also have finite resources and may arrive late at the scene, have limited access, and are sometimes slow to produce their reports. And like many private groups, dependent on external fund raising, each has its separate mandate and agenda.

Relief and aid workers in the field have become the eyes and ears of the world in conflict zones. Usually, they are the first on the scene and the last to leave. But their mandate and their training usually does not encompass trying to stop or even report on war crimes, and they are at risk of expulsion, with all that this entails for the endangered populations they are trying to serve, if they publicly cross that line. Yet knowledge of what is legal, illegal, and criminal in warfare will permit them or any other observers to alert those who do have the mandate and the means to inform the world or to act.

For the general public, *Crimes of War* should make it possible to become better informed consumers of the news by laying out the benchmarks for monitoring the watchdogs and governments. Just what steps governments should take to counter wholesale violations of the codes of war is not the subject of this book. Sometimes merely turning the spotlight on gross violations of humanitarian law can affect behavior in a small theater of war; other times, as in the Balkans, only military intervention or the threat of it can do any good. Our hope is that if the principles of law are widely understood, and if the news media and other observers present the relevant facts to the public, informed debate will provide the answers.

Joseph Pulitzer put it most succinctly when he wrote, "There is not a crime which does not live in secrecy. Get these things out in the open, describe them, attack them, ridicule them in the press, and sooner or later, public opinion will sweep them away." That, at least, is the hope of those who have contributed to this book.

Auschwitz, Poland, 1979.

FOREWORD

By Richard Goldstone

Reporters and other observers at the frontline of conflict often voice frustration that their reports and efforts hardly dent the public consciousness and do little to change an intolerable situation; but the fact is that accurate, timely, and thoughtful coverage of war crimes can have an impact far beyond any immediate calculation.

Perhaps the most dramatic recent example of the impact of that kind of reporting is the establishment of the United Nations International Criminal Tribunal for the Former Yugoslavia. Visual and written reports of the plight of the victims of ethnic cleansing in Bosnia jolted the Security Council into taking the unprecedented step of creating a court as its own sub-organ. Never before had it even been contemplated or suggested that it should use its peacekeeping powers to that end. That ethnic cleansing was happening in Europe and that the Cold War had come to an end were crucial to the endeavor. There can be no doubt, however, that it was media exposure that triggered the decision.

When I arrived in The Hague as the first chief prosecutor of the tribunal, its credibility was at a low ebb in consequence of the unconscionable delays by the UN in committing the resources necessary to enable it to begin its work properly. Many in the international community doubted whether the politicians really intended or wished it to become an effective body. I was keenly aware that without media support the tribunal would have floundered. In my first year in office I spent a substantial part of my time briefing journalists from many countries. With very few exceptions they wished the tribunal to succeed and they responded to my calls for positive and supportive coverage.

Even our early small advances received wide media coverage. I refer, for example, to Germany deferring to the jurisdiction of the tribunal in the case of Dusko Tadic, who was accused of war crimes and crimes against humanity in the Bosnian War; and the publicity given to the earlier indictments albeit against so-called small fish. The nongovernmental organization (NGO) community added its voice in helping to mobilize public opinion and pressurize governments. This support played a vital role in convincing the General Assembly to devote considerable funds to the tribunal. As a result, too, some governments began to take their obligations more seriously. Domestic legislation was passed by the parliaments of a number of countries to enable their authorities to comply with requests and orders of the tribunal. Pressure was placed on the warring parties to cooperate with the prosecutor's office—

some did so, and that made it more difficult for others not to. That there was nothing like full compliance was a source of frustration and disappointment. The point is that without the public attention the tribunal would have failed early in its life.

Now that the international community is on the way to creating a permanent criminal court and the work of the two ad hoc tribunals continues apace, it is time to ask what lessons have already been learned. Perhaps the most important concerns the difficult challenge of combining high quality reporting of situations of conflict with news value. There is a general lack of public understanding of humanitarian law, which places an additional burden on journalists reporting on these matters. Also, the relationship between war correspondents and international courts has already created a tension.

As international tribunals are established, journalism has gained a new and as yet undefined dimension. Journalists have very different mandates, modes of operating, routes to access information, and thresholds of proof in comparison with judicial bodies. The two functions should not be confused. It is important that reporters stay reporters—that is, uncover and write the story (and the story behind the story) for the general public.

Yet often there is overlap. A practical example: In 1991 a group of South African policemen shot into crowd of fifty thousand demonstrators outside Johannesburg. Many were killed and many more injured. As usual in such situations there were contradictory accounts of what gave rise to the shooting. I was appointed by then-President de Klerk to investigate the incident. A few days before the public inquiry was due to begin a videotape was delivered anonymously to my chambers at the courthouse. It showed the police lining up and the front of the crowd in the minutes before and at the time of the shooting. This footage played a material role in enabling me to conclude that the shooting was unjustified and that the policemen who fired were criminally responsible for their conduct. The policemen were prosecuted and the government paid substantial damages to the victims and survivors. One can imagine the agonizing which preceded the decision on the part of the reporting team to send me the videotape—how they weighed the general rule of not providing such evidence for court proceedings against the unique proof they had of the events in question. Judging by the crowd's reaction to them, I had a strong suspicion that the film was produced by a crew of an American television company. Whoever they were, I was most grateful for their action, which enabled many innocent victims to obtain a large measure of justice. So far as I am aware, the video was never broadcast, and this illustrates the uncertain tension that journalists feel about publishing or broadcasting controversial events without knowing the precise limits of the law or law enforcement.

A better knowledge of the laws of war, to which this book makes a unique contribution, will improve the quality of reporting and enhance public awareness. The parties to conflict usually know what is legal, what is illegal, and what is criminal conduct in war. But reporters do not and they should, as should the public. War is likely to be with us for some time to come. Humanitarian law pragmatically accepts the reality of war, as must we all. If carefully applied, knowledge of that law will assist the public in grasping a critical but often hidden dynamic in conflict.

Injudicious use of the terminology of the laws of war runs the risk for the observer of missing the mark, diluting the impact. Parties to a conflict, particularly those accused of war crimes, may actually stage the commission of atrocities, complete with witnesses, photos, and tapes, as part of a ruthless propaganda campaign to win sympathy and political support. A knowledge of the relevant law would enable reporters to ask pertinent questions and help them determine what is important to investigate—most likely, of course, at great risk to themselves. Hence there's an even greater need for measures to protect journalists.

There are now added reasons to encourage interest in this body of law. One is the rapid development of humanitarian law, especially since the atrocities in the former Yugoslavia and Rwanda, and the work of the two tribunals in interpreting what had been vague, often contradictory or confusing statements of the law.

Should the role of reporters extend to taking part in tribunal prosecutions? This is not covered in the conventions, nor is it likely to be. Not infrequently journalists come across evidence of war crimes—as eyewitnesses, in discovering a mass grave, or through being privy to statements made by commanders in the heat of action. Like aid workers and Red Cross or Red Crescent delegates, if reporters become identified as would-be witnesses, their safety and future ability to be present at a field of battle will be compromised. In my opinion the law takes too little account of that reality.

I would therefore support a rule of law to protect journalists from becoming unwilling witnesses in situations that would place them or their colleagues in future jeopardy. As already indicated, the same should apply to humanitarian aid workers and Red Cross or Red Crescent delegates. They should not be compelled to testify lest they give up their ability to work in the field, but they may of course testify voluntarily.

As this century comes to an end there is a paradox. Humanitarian law and international human rights law have never been more developed; yet never before have so many innocent civilians been the victims of war crimes, and never before have human rights been violated more frequently. This state of affairs will not improve absent a mechanism to enforce those laws and the norms they embody. The international community is coming to realize this— hence the two ad hoc tribunals and the move toward a permanent International Criminal Court. Reporters are entitled to much credit for these positive developments. If these new enforcement mechanisms are to succeed they will need the continued vigilance of the media and greater public awareness. To that end this unique publication is an invaluable resource.

Near the Rwandan border, Zaire, 1994.

International Humanitarian Law: An Overview

By Lawrence Weschler

Justice may be many things these days at the Yugoslavia War Crimes Tribunal in The Hague, but one thing it decidedly is not is swift. At times the pace of the proceedings in the court's main hearing chamber— a gleaming, light-filled, technologically almost-futuristic cubicle encapsulated behind a wall of bulletproof glass—can seem positively Dickensian. The proceedings tend to lurch forward and then become bogged down in a thicket of minute-seeming legalistic distinctions, and there are mornings when even the most attentive mind can wander.

One such morning a while back I found my own attention wandering into a book of history I'd brought along just in case—though of Holland, as it happened, not of Yugoslavia. I was reading about the earliest stages of human habitation of the Netherlands in the lowland marshes and swampfields north of the Rhine River delta, terrain much of whose elevation is pitched so low that it was regularly subject to catastrophic flooding. It was not all that surprising, therefore, to learn that through many centuries this muddy floodplain went largely uninhabited and that it wasn't until around the year 800 that the first tentative forays at serious colonization were undertaken as tiny communities pitched precarious clusters of hovels atop artificially piled mounds, known as terps.

With the passing generations, some of these terps were in turn joined together by painstakingly raised landbridges, which served both as connecting paths and as protective dikes. Any given triangle, say, of such dikes, joining together three outlying terps, incidentally proved capable of shielding the terrain it enclosed from outside flooding, but that only led to a new problem: what to do with all the rain and groundwater trapped and festering within the enclosure. Initial attempts at draining these patches of pestilential marshland, the so-called polders, have been documented as early as 1150, but the real breakthrough came with the introduction of windmills in the fifteenth and especially the sixteenth centuries. Eventually "gangs" of dozens of coordinated windmills were being deployed, each in turn raising the stagnant marshwaters a few inches up and over the dikes and into a surrounding network of irrigation and navigation canals. Polder after polder was thus reclaimed—hundreds, thousands, and presently hundreds of thousands of acres of uncommonly fertile land in a process that continues to this day.

Half-listening to the drone of the ongoing trial, I suddenly realized how in a sense the judges and prosecutors and investigators there in The Hague had set themselves a remarkably similar sort of reclamatory challenge. The tribunal's founding president and chief judge, the Italian Antonio Cassese; its founding prosecutor, the South African Richard Goldstone; and his replacement, the Canadian Louise Arbour, have all repeatedly cast their work in terms of an attempt to stem the historic cycle of floodtides of ethnic bloodletting that recurrently afflict places like the former Yugoslavia, or Rwanda, the other principal locus of the tribunal's mandate. In both places, these jurists have repeatedly insisted, the propensity for ethnic mayhem is far from endemic or inevitable. "For the great majority of their histories," as Justice Goldstone insisted early on, "the Croats and Serbs and Muslims, and the Tutsis and the Hutus, have lived in relative peace with one another, and they were all doing so relatively nicely until just recently. Such interethnic violence usually gets stoked by specific individuals intent on immediate political or material advantage, who then call forth the legacies of earlier and previously unaddressed grievances. . . . It is they, not the group as a whole, who need to be held to account, through a fair and meticulously detailed presentation of the evidence, precisely so that the next time around no one will be able to claim that all Serbs did this, or all Croats or all Hutus—so that people will be able to see how it is specific individuals in their communities who are continually endeavoring to manipulate them in that fashion. I really believe that is the only way the cycle can be broken."

In this context, it occurred to me that each of these individual prosecutions was like a single mound, a terp cast out upon the moral swampland of the war's aftermath—and the entire tribunal enterprise a system of interconnected dikes and sluices and pumps and windmills and canals designed to reclaim for each of the regions the possibility of a fertile regeneration.

But the tribunals weren't merely attempting to reclaim such a possibility for Yugoslavia and Rwanda alone. Sitting there in the spectator's gallery at the tribunal, I recalled that old jurists' saw to the effect that if international law exists at the vanishing point of law, the law of war exists, even more emphatically, at the vanishing point of international law; and it occurred to me how there, on the infinite marshy borderland, these jurists and lawyers and investigators, and the diplomats who'd carved out the immediate occasion for their labors, and the human rights monitors and (yes) the journalists who'd painstakingly (and often at great risk) gathered up the initial shards and planks required for their effort, were all engaged—fact by fact, testimony by testimony, case by case—in the latest instance of a decades-long, at times maddeningly halting, vexed, and compromised effort to expand the territory of law itself.

I say "decades-long," but in fact people have been working this border terrain for centuries and indeed millennia. The marshland into which the current pioneers have been inserting their tentative new foundations is hardly virgin territory, and they have continually been coming upon the waterlogged ruins of earlier efforts, bulwarks that seemed to hold for a time but then crumpled and are now having to be reconceived. We moderns pride ourselves on our various treaties, conventions, proclamations, and protocols—as though we were the first ever to have conceived of such a daft and brilliant scheme (the placing, after all, of humane constraints upon the very practice of war!)—but centuries ago there were already entire systems in place (the product, in part of carefully elaborated disputations by thinkers ranging from Augustine through Aquinas). Consider, for example, the remarkable sway of chivalry in medieval Europe (or, alternatively, of the various samurai codes in Tokugawa Japan): the way everything from the requirements for proper warning through behavior on the battlefield, treatment of noncombatants, the

protection of prisoners, and the victor's responsibilities following his opponent's surrender were all meticulously stipulated, stipulations which in turn
were often rigorously observed for fear of loss of knightly honor (a disgrace
more scathing, in some instances, than defeat itself). Of course, such codes
had their limits. For one thing, in the case of chivalry, they tended to rely on
fairly stylized face-to-face relations between combatants (as much a product
of the imperatives of ransom as those of mercy) and hence failed to survive
the introduction of munitions and artillery into the battlefield. Beyond that,
they were tied to notions of Christian nobility and therefore tended to get
jettisoned when the war-making involved non-Christian opponents, as in the
unspeakably gruesome Crusades. And when Christendom itself began breaking
up, with the onset of the Protestant Reformation, Christians took to treating
each other as heathen heretics. The wars of religion that ravaged sixteenth
and seventeenth century Europe were among the most harrowing and anarchic of all time, and much of the early theorizing behind what was to become
the modern law of war (from Grotius through Montaigne and Rousseau) arose
in the appalled shadow of such seemingly limitless mayhem.

The most recent campaign to plot and posit an international humanitarian legal order (a law, that is, of war, governing the interactions between
combatant forces and between those forces and noncombatants during times
of military conflict—as opposed to the doctrine of human rights more generally conceived, which is understood to apply to all people at all times) is
generally thought to have gotten launched in the mid-nineteenth century,
in part as a response to the exponential increase in the potential for mayhem
occasioned by the convergence of mass conscription and technological
progress. During the Crimean War of 1854, for example, eighty thousand
members of the three hundred thousand in the Franco-British expeditionary
force perished under conditions of horrendous disorder and distress. Five
years later, in June 1859, when a huge Austrian army clashed with a Franco-
Italian force in the Battle of Solferino, close to forty thousand died within
just a few days—with the majority, perhaps, expiring due to untreated
wounds. A young Swiss businessman named Jean-Henri Dunant, happening
upon the scene, was so "seized with horror and pity" that he dedicated the
rest of his life to addressing the appalling situation. He established the
International Committee of the Red Cross in 1863 and then convened an
international conference that culminated in the Geneva Convention of 1864
"for the amelioration of the conditions of the wounded in armies in the
field." During those same years, in America, with the Civil War raging,
though with a specific eye toward the requirements of the peace that would
need to follow, President Abraham Lincoln authorized a New York professor,
Francis Lieber, to prepare a draft of the rules of military engagement, especially as regards the treatment of prisoners of war; the Lieber Code, which
Lincoln thereupon promulgated as binding on all Union forces, was to have
a profound effect on subsequent such codifications.

International humanitarian law, as it was to develop over the next century, was determinedly agnostic on the question of the legality of war itself.
Phrased differently, it assumed war as a given and strove to channel its
excesses. For a long while, the principal tracks upon which this process
occurred were associated with two cities—The Hague, where conferences in
1899 and 1907 tended to focus on the conduct of war (permissible weapons
and the like); and Geneva, where further conventions, under the auspices of
the League of Nations in 1925 and the International Committee of the Red
Cross in 1929, 1949, and 1977, built on the work of the original 1864 convention. These conferences often tended to address the toxic legacy of the

immediately prior war. The 1925 Geneva Protocol, for example, prohibited the use of poisonous gases and biological weapons. The four Geneva Conventions of 1949 dealt, respectively, with the wounded and sick on land; the wounded, sick, and shipwrecked at sea; prisoners of war; and perhaps most significantly, the fate of civilian noncombatants. A 1954 convention in The Hague addressed the protection of cultural monuments. And two 1977 protocols to the 1949 Geneva Conventions, the fruit of a marathon three-year drafting session, among other things partially extended the terms of those earlier conventions on international conflicts to wars of national liberation and civil wars. The Nuremberg Tribunals of Nazi leaders (and to a lesser extent the Tokyo Trials of Japanese officials) staked out new territory with the development and promulgation of the notion of "crimes against humanity," territory further consolidated in 1948 with the United Nations Convention on the Prevention and Punishment of the Crime of Genocide.

The past century and a half, in short, has seen a remarkable project of constructive expansion out there on the infinite borderland. Indeed, the interconnecting bulwarks and dikes and bastions of international humanitarian law constitute one of the true wonders of our age—the astonishing and heartening achievement of generations of legal and diplomatic artisans. Their masterful monument has proven, at best, of only middling effectiveness. The porous ramparts sag and leak, and seem subject to random collapse.

Although the various conventions and codes project a magisterial all-inclusiveness, what they've most pointedly lacked, at least until recently, has been any effective means of enforcing their magisterial norms, and specifically of holding individuals criminally accountable, both to their victims and to the entire world community, for their violation. True, such individual prosecutions formed the core of the Nuremberg and Tokyo trials, but those prosecutions were arguably instances of victor's justice and in any case there weren't any other such trials for almost fifty years thereafter. There have been internal national human rights prosecutions following the collapse of dictatorships—Greece, Argentina, Ethiopia—and there have been cases where governments as such, though not individuals, have been ruled in violation of various human rights norms: Turkey, Honduras, Uruguay.

But the vast armature of international humanitarian law has stood largely mute, palsied in part by the fear of most national governing elites— and in particular the successive leaderships of the five permanent Security Council members most in a position to invoke those norms—that the glare of such attention might one day be turned on their own actions. (In the United States this tenor of concern often took the form of the anxious assertion that "by that logic Henry Kissinger could have been held liable for the Christmas bombing of Hanoi"—as well he might have been.)

Against this backdrop, the sudden lurch forward with the establishment of the two ad hoc criminal tribunals on Yugoslavia and Rwanda during the mid-1990s came as virtually a fluke (notwithstanding the years and years of prior lobbying by committed human rights lawyers and activists for State accountability and an end to individual impunity), their establishment arguably having primarily grown out of the panicky overreaction of the Security Council's permanent five, shamed at the spectacle of their own gaping failure to take any more consequent action to stop the carnage itself as it was happening. (At least this way they could be seen to be doing something.) No sooner had the tribunals been constituted than several of the permanent five, perhaps realizing the implications of their mistake, seemed to think better of the entire project. They filibustered the appointment of the permanent prosecutor for over a year and then imposed all sorts of procedural and budgetary constraints on the efficient operation of the Yugoslav tribunal. In particular, for a long while, the international peacekeeping forces on the ground were ordered to bend over backward to avoid even encountering, let alone arresting, the indicted war criminals plainly in their midst. And yet, somehow, the tribunals persisted, against enormous odds.

Perhaps most significantly, ad hoc though they were, they seemed to be steadily expanding the terrain of the possible along the borderland of international humanitarian legal practice. And meanwhile, to everyone's astonishment, the rudiments of a permanent International Criminal Court seemed to be taking shape, most notably in the summer of 1998 in Rome, where an international diplomatic conference eventually brokered a treaty calling for an establishment of a modest, admittedly compromised, though still surprisingly robust version of just such a tribunal (even though the United States, initially one of the fiercest rhetorical advocates of a permanent court, seemed to become spooked all over again by perceived threats to its own sovereignty and at least initially demurred).

Suddenly, improbably, unlike anything anyone had seen in almost fifty years, there were all kinds of concrete activity taking place out there along the infinite borderland.

It is against that backdrop, that a consortium of international journalists—many of them longtime frontline war correspondents—came up with the idea for the guide you hold in your hands. Although they'd witnessed and reported on many war crimes, as technically defined, over the years, they'd done so without any particular expectation that the perpetrators would ever be brought to justice. No, stronger than that: they'd done so in the near-certainty that the perpetrators, as usual, would get off scot-free, and that the regime of impunity would persist inviolate.

Suddenly, however, that sorry state of affairs seems to be changing. Suddenly, it's going to matter whether, say, there was or wasn't a machine gun emplacement nestled in the rafters of that hospital, or a cannon in its courtyard. It's going to matter whether armed troops were accompanying the column of refugees fleeing that collapsing enclave, or whether the defenders had raised a white flag and were attempting to surrender when they were shot. By virtue of their profession, war correspondents may well find themselves among the first outside witnesses on the scene at war crimes. As such, they're going to need to be informed witnesses, and the rest of us are going to have to become a far better informed and engaged public.

Hence this book.

NOTE: Terms in bold face are cross references to other articles.

A

Act of War

By David Turns

Until 1945, an act of war in the traditional and historical sense was under-stood to mean any act by a State that would effectively terminate the normal international law of peacetime and activate the international law of war. The decision was invariably that of the target State and was generally preceded by a statement warning that certain acts would be considered acts of war and would trigger hostilities. Belligerent and neutral States also used the term. Belligerents would interpret as acts of war any action that seemed to assist the enemy; neutrals, any infringement of their neutrality.

In 1945, the United Nations Charter banned the first use of force, putting an end to declarations of war. "All members shall refrain in their international relations from the threat or use of force against the territorial integrity or political independence of any State," states Article 2 of the char-ter. The last declaration of war was made by the Soviet Union against Japan in 1945. An example of modern State practice is provided by the United Kingdom, which during the Suez War of 1956 and the Falkland Islands War of 1982 strenuously denied that it was at war with, respectively, Egypt and Argentina. Britain applied the laws of armed conflict in its military opera-tions, nevertheless.

The term *act of **aggression*** has to all intents and purposes subsumed the legal term *act of war* and made it irrelevant, although act of war is still used rhetorically by States that feel threatened. The People's Republic of China stated in 1997 that any attempt by the Republic of China (Taiwan) to declare independence would be regarded as an act of war; and in August 1998, the U.S. Secretary of State, Madeleine Albright, said Osama bin Laden, the reputed mastermind of truck-bomb attacks on two U.S. embassies in Africa, had "declared war on the United States and struck first." In the domestic law of many States, act of war is also used in some contexts, such as insurance and reparations claims, to refer to any use of force in any armed conflict.

Aggression

By Steven R. Ratner

Aggression in international law is defined as the use of force by one State against another, not justified by self-defense or other legally recognized exceptions. The illegality of aggression is perhaps the most fundamental norm of modern international law and its prevention the chief purpose of the United Nations. Even before the UN, the League of Nations made the prevention of aggression a core aim; and the post–World War II Allied tribunals regarded aggression as a crime under the rubric **crimes against peace**.

The most authoritative definition comes from the UN General Assembly. (The UN Charter never defines the term, instead banning the threat or use of force.) In 1974, it completed a twenty-year project to define aggression. Member States claimed that a definition would help the UN—principally the Security Council, charged by the charter with addressing aggression—in responding more consistently and promptly. While it reflects a broad international consensus, it is not a treaty, though it may represent **customary international law.**

The definition begins by stating that "[t]he first use of armed force by a State in contravention of the Charter" constitutes *prima facie* evidence of aggression. The definition is somewhat limiting, and perhaps circular, in that the first use of force by a State would not be aggression if undertaken in a way consistent with the charter. Thus, for example, the deployment of U.S. forces to Somalia in 1992, while the first use of force, would not be aggression because it was authorized by the Security Council under Chapter VII of the charter. A number of States have accepted that a State's first use of force to extricate its citizens from another State when they are in imminent danger, and the other State is not able to protect them, is not aggression (e.g., Israel's 1976 Entebbe raid) and may be a form of self-defense. Some scholars and human rights activists have advocated a broader right of non-UN-approved intervention to prevent large-scale human rights abuses.

Second, the definition offers an illustrative list of acts of aggression: invasion, attack, or occupation of whatever duration; bombardment; blockade; attack on another State's armed forces; unauthorized use of military forces stationed in a foreign State; allowing territory to be used for aggression; and sending armed bands or similar groups to carry out aggression or substantial involvement therein.

Acts of aggression such as these trigger the two key lawful uses of force mentioned in the charter: (a) individual or collective self-defense; and (b) force approved by the UN itself. Thus, the Iraqi invasion of Kuwait triggered the right of Kuwait and its allies to engage in self-defense, as well as the right of the UN to approve the use of force against Iraq under Chapter VII.

Despite its prohibition in international law, aggression remains a feature of international life. Although the classic attack on another State is not as rampant as before World War II, more subtle forms of armed intervention persist, and the responses of the international community remain plagued by timidity and inconsistency.

(See **humanitarian intervention; just and unjust war.**)

A

Apartheid

By Steven R. Ratner

Nelson Mandela described apartheid as "the color line that all too often determines who is rich and who is poor . . . who lives in luxury and who lives in squalor . . . who shall get food, clothing, and health care . . . and who will live and who will die."

Apartheid was the system of racial discrimination and separation that governed South Africa from 1948 until its abolition in the early 1990s. Building on years of discrimination against blacks, the National Party adopted apartheid as a model for separate development of races, though it served only to preserve white superiority. It classified persons as either white, Bantu (black), colored (mixed race), or Asian. Its manifestations included ineligibility from voting, separate living areas and schools, internal travel passes for blacks, and white control of the legal system.

As part of its decades-long efforts to eliminate the practice, the UN adopted in 1973 the International Convention on the Suppression and Punishment of the Crime of Apartheid, which 101 States have ratified. It characterizes apartheid as a crime for which individuals can be held accountable. The convention defines apartheid as a series of "inhuman acts committed for the purpose of establishing and maintaining domination by one racial group of persons over any other racial group of persons and systematically oppressing them." These include denial of the right to life and liberty, imposition of living conditions designed to destroy the group, legislative measures to prevent the group's participation in national life, division of the population along racial lines, and exploitation of the group's labor force. It also declares apartheid a **crime against humanity**.

The Geneva Conventions commit States to a policy of nondiscrimination in treating the sick and wounded, the shipwrecked and stranded, captured combatants and civilians under an occupation regime or caught up in conflict. Apartheid has also been labeled a **war crime** in international conflicts under Additional Protocol I to the Geneva Conventions. Protocol I lists as grave breaches apartheid "and other inhuman and degrading practices involving outrages upon personal dignity, based on racial discrimination," though these would only be grave breaches during international armed conflict. The inclusion of apartheid as a grave breach stemmed from the international campaign to isolate South Africa and was opposed by several Western powers as not sufficiently connected to armed conflict. The International Committee of the Red Cross (ICRC) has noted that its presence on the list of grave breaches does not expand the scope of war crimes significantly as many of the worst practices of apartheid would qualify as war crimes if committed in armed conflict. But some acts that were perhaps not criminal previously (though they were unlawful) clearly became such with apartheid's inclusion—e.g., segregating prisoners of war or civilians by race.

The most recent attempt to criminalize apartheid took place in the context of the UN's International Law Commission's 1996 draft code of international crimes, which includes as a crime against humanity an offense called "institutionalized discrimination," a sort of generic version of apartheid; and the Rome Statute of the International Criminal Court (ICC),

Apartheid made work for sign writers as even the most mundane activity was racially separated—with little pretense of equality.

which also lists apartheid as a crime against humanity, defining it generically as inhumane acts "committed in the context of an institutionalized regime of systematic oppression and domination by one racial group over any other racial group or groups . . . with the intention of maintaining that regime."

Despite the Apartheid Convention's (and now the ICC's) geographically unconfined definition, states and nongovernmental organizations (NGOs)have only rarely referred to systems outside South Africa as apartheid. Groups such as the Kurds, the Tamils, the South Sudanese, or other indigenous peoples do suffer systematic discrimination that might well meet the definition of apartheid, even if those practices lack all the legal trappings of the South African model. But the term has not been invoked by victims or their advocates, no doubt because it is still associated with South Africa. Thus, the likelihood that individuals will be prosecuted domestically or internationally in the near future for apartheid remains small.

Arab-Israeli War Benny Morris

On November 2, 1948, an Israel Defense Forces (IDF) patrol visited the campsite of a small Bedouin subtribe, Arab al Mawasa, just west of the Sea of Galilee in northern Israel. The area, along with the rest of upper central Galilee, had been conquered by the IDF three to four days before in an armored offensive code-named Operation Hiram.

The patrol, in search of arms, scoured the area. On nearby "Hill 213" the troops found the decapitated remains of two Israeli soldiers who had been missing since a skirmish one month before. According to the 103rd Battalion's patrol report, "The men [then] torched the Arabs' homes [tents?]. The men returned to base with 19 Arab males. At the base the males were sorted out and those who had taken part in enemy operations against our army were identified and then taken under Haim [Hayun]'s command to a designated place and there 14 of them were tr̶ ̶ated. The rest are being transferred to a prisoner of war camp."[1]

Few such documents have surfaced in Israel's archives during the past fifty years, partly because soldiers and officers who committed atrocities rarely left written descriptions behind, partly because those that do exist are mostly deposited in the IDF Archive, where internal censors make sure that documents explicitly pertaining to massacres or expulsions never see the light of day. But occasionally slips occur.

We now know, on the basis of United Nations, American, and British documents and a handful that surfaced in Israel's civilian archives (the Israel State Archive, party political archives, private papers collections, etc.) during the 1980s and 1990s, of more than a dozen massacres of Arabs by Jewish troops in the course of the first Arab-Israeli war of 1948. These range in size from the shooting of a handful or several dozen civilians arbitrarily selected and lined up against a village wall after its conquest (as occurred, for example, in Majd al Kurum, Bi'na and Dir al Assad, Ilaboun, Jish, Saliha, Safsaf, and Sasa during Hiram) to the slaughter of some 250 civilians and detainees

Palestinian children raise toy guns in precocious defiance. All too often their contemporaries were killed or maimed by the real thing. Gaza, 1993.

during a firefight in the town of Lydda, southeast of Tel Aviv, on the afternoon of July 12, 1948.

Over the years, the release of new documents and newspaper interviews
with witnesses and participants has uncovered Israeli massacres of Arab civilians and prisoners of war in the subsequent wars of 1956, 1967, 1973, and
1982. The revelations came as a shock to much of the Israeli public, which
was nurtured on a belief in its own moral superiority and on a doctrine of
"purity of arms." Jewish troops, it was believed, in the mainstream Jewish
underground, the Haganah, before 1948, and in the IDF since then, had been
trained not to sully their arms by committing atrocities. When an atrocity
nonetheless came to light, it was always dismissed as a rare exception, a
unique occurrence.

The truth is otherwise—and not surprisingly. Underlying the series of
Arab-Israeli wars has been a deep hatred by each side of the other and deep
existential fears, both among Israeli Jews and Palestinian Arabs. Moreover,
the wars have been at least partly fought in areas crowded with civilians
(the whole of Palestine in 1948, the Gaza Strip in 1956 and 1967, the West
Bank and Golan Heights in 1967, and southern Lebanon and Beirut in 1982).
Almost inevitably, civilians were hurt and killed, sometimes deliberately,
more often unintentionally.

The bloodiest and most atrocity-ridden of these wars was, without
doubt, the 1948 war of independence, which began, from November 1947 to
May 1948, as a civil/guerrilla war between Palestine's thoroughly intermixed
Arab and Jewish communities, but ended, from May 1948 to January 1949,
as a conventional war between the invading Arab States' armies and the
newborn State of Israel. The fact that the Arabs had launched the war—the
Palestinian Arabs in November–December 1947 and the Arab States in May
1948—and that the war was protracted and extremely costly for the Jews
(who lost six thousand dead, or 1 percent of a total population of 650,000)
only exacerbated anger toward the Arabs and heightened the propensity to
commit atrocities. The willingness to commit atrocities on each side was also
fed by reports—sometimes accurate, sometimes fantastic—of atrocities committed by the other side; retaliation was a frequent motive for Arabs and
Israelis alike.

Two out of the three massacres committed by Arabs against Jews during
the 1948 war were triggered by Jewish atrocities against Arabs. On December
30, 1947, Irgun Zvai Leumi (National Military Organization, or IZL) terrorists
threw a bomb at an Arab bus stop at the entrance to the Haifa Oil Refinery
outside Haifa. Half a dozen Arabs were killed, and more were injured. The
Arab workers inside the refinery immediately retaliated by turning on their
Jewish coworkers with knives, crowbars, and sticks, killing thirty-nine of
them. (In turn, the Haganah responded on the night of December 31 by raid-
ing the nearby Arab village of Balad ash Sheikh, where many of the workers
lived, blowing up several dozen houses and killing about sixty Arabs.)

Similarly, the Arab irregulars' attack on the convoy of doctors, nurses,
students, and Haganah militiamen making its way through East Jerusalem to
Mount Scopus (the Mount Scopus Convoy) on April 13 was also a retaliation
for the assault by Jewish (IZL-Lehi-Haganah) troops on the Arab village of
Deir Yassin, just west of Jerusalem, on April 9, 1948, in which about one
hundred villagers were killed during the fighting or just afterward.

The third and largest Arab atrocity of the war, the massacre by irregulars
of dozens of surrendering Haganah troops, including some twenty women, at
Kfar Etzion in the Etzion Bloc of settlements just north of Hebron, on May
13, was unprovoked by any immediate Jewish attack or atrocity.

The funeral of an Israeli watchman killed during a border incident in 1953.

But overall, the Jewish forces—Haganah, IZL, Lehi (Lohamei Herut Yisrael, or Freedom Fighters of Israel, or "Stern Gang," as the British authorities called them), and IDF—committed far more atrocities in 1948 than did Arab forces, if only because they were in a far better position to do so.

The Haganah, and subsequently the IDF, overran large Arab-populated areas—some four hundred villages and towns—whereas Arab forces conquered or overran fewer than a dozen Jewish settlements in the course of the war. To this must be added the fact that the civil war in Palestine, which ended in mid-May 1948, raged in a country nominally ruled by a British administration. Neither Jews nor Arabs could legally hold prisoners and, for months, neither had facilities to hold large numbers, so prisoners either were not taken or were shot.

Massacres apart, 1948 was characterized by a great deal of random killing by Jewish troops of Arab civilians. Patrols and ambushes would randomly kill civilians scavenging for food or trying to cross the front lines for other reasons.

From the available evidence, it would appear that not one Jewish soldier or officer was ever punished in connection with these atrocities. Similarly, so far as the evidence allows, no Arab irregular or regular soldier was ever tried or punished for murdering Israelis.

The atrocities did not stop at killings; many Arab villagers and towns-people were expelled from their homes by conquering Jewish units. The largest of these expulsions took place in the towns of Lydda and Ramle on July 12 and 13, when upward of fifty thousand people were dispatched onto roads eastward. In retrospect, it is clear that what occurred in 1948 in Palestine was a variety of **ethnic cleansing** of Arab areas by Jews. It is impossible to say how many of the 700,000 or so Palestinians who became refugees in 1948 were physically expelled, as distinct from simply fleeing a combat zone. What is certain is that almost all were barred by the Israeli government decision of June 1948 and, consequently, by IDF fire, from returning to their homes or areas. Similarly, almost all of the four hundred or so Arab villages overrun and depopulated by Israel were in the course of 1948 or immediately thereafter razed to the ground, partly in order to pre-vent the refugees from returning. No Jewish soldier or commander was ever tried or punished for expelling an Arab community or destroying an Arab vil-lage (though as far as the evidence allows, neither was any Jewish soldier or official ever tried or punished for not expelling Arabs or for not destroying an Arab village or urban neighborhood).

In the course of the war Arab soldiers or irregulars expelled a handful of Jewish communities. Indeed, Arabs expelled Jewish communities from every site they overran, but there were less than a dozen such sites. These included the Jewish Quarter of the Old City of Jerusalem, most of whose buildings were subsequently razed; the Etzion Bloc of settlements—Kfar Etzion, Massu'ot Yitzhak, Revadim, and Ein Tzurim (again, the buildings were razed to the ground by their looters-conquerors); and Kfar Darom, in the Gaza Strip. (All these sites were resettled by Jews after Israel conquered the West Bank and Gaza Strip in the 1967 war. On the other hand, the hundreds of sites from which Arabs were driven out in 1948, and the buildings razed, remained uninhabited or were resettled with Jews.)

Following 1948, IDF discipline and ethics gradually improved. There-after, in each subsequent war, and in the interregnum between wars, there were progressively fewer atrocities, a point Gen. Rafael Eitan, the IDF chief of general staff, went out of his way to make when assailed for his troops' behavior during the 1982 invasion of Lebanon.

In October–November 1956, the IDF overran the Gaza Strip, where it remained in control until March 1957. During the battle for this heavily pop-ulated zone and during the first weeks of occupation, the IDF killed some five hundred civilians, either in actual combat or in a subsequent series of massacres. Elsewhere during the Sinai-Suez War, IDF troops reportedly killed fleeing, and often unarmed, Egyptian troops by the hundreds and, occasion-ally, Egyptian prisoners of war. For example, at the end of October 1956, the IDF Paratroop Brigade killed some three dozen POWs near the Mitle Pass. Revelation of this affair in 1995 prompted Egyptian protests to Jerusalem and a demand for an investigation (whose results were never made public).

During the 1967 Six-Day and October 1973 wars, there were cases of IDF troops killing fleeing, and often unarmed, Arab troops and murdering POWs. Again, the victorious Israelis had greater opportunity to commit atrocities than their Arab foes, but there is evidence also that Arab troops, when given the chance, killed off surrendering Israelis and POWs. Such incidents occurred in the 1973 war's first days, when the Syrians overran part of the Golan Heights and the Egyptians overran the IDF's Bar-Lev Line along the east bank of the Suez Canal. Arab civilians and security forces also killed downed Israeli pilots on both fronts.

On the other hand, in the aftermath of these two wars there were almost no reports of atrocities by IDF troops vis-à-vis Arab civilians. Indeed, both the 1967 war (when the IDF overran crowded cities in the West Bank and Gaza Strip) and the 1973 war (when the IDF conquered the populated west bank of the Suez Canal) were marked by almost no civilian casualties. However, in the immediate wake of the June 1967 war, the IDF destroyed more than half a dozen Arab villages in the West Bank (Imwas, Yalu, Beit Nuba, Khirbet Beit Mirsim, Nabi Samwil, etc.) and expelled their inhabitants.

Israeli soldiers with Egyptian prisoners of war under Egyptian artillery fire during the Yom Kippur War. Sinai, 1973.

The area of the first three villages was subsequently turned into a nature reserve, Park Canada, which remains to this day a favorite Israeli picnic spot.

Altogether, during and in the immediate aftermath of the 1967 war some 200,000 to 300,000 Palestinians left the West Bank and Gaza Strip for Jordan, many of them refugees for the second time, having moved to the West Bank in 1948 from areas that had become Israeli. In addition, fifty thousand to ninety thousand Syrian civilians (the exact number is disputed) fled their homes or were driven out of the Golan Heights during the IDF conquest. As in 1948, very few of these refugees, from the West Bank, Gaza, and the Golan, were allowed back by Israel, and most still live in camps in Jordan and Syria.

In 1982, as well, the IDF troops who overran southern Lebanon, including Beirut and much of the Beirut–Damascus road, committed few deliberate atrocities, despite the fact that the war was waged in a heavily populated area in which there were more than half a dozen Palestinian refugee camps that stiffly resisted the invaders. Nonetheless, thousands of Palestinian and

Lebanese civilians were killed by Israeli airmen, guns, and tanks as the invading force slowly pushed northward, laying down before it a curtain of fire in order to soften resistance and keep down IDF casualties. The exact number of Arab civilians killed is a matter of dispute (Israeli officials spoke of "hundreds"; the Lebanese and Palestinians of "thousands," and even, in one report, of as many as eighteen thousand). What is not disputed is that whole streets and blocks of Lebanese cities—Tyre, Sidon, and Beirut—were destroyed and a number of refugee camps were largely demolished (Rashidiye near Tyre, Ein al Hilwe near Sidon, and others) during the fighting.

Israel's invasion of Lebanon, according to Israeli government spokesmen, was caused or provoked by Palestinian "terrorism" against Israeli targets from southern Lebanon. In fact, during the years between July 1981 and June 1982, when the invasion was launched, there had been practically no terrorist attacks from Lebanon against Israel. But between 1969 and 1981, southern Lebanon had served as a base for Palestine Liberation Organization (PLO) attacks against Israeli targets, the most famous of which was the Coast Road Raid of March 1978, when seaborne Palestinian terrorists from Lebanon commandeered an Israeli bus on the road between Tel Aviv and Haifa and killed more than thirty of its passengers.

In September 1982, the largest deliberate atrocity of the Lebanon War took place, the massacre of several hundred Palestinian refugees (again the exact number is disputed, though apparently some five hundred died) in the Sabra and Shatilla camps or neighborhoods of southern Beirut at the hands of Lebanese Christian militiamen of the Phalange Party. While these militiamen, who were Israel's allies, had been let or sent into the camps by the occupying Israeli troops, the Israelis had not intended or planned the massacre, though Israel's defense minister, Ariel Sharon, was subsequently removed from his post on the recommendation of a commission of inquiry. The Kahan Commission found him "negligent" and indirectly responsible for what had happened. The massacre, and the previous destruction of the refugee camps in the south, had meshed with Sharon's policy of pushing the refugee communities as far northward and away from Israel's border as possible, and with the Phalange desire to rid Lebanon altogether of its (largely Muslim) Palestinian population.

In the years since, reports of only two deliberate atrocities, in which a handful of Lebanese villagers and Palestinians died, have surfaced in the Israeli press, and it is doubtful whether many more actually occurred. But during the years 1982–1985, as Israel's security forces struggled unsuccessfully to suppress the Shiite resistance campaign against their occupation of southern Lebanon, Shiite militants were occasionally executed by Israeli security men, thousands of suspects were detained without trial, **torture** was used systematically against suspects, and houses of resistance fighters were occasionally demolished.

The Arab-Israeli wars also gave rise, of course, to Israel's control of a foreign-populated territory (whether or not technically regarded as occupation of enemy territory in the West Bank and Gaza), resulting in resistance to that presence and Israeli efforts to suppress it.

From 1967 until 1995, Israel occupied and governed the Palestinian-populated West Bank and Gaza Strip, with the population increasing in number during this period from about 1 million to 2 million.

Periodically, groups of local inhabitants banded together to resist the occupation, occasionally using nonviolent political measures (strikes, school closures, demonstrations), at other times employing violence—which the Palestinians called "armed resistance" and the Israelis **"terrorism."** These acts, both within the occupied territories and in Israel proper, as well as along Israel's borders with Jordan and Lebanon, often involved deliberate attacks on civilians, which would qualify as terrorism on any ordinary definition. For example, in the bouts of Palestinian Islamic fundamentalist terrorism during 1994–1996, suicide bombers destroyed Israeli buses in the centers of Tel Aviv and Jerusalem, killing dozens of Israeli civilians.

Israel responded to both forms of activism, violent and nonviolent, with a range of measures, many of which violated international law and human rights conventions. Over the decades, for example, Israel has expelled without trial from the territories hundreds of political activists, some of whom were suspected of links to "terrorism"; others were merely suspected of political "agitation" and "incitement."

Severe punishments were usually reserved for persons suspected of what Israeli authorities characterized as terrorism or abetting terrorism. In the course of 1967–1981, the Israeli authorities demolished or sealed some thirteen hundred homes, usually of suspected terrorists. Another seven hundred or so homes were destroyed or sealed off during the Intifada, the semiviolent Palestinian uprising of 1987–1993. The homes in question generally also housed brothers and sisters, parents, and children of the suspects, rendering the measure a limited form of **collective punishment.** Usually, the families were not allowed to rebuild their homes. The homes were usually demolished before the suspect was brought to trial or convicted of any crime.

By far the most common antiresistance measure was arrest. During the thirty years of occupation more than fifty thousand Palestinians passed through the Israeli prison system, most of them during the Intifada years. Thousands more were detained on administrative orders, meaning that they were never tried or convicted by any court of law. The military authorities have the power to detain persons for six months without trial, renewable with a judge's permission. Israel's jails still hold more than one hundred administrative detainees, a few of whom have spent years in prison without ever having stood trial.

But most of the prisoners—Israel's prisons today hold about five thousand Palestinian prisoners—were tried by military courts. The courts freed very few suspects, and sentences have often been criticized as being unreasonably severe. A boy of fifteen could spend a year or two in jail for throwing a stone at a car. On the other hand, Israeli military and civilian courts have tended to be extremely lenient toward Israeli soldiers or civilians who killed Palestinians, often making do with suspended sentences or orders to do community service. Israel's General Security Service (and, less frequently, IDF and police units) has systematically employed various forms of **torture**, such as sleep deprivation, beatings, cold showers, and painful postures, against terrorist suspects over the years.[2]

In the course of the Intifada, IDF troops killed with regular and plastic-coated bullets about one thousand Palestinians, many of them minors. Most were killed during clashes between soldiers and stone-throwing rioters.

During the Intifada, dozens of suspected terrorists were killed by Israeli military and police undercover units who were often accused of acting like **death squads.** Israeli spokesmen countered that the peculiar conditions of operation of such units—small squads dressed as Arabs operating in the middle of Arab towns and without close support of regular troops—made haste with the trigger finger an imperative of survival. But over the six years of the Intifada, only a handful of such undercover troops were ever killed or injured by Arabs, raising questions as to whether they were typically in great peril during their operations.

Traumatized patients in Palestinian psychiatric hospital after it was hit by Israeli shells during the Siege of Beirut, 1982.

Apart from specific action against suspected terrorists and their supporters, IDF troops frequently resorted to wholesale collective measures in order to suppress rebelliousness among the West Bank and Gaza populations. Often, twenty-four-hour or dusk-to-dawn curfews were imposed on whole cities or villages—preventing the inhabitants from going to work or otherwise living a normal life for days on end. Occasionally—such as during or after a nationally motivated strike—the authorities would close down schools, universities, or businesses. Sometimes the troops would cut off water, electricity, or telephone lines to specific localities as a form of punishment. Lastly, the security forces often arrested, and subjected to interrogation, family members of suspected terrorists in order to discover the

Israel's administration of the occupied territories has been a target of criticism, in part because Israel claims that it is not legally obliged to implement provisions of the Fourth Geneva Convention relating to the occupation of territory. Israel is a party to all four Geneva Conventions but did not sign the two Additional Protocols of 1977.

The Government says in actual practice it applies what it calls the "humanitarian provisions" of the Fourth Convention to the territories, without specifying which provisions are "humanitarian." The position has been assailed by Palestinians and the Arab States and is not accepted by Israel's principal ally, the United States, or any other major power.

One reason that Israel refused to apply the Fourth Geneva Convention as a matter of law, is that the Labor government in power in 1967 feared that by applying the convention, whose second article refers to "all cases of partial or total occupation of the territory of a High Contracting Party," it would effectively acknowledge Jordan as the previous sovereign. Israel viewed Jordan as a belligerent occupier that had unlawfully invaded and illegally annexed the West Bank.

In common practice, Israeli courts, guided by Supreme Court guidelines, operate in light of accepted international customary law and those international conventions adopted into internal Israeli law. Thus there is something of a dichotomy between Israel's official public position in international forums and legal practice vis-à-vis the territories.

In summation, the Arab-Israeli wars, like most wars, have resulted in atrocities, mostly committed by the winning side or the side in a position to commit such atrocities, both against soldiers and civilians. The number and frequency of the atrocities has diminished over the years, in part because the wars have been shorter (the 1948 war lasted a full year, the 1967 war a bare six days), in part because of greater discipline among the Israeli troops. On the other hand, the increased firepower in Israeli hands has meant that troops, when advancing through built-up areas, as in 1982, have tended to lay down curtains of fire that have resulted in large numbers of civilian casualties, something that did not occur in the previous wars, when the IDF had less firepower or was not engaged in built-up areas.

At the same time, the decades of Israeli occupation of the West Bank, Gaza Strip, and Golan Heights has resulted in the systematic deployment of a variety of measures that are contrary to international humanitarian law, including torture of suspected terrorists, house demolitions, administrative detention without **due process**, and **deportations**.

1. "C Company," 103rd Battalion report, signature illegible, November 2, 1948, IDF Archive 1096\49\\65.
2. B'Tselem, *The Interrogation of Palestinians during the Intifada*, 1991, Jerusalem; also B'Tselem, *Routine Torture: Interrogation Methods of the General Security Service*, Jerusalem, 1998.

Israel's Views of the Application of IHL to the West Bank and Gaza Strip

By Kenneth Anderson

Although the West Bank and Gaza are referred to by nearly all other States as "occupied territories," implying that all Israeli activities in them are governed by the Fourth Geneva Convention of 1949, Israel calls them "administered areas" and has a different view of its obligations and their legal status.

The Israeli government view, laid out in legal memoranda issued by its Ministry of Foreign Affairs, is that the territories did not belong to any sovereign State at the time Israel captured them during the 1967 war. That is, Egypt did not claim the Gaza Strip, and Jordan may have claimed the West Bank, but Israel and the great majority of States did not recognize that claim; and Palestinians did not assert sovereignty to the territory at that time. In addition, UN resolutions 242 and 338, which call upon Israel to withdraw from occupied territory, did not say that other States claimed sovereignty at the time. Israel further argues that any Palestinian claims to sovereignty over the territories based upon the UN General Assembly partition resolution of 1947 were rendered invalid because the Palestinians and allied Arab states rejected the resolution and took up arms against it.

Accordingly, in the Israeli view, the Fourth Convention is inapplicable on its face, since under the second paragraph of Article 2 common to all fo Conventions of 1949, the Conventions apply only to "occupation of the ter tory of a High Contracting Party." Formal recognition of the applicability of the Convention, Israel argued, implied a recognition of the sovereignty of the former administration.

Nevertheless, the Israel government in official statements has pledged compliance with what it views as the humanitarian and customary provision of the Convention—but without stipulating which articles it has in mind. Israel claims it has gone further than required in its protection of the local population of the territories. For example, although the Convention accepts the legality of the death penalty, it is not applied even to horrific acts of terrorism. Similarly, the Convention does not require that any provision be made for movement of the local population to and from territories, whereas Israel, within limits, permits such travel and trade, even to countries in a legal state of war with Israel.

The United Nations Security Council, the International Committee of t Red Cross, States, and scholars have criticized Israel's legal position. Critics note that Article 1 of the Fourth Geneva Convention requires a High Contracting Party to "respect and ensure respect" for the Convention "in al circumstances." Moreover, Article 4 stipulates that "persons protected by th Convention are those who, at any given moment, and in any manner whats ever, find themselves, in case of a conflict or occupation, in the hands of a Party to the conflict or occupying power of which they are not nationals." Thus, critics agree, Israel should apply the full Convention, and it is an exa geration to claim that accepting the applicability of the Convention implies

Armistice

By Howard S. Levie

An armistice is not a peace treaty. While its main objective is to bring about a cease-fire, a halt to hostilities, that halt may be indefinite or for a specified period of time only. An armistice agreement does not terminate the state of war between the belligerents. A state of war continues to exist with all of its implications for the belligerents and for the neutrals. (The Korean Armistice Agreement did not specify a time period—and thus was subject to termination by either party. North Korea in fact, denounced it in 1997.)

In time past, brief, local cease-fire agreements frequently were used for the purpose of removing the dead and the wounded from the battlefield.

In recent decades the armistice agreement has gained in importance because in a majority of cases it has not been succeeded by a treaty of peace as was formerly the almost universal custom, but remains as the only agreement entered into by the hostile nations bringing hostilities to an end.

The U.S. Army's "The Law of Land Warfare," issued in 1956, defines armistice and the subjects that it should cover. "An armistice (or truce, as it is sometimes called) is the cessation of active hostilities for a period agreed upon by the belligerents. It is not a partial or temporary peace; it is only the suspension of military operations to the extent agreed upon by the parties."

Of course, the parties may also include such provisions as they may desire and agree upon; it is extremely rare that armistice agreements impose obligations to address violations of the laws of armed conflict.

Effective Date and Time: It is particularly important to allow time for the information to reach outposts that would otherwise unwittingly violate the armistice agreement by continuing hostilities after it had become effective. Even in an era of instant communications, not every soldier or group of soldiers will be equipped to receive the information immediately.

Duration: In former days it was customary (but not required) to specify the length of time that the armistice agreement was to remain in force. In modern times such a provision has frequently been omitted, probably on the assumption that a peace treaty will be forthcoming in the not-too-distant future. When an armistice agreement contains no specific period of duration it remains in effect until formally denounced by one side. While there is no law requiring it, certainly it should be expected that the denunciation will be announced as becoming effective only after a specified period of time or at a specified future time, and not by the arrival of an artillery bombardment!

Line of Demarcation and Neutral Zone: While there is no specific provision in any convention on the law of war providing for a demarcation line and a neutral zone (the latter sometimes referred to as "no-man's land"), inclusion of these items will go far in preventing incidents that neither side really wants and which can inadvertently and unintentionally result in the resumption of hostilities.

Relations with Inhabitants: In almost every armistice one side will be occupying some of the territory of the other side. This means that there will be enemy civilians in part of the territory it controls. The U.S. Army's Land Warfare Manual states that if there is no provision on this subject in the armistice agreement these relations remain unchanged, each belligerent "continuing to exercise the same rights as before, including the right to prevent or control all intercourse between the inhabitants within his lines and persons within the enemy lines."

Prohibited Acts: Rarely do armistice agreements prohibit specific acts by the belligerents other than the basic act of hostilities; and rarely is any action taken by the other belligerent when the opposing force has taken an action that it believes to be prohibited. However, any violation of the armistice agreement, including any hostile act, would certainly fall within the definition of being a "prohibited act." Although not specifically set forth in the Korean Armistice Agreement, certainly the frequent violations of the demilitarized zone by the North Koreans, the construction of tunnels under that zone, and the landing of commandos in South Korea, with such missions as to assassinate the president of the Republic of Korea, are prohibited acts.

Prisoners of War: This was the most difficult problem that confronted the negotiators during the negotiation of the Korean Armistice Agreement, and its solution took well over a year. The United Nations Command insisted on "voluntary repatriation," which meant that the prisoner of war was free to return to the army in which he was serving when captured, or to go elsewhere if he preferred. This was primarily because while the North Koreans occupied most of South Korea early in the conflict, they conscripted into their army all South Koreans of military age who had been captured or had surrendered. These men had no desire to be "repatriated" to North Korea. "Voluntary repatriation" is now accepted international law and a provision to that effect will undoubtedly be found in future armistice agreements.

Consultative Machinery: Provisions of the Korean Armistice Agreement furnish a good example of the commissions set up by armistice agreements. There was a Neutral Nations Repatriation Commission to oversee the armistice with respect to prisoners of war; a Military Armistice Commission (with joint observer teams) to oversee the implementation of the armistice itself; and a Neutral Nations Supervisory Commission (with its own inspection teams) to ensure compliance with certain of the provisions of the armistice agreement.

Miscellaneous Political-Military Matters: There are times when the negotiators of an armistice agreement are authorized by their governments to discuss political matters. (At times, governments have used diplomats in armistice negotiations. The Korean Armistice Agreement, for example, was negotiated by military officers, while the Agreement for the Cessation of Hostilities in Vietnam was negotiated by diplomats.) Thus, while the United Nations Command Delegation insisted that it could discuss military matters and not political matters, Article 4 of the Korean Armistice Agreement contained a provision by which the military commanders recommended to the governments that within three months of signing the Parties convene a political conference to settle certain questions beyond the authority of the military commanders.

In recent decades the armistice agreement has gained in importance as an international agreement because of the fact that in a majority of cases it has not been succeeded by a treaty of peace as was formerly the most universal custom, but remains as the only agreement entered into by the hostile nations bringing hostilities to an end.

B

Belligerent Status

By Ewen Allison and Robert K. Goldman

Historically, rebel groups seeking to overthrow a recognized government or to secede from a State have sought "belligerent status"—a legal standing akin to that accorded a government and bringing the law of international armed conflict into play for both sides.

A rebel group gained "belligerent status" when *all* of the following had occurred: it controlled territory in the State against which it was rebelling; it declared independence, if its goal was secession; it had well-organized armed forces; it began hostilities against the government; and, importantly, the government recognized it as a belligerent.

In more recent times, however, governments have simply refused to grant recognition to groups rebelling against them. Governments are loath to admit that they have lost effective control of territory, nor are they anxious to grant legal standing to rebel groups.

This refusal has serious legal and humanitarian consequences. Without belligerent status a government would not be bound to treat insurgents according to the law of international armed conflicts, thus often paving the way for savage and inhumane incidents.

As a countermeasure, the international community has arranged for certain minimum standards of humanitarian law to be triggered by facts on the ground without waiting for governments to recognize belligerents or a state of belligerency. A confrontation is deemed to be an internal armed conflict when the fighting is intense, organized, and protracted enough to go beyond temporal disturbances and tensions. Additionally, the conflict must be confined within a State's borders and generally not involve foreign parties. As soon as the situation on the ground meets these criteria, parties are expected to conform to a distinct body of humanitarian law crystallized most notably in Common Article 3 of the Geneva Conventions of 1949 and in Additional Protocol II. These rules apply regardless of the legal standing of the parties.

In effect, humanitarian law sidesteps entirely the sensitive issue of recognition.

(See **international vs. internal armed conflict**.)

Biological Experiments

By Sheldon H. Harris

The Nazis were not the only nation to build death camps in the period leading up to World War II. The Japanese, too, had their concentration camps. The object was not, as with the Germans, the extermination of a people, but instead was to use incarcerated common criminals and prisoners of war as guinea pigs in biological and, to a lesser extent, chemical warfare experiments.

The rationale was simple. The fanatical, right-wing militarists who dominated Japanese society from the late 1920s to the end of World War II believed that in order to achieve their goal of Japanese domination of East Asia, they would have to rely upon exotic weapons of war such as pathogenic and chemical arms. That was horrible enough. But those who originated the program did not believe that these weapons could simply be developed in laboratories and let loose against enemies on the battlefield. They had to be tried out on human subjects.

And so a vast network of death factories was constructed that, by the time World War II had begun, stretched from the remote steppes of Inner Mongolia to Singapore, and from Bangkok to Manila. The center of this empire of death was Ping Fan, a suburb of the city of Harbin in north China, where the architect of Japan's chemical and biological warfare program, Lt. Gen. Shiro Ishii, had his headquarters.

Each factory employed at least two thousand people, including (apart from the ordinary soldiers used to guard the facilities) some twenty thousand physicians, microbiologists, veterinarians, zoologists, and plant biologists. At a conservative estimate, their diabolical research project of testing prospective pathogens and biological weapons on the camps' inmates involved between twelve and fifteen thousand men, women, and children.

Tens of thousands of others were killed in field tests that consisted of distributing food tainted with deadly pathogens; lacing water wells, streams, and reservoirs with other pathogens; creating cholera epidemics by injecting cholera into the veins of unsuspecting peasants, who were told they were being inoculated against the disease; and spraying or dropping various biological weapons on villages, towns, and cities from the air.

With the exception of few lesser participants, who were brought before a show trial by the Soviet authorities, most of the architects of Japan's biological warfare programs were never prosecuted for their crimes. The reason for this was that after the U.S. occupation of Japan, American scientists eager to acquire the experimental data garnered from these biological experiments argued successfully that their Japanese colleagues had gained invaluable insights into how the human body reacted to certain pathogens— information that would greatly assist American biological weapons programs. The result was that the U.S. occupation authorities colluded in a cover-up of what had taken place.

The use of "bacteriological methods of warfare" has been banned under international law since the 1925 Geneva Protocol on chemical and biological weapons, which was a response to the horrors of poison gas as employed in World War I. In the so-called medical case at the Nuremberg War Crimes Trials two decades later, the defendants were charged with conducting medical and biological experiments on thousands of German and non-German subjects. The tribunal ruled that whatever right Germany had to experiment on German nationals who were prisoners, that right "may not be extended . . . to permit the practice upon nationals of other countries who . . . are subjected to experiments without their consent and under the most brutal and senseless conditions. . . . To the extent that these experiments did not constitute war crimes, they constituted crimes against humanity."

These statutes alone should have made prosecutions of the architects of the Japanese biological warfare program almost mandatory. But they had everything to do with the Cold War and almost nothing to do with the state of international humanitarian law. That said, subsequent laws have only strengthened the prohibitions against the kinds of grave breaches of which the Japanese were guilty. Protocol I of the 1977 Additional Protocols to the Geneva Conventions explicitly forbids "medical and scientific experiments"

A Chinese woman, raped and impregnated by a Unit 731 researcher named Kobayashi, is vivisected along with her fetus in the laboratory at Pingfang.

even with the consent of the subject. And in the arms control field, the 1972 Biological Weapons Convention forbids "develop[ing] . . . microbial or biological agents or toxins [and] equipment" designed to use or deliver "such agents or toxins for hostile purposes or in an armed conflict."

But leaving aside prosecutions, the truth is hard enough to come by. Until the 1980s, the Japanese government denied the crimes committed by its doctors and scientists had even taken place. When the overwhelming weight of the evidence forced it to concede something had indeed occurred, the Japanese authorities insisted the program had been the work of renegade militarists. The government neither apologized nor offered compensation to those still alive who had been exposed to the germ warfare experiments, or to the families and heirs of those who had not survived them.

(See **biological weapons**; **chemical weapons**; **medical experiments on POWs**.)

B Biological Weapons

By Terence Taylor

Potentially, biological weapons (BW) can cause many thousands of casualties with the use of a very small quantity of material. In terms of a threat to human life they are on a scale comparable to a nuclear weapon as a weapon of mass destruction, and some major powers view them as the strategic equivalent.

Prior to the U.S.-led Desert Storm assault to liberate Kuwait in 1991, James Baker, the U.S. Secretary of State, warned Tariq Aziz, his Iraqi counterpart, that if Iraq used any weapon of mass destruction, it would suffer a blow from which it would take years to recover. At the time, Iraq had operational biological and chemical weapons, though its nuclear program was not complete.

Iraq interpreted this as a threat to use nuclear weapons, and its leadership decided not to make first use of mass destructive weapons.

Biological weapons can be developed using living organisms (for example, bacteria and viruses) or toxins (poisons) obtained from these organisms. Given the right technological expertise they are cheaper and easier to produce than nuclear weapons. Recent developments in biotechnology in civil industry, mainly in the pharmaceutical and veterinary medicine sectors, have made possible the easier production, storage, and weaponisation of some types of pathogenic organisms. Until the mid-1970s, while BW had some military value, their state of scientific technological development was such that their effects were too unpredictable and the problems of their storage and handling too great; consequently, other weapons conferred greater advantages. The advances in civil industry, mainly in the past twenty years, have made possible the production of weapons that are more effective and have more predictable results.

It is also easier to hide a BW program in civilian research and production facilities than either a nuclear or chemical one. The two biggest known post–World War II clandestine programs, in Russia (beginning in the days of the Soviet Union) and Iraq, used this technique. The hardest part of a BW program to conceal is the weapons end of the process, when the organism or toxin is put into a missile warhead, bomb, artillery round, or aerial spray tank. However, this activity can be done shortly prior to intended use to achieve maximum surprise. Most at risk to these deadly weapons are unprotected civilian populations. For example, studies have shown that a missile delivering 30 kilograms of anthrax spores overhead an urban area could kill between 80,000 and 100,000 people if they had no special protection in an area of some 10 kilometers. In comparison, a 12.5 kilo ton (Hiroshima-size) nuclear weapon delivered over a similar area of a size of 7.8 square kilometers could kill between 23,000 and 80,000 people (but also cause severe structural damage). For a chemical agent to be delivered to achieve a similar casualty toll to the BW delivery described above, many more kilograms of agent would be required. For example, even three hundred kilograms of a highly lethal chemical agent, such as sarin nerve gas, delivered over a similar target could kill perhaps only 80 to 200 people and cover an area only a fraction of that covered by ten times less (in weight) of anthrax.

The Biological Weapons Convention (BWC), which entered into force in

1975, bans the research, development, production, stockpiling, or acquisition of biological and toxic weapons. The convention similarly bans delivery systems specifically designed for such weapons. While the BWC deals only with possession of these weapons, first use in warfare was banned by the 1925 Geneva Protocol (which also dealt with the use of chemical weapons). This protocol was itself derived from an ancient customary law of war restricting the use of "poisonous" weapons or substances in armed conflict that had first been codified in the Hague Conventions of 1899 and 1907. To date 149 countries have joined the BWC.

The BWC contains no provision for monitoring, but there is a nonbinding "confidence-building" regime under which States may make declarations about their facilities that handle highly pathogenic organisms and give lists of publications which deal with them. Although a group of treaty members has begun drafting a legally binding protocol for verification, I and others with field experience believe that it is not possible to have a global measure that can work with any degree of confidence. It is more likely to give a sense of false security, which may be worse than the existing situation.

While the United States and Britain had dismantled their BW programs well before the BWC came into force, it came to light by 1990 that the Soviet Union had been running an extensive illegal BW program. They took advantage of the more recent developments in biotechnology to carry their program forward to a much more advanced level. In April 1992, President Boris Yeltsin of Russia publicly admitted to the BW program and announced a decree ending it. Convincing proof that the program has been fully dismantled has yet to be provided.

Iraq, although a signatory to the BWC, never ratified it and developed an advanced program using viruses, bacteria, and toxins. By the time of Operation Desert Storm in 1991, which resulted in the liberation of Kuwait, Iraq had missiles, aerial bombs, and artillery filled with biological agents and ready to use. They also had research and development programs on new agents and delivery means in progress. Neither the United States nor Britain knew the scale and scope of the program, but both took precautions, such as anthrax vaccination programs for the troops and prophylactics against nerve agent attacks. Britain also fielded a biological agent warning and detection system. Coalition bombing targeted chemical weapons plants but left the main BW sites untouched as the coalition was unaware of them.

Iraq only admitted to having a BW program after four years of investigations by United Nations inspectors. However, Iraq still continued to hide important aspects of this weapons program.

Other smaller programs existed or still exist in other parts of the world. An example of one, now ended, was that in South Africa run by the apartheid regime until the early 1990s. This was a relatively small program aimed at assassination targets. However, it used advanced biotechnological techniques and it is likely that some of those who worked on the program have exported their skills elsewhere.

B

Blockade as Act of War

By Christopher Greenwood

Under the traditional concept of *blockade*, a belligerent was entitled to pro-
claim a blockade of all or part of the enemy's coast and to use warships to
enforce that blockade. There was no legal obligation to comply with a blockade, but any merchant ship, whether belligerent or neutral, that was
intercepted by the blockading State while attempting to run the blockade
was liable to capture. Following the decision of a prize court, ship and cargo
became the property of the blockading power. The traditional concept of the
blockade was confined, therefore, to the law of naval warfare. *Blockade* today
is a technical legal term that most people, including lawyers, use without
much precision to describe a variety of conduct beyond maritime operations.

In order to be lawful, a naval blockade had to be formally declared and
had to be effective, that is to say it had to be properly enforced by warships
of the blockading State. At one time this meant stationing warships just off
the coast of the State that was subject to blockade, but by the time of the
two World Wars, blockades were often administered from a long distance. An
effective blockade allowed a belligerent to cut off all maritime commerce
between its enemy and the rest of the world. The purpose was not only to
prevent goods from reaching the enemy (to a large extent that could be done
without a blockade in any event) but also to prevent the enemy from export-
ing to the outside world and thereby sustaining its war economy. Blockades
were used to great effect during the American Civil War and the two World
Wars, but since 1945 there have been very few instances of anything that
could properly be described as a blockade in this technical sense.

Today, however, the term *blockade* is frequently applied to maritime
operations undertaken at the behest of the United Nations Security Council.
The council has on several occasions authorized warships to intercept shipping suspected of violating economic sanctions. Following Iraq's invasion of
Kuwait in 1990, for example, Resolution 661 imposed a ban on imports to,
or exports from, Iraq and occupied Kuwait. Shortly afterward, Resolution 665
authorized states with naval forces in the region cooperating with the government of Kuwait to intercept shipping suspected of violating these
sanctions. The result was in many ways very similar to that of a wartime
blockade. Warships from several navies intercepted over ten thousand vessels
between the summer of 1990 and the end of hostilities, and all maritime
trade with Iraq and Kuwait was effectively cut off.

Nevertheless, operations of this kind differ from the traditional blockade
in a number of ways. First, there is a legal duty resulting from the Security
Council resolutions not to engage in **sanctions** breaking and any form of
sanctions breaking is likely to lead to penalties. Second, the obligation to
comply with the UN sanctions resolutions prevails over existing contracts and
international agreements regarding shipping. Third, warships policing UN
embargo operations of this kind are entitled to stop and search merchant
shipping and to turn back ships suspected of sanctions breaking, but there
are no provisions for the capture of ships or for prize court proceedings. For
example, the owners of a Greek ship stopped by an American warship while
trying to enter a Yugoslav port during the Yugoslav sanctions would probably
be liable to penalties in the Greek courts but not in those of the United

States. Finally, the imposition of a traditional blockade was generally regarded as an **act of war**, whereas enforcement of United Nations sanctions is a rather different act. Although sometimes there may be an armed conflict in place between the States whose warships are used to enforce sanctions and the target State (as was clearly the case in the **Gulf War** in 1991, and perhaps in the period leading up to it), that will not always be so. The enforcement of legal sanctions even by means of maritime embargoes is not necessarily an act of war.

In recent times, some commentators have also used the term *blockade* to describe land-based operations designed to cut off supplies to a particular town or area. These operations, which are more like the **sieges** of the past, are not really blockades at all. The large body of law relating to naval blockades is not applicable to them, there is no provision for the confiscation of property from those seeking to supply the besieged area, and the emphasis is on stopping supplies from getting in, rather than cutting off exports. There is also, as a result of Additional Protocol I to the Geneva Conventions, an obligation not to deprive the civilian population of the basic means of survival. The effect of this rule is far less clear-cut in naval operations, although a blockade that had as its sole purpose depriving the enemy population of food and other humanitarian supplies would be unlawful today. (See **humanitarian aid, blocking of; starvation.**)

B

Bosnia Florence Hartmann

The conflict in Bosnia-Herzegovina, which began in April 1992 and ended in November 1995, has come to be seen as the model for wars of ethnic cleansing throughout the world. This was the most violent event Europe experienced since World War II, and the devastation of the small multiethnic state recalled the ruins of Germany after the Allied bombing. The methods of ethnic cleansing, used for conquest of territory were a repudiation of the lessons of World War II as codified in the Geneva Conventions. Practically the only saving grace in Western policy making during the three-and-a-half-year war was the decision to launch an international war crimes tribunal to indict and try some of those responsible.

Everyone knows by now that the war was both the result of Yugoslavia's collapse and the event that ensured it could never be reconstituted. Long

before the war began, Slobodan Milosevic in Serbia and, following his example, Franjo Tudjman in Croatia, had turned their backs on the Yugoslav ideal
of an ethnically mixed federal State and set about carving out their own ethnically homogeneous States. With Milosevic's failure, in 1991, to take control
of all of Yugoslavia, the die was cast for war.

Flatly rejecting proposals for a loosely based federation, refusing to
adopt the democratic and Western market reforms that had swept the former
Soviet bloc, and facing challenges in the streets from students, Milosevic
opted for a military contest. He had effective control of the federal army and
police, an aroused Serbian diaspora in the republics heading for independence, with ultranationalists at the fore, and the ability to manipulate all the
key institutions in Serbia—the academics, the media, the Serbian Orthodox
Church. Thus the wars over the succession to multinational Yugoslavia illus-
trated perfectly Clausewitz's idea that war is a continuation of politics by
other means.

To strengthen his hold on the domestic power base, Milosevic made it
his mission to set Yugoslavia's ethnic and national groups against one

*Civilians sprint to evade Serb snipers in "Sniper Alley." All too many were not fast
enough. Sarajevo, 1992.*

another. In the end, he succeeded in chasing out of what remained of Yugoslavia all those national groups that refused to submit to the hegemony of the Serb people and of Milosevic's Socialist Party (the successor to the League of Communists).

The Serbian political project, first in Croatia, then in Bosnia-Herzegovina, envisioned the creation of ethnically homogeneous States, fashioned by seizing territory from other States. **Ethnic cleansing** meant using violence and deportations to remove any trace of the other ethnic communities who had previously cohabited with Serbs in the coveted territories. This "cleansing" was the goal of the war, not the unintended consequence. It was not the inability of the different ethnic groups to live together that brought on the conflict, but rather the political aim of separating them.

The violence unleashed grew directly out of the artificiality of the polit-

French UN peacekeepers explain ethnic divisions in Central Bosnia, 1990.

ical agenda, which stood in total contradiction to the centuries-old multiethnic history of the Balkans. Simply put, achieving ethnically homogeneous States in a region of historic mixing could not be achieved except through extreme violence. In Bosnia, cleansing clearly took the form of **genocide**, for it was aimed to eliminate enough of the population, starting with the annihilation of its elite, so it could no longer form a plurality. For the Serbs, war crimes served as a force multiplier—a means to achieve greater effect from other resources. They did not have enough military assets to achieve their ambitions otherwise.

Western governments, starting with the United States, chose not to intervene for three and a half years. In response to the atrocities reported by the media, relief organizations, and even their own diplomats, and to quell the public outcry over the haunting images of starved **concentration camp** inmates behind barbed wire, the Security Council passed resolutions its members then failed to implement and, in conjunction with the European Community, set up a diplomatic process which neither would back up by force. To evade their obligations under the 1948 Genocide Convention, which requires parties to prevent and punish genocide, Western leaders took frequent recourse to the term used by Serbian officials, *ethnic cleansing*, and then stated that all parties had committed the practice. They did not use the term *genocide* until the war had ended. The major powers recognized Bosnia-Herzegovina as a sovereign State, admitted it as a full member of the United Nations, and established diplomatic relations, meanwhile suspending the UN membership of the rump Yugoslavia and imposing sanctions on it for supporting the war. But they refused to identify the conflict as an international armed **aggression** and instead characterized it as a **civil war** and an ancient ethnic feud, a posture that permitted them to avoid their collective security obligations under the United Nations Charter. They also refused to document from their intelligence sources the links between the Serbian and Bosnian Serb Armies—an integrated command structure, a single logistical

ID pictures of recently killed city residents await to accompany obituaries in the daily newspaper Oslobodjene. *Sarajevo, Bosnia. 1994.*

infrastructure, and a common paymaster. A top American diplomat called the international failure to respond the worst crisis in European collective security since the 1930s.

The evidence of concentration camps, systematic rape, massacres, torture, and mass deportation of civilians was undeniable, and in February 1993, largely at American behest, the Security Council set up "an International Tribunal for the Prosecution of Persons Responsible for Serious Violations of International Humanitarian Law Committed in the Territory of the Former Yugoslavia Since 1991" (ICTY) in The Hague. But the major powers did not get around to naming a chief prosecutor until July 1994, and they gave no support to the Bosnian government when it brought a case for genocide against Serbia at the International Court of Justice in The Hague, and Western governments instead have repeatedly urged Bosnia to drop that case.

Prosecuting primarily lower-level officials, the ICTY was unable to unmask the silence of the West on the real nature of the enterprise. It was not until July 1995, when NATO intervention in Bosnia-Herzegovina was at hand, that the tribunal indicted political leader Radovan Karadzic and military commander Ratko Mladic for genocide. And when Dusko Tadic was put on trial in 1996 for crimes committed at the Omarska detention camp and elsewhere in Prijedor County, the tribunal, working with such evidence it was able to obtain from open sources, victims, and ever-balking major powers, analyzed the atrocities as if they had occurred during a military campaign and a civil war rather than in an international conflict. The tribunal had ample jurisdiction to indict him for an internal conflict, but the tight focus of its charges effectively shielded Serbia, which had organized the genocide in which Dusko Tadic took part, from direct accountability.

A key factor in **incitement** of ethnic hatreds, first in Serbia, and later in Croatia, was a media under the thumb of the political leaders. This psychological conditioning disguised the conflict in civil and ethnic terms by using

The tombs of unknown and known civilian children massacred by Serbs stand stark against the snow in the Lions Cemetery. Sarajevo, December 1995.

the supreme alibi, namely the impossibility of the people of the former Yugoslavia to live together on the same territory. But it also awakened that barbarity which sleeps in all of us, and pushed the people to commit these massive atrocities.

Historically, in conventional conflicts, defeating the enemy's army on the battlefield and seizing territory are usually each side's principal war aims. The killing and wounding of civilians, the destruction of property, and the creation of refugees or displaced people are often by-products of these aims. While much of this devastation is legal under international law, since the codes of war offer no complete guarantees for the safety of civilians caught in zones of combat, the essence of the laws of war is that suffering must be minimized. This makes it imperative that the civilian population should not be made the object of attack. Soldiers from proper armies who contravene these laws are subject to trial for war crimes. In Bosnia-Herzegovina, the killing of civilians was not a by-product of war, for the goal of ethnic cleansing was the annihilation of civilians.

By the time Yugoslavia collapsed, the reputation of the Yugoslav Federal Army was irreparably stained, for under Milosevic's guidance the army coordinated and supported many of the militias who did the dirty work.

These were not the isolated, sporadic acts committed by militia factions running amok. To the contrary, the manner in which they were perpetrated, their ritualization, duration, and the pattern of commission across the territory under army control all testify that they were the product of a systematic policy, planned and coordinated at the highest political and military levels of the Yugoslav government.

To accomplish the war aim, there was probably no other way. In a multi-ethnic society like the former Yugoslavia before 1991, the annexation of territories while necessary could not be sufficient. Too many members of rival ethnic communities would have remained, and the more territories were

conquered, the more difficult, paradoxically, it would become to occupy and administer. Only ethnic cleansing, that is, the elimination of the other ethnic communities present in the coveted territories, could bring to fruition the war aims of the Serbs, and, later, of the Croats as well. Both Milosevic and Tudjman realized this from the start. The horrors and the goals of the war were one, or, more precisely, the success of the war depended on its horrors.

The war began on April 6, 1992, with the assault on key cities such as Bijeljina and Zvornik on the Bosnian-Serbian border by the Yugoslav Army and its allied paramilitary groups, followed by the siege of Sarajevo. Though planned over a long period, the order to activate the impressive military might secretly put in place around the Bosnian capital was held until the recognition of Bosnia-Herzegovina's independence by the Europeans and Americans.

From the very beginning of the conflict, **terror** was the method used to separate the communities. The violations of international humanitarian law testify to the determination to reach this goal. Bombardments of the civilian population, first of Sarajevo, then of besieged villages; massacres during the conquest, then the forced evacuation of civilians to modify the ethnic structure of the particular area; illegal internment of the civilian population in concentration camps; torture; systematic rape; summary executions; appropriation and pillage of civilian property; systematic destruction of the cultural and religious heritage with the sole aim of eliminating any trace of non-Serbs in the conquered territories; using detainees as human shields on front lines and in minefields; and starvation of civilians who resisted—these were only some of the violations of international humanitarian law and the laws of war of which the Serbs were guilty.

Violence breeds violence. In 1993, emboldened by Milosevic's campaign of terror against the Muslims and the Western powers' consistent denial that genocide had taken place, the Croats entered the war against their former Muslim allies, using many of the same methods as the Serbs—terror, deportations, concentration camps, indiscriminate bombardments of civilians, massacres, the blocking of humanitarian aid, destruction of religious shrines, and appropriation of property.

They were encouraged by Slobodan Milosevic's support for a Greater Croatia (which would include western Herzegovina and a part of central Bosnia, where a majority of 800,000 Bosnian Croats lived). These grave breaches of the laws of armed conflict were always on a smaller scale than those of the Serbs.

Victims of a double aggression, the Muslims certainly committed violations of international humanitarian law. But the Sarajevo government never made ethnic cleansing their cardinal policy, as had their enemies. This does not excuse the acts of certain special units of the Bosnian Army, the summary executions of some Serbs in Sarajevo, and the establishment of several concentration camps in which sexual assaults, assassinations, and torture were reportedly regularly practiced.

In an exhaustive report to the United Nations, a special Commission of Experts, chaired by Cherif Bassiouni of DePaul University in Chicago, concluded that globally 90 percent of the crimes committed in Bosnia-Herzegovina were the responsibility of Serb extremists, 6 percent by Croat extremists, and 4 percent by Muslim extremists. These conform roughly to an assessment drafted by the American CIA.

Whatever the apportionment of blame, what is tragically clear is that the ethnic cleansers were all too successful in their work. Whether bringing the architects and perpetrators of these crimes to justice can reverse any of this remains to be seen.

(See **international vs. internal armed conflict; NATO and the Geneva Conventions; UN and the Geneva Conventions**.)

C

Cambodia Sydney Schanberg

For the last three decades, without surcease, Cambodia has been con-
sumed by war, genocide, slave labor, forced marches, starvation, disease,
and now civil conflict. It is to Asia what the Holocaust was to Europe.

Roughly the size of Missouri, bordered by Thailand, Laos, and Vietnam,
Cambodia had a population of perhaps 7 to 8 million in 1975 when the
maniacal Khmer Rouge guerrillas swept into Phnom Penh and began the
"purification" campaign that was the centerpiece of their extremist agrarian
revolution. Four years later, the Khmer Rouge were pushed back into the jungle, leaving behind their legacy: 1.5 to 2 million Cambodians dead in what
would become known to the world as "the Killing Fields." Twenty percent of
the population erased. In America that would be 50 to 60 million people.

Some scholars say that technically what happened in Cambodia cannot
be called a genocide because for the most part, it was Khmers killing other
Khmers, not someone trying to destroy a different "national, racial, ethnical
or religious group"—which is how international law defines genocide.

To make such semantic or legalistic distinctions, however, is sometimes
to forsake common sense -- after all, the Khmer Rouge set out to erase an
entire culture, a major foundation stone of which was Cambodia's religion,
Theravada Buddhism. And this may help explain why, over the years, the law
has proved so poor a guide to the reality of human slaughter. For, whether
you call the mass killing in Cambodia a **genocide** or simply a **crime against
humanity**, it was the same by either name. It was a visitation of evil.

One might thus reasonably pick Cambodia as a paradigm for the law's
weakness in dealing with such crimes. International law, after all depends for
its legitimacy on the willingness of the world's Nation-States to obey and
enforce it. In Cambodia's case most Nation-States expressed shock and horror
—and did nothing. Even after the Vietnamese Army pushed the Khmer Rouge
out of power in 1979, ended the genocide, were welcomed as liberators, and
installed a pro-Hanoi government in Phnom Penh, Western nations saw to it
that Cambodia's seat at the United Nations continued to be occupied for several years by those very same Khmer Rouge. Washington and its allies, while
denouncing the Khmer Rouge crimes, were still slaves to Cold War ideology;
they decided it was better to keep the Khmer Rouge in the UN seat than to
have it go to a government in the orbit of Vietnam and its mentor, the Soviet
Union. Realpolitik, not the law, was the governing force.

For the human record, let us examine exactly what the Khmer Rouge
did to the Cambodian population. Their first act, within hours of military
victory, was to kidnap it, herding everyone out of cities and towns into work
camps deep in the countryside. All villages that touched on roads were similarly emptied. Cambodia, in fact, was transformed into one giant forced-labor
camp under the fist of Angka, "the organization on high." That was the
mild part.

The Khmer Rouge had actively sealed off the country. The world could
not look in. The horror could begin. Led by Pol Pot, their Paris-educated,
Maoist-influenced "Brother Number One," the new rulers proceeded to completely shatter the three underpinnings of Cambodian society—the family,
the Buddhist religion, and the village. In grueling migrations, people were

14-5-7 8
ចានគម្រ្សុន-សា៦462

*Their only epitaph: With macabre bureaucratic precision the Khmer Rouge pho-
tographed their victims before torturing and killing them. This picture is all that
remains of a mother and child murdered in Tuol Sleng Prison sometime between
1975 and 1979. So were all of those on the following pages.*

marched to sites as far as possible from their home villages. Children were
separated from parents and placed in youth groups, where they were indoc-
trinated to inform on their parents and other adults for any infractions of
Angka's crushing rules. Marriage was forbidden except when arranged by
Angka. The schools were shuttered, currency abolished, factories abandoned.
Newspapers ceased to exist. Radio sets were taken away.

As for religion, Buddhist temples were razed or closed. Of the sixty
thousand Buddhist monks only three thousand were found alive after the
Khmer Rouge reign; the rest had either been massacred or succumbed to hard
labor, disease, or torture. The Chams, a Muslim minority, were also targets
for elimination.

Religion, however, was but a starting point. Simply put, the Khmer
Rouge marked for potential extinction all Cambodians they deemed not
"borisot" (pure)—meaning all those with an education, those raised in population centers, those "tainted" by anything foreign (including knowledge of a
foreign language), even those who wore glasses. Anyone, that is, suspected
of not being in step with their pathological agrarian master plan. All suspect

Cambodians were labeled "new people" and kept apart from the "pure" populations. In some instances, the "new people" were given special identifying neckerchiefs—reminiscent of the yellow Star of David—so they could always be picked out of a crowd, as they often were when taken away for execution.

The Khmer Rouge had a pet slogan: "To spare you is no profit; to destroy you, no loss." With this incantation, at least 1.5 million Cambodians were erased.

I was in Phnom Penh when the Khmer Rouge marched in victorious on April 17, 1975, their faces cold, a deadness in their eyes. They ordered the city evacuated. Everyone was to head for the countryside to join the glorious revolution. They killed those who argued against leaving. Two million frightened people started walking out of the capital. The guerrilla soldiers even ordered the wounded out of the overflowing hospitals, where the casualties had been so heavy in the final few days of the war that the floors were slick with blood. There was no time for anything but emergency surgery. When the doctors ran out of surgical gloves, they simply dipped their hands in bowls of antiseptic and moved on to the next operating table. Somewhere between five thousand and ten thousand wounded were in the city's hospitals when the order to evacuate came. Most couldn't walk so their relatives wheeled them out of the buildings on their beds, with plasma and serum bags attached, and began pushing them along the boulevards out of the city toward the "revolution."

Foreigners were allowed to take refuge in the French embassy compound. I watched many Cambodian friends being herded out of Phnom Penh. Most of them I never saw again. All of us felt like betrayers, like people who were protected and didn't do enough to save our friends. We felt shame. We still do.

Two weeks later, the Khmer Rouge expelled us from the country, shipping us out on two truck convoys to the border with Thailand. With this act, Cambodia was sealed. The world could not look in. The killing could begin.

But the story of Cambodia's misery did not start with the Khmer Rouge. It began in March 1970, when a pro-Western junta headed by Gen. Lon Nol, with Washington's blessing, deposed Prince Norodom Sihanouk, who was out of the country. Sihanouk, a neutralist, had kept Cambodia out of the Vietnam War by making concessions to appease both sides. He allowed the Americans to secretly bomb Viet Cong sanctuaries inside Cambodia while he allowed the Vietnamese Communists to use Cambodia's port city, Kompong Som (also called Sihanoukville) to ship in supplies for those sanctuaries.

With Sihanouk gone, the Lon Nol group in effect declared war on Hanoi; and President Richard Nixon, pleased to have partisans—not neutralists—in Phnom Penh, ordered American troops to push into Cambodia from Vietnam for a six-week assault on the Communist sanctuaries. However, not having real confidence in Lon Nol, the president didn't inform him of the invasion on his sovereign territory until after it had begun and after Nixon had informed the American public on national television.

This was probably the moment that marked Cambodia's transformation into a pawn of the Cold War, with the Chinese backing the Khmer Rouge, the Soviets backing Hanoi, and the Americans backing the Lon Nol regime—all of them turning the entire country into a surrogate Cold War battlefield. The great irony in this turn of events is that the Khmer Rouge were no serious threat in 1970, being a motley collection of ineffectual guerrilla bands totaling at most three thousand to five thousand men, who could never have grown into the murderous force of seventy thousand to 100,000 that swept into Phnom Penh five years later without the American intervention and the subsequent expansion of Chinese and Russian aid to the communist side. The enlarged war gave the Khmer Rouge status and recruitment power. It also gave them tutelage and advisory help from Hanoi's forces (at least for the first two years before deep rifts drove the two apart).

This five-year war was marked by barbarism by all sides. Cambodian warriors have a battlefield custom, going back centuries, of cutting the livers from the bodies of their vanquished foes, then cooking them in a stew and eating them. The belief is that this imparts strength and also provides talismanic protection against being killed by the enemy. In this and countless other ways, the international conventions that say respect must be shown to the fallen enemy were universally disregarded.

Early in the war, in a town south of Phnom Penh, Lon Nol troops had killed two Viet Cong and recovered their badly charred bodies, which they hung upside-down in the town square to swing gruesomely in the wind—thereby sending a message to all who might consider aiding the foe. Henry Kamm, my *New York Times* colleague, tried to tell the Lon Nol commander that treating the bodies in this manner violated the Geneva Conventions. The commander found this amusing. He left the bodies twisting.

With the Vietnamese Communist units moving deeper into Cambodia, the Lon Nol government began whipping up anti-Vietnamese fervor. This visited fear and worse upon the 200,000-strong ethnic Vietnamese community in the country who, though they were citizens of Cambodia and had lived there for generations, soon became the targets of a public frenzy. Massacres began occurring. Many of the Vietnamese lived along the rivers, earning their living as fishermen; their bodies were soon floating down the Mekong by the dozens. One government general, Sosthene Fernandez, a Cambodian of Filipino ancestry who later rose to become chief of the armed forces, began using ethnic Vietnamese civilians as protective shields for his advancing troops, marching them in front into the waiting guns of the Viet Cong. This, too, is against international law. Fernandez disagreed. "It is a new form of psychological warfare," he said.

Saigon raised bitter protests against these pogroms, and Cambodia's Vietnamese population was finally interned in protective custody in schools and other public buildings. Many were eventually moved under guard to South Vietnam as a temporary measure until emotions cooled.

As the war progressed, the country—at least the part held by the Lon Nol government—progressively shrank. The energized Khmer Rouge kept grabbing more and more territory until the area under government control, aside from the capital, was reduced to a handful of transport corridors and several province towns. The Phnom Penh airport and the Mekong River were its lone links to the outside world. To preserve these lines of supply, the Americans bombed Khmer Rouge and Viet Cong targets in the countryside on a daily basis. Since most of the raids were by giant, eight-engine B-52s, each carrying about twenty-five tons of bombs and thus laying down huge carpets of destruction, the bombing was anything but surgical, and frequently hit civilian villages. The result was thousands of refugees fleeing into Phnom Pehn and the province towns. The capital swelled from a population of 600,000 at the start of the war to 2 million at its end in 1975. The American embassy in Phnom Pehn—and Henry Kissinger's team in Washington—insisted that the refugees were fleeing only one thing: attacks by the brutal Khmer Rouge. But in fact they were fleeing both the Khmer Rouge and the American bombs. I visited refugee camps regularly and consistently heard both accounts. Some peasants didn't flee at all; the Khmer Rouge used their anger about the bombing to recruit them as soldiers and porters.

The bombing raids illustrate what is pretty much an axiom in all wars: i.e., that so-called "conventional" **weapons** not forbidden by international law can produce the same horrific results as banned weapons.

In Cambodia, the B-52s carried napalm and dart cluster-bombs (since discontinued by the Pentagon). The raids were carried out by three of the mammoth planes in formation. Each plane can carry twenty-five to thirty tons of bombs, making the total load of a formation seventy-five to ninety tons. B-52s drop their bombs to form a grid, or "box," of destruction on the ground; the grid (an average one might be one kilometer wide and two kilometers long) can be altered to fit the size and shape of the troop concentration. Soldiers who manage to survive these massive explosions (which sometimes throw bodies and dirt as much as one hundred feet in the air) are often rendered unfit for further duty, having been put in permanent shock or made deaf or simply frightened to the bone of every sharp sound or movement. Such raids were what destroyed the retreating Iraqi troops on the road to Basra at the end of that war in 1991—the road that became known as the "Highway of Death."

In 1973, an accidental B-52 bombing of Neak Loeung, a government-held Mekong river town, killed and wounded some four hundred Cambodians, most of them civilians. The American embassy apologized and gave monetary gifts to victims' families on a sliding scale—a few hundred dollars for the loss of a limb, more for multiple limbs, and still more for a death. When civilians die in wars, the military calls it unintentional, even though everyone knows civilian deaths are inevitable, especially when the weapons spray their lethality over large spaces. The phrase used by the Pentagon for civilian deaths is "collateral damage"—just as napalm was called "soft ordnance"—the idea being to give war a softer, sanitized sound for the lay public.

Napalm, incidentally, was dropped by B-52s in the Vietnam and Cambodian wars, in the form of CBUs—Cluster Bomb Units. (Other planes dropped napalm in different containers and forms.) A CBU is a large bomb, say 750 pounds, that carries hundreds of smaller projectiles. A typical CBU is rigged to open, in the manner of a clamshell, a short distance above the ground, releasing its hail of explosive bomblets on the enemy troops beneath it. One variety was the CBU-3; its bomblets carried napalm, which set fire to the troops or robbed the air of oxygen, thus asphyxiating them. Another version carried special darts, which ripped through flesh or pinned the victims to trees or the ground. Sometimes it is hard for the layman to discern any great difference between these weapons and, for instance, the chemical arms banned by international law and custom. Both have a terror component. The napalm and darts have since been taken out of the American CBU inventory—because of their bad image—but conventional-bomblet CBUs are still used, as in the 1991 Gulf war with Iraq.

And what about plain old rockets? Should all of them be banned, since they are frequently used as instruments of terror against civilians? The Khmer Rouge sent rockets shrieking into Phnom Penh throughout that five-year war. These were not precisely aimed munitions by any definition. They were crudely produced Chinese projectiles with a fan-shaped tail that whistled as it cut through the air overhead; you knew when it began its downward plummet because the whistling suddenly stopped. These rockets were launched from the city's environs, set off from hand-fashioned wooden platforms; there was no aiming at specific military targets—the effort was simply to get them to land somewhere, anywhere, in the refugee-packed city. And land they did—on markets, in school rooms, in backyards—spewing jagged metal and sliced limbs. The purpose was to demoralize the civilian population, and it worked.

An artillery piece can also be used as a weapon of terror against civilians. One afternoon in the summer of 1974, the Khmer Rouge trained a
captured American-made 105 mm howitzer on Phnom Penh and fanned its
muzzle across the city's southern edge. At first, as the shells fell in this half-
moon arc, they exploded without result, but then the arc came to a colony
of houses called Psar Deum Kor, and the death began. Fires started by the
shells broke out and the houses were quickly in flames, whipped by high
winds. Within a half hour, nearly two hundred people were dead and another
two hundred wounded, virtually all civilians. The bodies were carted off on
police pickup trucks. No military target was anywhere in the vicinity.

In the end—whether in Cambodia or any other killing field—there is
nothing new either about the barbarity of people destroying people or,
unfortunately, about its seeming inevitability in every age. One unchanging

"After" photos of the Khmer Rouge's torture victims. Phnom Penh, Cambodia, 1998.

lesson is that war or genocide or crimes against humanity are states of violence that, where they exist, remove all breath from such notions as the law
and civilized behavior.

Is it hopeless, then, to try to strengthen both the international law and
its enforcement? No, never hopeless, not if you believe in the possibility of
improvement, no matter how slight. Journalists are by blood and tradition
committed to the belief, or at least to the tenet, of trying to keep bad
things from getting any worse than they already are. Thus, this book.

Carpet or Area Bombing

By Horst Fischer

Air attacks on a city that treat it as a single **military objective** instead of clearly distinguishing military objectives and attacking them individually are an example of area bombardment, often called carpet bombing. Many of the World War II attacks on cities targeted an area rather than individual military objectives. Legal arguments and military rationales were given for the strategic bombing campaign, among them to destroy the enemy's industry, to weaken the morale of the population, or simply to punish the adversary for its previous violations. The destruction of Rotterdam, Dresden, and Hiroshima are prominent examples. The Nuremberg Tribunal did not discuss area bombardment in any detail, and the practice, which flies in the face of all the civilian protections in the Fourth Geneva Convention of 1949, continued into the Cold War. The U.S. aerial campaigns against North Vietnam—in particular the so-called Christmas bombing of 1972 against Hanoi and Haiphong—are believed to have been illegal area bombardments.

An explicit ban on area bombardment was first codified in the 1977 Additional Protocol I, which applies to bombardments of cities, towns, villages, or other areas containing a concentration of civilians. An attack by bombardment by any methods or means that treats as a single military objective a number of clearly separated and distinct military objectives is considered to be an **indiscriminate attack** and is prohibited. Launching such an attack in the knowledge that it will cause excessive loss of life, injury to civilians, or damage to civilian objects is considered a grave breach. Bombarding areas containing solely military targets is permitted. Important powers such as the United States, which are not party to Protocol I, accept this principle as binding **customary international law**.

Though the Protocol's wording makes it clear that attacks targeting cities as such are prohibited, declarations by States while negotiating the text suggest severe problems in applying it. States have made clear that "clearly separated" implies a significant distance between separate military objectives, but what is "significant" is highly subjective.

One obvious problem is the inaccuracy of aerial bombardment. This has been altered by newer precision-guided weapons; but these are available only to a few combatants, and then, only in limited quantities. So long as the party to the conflict attempting to distinguish between targets employs weapons that can be used discriminately, it will be able to claim it has avoided crossing the line into violations of humanitarian law.

From recent conflicts it can be concluded that belligerents are aware of the restraints on area bombardment even if they are not bound by the rules of Protocol I. The major allied forces in the **Gulf War** claimed to have implemented the standards of Protocol I in attacking Iraqi military targets although not bound to do so.

The U.S. military command has acknowledged that the bombing of the Iraqi Basra area by American B-52 bombers in 1991 was an area bombardment. As the attacks had been directed solely against the combatants of the so-called Iraqi Republican Guard, the United States believed the attacks to have been lawful.

Bomb craters from B-52 strikes. Near Saigon, Vietnam, 1968.

Chechnya Barry Renfrew

Russia's disastrous war in Chechnya saw butchery and savagery on a scale and intensity recalling World War II. Huge formations of tanks, artillery, and aircraft pounded Chechen cities and towns to charred ruins. Most of those killed or murdered were civilians. Human rights and international humanitarian law were meaningless to both sides.

Russian estimates of deaths during the twenty-one-month war range up to 90,000, mostly civilians. Some 600,000 people, half the population, fled or were driven from their homes. Both sides committed atrocities, although the far larger Russian military was guilty of the worse excesses. Russian troops indiscriminately attacked towns and villages, killing and raping civilians, pillaging and burning homes. Chechen fighters executed prisoners and civilian opponents, used civilians to shield their forces and military installations, and drove Russian civilians out of Chechnya in a systematic campaign.

There is no neat, simple answer as to why this war was so savage. It was a war inflamed by intense nationalism and ethnic hatred; a calamitously managed war that swiftly degenerated into a brutal campaign of suppression that only increased Chechen resistance; a war in which an ill-trained, disintegrating army, in truth little more than a mob, was pitted against a smaller, but highly motivated and skilled guerrilla force; a war in which a democratically elected government employed the ruthless methods and forces of Soviet totalitarianism against a civilian population. It was also a war between peoples and cultures that have waged merciless wars of conquest and extermination against each other for centuries with unrelenting medieval savagery.

Kill or be killed was the sole motivation of most soldiers in the disintegrating Russian Army, who were desperately fighting to stay alive rather than win a war. Win or die was the creed of Chechens inspired by fanatical patriotism and their Islamic belief in jihad, or holy war, against the traditional enemy. Many Russians see Chechens as swarthy, treacherous savages and

An internal conflict: Despite vastly superior weaponry, Russian troops, like this wounded soldier, suffered heavy casualties. So did the civilians.

habitual criminals. The Chechens saw the Russians as ruthless conquerors and despoilers of their motherland.

The West chose to see the war as an internal matter with no legal or practical basis for outside intervention. Although painfully aware that Russian forces were responsible for the deaths of thousands of civilians, the West believed it had to support Boris Yeltsin.

Russia is a disparate patchwork of conquered ethnic and national groups held together by force. Every Russian government, whatever its ideology, has believed that the existence of Russia depends on preserving this fractious empire—at any cost. Many Russian leaders and ordinary people were deeply aware that the dissolution of the Soviet Union had stripped away huge strips of territory and much of their national pride. Many feared that Russia was on the brink of disintegration.

The Chechens, an intensely nationalistic and martial people, were among the last to be conquered by czarist Russia in the nineteenth century. The Chechens never accepted Russian domination and Moscow's rule was correspondingly harsh. Soviet dictator Joseph Stalin deported virtually the entire Chechen nation, hundreds of thousands of men, women, and children, to Central Asia in the 1940s, where many perished in appalling conditions.

Chechnya declared independence after the Soviet Union collapsed in 1991. Some Chechens opposed the regime of Dzhokhar Dudayev, an ex-Soviet general, because of clan rivalries and a more modern squabble over power and wealth in a region straddling major oil pipelines. But most Chechens saw their right to independence as a fact of nature as indisputable as the mountains of their land. Chechens had no need to justify their claim of independence through international law or history. A Chechen asked such a question would give you either a look of pity because you were clearly a fool or else a threatening retort that you must be an enemy.

International law has little to say on whether the Chechens had the right to secede or whether Russia was justified in using force to stop them. (Although international treaties often refer broadly to the self-determination of peoples, it is usually construed to refer to anticolonial struggles of far-away peoples and not to parts of a nation.) But governments assert their sovereign right to preserve their territorial integrity, by force if necessary— tacitly accepting the right of other States to do likewise.

Internationally, the Chechen War was quickly deemed an internal matter. The United Nations said it could not intervene in a domestic problem. There were scattered calls for sanctions, but Western reaction was confined to appeals for restraint and occasional rebukes.

Western governments were unwilling or unable to do more because they had based their Russian policies on President Boris Yeltsin, the man who launched the war. Yeltsin was seen by the West as the best guarantor of moderate, pro-Western government in Moscow. But Russian democracy was in its infancy, and powerful Communist and nationalist groups in Russia were calling for Yeltsin's removal and a return to the country's totalitarian past.

Keenly aware of Russia's vast nuclear arsenal and haunted by the specter of a Russia in chaos or under a new authoritarian regime, the West wanted a friendly government in the Kremlin. The world was still celebrating the end of the Cold War and the fall of the Soviet Union, which had killed and imprisoned millions of its own people. Sustaining democratic reforms to ensure Russia did not slide backward was an overwhelming concern.

A democratic Russia, or at least the hope of it, outweighed the suffering of Chechnya.

Even if they had wanted to act, what could the United States and its allies have done to halt or moderate the war? Embargoes on weapons or other strategic items would have been futile against the huge Russian military, which still had many of the resources of a global power and could supply all its own needs. A business or financial embargo would have hurt pro-democratic market reforms. There seems little else the West could have done, even with hindsight. Today, preserving the hope of a democratic Russia seems more vital than ever as the country disintegrates and the threat of authoritarianism or fascism waits in the wings.

Russian soldiers were bewildered when they were sent into Chechnya in December 1994. Women and children tried to block the Russian tanks, begging the troops to turn back. One Russian general halted his forces, saying it was not the role of the army to fight its own citizens.

That early uncertainty evaporated as Chechen forces inflicted heavy

Chechen fighter with AK-47 rifle about to launch a grenade. Grozny, 1996.

losses on the Russians. The ill-trained, poorly led Russian troops were mowed down by the hundred in futile human-wave attacks against Chechen positions. What was supposed to be a swift police action turned into a gigantic disaster for the Russian military. Atrocities began almost at once, with Chechens literally tearing captured Russian airmen to bits while Russian forces indiscriminately bombed civilian settlements.

Grozny, the Chechen capital, was engulfed by a pitched battle. After infantry assaults failed, the Russian military set out to pulverize the city into submission. Russian aircraft bombarded Grozny while armored forces and artillery hammered the city from the ground.

I was walking back from the center of Grozny along a residential street with two colleagues at the height of the battle. Without warning, a Russian jet suddenly dived at us, firing a missile that shattered a large brick house a few yards away and knocked us over. The only other people on the street were two children. Earlier that day we had ducked Chechen sniper fire in the city center. Anything that moved had become a target.

The Russian assault fell mainly on Grozny's civilians, mostly ethnic

Russians. The city's small Chechen population had fled to surrounding villages. Separatist forces operated from buildings filled with Russian civilians as shields.

Under international humanitarian law, the Russians were justified in seeking to capture the city because it was the rebels' main base and the location of **legitimate military targets**, regardless of the presence of civilians. The fact that Chechen forces had fortified large parts of the city also meant that apartment blocks and other civilian structures were legitimate targets if they were being put to military use. And many civilians perished not because of the Russians, but because Chechen forces were using them as human **shields**, and, at times, prevented them from leaving the city or being evacuated. A Russian strategy of capturing Grozny by destroying it as a whole target was illegitimate, however, under the rules of war because tar-

Grozny under siege: Residents haul water from a spring in a park, while an amputee follows behind across the ice.

geting must be discriminate and aimed at discrete individual objectives. Combatants may not lawfully treat all the targets in an area, such as an entire city, as a single, giant target.

Reporting from Grozny during the battle, I could see clearly that both sides would do anything to win. Talk of law or humanitarian concerns was meaningless to most Russian and Chechen commanders, especially those who indifferently sent their own troops to be slaughtered day after day in a war of attrition.

Nor can it be said that the opposing sides did not know what they were doing or were unaware of the legal and moral responsibilities of professional soldiers. Top Chechen commanders had been senior officers in the Soviet Army, with the same professional outlook, years of training, and higher education as their ex-colleagues in the Russian military. But commanders on both sides also came from a Soviet tradition of the ruthless use of force to impose the will of the State and the virtual absence of human or civil rights.

After Grozny fell, the war moved to the countryside. Russian forces "pacified" Chechen villages, attacking them with tanks, artillery, and aircraft, often regardless of whether they resisted. Humanitarian and aid groups chronicled persistent patterns of Russian soldiers killing civilians, raping, and looting. Chechen bandits also robbed and killed civilians.

Russian forces randomly rounded up Chechen men in a systematic campaign to terrify the population. Survivors reported being tortured. Many Chechen families said their menfolk never returned, but there are no reliable estimates of how many people disappeared. Mass graves were found near Russian detention centers in Grozny.

Sergei Kovalyov, a prominent dissident in the Soviet era who was head of Russia's human rights commission, resigned in January 1996 to protest the government's actions. But he also criticized the Chechens for their treatment of Russian civilians.

"I can no longer work with a president whom I consider neither a supporter of democracy nor the guardian of the rights and freedoms of the citizens of my country," he said in a letter to Yeltsin.

Chechen fighters, as well as using civilians as shields in battle, killed prisoners and civilian opponents, especially supporters of pro-Moscow Chechen political groups, frequently torturing and mutilating victims. Some captured Russian soldiers were tortured and executed, while others were treated well and released.

Trying to take the war to the Russians, Chechen detachments attacked several Russian cities, again using civilian **hostages** as human shields, and in one case seizing a hospital that became the center of a major battle.

By the summer of 1996 the war appeared to be winding down with Moscow claiming victory. In August, the separatists captured much of Grozny in a surprise attack. Moscow, conscious of growing popular anger against the war and seeing no hope for a military victory, pulled its forces out and tried to save face by saying a decision on Chechen independence would be made by 2001. The Chechens said they were independent.

Russia has done its best to forget the war. Despite elections, Chechnya has been swallowed up by lawlessness and violence. Journalists can no longer visit Chechnya because of endemic kidnapping. The shattered country lives under the rule of the gun.

(See **civilian immunity; evacuation of civilians; indiscriminate attack; international vs. internal armed conflict; military objectives; pillage; wanton destruction; willful killing.**)

Chemical Weapons

By Peter Pringle

In March 1984, an Iranian soldier attacking Iraq during the conflict between those two States came under fire from artillery shells that emitted a heavy smoke smelling of garlic. Within a few minutes, the soldier's eyes burned and his skin began to itch, redden, and blister. Five days later the skin on his neck, chest, and shoulders began to peel off. Shortly afterward, the soldier died.

A UN investigation of several such instances concluded that chemical weapons, including mustard gas and the nerve agent known as Tabun, had been used. By the end of the war, Iran claimed tens of thousands of chemical weapons' casualties. There was no doubt that Iraq had broken the 1925 Geneva Protocol for the Prohibition of the Use of Asphyxiating, Poisonous, or other Gases, and of Bacteriological Methods of Warfare, nor that Iran had retaliated in kind, albeit briefly and less effectively.

Since then, Saddam Hussein has apparently stockpiled chemical and **biological weapons**, and there have been uncorroborated allegations of the use of such weapons by other States: the use of gas by South African-backed forces in Mozambique, by contestants in the conflict between Azerbaijan and Armenia, by Turks against Kurds, and in the Sudan civil war. More recently, there have been unverified claims by a Soviet-era defector that the Russians may have developed super-strains of germ weapons, and some of these may still exist in the Russian arsenal.

For the observer at the front line, accusations of the use of chemical and biological weapons are almost impossible to verify on the spot. Only after a prolonged investigation that involves examining the corpses of the victims, interviewing survivors, and searching for residues of the weapons ingredients and products of chemical reactions involving such ingredients, can the truth be known—and sometimes not even then.

One of the lingering military mysteries of the Cold War was Moscow's alleged use of so-called yellow rain against Hmong tribesmen in Laos. Yellow rain was said by the United States to be a deadly chemical and biological weapon that was sprayed from light aircraft and fell "like a yellow rain," but an independent inquiry by American and British scientists suggested a perfectly natural explanation: the defecation of honey bees. When bees defecate they leave the hive in a swarm, and the result, for anyone standing underneath the flight path, can be something like a yellow rain. The waste matter contains toxins that can make people ill. However, the U.S. government has not officially accepted the bee theory, nor dropped its charges of yellow rain.

Put together over the years, these reports of the use of banned weapons underscored the urgency of tightening international controls. The 1925 Geneva Protocol, eventually ratified by 149 states, prohibited only the "first use" of chemical and biological weapons. Countries were allowed to develop and stockpile chemical weapons for "defensive" purposes: the law did not prohibit reprisals with chemical weapons. The ban did not apply against a country's own nationals, nor tear gases, including CS gas. The 1972 Biological Weapons Convention renounced germ weapons totally, including their development and stockpiling. In 1993, the new Chemical Weapons

Convention was opened for signature in Paris. It entered into force on April 29, 1997, and 111 states have ratified it, including the U.S. and Russia.

The essence of the fifty-thousand-word treaty is that each State party undertakes never, in any circumstances, to develop, produce, otherwise acquire, stockpile, or retain chemical weapons, or transfer them directly or indirectly to anyone; never to use chemical weapons or engage in any preparations for doing so; and never to assist, encourage, or induce, in any way, anyone to engage in any activity prohibited by the treaty.

By "chemical weapons" the treaty means munitions or other devices using toxic chemicals to cause death, temporary incapacitation, or permanent harm to humans or animals. The treaty does not prohibit the development of toxic chemicals for industrial, agricultural, research, medical, pharmaceutical, or other peaceful purposes, or purposes related to protection

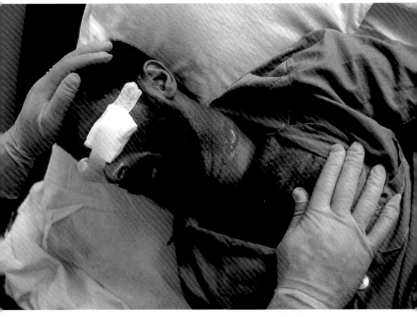

An Iranian victim of Iraqi chemical warfare is treated at a hospital in 1986.

against chemical weapons, and law enforcement including domestic riot control. Riot control agents, such as CS gas, cannot be used as a method of warfare, a distinction not always easy to make. (In a move to which no other party to the convention took exception, President Bill Clinton pledged to Congress that the United States will not be restricted in the use of riot control agents in two circumstances: conflicts to which the United States is not a party but is playing a peacekeeping role, or locations where U.S. troops are stationed with the approval of the host State.)

Each State undertakes to destroy, within ten years, its chemical stockpiles and production facilities that can produce more than one ton of chemical weapons per year.

The treaty set up a new international body, the Organization for the Prohibition of Chemical Weapons, headquartered in The Hague. It will oversee treaty compliance and investigate any claims of violation by treaty-member States. The Secretary-General of the United Nations is empowered by UN resolution to investigate any claims of violations by nonmember States.

Child Soldiers

By Anna Cataldi

The woman ran toward me, shouting and waving her arms, tears running down her face. It was a freezing November morning, and I was in a refugee camp in Turanj, a small, bombed-out town on the border between Bosnia and Croatia. A moment later, the woman shouted out what sounded like some kind of curse and then suddenly collapsed as if in a dead faint.

I could not understand what I had done to inspire such a reaction. A Polish United Nations soldier, who understood Serbo-Croatian, stepped forward and explained that the woman had not been raging at me but had been desperately seeking the help of the only journalist to have shown her face in the camp in days.

The previous night, soldiers from the forces of Fikret Abdic had come to the camp in search of new recruits. Abdic was a Bosnian businessman and warlord who, though a Muslim, had broken with the government in Sarajevo and was fighting a war within a war against it in northwest Bosnia. The fight was not going well, and he needed all the fighters he could get.

The woman had already sacrificed for Abdic's dubious cause. Both her husband and her two elder sons had been killed during the fighting in the previous several months. Now the fighters had taken her youngest boy. They had seized him and thrown him in a van treacherously marked with red crosses. He was only fourteen.

Occurrences like this took place all the time during the Bosnian War and are taking place in conflicts that are still going on all over the world. While the employment of children is anything but a recent phenomenon—for millennia, children have gone to war as drummer boys, messengers, porters, and servants—the escalating number of children bearing arms in contemporary conflicts is terrifying. Graca Machel, author of the United Nations Report on the Impact of Armed Conflict on Children, has estimated that in 1995 and 1996 alone, 250,000 children were serving either in government armies or in opposition forces. She has called the participation of child soldiers in war "one of the most alarming trends in armed conflicts."

The two Additional Protocols of 1977, applying to international and internal armed conflicts respectively, impose on the parties to a conflict the obligation "to take all feasible measures in order that children who have not attained the age of fifteen years do not take a direct part in hostilities" and to "refrain from recruiting them into their armed forces." The 1998 Rome Statute for an International Criminal Court lists as a war crime conscription or enlistment of children under the age of fifteen into a State's armed forces or using them to participate actively in hostilities.

Human rights law also addresses the issue of children in armed conflict. The 1989 Convention on the Rights of the Child (UNCRC), which has gained nearly universal acceptance—the holdouts are Oman, Somalia, the United Arab Emirates, and the United States—is the primary instrument. The con-

Child soldiers in war games. First row: Afghanistan, 1990; Sidon, 1982. Second row: Cambodia, 1973; Liberia, 1992; Afghanistan, 1985. Third row: Jordan, 1969; Iran, 1983. Bottom Row: Vietnam, 1968; Sri Lanka, 1995; Spain, 1936.

vention defines a child as a person below the age of eighteen, but sets fifteen as a minimum age for going to war. Some States want to set eighteen
as the minimum age for combatants, but the proposal has not received wide
support, least of all from those countries affected by internal conflicts of the
sort most likely to see the use of child soldiers. In such countries, particularly in Africa, typically half of the population is under the age of fifteen.
(See **perfidy and treachery**.)

Children as Killers

By Corinne Dufka

The Krahn militiamen, about two hundred of them, were advancing up Broad
Street. Armed with AK-47s, machetes, fishing harpoons, and kitchen utensils,
their objective was to take over the posh seaside neighborhood of Mamba
Point from Charles Taylor's National Patriotic Front of Liberia (NPFL) militia.
It was April 1996 and Monrovia, the Liberian capital, had plummeted into
urban chaos, leaving hundreds dead and causing tens of thousands to flee
the city in panic.

A commander heard a stirring within a building. "What's that?" the soldiers yelled excitedly. An unarmed man was pulled out from his hiding place
on the second floor. We knew him as the caretaker, surely trying to stay out
of harm's way. For the Krahn, he was the enemy.

Within minutes he was being chased like an animal by a group of ten
soldiers. They ran him around in circles stabbing him with bayonets until,
bleeding profusely, he was too tired to resist. The caretaker, a gentle but
strapping man, did not last long. He was soon shot in the back with a pistol,
and as he lay dying some of the soldiers took turns stabbing him in the back
with a six-inch-long butcher knife.

Perhaps the last image he had before slipping into death was of Double
Trouble, a nine-year-old boy soldier dressed in an oversize, faded, purple T-
shirt and flip-flops, grabbing the knife and having his turn at plunging it in
and out between the shoulders. He then grabbed an empty Coke bottle,

which like a *tira de gracia* was broken over the dying man's head. Double Trouble stood up and looked around for the approval of his mates. Like he had just hit a home run. The score, 1–0. They slapped him on the back and cheered.

"Where's your mama?" I asked him after the battle. He had a soft, childish face that hardened between the eyes as he responded. "She dead." "And your daddy?" "He dead too. Everybody dead." "How old are you?" I asked. "Old enough to kill a man," he replied.

Double Trouble. One of thousands of child soldiers in Liberia. Most have experienced more loss and pain before the age of eight than the rest of us do in a lifetime. Many watched their parents killed in front of them, or worse, were forced to kill their loved ones as some sort of perverse initiation rite.

In Liberia, Krahn militia men and boys spear a suspected NPFL member and beat him to death. Double Trouble is shown in flip-flops holding a stick.

But every child needs a family and soon the militia became theirs.

A few days later, a brief cease-fire between the two warring sides was agreed upon. The fighters relaxed. Boys will be boys, I thought, as I came upon a group of five NPFL child soldiers, the eldest not more than twelve, playing soccer on one of the most heavily contested corners of the urban war. I saw their rifles discarded on the street below a rain-soaked Liberian flag, and only then did it become clear that the white "ball" they maneuvered was a human skull. The decaying body lay some twenty meters away.

They kicked the "ball" over the debris of war—spent cartridges, old wallets, clothes dropped by fleeing civilians, and old photographs—and squealed with delight as it entered the goal posts marked by two rusting sardine cans. A glimpse of childhood and they were back behind the barricades the next morning. "Hey, white woman," a boy of about eleven with oversize tennis shoes, a looted hat with yellow flowers, and an AK-47 half his height yelled at me from behind a bullet-pocked wall. "No school today. Nope. Today we gunna kill da Krahn."

Civil Defense

By Heike Spieker

Civil defense refers to a variety of practical measures to protect civilians in wars and natural disasters. The purpose of civil defense is to ensure the survival of the civilian population, including the buildings, vehicles, facilities, and other objects necessary for survival. For example, Israel after the Scud bombardment during the **Gulf War** strengthened its civil defense system by stepping up the construction of air-raid shelters.

Civil defense can be carried out by civilians or the military either in occupied territory or in any part of territories of parties to the conflict. Among the activities covered are warning systems; arrangements for evacuation; management of shelters; fire fighting and rescue; medical services including first aid; religious counseling; the provision of emergency accommodation and supplies; the repair of indispensable public utilities; and safeguarding objects essential for survival.

Explicit rules for the protection of civil defense in occupied territory were codified in the Fourth Geneva Convention of 1949 and Additional Protocol I of 1977. These provide narrowly defined legal protection that applies principally where civil defense is carried out by civilians, be they officials or private citizens. This protection balances the diverging interests of civil defense organizations, civilian population and occupying power.

Under Article 63 of the Fourth Geneva Convention, civilian civil defense organizations "shall be able to pursue their activities . . . by the maintenance of the essential public utility services, by the distribution of relief and by the organization of rescues." The occupying power may not impose "temporary and exceptional measures" except for "urgent reasons of security" and may not require changes in the personnel or structure of civilian civil defense organizations that would be disadvantageous to their activities.

Protocol I further strengthens civilian protections and states that civilian civil defense organizations shall be "respected and protected" and are entitled to perform their tasks except in cases of imperative **military necessity**. Units and personnel must display a distinctive insignia (a blue triangle in an orange square) and only the owners of civil defense facilities and equipment have the right to destroy or divert them from their proper use.

Occupying powers are obliged to grant civilian civil defense organizations the necessary facilities and not to divert buildings nor matériel if this would harm the civilian population. Military units assigned to civil defense are also to be "respected and protected" if they are permanently assigned and exclusively devoted to the tasks, perform no other military duties, during the conflict, and display the insignia.

Violating the protections of Protocol I constitutes an **illegal act** by the State and constitutes a grave breach if civilian personnel of a civil defense organization are made the object of attack.

If civilian civil defense organizations, their personnel, buildings, shelters, and matériel are used to harm the enemy, their protection ceases. But organizing civil defense at the direction of military authorities, cooperating with the military in civil defense tasks, and organizing along military lines do not constitute "acts harmful to the enemy."

Civil Patrols

By Ewen Allison and Robert K. Goldman

C

In 1982, an army colonel ordered the Guatemalan village of Chichicastenango to form a "Civil Defense Patrol" to help put down an ongoing insurrection. The colonel made it clear that those who refused to sign a commitment to civil patrols would be seen as subversives and killed. The villagers signed.

Hundreds of thousands of Guatemalan civilians had to serve in civil patrols, essentially **paramilitary** groups formed from the civilian population as a means to control them and gain their assistance in the civil war. Already poor, patrollers were forced to purchase weapons and uniform shirts from the army. Members had to patrol continuously for up to twenty-four hours a week, and sometimes went on army-accompanied sweeps that lasted up to several weeks. Males of nearly all ages—even eight-year-olds—were compelled into service. Besides their combat duties, patrollers had to work as laborers for army soldiers. Those who refused to participate had to pay a fine, find a replacement, or face beatings and other severe punishments or even execution, all without trial. Recalcitrant villagers in Chichicastenango were put into a specially dug well fifteen meters deep.

Humanitarian law does not interfere with a government's right to suppress insurrections and implicitly allows a military draft. Human rights law takes a dim view of forcing people to serve in civil patrols. The Inter-American Commission on Human Rights has repeatedly declared that the institution of civil patrols in Guatemala was a restriction of liberty and a form of involuntary servitude, in violation of Articles 6, 7, and 22 of the American Convention on Human Rights.

Yet civil patrollers are not only victims, they are also victimizers. Patrollers in Guatemala beat, tortured, and even killed thousands of suspected subversives, even those who merely refused to serve in the patrols. Sometimes civil patrols were ordered to do these things by army or government officials, sometimes the patrols acted on their own initiative. In either case, patrollers violated not only the human rights of the victims but also the rules of internal armed conflict that call for humane treatment of noncombatants.

Governments are usually held responsible for violations of both humanitarian and human rights law perpetrated by patrollers. This is especially the case when the patrols are organized by government or army officials. Also, governments are held responsible under human rights law when they fail to suppress violations by privately organized armed groups.

(See **compelling military service**; **irregulars**.)

Civil War

C

By A. P. V. Rogers

Treaties on the laws of war were developed to deal with wars between States, not civil wars (or internal armed conflicts as they are now known). They only applied to the latter in the unlikely event that the **belligerent status** of the insurgents was recognized. It was not until after World War II that treaties started to include some provisions on internal armed conflicts to ensure some protection for the victims of those conflicts.

It is never easy to determine when a violent confrontation within a State goes beyond the realms of domestic criminal law and becomes an armed conflict to which international law applies. This is especially the case as the State will be reluctant to admit that it does not have the situation under control, yet dissidents will be quick to claim that theirs is a cause of international concern.

Assuming that threshold is crossed, the international legal rules governing internal armed conflicts are much less developed than those applying to armed conflicts between States. The rules are to be found in basic customary law principles and in Common Article 3 of the 1949 Geneva Conventions. Additionally, certain fundamental (known as "non-derogable") principles of human rights law provide protection for the victims of these conflicts. If dissident forces exercise sufficient control over part of the State's territory as to enable them to carry out sustained and concerted military operations and comply with their obligations under it, Protocol II of 1977 also applies.

The following are the most important rules that apply to all parties to internal armed conflicts:

1. All combat activity must be justified on military grounds; activity that is not militarily necessary is prohibited.

2. Attacks may be directed *only* against objects that make a contribution to the enemy's military effort and hence are of tactical or strategic importance. Incidental loss and damage must be minimized.

3. A distinction must always be made between combatants, who may take a direct part in hostilities and be attacked themselves, and noncombatants, who may not take a direct part in hostilities and may not be attacked or used as shields.

4. Noncombatants and their property must be spared as far as possible from the incidental effects of military operations. Stealing is an offense in war as in peace.

5. Prisoner of war status does not arise in internal armed conflict. Captured persons can be tried under the law of the State where the internal armed conflict is going on for any offenses they may have committed against that law. They have the protections listed in paragraph 6 and under human rights law. Sentences may only be carried out after a proper trial by a properly constituted court.

6. Persons who take no active part in hostilities (noncombatants, captured persons, the wounded, sick, and shipwrecked) are to be treated humanely and equally, irrespective of race, color, religion, sex, wealth, etc. That means there must be no murder, mutilation, cruel treatment, torture, rape, sexual assault, or other outrages on personal dignity, or humiliating or degrading treatment.

Ibo troops retreat during the Nigerian Civil War over the secession of Biafra, 1968.

7. Hostage taking is prohibited.

8. Starvation of noncombatants as a method of warfare is prohibited.

9. The wounded, sick, and shipwrecked must be collected and cared for.

10. Although it may be necessary to evacuate noncombatants from areas of danger, it is prohibited to move them for discriminatory reasons or to shield military targets from attack.

In internal armed conflicts to which Protocol II applies, the above rules are supplemented by more detailed provisions on the protection of the civilian population, especially children, the treatment of detainees, and the conduct of criminal prosecutions.

(See **international vs. internal armed conflict**.)

Civilian Immunity

By Heike Spieker

The principle of distinction is a technical term in the laws of armed conflict intended to protect civilian persons and objects. Under this principle, parties to an armed conflict must always distinguish between civilians and civilian objects on the one hand, and combatants and military targets on the other.

The meaning of the term was spelled out in Additional Protocol I of 1977. While a number of States have not ratified Protocol I, the obligation to uphold the principle of distinction is also valid as customary law.

The civilian population enjoys **immunity** insofar as it shall "enjoy general protection against dangers arising from military operations" and "shall not be the object of attack." The Protocol prohibits actions whose primary purpose is to spread terror among the civilian population. It also prohibits so called **indiscriminate attacks**, thereby obliging each party to an armed conflict under all circumstances to distinguish at all times between the **combatants** and **military objectives**, and civilians or civilian objects.

Examples of indiscriminate attack include **carpet bombing** or an attack which may be expected to cause **collateral damage** to civilian persons or objects "which would be excessive in relation to the concrete and direct military advantage anticipated."

Several experts in international law believe that the customary law principle of distinction applies in all internal armed conflicts, but the black letter law is much less explicit than for an international conflict.

Under Protocol II, civilians, i.e., all persons "affected" by a noninternational conflict, "shall enjoy the general protection against the dangers arising from military operations" in the course of noninternational armed conflicts "unless and for such time as they take a direct part in hostilities."

This Protocol, which addresses exclusively noninternational armed conflict, does not explicitly distinguish clearly between civilians and combatants, and does not even mention the term *combatant*. Still, it prohibits making civilians as such the object of attack or undertaking acts or threats of violence the primary purpose of which is to spread terror among the civilian population. A prohibition of indiscriminate attacks is not codified as such.

For example, Iraq's bombardment of Israeli cities with Scud missiles during the **Gulf War** was an indiscriminate attack since these missiles, due to their construction, could not be precisely directed at a specific military target. Had Iraq directed the same missiles against Kurdish towns in northern Iraq, the attacks could not easily have been been characterized as unlawful indiscriminate attacks, provided Iraq had claimed to direct them against insurgents.

(See **international vs. internal armed conflict**)

Civilians, Illegal Targeting of

C

By Joel Greenberg

On July 25, 1993, Israel launched a massive retaliatory strike against Shiite Muslim guerrillas who had rocketed northern Israeli towns and killed seven Israeli soldiers in a month in the Israeli occupation zone in southern Lebanon.

Operation Accountability began with wide-ranging air strikes across Lebanon and ended six days later with an American-brokered cease-fire. Intensive Israeli air and artillery bombardments forced hundreds of thousands of civilians in southern Lebanon out of their towns and villages.

Israel's openly declared aim was to stop attacks by the Iranian-backed Hizbollah group through the massive displacement of Lebanese civilians. The plight of the refugees streaming north toward Beirut, it was hoped, would compel the Lebanese government and its patron, Syria, to rein in Hizbollah.

Yitzhak Rabin, the Israeli prime minister, put it this way: "The goal of the operation is to get the southern Lebanese population to move northward, hoping that this will tell the Lebanese government something about the refugees who may get as far north as Beirut."

After issuing warnings, Israel proceeded to attack the hearts of villages, causing civilian casualties. Human Rights Watch said the Israeli Army also executed "what appear to have been calculated direct attacks on purely civilian targets."

The direct targeting of civilians is a breach of the laws of armed conflict. "The civilian population as such, as well as individual civilians, shall not be the object of attack. Acts or threats of violence the primary purpose of which is to spread terror among the civilian population are prohibited," states Additional Protocol I of 1977. Israel has not ratified Protocol I, but this provision, prohibiting direct attacks on civilians, is generally recognized as customary law, universally applicable regardless of ratification.

Nearly three years later, on April 11, 1996, Israel unleashed a similar offensive against Hizbollah, which led to another mass exodus of civilians in southern Lebanon. Operation Grapes of Wrath began with surgical air strikes and ended seventeen days later after an Israeli artillery barrage killed more than one hundred Lebanese refugees sheltering in a United Nations base.

As the bombardment by Israeli warplanes, gunships, and artillery spread northward, some 400,000 people fled their villages and towns, urged on by radio broadcasts and leaflets that warned them to leave or risk being hit. Amnesty International said that the language of the warnings was intended to threaten civilians, some of whom could not leave because they were too old or too sick to leave, or lacked transport, while others chose to remain to safeguard their property.

A warning broadcast on April 11 over the Voice of the South radio station of the Israeli-backed South Lebanon Army militia said: "If Hizbollah men happen to be near anybody's house, it will be hit." An April 13 message to residents of forty-five villages warned that "any presence in these villages will be regarded as subversive; that is, the subversive elements and whoever

85

happens to be with them will be hit."

The warnings seemed to suggest that the civilians and civilian objects were being targeted as punishment for their association with Hizbollah, rather than being destroyed incident to a legitimate attack on Hizbollah. Whether this or the other possible interpretation—that Israeli authorities were simply cautioning they would hit Hizbollah targets and anyone in the way might well become regrettable civilian collateral damage—the warnings carried an echo of the American **free fire zone** doctrine in Vietnam.

Israeli public statements were more circumspect. When civilians stayed behind in Nabatiyeh al-Fowqa, and were killed in fighter-bomber rocket attacks, Prime Minister Shimon Peres declared: "We only hit at those buildings from which Katyushas were fired. . . . But naturally Nabatiyeh was supposed to be vacant."

Brig. Gen. Giora Inbar, the commander of the Israeli army's liaison unit in southern Lebanon, indicated that the population displacement was not for military advantage but to send a political message: "The residents of southern Lebanon are under pressure. . . . If they understand that the address for peace and quiet is the government of Lebanon, which will impose its authority on Hizbollah, then this pressure is worthwhile."

More bluntly, an Israeli colonel, identified only as "Z", told the Israeli newspaper *Ha'aretz* that if Lebanese leaders "cared about the 400,000 refugees from the south, they would have acted to stop the fighting, but it seems that until thousands of refugees don't leave [the city of] Sidon for Beirut, they won't care."

And *The Wall Street Journal* quoted an unnamed official as saying: "Even if you tie me up and whip me, I'm not going to admit on-the-record that our policy is to force out civilians to put pressure on the Lebanese government. But let's just say we hope Lebanon understands the message."

Displacement of civilians is permitted under the laws of war if it is for their own protection or required for imperative military reasons. In this instance, the International Committee of the Red Cross (ICRC) publicly criticized the attacks as "contrary to international humanitarian law." The ICRC said its rationale drew from the 1899 and 1907 Hague Conventions and Protocol I, Articles 51, 52, and 57, which prohibit: acts or threats of violence, the primary purpose of which is to spread terror among the civilian population; attacks which may be expected to cause incidental loss of civilian life, injury to civilians; damage to civilian objects or a combination thereof, which would be excessive in relation to the concrete and direct military advantage anticipated; and attacks by bombardment by any methods or means which treat as a single military objective a number of clearly separated and distinct military objectives located in a city, town, village or area containing a similar concentration of civilians or civilian objects.
(See **collateral damage**; **indiscriminate attack**.)

For sixteen days in April, 1996, Israel pounded Lebanon during "Grapes of Wrath," a blitzkrieg against the Hizbollah movement. Here Ibrahim Alayan is pulled from the rubble of his home in Nabatiye, north of Tyre, which was hit by a missile.

Collateral Damage

By Horst Fischer

Collateral or incidental damage occurs when attacks targeted at **military objectives** cause civilian casualties and damage to civilian objects. It often occurs if military objectives such as military equipment or soldiers are situated in cities or villages or close to civilians. Attacks that are expected to cause collateral damage are not prohibited *per se*, but the laws of armed conflict restrict **indiscriminate attacks**. Article 57 of the 1977 Additional Protocol I to the 1949 Geneva Conventions states that, in an international conflict, "constant care shall be taken to spare the civilian population, civilians, and civilian objects." In addition, under Article 51, **carpet bombing** is prohibited, as are attacks that employ methods and means of combat whose effects cannot be controlled. Finally, attacks are prohibited if the collateral damage expected from any attack is not proportional to the military advantage anticipated. Military commanders in deciding about attacks have to be aware of these rules and either refrain from launching an attack, suspend an attack if the principle of **proportionality** is likely to be violated, or replan an attack so that it complies with the laws of armed conflict.

In internal conflict, civilians have little legal protection from collateral or incidental damage. Additional Protocol II requires that, so long as they do not take part in hostilities, the civilian population and individual civilians "shall enjoy general protection against the dangers arising from military operations" and "shall not be the object of attack." Protocol II also prohibits acts or threats of violence whose primary purpose is "to spread terror among the civilian population."

Parties to recent major armed conflicts, such as the **Gulf War** and the wars in the former Yugoslavia, have used the term *collateral damage* as part of an effort to demonstrate that their attacks were lawful. The claim is either that no collateral damage was caused or that the damage was minimal or proportional. Neutral observers might reach different conclusions than the parties to these conflicts. The death of many civilians in Iraq during the Gulf War due to the the lack of electricity in hospitals, which was the result of the destruction of almost all Iraqi power plants by allied air attacks, has been asserted by Iraq as disproportionate collateral damage. On the other hand, NATO officials in spring and summer 1995 quite rightly claimed that NATO attacks on Bosnian Serb military targets in Bosnia-Herzegovina did not kill civilians in a disproportionate manner and that therefore collateral damage was proportional.

Thus, besides having legal implications, the term is often used to win political support for a specific method of warfare or to counter allegations of violations of humanitarian law. The observer is reminded that whatever the claims of governments or armed forces, attacks directly targeted at the civilian population are in violation of the basic principle of distinction and cannot be referred to as having caused collateral damage.

(See **civilian immunity**.)

Collective Punishment

By Daoud Kuttab

C

For fourteen years, George Qumsieh, a stonecutter, worked to build a three-story stone home in the West Bank town of Beit Sahour. In February 1981, he and his family—his wife, four daughters, and three sons—moved into their new home. Nine months later, Israeli soldiers arrived at the home to arrest their youngest son, Walid, age fifteen. The army accused Walid of having thrown stones at an Israeli military vehicle four days earlier, in which a side window was broken. No soldiers were reported to have been injured in the incident.

The following day, and before the Shin Bet (General Security Service) had completed interrogating Walid, more troops arrived at the Qumsieh home. Ariel Sharon, the newly appointed Likud defense minister had promised an "iron fist" policy against Palestinians. Members of an Israeli engineering brigade placed the explosives and blew up the Qumsieh stone house. Months later, Walid was sentenced to seven years in jail based on the confession of his friends.

Under the 1949 Geneva Conventions, collective punishments are a war crime. Article 33 of the Fourth Convention states: "No protected person may be punished for an offense he or she has not personally committed," and "collective penalties and likewise all measures of intimidation or of terrorism are prohibited." Israel, however, does not accept that the Fourth Geneva Convention or the Additional Protocols apply to the West Bank *de jure*, but says it abides by the humanitarian provisions without specifying what the humanitarian provisions are.

By collective punishment, the drafters of the Geneva Conventions had in mind the **reprisal killings** of World Wars I and II. In the First World War, Germans executed Belgian villagers in mass retribution for resistance activity. In World War II, Nazis carried out a form of collective punishment to suppress resistance. Entire villages or towns or districts were held responsible for any resistance activity that took place there. The conventions, to counter this, reiterated the principle of individual responsibility. The International Committee of the Red Cross (ICRC) Commentary to the conventions states that parties to a conflict often would resort to "intimidatory measures to terrorize the population" in hopes of preventing hostile acts, but such practices "strike at guilty and innocent alike. They are opposed to all principles based on humanity and justice."

The law of armed conflict applies similar protections to an internal conflict. Common Article 3 of the four Geneva Conventions of 1949 requires fair trials for all individuals before punishments; and Additional Protocol II of 1977 explicitly forbids collective punishment.

Israel's occupation of the West Bank differs from almost anywhere else because it has continued for more than one generation. Demolition of Palestinian houses has been a regular event in the occupied territories. Most often, the army acts following a bombing directed against Israeli civilians. On July 30, 1997, a bomb exploded in West Jerusalem, killing fifteen, including two suicide bombers, and injuring 170. The army responded by punishing the families of those suspected of carrying out the bombing as well as the village where they came from. Homes of the families of four residents were completely demolished, as were eight homes in East Jerusalem. For one month, Israeli soldiers barred almost everyone from entering or exiting the West Bank.

Officially, the army destroyed the houses because they were built illegally. However, an unnamed defense official stated that the demolitions were meant as a signal to the Palestinian authorities that they could not "resume normal life until they take certain measures to combat terrorism."

Other security measures by the Israeli Army are no less controversial but are more ambiguous under international law.

Take travel restrictions. Issa from Bethlehem and his fiancée, Farida, from Jerusalem decided to get married on September 13, 1997, in the Mar Elias Christian Church south of Jerusalem. Following the July explosion, the Israeli Army announced a tight closure of the territory under control of the Palestinian Authority. So a Palestinian from Bethlehem could not obtain permission to travel to Jerusalem; and had they decided to move the wedding to Bethlehem, Farida could not have gotten permission to enter the area under Palestinian Authority control. After three abortive attempts to cross Israeli checkpoints, the groom, dressed in his wedding finest, circumvented the restrictions, climbed walls, and walked hours on dirt roads to make the ceremony. Most of the guests stayed home. Most of the restrictions on Palestinians began after Israel annexed the West Bank in the 1967 war, but they were largely ignored until the Gulf War. In March 1993, after a series of stabbings in Israel, the government there established a permanent checkpoint between the rest of the West Bank and Israel, and began routinely sealing off the occupied territories. The closure blocked the movement of Palestinians and of goods into or out of the territories, except for those with valid permits. Since then, Israel has repeatedly imposed a "total closure," banning Palestinians from reaching hospitals, schools, educational institutions, diplomatic missions, and places of worship in Jerusalem. Travel restrictions, while taken as punishment by those suffering under them, can be but are not necessarily a collective punishment; they may be a security measure in response to a security breach. Some advocates have argued that semipermanent restrictions border on collective punishment.

Two Palestinian brothers stand in the ruins of their home in Gaza, demolished by the Israeli Army because a suspect lived next door.

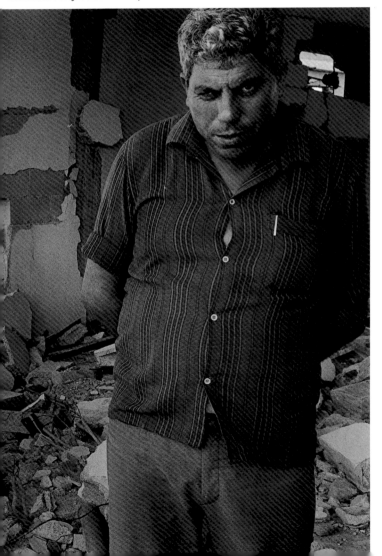

olombia is undergoing one of the world's most complex armed conflicts. Unlike other guerrilla wars in Central and South America, the fighting in Colombia does not so much pit a government army against guerrilla forces but paramilitaries against guerrillas with the army on the sidelines.

Observers inside and outside Colombia believe that, at their inception, these paramilitary groups were the means through which the government and the military authorities could unleash a dirty war without any obvious State involvement. But things have long since gotten to the point where the total war being fought in Colombia is one in which civilians are the principal targets. In Colombia, despite the fact that the army can point to a decline in the number of its violations of humanitarian law, the entire notion of the laws of war seems to be breaking down. The most elementary distinctions— between combatant and noncombatant, civilian and soldier—are no longer being respected. And in recent years, things have only gotten worse.

Colombia has a long history of bloody political fighting, including the quasi **civil war** of the 1940s and 1950s known as *La Violencia,* which pitted armed militias of the Liberal and Conservative parties and nearly destroyed the country. The violence never entirely ceased. It was remnants of the Liberal party militia that formed the first guerrilla movement, the Revolutionary Armed Forces of Colombia (FARC), in the 1960s. And it was in response to the rekindled guerrilla threat, first from the FARC and then from the National Liberation Army (ELN), that the first paramilitary formations were set up as ancillary units to the Colombian army.

Colombia, then, has remained mired in a vicious circle of violence and retaliation for several decades. Much of it was cyclical and retaliatory in nature. Both the **guerrillas** and the **paramilitaries** regularly resorted to killing members of one another's families. And as they did so, the violence progressively grew more personal and unstoppable. But however bad the violence was in the past, the access of all sides to tens of millions of dollars of drug traffickers' money has made the current round of internecine fighting and political violence that began in the early 1980s more wide-reaching and less discriminating than ever before.

The money obtained from drug trafficking gives the guerrillas and the paramilitaries access to the international arms market while freeing them from previous constraints on how they use the new weapons they have acquired. Their tactics have changed as well, although this would probably have happened with or without the involvement of the narcotraffickers. Freed from dependence on States which once supported them as liberation movements (and which might have been expected to pressure them to refrain from certain types of operations), guerrilla groups like the FARC and ELN have increasingly resorted to kidnappings, assassinations of elected officials, and attacks on oil pipelines. The result has been further, massive displacement of the civilian population. For their part, the paramilitaries engaged in counterinsurgency have carried out massacres and forcibly recruited young men and women into service in a war they do not want to fight. And whereas in

Death Squads dump their victims on a hillside overlooking Bogota. The police refer to mass killings as the "Clean Up Scheme," or the "Rehabilitation Program."

earlier spasms of violence, the paramilitaries were utterly dependent on the Colombian army, now, while they still depend on it for protection from prosecution, they are financially independent from it and have become the principal armed opponents of the guerrillas.

These developments have caused a further deterioration in the situation of the civilian population and led to a major humanitarian crisis, one that is largely unknown outside Colombia. Over 600,000 people have become internally displaced from their homes in the last decade.

The Colombian crisis would exist with or without the drug traffickers. But while they are not at the root of the war, or of the social and historical events that provoked it, they are at the root of the criminalization of the conflict, itself a malign development in contemporary Colombian history. The drug traffickers have shown themselves willing to work with and finance both

San Jose de Apartado. The villagers have erected a monument to those killed by the paramilitaries. Colombia, 1998.

sides. The situation is far from the ideological contest that marked the Colombian conflict thirty years ago. Guerrillas and paramilitaries alike grow rich off the war, and the profits that the war has engendered make the prospect of peace that much more elusive.

In the wake of the narcotraffickers have come common criminals who are willing to work for any group willing to pay for their services, and, of course, are even less mindful of the laws of war than the guerrillas and paramilitaries themselves. Perhaps predictably, the violence of the conflict has spilled over into almost every corner of Colombian life. The country is now among the most violent in the world, with an annual homicide rate of about seventy per 100,000 inhabitants. In contrast, the homicide rate in the United States, the most violent of all developed countries, is about eleven per 100,000 inhabitants.

This mixture of war and crime—the fighting can be shown to wax and wane according to the amount of narcotics money being channeled to both sides—makes the Colombian conflict very difficult to understand. What is clear, however, is the readiness of all sides to commit grave violations of humanitarian law, although certain groups tend to commit some violations more than others.

For example, while all sides rely on forced abductions, the FARC, and to a lesser extent the ELN, have come to use kidnapping and hostage taking of civilians both as a political weapon and as a means of obtaining funds. The FARC tends to target politicians and land owners, while the ELN is more prone to kidnap foreigners, especially those whom they believe can be ransomed for large sums. But there are no hard and fast rules. The ELN at times resorts to political kidnappings, while the FARC continues to hold three American missionaries it seized in 1993. And while kidnapping remains primarily the tool of the guerrillas, the tactic is being resorted to more and more frequently by right-wing paramilitary organizations.

Funeral for 2nd Lieutenant Perez, 23, killed on the street by snipers. Colombia.

No one knows how many kidnappings occur each year because only a percentage of them are reported to the authorities. If, as the Colombian authorities estimate, at most about 20 percent of the kidnappings are reported and there are about nine hundred reported abductions a year, the total would be destabilizing by any measure. The overall statistics for the past two years of persons killed by the violence is staggering.

Summary executions are another instance of a tactic which, while engaged in by all sides, is more commonly engaged in by one of the belligerents. It has been the paramilitary squads, according to most recent human rights reports, that have been the main offenders. Fighters loyal to two of the top paramilitary leaders, the brothers Fidel and Carlos Castano, have been singled out as users of the tactic. As has so often been the case in Colombia, the Castanos' war against the guerrillas has been motivated in large part by family history. The brothers' father was kidnapped by the FARC in the 1970s and held for ransom. The family negotiated with the guerrillas and eventually paid a ransom, but the father was killed anyway, and his body dumped on family property. It is not surprising, in the Colombian context that upon reaching manhood the Castano brothers founded paramilitary organizations that continue to this day to carry out some of the worst massacres Colombia has ever known.

In the case of the Castanos, political violence and crime soon became all but impossible to separate. Their forces were financed by the sale of cocaine, and, in late 1997, Carlos Castano was identified by the U.S. Drug Enforcement Administration (DEA) as a major drug trafficker. In the field, the Castanos' fighters have made a practice of going in the middle of the night to a civilian area with a list of suspected leftists, dragging those they could find from their homes, executing them, and dumping the bodies where they will be seen by as many people as possible. Apparently, it was in retaliation for these acts that the FARC kidnapped and then reportedly killed Fidel Castano.

But, as in the case of kidnappings, while the paramilitary organizations have been responsible for most of the recent large-scale massacres, both the FARC and the ELN have summarily executed political officials in towns where the insurgents wanted to seize control. And in any case, determining who is responsible for any given massacre, or even why it occurred, is often complicated because groups routinely operate at the behest of other parties, especially the drug traffickers themselves. For example, the paramilitary units not only kill suspected leftists but also members of the drug cartels who know too much or are suspected of disloyalty. The guerrillas have also executed people working in the coca fields or in drug laboratories at the behest of the cartels for the same reasons.

The practice of carrying out summary executions is routinely compounded by the use of **torture**. Torture is used to extract information, but it is also employed as a punishment and as a deterrent to others. Such killings are only one element in the pattern of direct and indiscriminate attacks against the civilian populations in which all sides regularly engage. The result of these attacks, which have been little reported even in the Colombian press, has been hundreds of thousands of internally displaced people both in areas controlled by the guerrillas and areas controlled by the paramilitaries. This toll of internally displaced may be the most catastrophic human effect of all of the Colombian conflict. Even less noted has been the environmental disaster the fighting has caused. Despite widespread international protests, the ELN continues to blow up oil pipelines that run through virgin jungle. Tens of thousands of gallons of crude oil are spilled each year, fouling waterways, killing wildlife, and making cleanup virtually impossible, even if the will or resources to try were available.

The prospects are bleak. Colombia, despite its riches and the talents of its people, is a society totally permeated now by the culture of death. In one sense, it is a very special case. But, at least to a degree, the war being fought in Colombia resembles some of the recent conflicts in Africa in which the decline of the State, and the triumph of a murderous criminality, has led to a fundamental undercutting of the very bases of humanitarian law.

Combatant Status

By A. P. V. Rogers

During an armed conflict, only "combatants" are permitted to "take a direct part in hostilities." Noncombatants who do so commit a war crime and lose any protected status that they might have—that is, they are not entitled to be treated as prisoners of war, and any attacks on people or property may be prosecuted as common crime.

Combatants are all members of the armed forces of a party to the conflict except medical and religious personnel. They cannot be punished for their hostile acts and if captured can only be held as POWs until the end of hostilities.

Taking a direct part in hostilities usually means attacking enemy combatants or military objectives.

The armed forces consist of all organized armed forces, groups, and units that: are under a command responsible for the conduct of its subordinates to a party to the conflict; are subject to an internal disciplinary system that enforces compliance with the law of armed conflict; and whose members, at least when deployed on military operations, wear uniform or combat gear that distinguishes them from the civilian population.

Medical and religious personnel, like civilians, are noncombatants. They may not take a direct part in hostilities and so long as they do not, are legally protected from attack. Medical personnel may, however, use small arms in self-defense if unlawfully attacked. Religious personnel are not armed.

The composition of the armed forces is a matter for the state or faction concerned. Its components may be regular units, reservists, territorial defense units, citizens called up for part-time service, or full-time soldiers as long as the conditions set out above are fulfilled. It is normal for members of the armed forces to have ranks, the more senior ranks having power to give orders to, and discipline over, their subordinates.

Violation of the law of armed conflict does not mean loss of combatant status so long as those responsible are tried and punished. If members of an armed group consistently violate the law of armed conflict and are not punished, that is strong evidence that the group does not qualify as "armed forces," since it fails to meet the criterion of an internal disciplinary system, and that its members do not have combatant status.
(See **irregulars; paramilitaries**.)

Command Responsibility

C

By Nomi Bar-Yaacov

In January 1988, barely one month into the Intifada uprising against Israeli occupation of the West Bank and Gaza Strip, Col. Yehuda Meir ordered troops under his command to round up twenty Palestinian men from Hawara and Beita, two Arab villages in the West Bank, bind them in handcuffs and blindfolds, and break their bones. The unit commander reporting to Meir passed on the order to his troops, but told them he did not require them to comply. Some soldiers refrained from doing so, but others carried out the order with such zeal that they broke their truncheons. The defense minister at the time, Yitzhak Rabin, publicly spoke of the need to "break the bones of Intifada rioters."

Although Meir was not present during the incident, he was the superior commanding officer in the area.

It took some months before military police, following a request by the International Committee of the Red Cross (ICRC), launched an investigation. The army chief of staff summoned Meir and offered him the choice: to appear before a disciplinary military court for a severe reprimand and discharge from the army, or to face a court martial. Meir accepted the first option, under which he was to go to work for the State security service until he could begin retirement on his colonel's pension.

When word of the behind-the-scenes deal became public, the Association for Civil Rights in Israel petitioned the Israeli High Court of Justice, demanding that Meir be court-martialed.

The High Court ruled unanimously that Meir should be tried in a special military tribunal for torture, intentionally causing bodily harm, grievous assault—all, incidentally, grave breaches of the Geneva Conventions—and unbecoming conduct.

"These actions outrage every civilized person, and no lack of clarity can cover it up" Justice Moshe Bejski said. "Certainly, if the order is given by a senior officer, that officer must be aware that the morality of the Israeli Defense Forces forbids such behavior."

Following the High Court's decision, Meir went on trial before a special military tribunal in Tel Aviv in April 1991. He was found guilty, demoted to private's rank, and deprived of his colonel's pension.

Meir's case points to two critical issues of international humanitarian law (IHL). Can obedience to superior orders be a defense against allegations of war crimes? And how far up the chain of command does "command responsibility" reach?

The answer to the first question is that a claim of superior orders cannot serve as a defense against an allegation of grave breaches or other serious violations of IHL. It should be noted, however, that the illegality of the orders was blatant and undeniable in Meir's case. In other cases, the illegality may not be so apparent, and a war crimes prosecution may fail if the subordinate is not shown to have acted "willfully" in the sense of knowing or having reason to know that the order was illegal. In addition, although a claim of superior orders cannot serve as an affirmative defense, it may be part of a claim of duress—such as a threat to execute the subordinate for failure to carry out orders—that may be offered in mitigation.

The second issue is how far up the chain of command responsibility may extend for ordering a war crime. Article 86 of Additional Protocol I to the 1949 Geneva Conventions states: "the fact that a breach of the Conventions or of this Protocol was committed by a subordinate does not absolve his superiors from penal disciplinary responsibility as the case may be if they knew, or had information which would have enabled them to conclude in the circumstances at the time that he was committing or was going to commit such a breach and if they did not take all feasible measures within their power to prevent or repress the breach."

This rule applies to officers. Therefore command responsibility extends as high as any officer in the chain of command who knows or has reason to know that his subordinates are committing war crimes and failed to act to stop them. Although Israel has not ratified Additional Protocol I, it is clear from Israeli Supreme Court practice that its domestic law embraces these internationally recognized standards for superior orders and command responsibility.

Under the 1998 statute of the new International Criminal Court, a military commander is liable for crimes that he "knew or should have known" about under circumstances at the time, and only for those crimes committed by forces under his "effective command and control." He is liable if he "failed to take all necessary and reasonable measures" to prevent and repress such crimes that subordinates "were committing or about to commit" or for failing to report such crimes to proper authorities.

Various cases have raised difficult questions, starting with the famous Yamashita case heard by the International Military Tribunal in Tokyo following World War II. This Tribunal held a senior enemy commander to what many critics, including a dissenting U.S. Supreme Court opinion, thought to be an extraordinarily high standard of responsibility for actions of subordinates, even under circumstances where Admiral Yamashita had lost almost all command, control, and communications over his subordinates. In practical terms, command responsibility is not taken to extend as far up the chain of command as might logically be implied, that is, to commanders in chief, and is generally confined to officers in some meaningful supervisory capacity.

Meir argued in his own defense that he was acting in accord with his understanding of orders given by his superiors. The tribunal rejected his argument. The judges concluded that political and high-ranking military officials had not given orders to break bones. Consequently, the State prosecutor's office decided not to pursue charges against Ehud Barak, the chief of staff at the time, Rabin, the minister of defense, or Maj. Gen. Yitzhak Mordechai, the commanding officer of the central zone.

Officers and soldiers who carried out Meir's orders in the Hawara and Beita affair were tried in special military courts. Their arguments that they were merely "obeying orders" were rejected and they served time in prison. (See **Arab-Israeli wars**; **willfulness**)

Compelling Military Service

C

By Patrick J. Sloyan

It was the standard practice for American infantry in Vietnam, where boobytraps and minefields threatened unspeakable horrors. Lt. William Diehl still remembers the day as a platoon leader on a jungle patrol.

One of their prisoners, a suspected Viet Cong guerrilla, was brought to the front of the line of soldiers. A rope was placed around the prisoner's neck and the platoon point man prodded the prisoner to lead the way. They had not gone far when the human mine detector broke a tripwire and set off a buried shell. This time, however, the tactic failed. The blast was so powerful that it killed the point man, ripping his heart from his chest. It also wounded Diehl. Some nights, Diehl can still see the point man's heart pulsating on the jungle trail. He was certain some Vietnamese children, their mothers and grandparents living nearby were responsible. "We always believed the mines were planted by the villagers," Diehl said.

Diehl's unit violated U.S. Army training and at least three of the laws of war. Prisoners, whether military POWs or enemy civilians, cannot be forced to serve in military operations, be involved in dangerous work, or be subjected to cruel or inhumane treatments. What Diehl observed in Vietnam was specifically banned by Article 52 of the Third Geneva Convention of 1949.

Using human mine detectors had become commonplace during the ten-year war. In the My Lai massacre on March 16, 1968, troops of the Americal Division destroyed an entire village and killed more than five hundred old men, women, children, and infants. Only about twenty were spared; "In case we hit the minefield," Lt. William Calley later told an Army court-martial.

The motive for making civilians walk through minefields was survival. Almost a third of the fifty-eight thousand American soldiers who died in Vietnam were killed by a boobytrap or a mine; 40 per cent of the 153,000 wounded fell to a similar weapon. But the Geneva Conventions of 1949, which cover international, and, as in the case of Vietnam, "internationalized" conflicts, leave no doubt it is a war crime to force a captured soldier or civilian to "walk the point."

"Compelling a prisoner of war to serve in the forces of the hostile power" is a grave breach, according to the Third Geneva Convention. Unless he volunteers, employing a POW on unhealthy or dangerous labor is banned. The Third Convention specifies that the "removal of mines or similar devices shall be considered as dangerous labor." POWs also cannot be forced to do dangerous work or work for which they are physically unsuited; they can only be forced to work in sectors that are not military in nature or purpose.

Under the Fourth Geneva Convention, civilians cannot be forced into military service but can be interned and compelled to work under the same conditions as nationals of the occupying party. Internees may volunteer to work for the "needs of the army of occupation" but not its "strategic or tactical requirements" such as digging trenches, or building fortifications and bases. Noninternees may not be compelled to work.

The U.S. Army was well aware of the practice of using enemy POWs and civilians to clear mines during the war and of its criminal nature. By the time of Calley's trial, the Infantry School at Fort Benning had produced a training film showing an army platoon in a Vietnamese village. The lieutenant tells his sergeant to take some of the villagers and run them through a suspected area. "You want me, Lieutenant, to take the villagers and run them through a minefield?" the sergeant asks. Pressed to repeat the order, the officer backs down.

During the 1991 **Gulf War**, the lesson was remembered. Norman Schwarzkopf, a lieutenant colonel in Calley's Americal division in Vietnam, was in command. Confronted by desert belts of Iraqi landmines and aware that thousands of Iraqi prisoners would surrender rather than fight, Schwarzkopf ordered perhaps the most ambitious effort to prevent war crimes ever conducted on a battlefield. Every officer and enlisted soldier was lectured on the rules of land warfare and the proper treatment of prisoners. According to personnel in the International Committee of the Red Cross

My Lai massacre victims: Approximately twenty villagers survived, only to be used as human mine detectors.

(ICRC) legal division, they were contacted almost daily by members of Schwarzkopf's staff on the finer points of the laws of war.
(See **forced labor**.)

Concentration Camps

By Ed Vulliamy

The laws governing warfare and conflict make no reference to concentration camps. But for more than a century, concentration camps have been a venue for wholesale war crimes and the symbol of the worst abuses against civilians in wartime.

It was a Spanish general, Valeriano Weyler, who established the first *reconcentrados* or "concentration centers" in Cuba in his drive to suppress the 1895 rebellion. Britain introduced concentration camps on a massive scale during the Boer War from 1899 to 1902. To deny the Boer guerrillas food and intelligence, Gen. Lord Kitchener ordered the British Army to sweep the Transvaal and Orange River territories of South Africa "clean." Civilians—women, children, the elderly, and some men of fighting age—were herded from their homes and concentrated in camps along railway lines, with a view to their eventual removal from the territory. The Boers, to whom these camps became a symbol of genocide, called them *laagers*.

The Nazis developed a vast network of *Konzentrationslager*, using them at first to hold political prisoners, later slave labor, and finally to annihilate European Jewry and to kill large numbers of Poles, Russians, and Gypsies. Of the nearly 6 million Jews killed under Hitler's "Final Solution," 2 million died in Auschwitz, the main extermination center.

No one in the post–World War II generation could have anticipated the reappearance of such camps in Europe. On that August 1992 day when my colleagues and I from the British television network ITN alighted from our vans, it was hard to gauge who was more amazed to see whom. Before us, there was a landscape of human misery that seemed to recall another time: men, some of them skeletal, lined up behind a barbed wire fence, with lantern jaws and xylophone ribcages visible beneath their putrefied skin. They, in turn, saw a camera crew and a clutch of reporters advancing across the withered summer grass.

This was Logor Trnopolje, a teeming mass of wretched humanity—scared, sunburned, and driven out of house and home. Among them was the figure of Fikret Alic, whose emaciated torso behind sharp knots of wire would become the enduring symbol of Bosnia's war, of its cruelty and its echo of the worst calamities of our century. Alic had come from yet another camp, Kereterm, where he had broken down in tears, having been ordered to help clear up some 150 corpses, the result of the previous night's massacre.

I ventured into Trnopolje, past families crammed against one another on the floor of what had been a school, past stinking holes dug into the ground for what were intended to be cesspits. "I can't tell you everything that goes on," said one young inmate, Ibrahim Demirovic, "but they do whatever they want." A gracious doctor, Idriz, had been put in charge of a "medical center" where he gave us an undeveloped film—it showed his patients, beaten literally black and blue.

The day after the discovery of Trnopolje and Omarska, I shied from calling them concentration camps because of the inevitable association with the bestial policies of the Third Reich. I reasoned that we must take extreme care in relating genocides of our lifetime and the Holocaust, which was singular and inimitable. While thousands were purposefully killed in the gulag of Serbian camps, did that equate with the Nazis' industrial mass murder of Jews and others?

On reflection, *concentration camp* is exactly the right term for what we uncovered that day. For here civilian populations were literally *concentrated* —frog-marched in columns or bused to locations for illegal purposes of mal-treatment, torture, abuse, killing, and, crucially, enforced transfer, or **ethnic cleansing**. Indeed, The UN's independent Commission of Experts determined after a year long study that Trnopolje was a concentration camp, and Omarska and Keraterm "de facto death camps."

In general, the laws which would apply to concentration camps address the topic piecemeal, and the principal element is **unlawful confinement**, a grave breach of the Fourth Geneva Convention. Confinement of civilians is not necessarily unlawful. "Foreign" civilians who pose a threat to a party to a conflict may be put in "places of internment" or given an "assigned residence." However, the threat they pose must be genuine, evidenced by some clear action, not merely by their nationality. It is also lawful to remove civilians for their own security in an emergency, such as an impending battle, and set up temporary shelters for them. Even so, they must be returned home as soon as it is safe to do so and be well cared for in the meantime. Also, some civilians may be held or imprisoned as suspects or criminals, so long as they are given **due process**. In an internal conflict, noncombatants may be interned but are entitled to humane treatment and the judicial protections guaranteed by a regularly constituted court. None of these safeguards exist in concentration camps. Confinement under such conditions is thus unlawful. The arbitrary imprisonment of large numbers of civilians during conflicts— internal or international—can be a crime against humanity.

The themes of the "concentration" and "clearance" of civilians came to dominate the last phase of the Boer War, just as they dominated the entire Bosnian War, most notably in its early stages. As we know, the removal of Muslims and Croats from Serbian terrain was not a by-product of a war between armies, it was the *raw material*, the declared aim, of the Serbs.

The Boer War concentration camps aroused outrage and fury back in Britain, led by temperance crusader Emily Hobhouse. She described "deportations . . . a burned-out population brought in by hundreds of convoys . . . semi-starvation in the camps . . . fever-stricken children lying on the bare earth . . . appalling mortality."

The camps provoked Lloyd George to thunder, "When is a war not a war? When it is carried on by methods of barbarism." Even the all-woman Fawcett Committee, which supported the British war but made intrepid inspections of the concentration camps, was struck by the conditions at Mafeking, where women were washing clothes in water fouled by excreta, or at Brandfort, where an epidemic killed 337 people in three weeks. These places were by no means Auschwitz or Belsen, but they *were* concentration camps.

The term concentration camp implies not so much a prison or assigned residence for POWs or even civilians, but a role in an overall process of "clearance." The fact that the Serbs sought to defend Trnopolje by describing it as a "transit camp" confirms the point: there is an entwinement between concentration camps and the forced movement or clearance of population.

In their description of Trnopolje in the trial verdict against Dusko Tadic, judges in The Hague noted that "there was no regular regime of interrogations or beating, as in other camps, but beatings and killings did occur." They referred to testimony about "dead people wrapped in paper and wired together, their tongues pulled out . . . and the slaughtered bodies of young girls and old men." The judges acknowledged that some inmates were allowed to forage for food in the village beyond the camp. But this "in effect amounted to imprisonment," since many were killed during these excursions, and survivors feared repeating them.

Moreover, "because this camp housed the largest number of women and girls, there were more rapes at this camp than any other. Girls between the ages of 16 and 19 were at the greatest risk . . . the youngest girl being 12 years of age." One girl serially raped by seven Serbian soldiers suffered "terrible pains . . . and hemorrhaging."

But what hallmarked Trnopolje was the fact that the camp was, as the judges said, "the culmination of the campaign of ethnic cleansing, since those Muslims and Croats who were not killed at the Omarska and Kereterm camps were, from Trnopolje, deported." This is one of the defining essences of concentration camps—that the detaining power wishes to be rid of their inmates, either by killing them, or else by enforced transit elsewhere.

Images like these from the Trnopolje Camp in August 1992 brought back memories of the Nazi Camps. But these were run by Serbs, for Bosnians.

In the case of Trnopolje, these transits—the concentration camp's purpose—were utterly terrifying. I went on one of them, in this instance of Muslims from the town of Sanski Most. Because they were **internal displacements**, from Serb-controlled northern Bosnia into government-held regions, they attracted little attention aside from the news media.

A year later, in September 1993, I found myself uncovering another concentration camp: Dretelj. This time the inmates were Muslims, their guards Bosnian-Croat. Most of the prisoners were locked away in the dank darkness of two underground hangars, dug into facing hillsides. The metal doors had been slid open for our visit, but many men preferred to stay inside, staring as though blind into the ether. "We're not really allowed out," said one. These men had been locked in here for up to seventy-two hours at a time, without food or water, drinking their own urine to survive. They all remembered the night in July 1993 when the Croat guards got drunk and began firing through the doors—between ten and twelve men died that night; the back wall of the hangar was pockmarked with bullets.

The plan was simple; the Bosnian Croat authorities explained them to the United Nations High Commission for Refugees (UNHCR) at a meeting in the coastal resort of Makarska during the week before our discovery of the camp. The proposal was to ship fifty thousand Muslim men to a transit camp at nearby Ljubuski, and thence to third countries. The Croatian Foreign Minister Mate Granic said his country would do all it could to help. Would the UNHCR? The aid workers were flabbergasted, caught in a heinous dilemma: to cooperate with the aim of Dretelij and three other concentration camps, or else to leave the men festering in conditions which had been hidden from the International Committee of the Red Cross for two months.

Any such fulfillment of the concentrations camps' goal is illegal **deportation** anyway. But in addition to its laws on confinement, the Geneva Convention of 1949 does regulate the transfer of internees—to take the Serbs' and Croats' own sanitized description of their concentration camps. This shall, says Article 127, "always be effected humanely," and as a general rule by rail or other means of transport. "If, as an exceptional measure, such removals have to be effected on foot, they may not take place unless the internees are in a fit state of health."

The convention continues: "When making decisions regarding the transfer of internees, the detaining power shall take their interests into account, and in particular shall not do anything to increase the difficulties of repatriating them or returning them to their own homes." At the time of writing, that provision, with regard to those "concentrated" at Trnopolje and Dretelj, remains infamously and horribly unfulfilled.

Crimes against Humanity

By M. Cherif Bassiouni

The term *crimes against humanity* has come to mean anything atrocious committed on a large scale. This is not, however, the original meaning nor the technical one. The term originated in the 1907 Hague Convention preamble, which codified the customary law of armed conflict. This codification was based on existing State practices that derived from those values and principles deemed to constitute the "laws of humanity," as reflected throughout history in different cultures.

After World War I, the Allies, in connection with the Treaty of Versailles, established in 1919 a commission to investigate war crimes that relied on the 1907 Hague Convention as the applicable law. In addition to war crimes committed by the Germans, the commission also found that Turkish officials committed "crimes against the laws of humanity" for killing Armenian nationals and residents during the period of the war. The United States and Japan strongly opposed the criminalization of such conduct on the grounds that crimes against the laws of humanity were violations of moral and not positive law.

In 1945, the United States and other Allies developed the Agreement for the Prosecution and Punishment of the Major War Criminals of the European Axis and Charter of the International Military Tribunal (IMT), sitting at Nuremberg, which contained the following definition of crimes against humanity in Article 6(c):

> Crimes against humanity: murder, extermination, enslavement, deportation, and other inhumane acts committed against civilian populations, before or during the war; or persecutions on political, racial or religious grounds in execution of or in connection with any crime within the jurisdiction of the Tribunal, whether or not in violation of the domestic law of the country where perpetrated.

The Nuremberg Charter represents the first time that crimes against humanity were established in positive international law. The International Military Tribunal for the Far East, at Tokyo, followed the Nuremberg Charter, as did Control Council Law No. 10 of Germany, under which the Allies prosecuted Germans in their respective zones of occupation. Curiously, however, there has been no specialized international convention since then on crimes against humanity. Still, that category of crimes has been included in the statutes of the International Criminal Tribunal for the Former Yugoslavia (ICTY) and the International Criminal Tribunal for Rwanda (ICTR), as well as in the statute of the International Criminal Court (ICC). In fact, there are eleven international texts defining crimes against humanity, but they all differ slightly as to their definition of that crime and its legal elements. However, what all of these definitions have in common is: (1) they refer to specific acts of violence against persons irrespective of whether the person is a national or nonnational and irrespective of whether these acts are committed in time of war or time of peace, and (2) these acts must be the product of persecution against an identifiable group of persons irrespective of the make-up of that group or the purpose of the persecution. Such a policy can

also be manifested by the "widespread or systematic" conduct of the perpetrators, which results in the commission of the specific crimes contained in
the definition.

The list of the specific crimes contained within the meaning of crimes
against humanity has been expanded since Article 6(c) of the IMT to include,
in the ICTY and the ICTR, rape and torture. The statute of the ICC also
expands the list of specific acts. In particular, the ICC statute adds the
crimes of enforced disappearance of persons and apartheid. Further, the ICC
statute contains clarifying language with respect to the specific crimes of
extermination, enslavement, deportation or forcible transfer of population,
torture, and forced pregnancy.

To some extent, crimes against humanity overlap with genocide and war
crimes. But crimes against humanity are distinguishable from genocide in
that they do not require an intent to "destroy in whole or in part," as cited
in the 1948 Genocide Convention, but only target a given group and carry
out a policy of "widespread or systematic" violations. Crimes against humanity are also distinguishable from war crimes in that they not only apply in the
context of war—they apply in times of war *and* peace.

Crimes against humanity have existed in customary international law for
over half a century and are also evidenced in prosecutions before some
national courts. The most notable of these trials include those of Paul
Touvier, Klaus Barbie, and Maurice Papon in France, and Imre Finta in Canada.
But crimes against humanity are also deemed to be part of *jus cogens*—the
highest standing in international legal norms. Thus, they constitute a non-
derogable rule of international law. The implication of this standing is that
they are subject to universal **jurisdiction**, meaning that all States can exercise their jurisdiction in prosecuting a perpetrator irrespective of where the
crime was committed. It also means that all States have the duty to prosecute or extradite, that no person charged with that crime can claim the
"political offense exception" to extradition, and that States have the duty
to assist each other in securing evidence needed to prosecute. But of greater
importance is the fact that no perpetrator can claim the "defense of obedience to superior orders" and that no statute of limitation contained in the
laws of any State can apply. Lastly, no one is immune from prosecution for
such crimes, even a head of State.

(See **command responsibility**.)

Crimes against Peace

By Steven R. Ratner

C

Crimes against peace, as described by the Nuremberg Tribunal in 1946, are "the supreme international crime, differing only from other war crimes in that it contains within itself the accumulated evil of the whole."

Also known as the crime of **aggression**, crimes against peace formed the first charge against the Nazis in the 1945 Charter of the International Military Tribunal at Nuremberg. The charter defined them as "planning, preparation, initiation or waging of a war of aggression, or a war in violation of international treaties, agreements or assurances, or participation in a common plan or conspiracy [to do so]." Crimes against peace are not war crimes *per se*, which involve unlawful conduct *during* war.

The idea of charging the Nazis with the crime of starting World War II was controversial at the time and has remained so ever since. For the Americans, crimes against peace were the chief offense of the Nazis, and the criminality of aggressive war needed to be enshrined in international law. But starting a war had not been regarded as criminal up to that time. The Kellogg-Briand Pact of 1928, which outlawed war (not too successfully, to say the least), only rendered aggression an *illegal* act for States, not a *criminal* act for which *individuals* could be tried. The French resisted the concept for this reason; the Soviets, for their part, were concerned about criminalizing aggressive war given their invasions of Finland and annexation of parts of Poland. The American view prevailed—though the tribunal's jurisdiction was limited to *Axis* aggression—leading to the conviction of leading Nazis for crimes against peace. Afterward, a fierce debate raged in legal circles as to whether the Allies had applied criminal law retroactively.

Although UN bodies have restated the importance of crimes against peace since World War II, the UN's members—especially Western States—have noted serious obstacles to actually prosecuting individuals. First, a definition of aggression specific enough for prosecutions of governmental officials remains elusive. Second, since wars are typically planned by many people in State bureaucracies, drawing a line of guilt might prove difficult. Third, criminal cases could encompass complex, politically laden factual inquiries ill-suited for courts. While some cases of aggression are as stark as Iraq's invasion of Kuwait, other incidents demand more careful scrutiny.

One clear manifestation of these concerns was the Security Council's unwillingness to give the UN's Yugoslavia Tribunal jurisdiction over this crime. Another was the decision by the States drafting the Rome Statute of the International Criminal Court (ICC) to give the ICC jurisdiction over crimes against peace only if States formally amend that statute to add a definition of the crime and the conditions for the exercise of jurisdiction. States thus seem to say that aggression is a crime in the abstract, but are reluctant to prosecute it. The concept of crimes against peace still has some effect on international law, as States want to recognize the illegality of aggression in the strongest way—by proclaiming that leaders can be held accountable for it. But the dim prospects of actually prosecuting anyone make impunity the norm and crimes against peace somewhat of a dead letter.
(See **crimes against humanity**; **war crimes**)

Cultural Property and Historical Monuments

By Peter Maass

**The mosque was on death row. An execution date had not been pro-
nounced, of course, but the Ferhad Pasha mosque was living on borrowed
time when I walked through its front gate in the summer of 1992.
Nationalist Serbs controlled Banja Luka and were well on their way to
destroying all symbols of Muslim culture, and none was so historic or
important as Ferhad Pasha, built in 1583 during the Ottoman Empire.**

It was one of the oldest mosques in Bosnia, and it was beautiful, and
because of that, it was in greater peril than the handful of frightened
Muslims who had just ended an afternoon prayer session. "Yes, I will talk to

you," one of them told me. "But please, we must leave this place now." The mosque had survived four centuries of Balkan tumult, but it would be best not to linger in its doomed shadow.

A few months later, on May 7, 1993, people who lived near the mosque were woken from their sleep by an explosion that made the earth tremble under their homes. Antitank mines were detonated under the ancient building's foundations, turning it to rubble, which was carted away to a secret dump. All that was left behind was a blackened patch of ground. The "ethnic cleansers" hoped that destroying the spiritual heart of their community would ensure Muslims would leave their homes and never return. Across Bosnia this was done, as one mosque after another was turned to pebbles and dust. With each explosion, a war crime was committed.

International guidelines protecting cultural property against damage and theft date back to the American Civil War. The carnage of that war led to the 1863 Lieber Code, which gave protected status to libraries, scientific collections, and art works. The code applied only to American troops but

Before and after: In November 1993, Bosnian Croats shelled and destroyed the four-century-old Neretva Bridge in Mostar. It had been used by the beleaguered Bosnians, but its major "offense" was that it was built under Ottoman rule.

influenced a series of international accords leading to the 1954 Convention for the Protection of Cultural Property. The convention's definition of cultural property is broad, including significant architectural monuments, art works, books or manuscripts of artistic or historical significance, museums, large libraries, archives, archaeological sites, and historic buildings. The convention was strengthened by the Additional Protocols of 1977, of which Article 53 prohibits "any acts of hostility directed against the historic monuments, works of art or places of worship which constitute the cultural or spiritual heritage of peoples." It's important to note that the protocols established protections against the destruction of other types of civilian property not linked to military actions or uses.

Article 53 also prohibits the use of cultural property "in support of the military effort"—for example, using a national historical building as a command center. In such cases, destruction or damage of cultural property is not necessarily a war crime. The 1954 convention states that the obligation to not harm cultural property "may be waived only in cases where military necessity imperatively requires such a waiver." The phrase "military necessity" is not defined in the convention, though it would likely apply, for example, to a church damaged during a bombing raid on an adjacent weapons factory, or a museum destroyed because it was being used as an arms depot.

The Nuremberg Trials after World War II marked the first time that individuals were held accountable for cultural war crimes. Several Nazi officials were sentenced to death for a panoply of violations that included the destruction of cultural property. Following that precedent, the Yugoslavia War Crimes Tribunal was empowered to prosecute individuals deemed responsible for the "seizure of, destruction or wilful damage done to institutions dedicated to religion, charity and education, the arts and sciences, historic monuments and works of art and science." However, the conventions related to cultural war crimes do not spell out the penalties that should be handed down for violations.

The destruction of the Ferhad Pasha mosque easily qualifies as a war crime. At the time, Banja Luka was under the firm political and military control of Serbs, and there was no fighting in the city or in the area immediately around it. The historic mosque could not be regarded as a military target; the few Muslims who remained in Banja Luka were using it only as a house of worship. Nonetheless, it was destroyed.

Customary Law

By Theodor Meron

Together with treaties, customary law is one of the principal sources or components of international humanitarian law (IHL). It results from a general and consistent practice of States that is followed by them from a sense of legal obligation. The most obvious significance of a norm—a principle or rule—of a customary character is that it binds States that are not parties to the treaty in which the norm is restated. It is, of course, not the treaty provision, but the customary norm with identical content that binds such States. Customary law is important also for filling in matters inadequately covered by humanitarian law treaties. The fact that a norm is customary has also a significance for the applicable rules of interpretation and may have the beneficial effect of limiting the power of States to make reservations or to denounce those treaties of IHL which have a high customary law content. A State cannot opt out of its duty to conform to a general international law. The recognition that an IHL treaty states customary law strengthens the moral claim of the international community for its observance by emphasizing its moral character and deep roots in community values.

The decisions on customary humanitarian law of the Hague Tribunal for the Former Yugoslavia are the linear successors to the decisions of the Nuremberg Tribunals. In both Nuremberg and The Hague, the tribunals looked primarily to the belief of States that certain principles are legally binding rather than to the practice of States in reaching their decisions. These decisions were supportive of an expansive view of customary law. Courts and tribunals tend to rely not on battlefield practice but on verbal statements in which States or institutions (for example, UN organs) express support for principles of IHL. Although they adhere to the traditional twin requirements (practice and the psychological belief that such practice is legally binding) for the formation of customary humanitarian law, in effect they weigh statements both as evidence of practice and as articulation of the psychological belief, which in the formation of humanitarian and human rights law is critical. The emphasis on the psychological element helps compensate for scarcity of supporting practice.

How to treat violations continues to be an important question. Both scholarly and judicial sources have shown reluctance to reject as customary norms—because of contrary practice—rules whose content merits customary law status perhaps because of the recognition that humanitarian principles express basic community values and are essential for the preservation of public order. Even repeated violations are often not regarded as negations of customary law provided they are responded to by protests or condemnations by other States or international organizations, and that the State accused either denies the facts of its questionable conduct or appeals to exceptions or justifications contained in the rule itself.

There is considerable judicial and scholarly support, which is also endorsed by the International Committee of the Red Cross (ICRC), that the rules contained in the four Geneva Conventions of 1949 for the Protection of Victims of War and in the Hague Convention (IV) of 1907 on the Laws and Customs of War on Land (except for administrative, technical, and logistical provisions) reflect customary law. It is also widely recognized that many, perhaps even most, of the provisions, principles, and rules contained in Additional Protocol I to the Geneva Conventions and some, perhaps even many, of the provisions contained in Additional Protocol II reflect customary law. Several rules pertaining to types of weapons, and especially the prohibition on the use of chemical weapons, are regarded as customary.

A declaration of the significance of customary law is incorporated into several IHL treaties, most notably in the so-called Martens clause, named for its drafter, Feodor de Martens, the adviser to the Russian Foreign Ministry at the beginning of the century. First inserted in the preamble of the 1899 Hague Convention II, this provides a minimum threshold of humanitarian treatment by combatants even in the absence of specific treaty language. "Until a more complete code of the laws of war is issued, the High Contracting Parties think it right to declare that in cases not included in the Regulations adopted by them, populations and belligerents remain under the protection and the empire of the principles of international law, as they result from the usages established between civilized nations, from the laws of humanity, and the requirements of the public conscience."

A study of customary rules of IHL presently being carried out by the ICRC is likely to recognize many additional rules of IHL applicable in international and, what is of particular importance, in noninternational armed conflicts, as customary law. The Rome Statute of the International Criminal Court codifies many rules and principles of IHL as customary criminal law.

In any discussion of customary law, sight must not be lost of the fact that the Geneva Conventions have attained practically universal ratification and that the Additional Protocols have gained many ratifications. For States parties to the IHL treaties, all treaty provisions, no matter whether they reflect customary law or not, are of course binding. In the national law of many countries, however, customary law is a part of the law of the land. As such, it may be invoked by victims of violations of IHL or human rights law.

Dangerous Forces: Dams, Dikes, and Nuclear Stations

By Erich Rathfelder

It was with worried expressions that the people of Omis, a small coastal town on the Adriatic, watched the Cretina River. In that bitter winter of 1993, it seemed as if death and destruction could come roaring down from the river at any time. The citizens of Omis, as well as villagers in the surrounding area, held their collective breath.

The danger of a deluge came from the Peruca Dam, a huge edifice that lay some forty kilometers inland, and that, before the breakup of Yugoslavia, had been part of the country's second biggest hydroelectric complex. Serb forces had controlled it since the beginning of the Croatian War in 1991. Now, Croatian forces were massing for an attack on Peruca and the 641 million cubic meters of water behind the dam represented mortal danger to civilians in the town below.

On January 28, Serb troops had detonated between thirty and thirty-seven tons of explosives in different parts of the dam. Peruca had been shaken to its foundations, but it seemed to be holding. Had its walls been breached, the mass of water would have raced in a giant wave down the river canyon, crushing the villages downriver and completely wiping out Omis.

Fortunately for the people of Omis, a Croatian counterattack was successful. Croatian military engineers reached the dam, opened its sluice gates, and allowed the water level to fall and the pressure to abate. Their action, and that of Capt. Mark Gray, a British officer serving with the United Nations as a military observer, probably saved the lives of between twenty thousand and thirty thousand people. In October 1992, while the Serbs still held Peruca, Gray, on his own initiative, opened one of the sluice gates following heavy rains, thus lowering the water level by six meters.

The Serb military actions were subject to two fundamental principles governing the impact of armed conflict on civilians as well as special rules that apply to "dangerous forces." First, civilians may not be made the direct object of attack. If the aim of the attack on the dam was to wipe out the civilians of Omis it was a grave breach. If it was to cause them under threat of destruction to abandon the area for reasons not strictly related to military necessity or their safety, then the attack was a serious violation.

Even if the attack upon the dam was not undertaken in order to affect civilians directly, if the resulting damage to civilians and civilian objects was not justified by **military necessity**, and would have been disproportionate to the concrete military advantages gained through it, the attack would also be a violation of the laws of armed conflict.

In addition, a special set of rules apply in this case.

According to Article 56 of the 1977 Additional Protocol I to the Geneva Conventions, "works or installations containing dangerous forces, namely dams, dikes and nuclear electrical generating stations, shall not be made the object of attack, even when these objects are **military objectives**, if such attack may cause the release of dangerous forces and consequent severe losses among the civilian population."

On the face of things, it would therefore appear that what the Serbs did was a violation of the laws of armed conflict. However, as with so many prohibitions in international humanitarian law, Article 56 of Protocol I is subject to important caveats. In other words, even so seemingly gross a violation as detonating explosives in a dam that causes severe losses among civilians is not always forbidden to soldiers.

Traditionally, the laws and customs of war allow the destruction of dams and dikes to stop an enemy's advance. And Article 56 does specify three exceptions to the prohibition against attacking or destroying works or installations containing dangerous forces. Where dams or dikes are concerned, the exception occurs when the installation is used for "other than its normal function and in regular, significant and direct support of military operations and if such attack is the only feasible way to terminate such support."

In other words, the article places obligations not only upon attacking forces but also defenders who might decide to utilize those installations or the nearby areas for "regular, significant, and direct" support of military operations.

The exceptions to the prohibition would appear not to apply in this instance, since the Croatian forces did not hold the dam and could not be said to have been using it as a military installation. The Serbs could also could not claim that destroying the dam allowed them to fend off the Croatian offensive. It would appear, rather, that the Serb attacks upon the dam were a clear violation of the obligation for the Serbs to take "all practical precautions . . . to avoid the release of dangerous forces."

(See **proportionality**)

Dead and Wounded

By H. Wayne Elliott

D In 1967 a U.S. Army sergeant in Vietnam posed for a photograph. The photograph, later published nationally, showed the sergeant holding the decapitated heads of two enemy corpses. The soldier was court-martialed and convicted of "conduct prejudicial to good order and discipline." There were other reports of U.S. soldiers cutting the ears and fingers off the enemy dead. Gen. William Westmoreland, commander of U.S. forces in Vietnam, denounced the mutilation of dead bodies as "subhuman" and "contrary to all policy and below the minimum standards of human decency." Not only is the mistreatment of dead bodies "contrary to all policy," it is also a violation of the laws of war.

One of the consequences of war is the death of some of those who get caught up in it. From time immemorial, the proper disposal of the dead has been a military concern. In earlier times the proper disposal of the battlefield dead often had religious overtones. Also, the dead on the battlefield were an immediate hygienic problem. Often, the need to avoid the diseases which could come from the untended dead was enough to force some humane disposal of the bodies. But, the law does not rely solely on the religious practices or the health concerns of the living. The proper disposal of the dead is now mandated by law.

The main obligation to the dead is now found in Article 15 of the First Geneva Convention. The thrust of that article is the need to aid the wounded. However, it also provides that the parties must "at all times, and particularly after an engagement . . . search for the dead and prevent their being despoiled." The article also says that "whenever circumstances permit," an armistice should be concluded so as to facilitate the search for the wounded. Of course, while searching for the wounded, the dead would also be found.

The International Committee of the Red Cross (ICRC) Commentary to the Geneva Convention says that the dead must be brought back along with the wounded. One reason for this is that in the highly charged atmosphere of the battlefield, it might not always be possible to determine who is really dead and who is seriously wounded. Another reason is that the laws of war require that an effort be made to identify the dead and to provide a proper burial.

The treatment of the battlefield dead can be divided into two aspects. First, there is a prohibition on deliberate mistreatment of the body, either through failure to treat it with appropriate respect or through mutilation. Second, there is a prohibition on pillaging the dead. These mandates concerning the dead are as much derived from the customary laws of war as from the Geneva Conventions.

The Geneva Conventions take the customary rules further. In Article 16 of the First Geneva Convention, we find an obligation for the party that has the body to send to the other party (usually through a neutral power or the ICRC) written evidence of death. Where the body is identified with the required double identity disk, one half of the disk, along with any personal effects found on the body, is to be sent to the other side.

Article 17 of the First Geneva Convention is concerned specifically with the burial of the battlefield dead. The bodies are to be examined, preferably

En route to a burial site, U.S. troops drag the body of a Viet Cong soldier behind an armored vehicle. Tan Binh, Vietnam, 1966.

by a person with medical skills, so as to confirm death. Burial is to be, where possible, in individual graves. The idea is that individual graves would be more consistent with the general requirement that the dead be respected, and also that individual burial would make subsequent exhumation easier. The requirement, however, is not absolute. Climate, sanitation, and hygiene may make mass burial the only proper action. The remaining half of the double identity disk must remain with the body. Cremation is prohibited except where it is based on the religion of the deceased or where imperative reasons of hygiene justify cremation.

Where possible, the burial or cremation is to be done in accordance with the religious rites of the deceased. The bodies are to be grouped according to nationality and the cemeteries mapped in such a way as to make later exhumation easier. This is the core of the Geneva Convention duty to the dead—they are to be treated honorably and their graves protected.

Mutilation of the dead is actually a fairly rare occurrence in well-disciplined armies. This is probably as much the result of a general revulsion at such conduct as from a fear of criminal punishment. However, pillaging the dead is a greater problem. In World War II the U.S. Army prohibited soldiers taking as "war trophies" any item that evidenced disrespectful treatment of the dead. A similar prohibition exists today. Nonetheless, there is a recognized right to search the dead for information that might be of some intelligence value. But private property of the deceased must be safeguarded for later delivery to the deceased's own military authorities.

As this summary indicates, the duty owed to the dead is somewhat subjective. What sort of conduct constitutes disrespect? How can we determine when neglect of the dead has ceased to be mandated by considerations of military necessity and become evidence of the war crime of mistreatment of the dead? There are no hard and fast answers to these questions. However, if the dead are left on the battlefield for some time after the fighting has ended, their very presence is evidence of failure to meet the obligations imposed by law. If the dead are left on the field solely so that they might be seen by journalists or photographed, that is stronger evidence that the threshold of mistreatment is near. If the dead are placed on display as propaganda (dragging the bodies through the streets as occurred in Somalia is a ready example), then the threshold has been crossed and a war crime has been clearly committed.

The laws of war accept that death is an inherent part of war. They also recognize that the disposal of the dead will be given less immediacy than the care of the living.

The *raison d'etre* for protecting and honoring the dead is captured in the inscription on the Tomb of the Unknowns in Arlington Cemetery: "Here Rests in Honored Glory an American Soldier Known But to God." That sentiment is not one peculiar to Americans.

Death Squads

By Jean-Marie Simon

D

They lounged outside police detective headquarters in Guatemala City, wearing mismatched suits and leaning on their machine guns as if they were umbrellas. They were experts in torture, disappearances, and executions. During the Guatemalan military government's undeclared civil war against its own people, which reached its height in the early 1980s, these men, who composed the death squads, terrorized Guatemala.

Salvadorean death squads leave their Mano Blanca "white hand" symbol on a victim's door.

Death squads were literally called *escuadrones de la muerte* but often were known as *judiciales,* a misnomer, as there was nothing judicial about them.

On Christmas Day, 1980, a *judicial* followed me out of a movie theater and told me I could accompany him either to McDonald's for a Big Mac or to police headquarters. Since the police station was a torture center, where passers-by heard screams coming from the basement, I opted for a brief date with a death squad agent. On another occasion, four heavily armed men in a Bronco Jeep followed two colleagues and me down a deserted street one night. When a friend, a well-connected politician, looked into the matter, he reported that, yes, the men had been after us, but it was just a scare tactic. ("If they had wanted to kill you, you'd be dead," he reassured me.)

Tens of thousands of people died in Guatemala, either in rural massacres conducted by uniformed army troops or, in the cities, in the form of "**disappearances**" at the hands of death squads.

Some were members of the military who donned civilian clothing to carry out the kidnappings. Others, however, were former soldiers, police,

121

bodyguards, or unemployed civilians deputized to do the army's dirty work for pay. *Judiciales* were rural peasants recruited into so-called **civil patrols** whom the army told to denounce their neighbors in return for a gun, some land, some money, or immunity from becoming army targets themselves. For most of them, it was nothing political, just money; if you told a *judicial* you would pay him twice as much to wash cars, he would wash cars instead.

Death squads kidnap and kill because someone in the government or the military commands, sanctions, or condones their behavior. Governments, armed forces, and political organizations have a practical reason to utilize death squads—deniability—but it is rarely plausible.

Death squad executions violate the laws of armed conflict as well as many human rights covenants. A related crime, forced disappearances, is now considered a **crime against humanity** under specific circumstances.

The laws of armed conflict as codified in the Four Geneva Conventions of 1949 explicitly prohibit executions without a fair trial. Common Article 3, which applies in internal conflict, forbids "violence to life and person, in particular murder of all kinds, mutilation, cruel treatment and torture" of persons who have not taken part in hostilities. It also forbids "the passing of sentences and the carrying out of executions without previous judgment pronounced by a regularly constituted court, affording all the judicial guarantees which are recognized as indispensable by civilized peoples."

Additional Protocol II of 1977, covering internal armed conflict, states that the court must offer "the essential guarantees of independence and impartiality." The court must inform the accused without delay of the particulars of the offense and provide necessary rights and defense; no one shall be accused except for individual penal responsibility; no one shall be held guilty for a criminal offense which did not exist in law at the time it was committed; those charged with offenses are presumed innocent until proven guilty; anyone charged has the right to be tried in his presence and not to be compelled to testify against himself. Although the protocol is less widely accepted than the 1949 Conventions, Guatemala became a party in 1987.

The Organization of American States in 1994 declared the systematic practice of forced disappearances a crime against humanity, a standard adopted by the 1998 Rome Statute of the International Criminal Court. Human rights covenants, which apply in situations of riots or disturbances but may legally be restricted and temporarily suspended during armed conflict, prohibit the death sentence without a judgment by a competent court.

The situation in Guatemala was clearly an internal armed conflict, and humanitarian law applied. Therefore, the government, army, death squads, and anyone else using force for the government were bound by its terms.

The death squads left very few survivors, and most of these either escaped captivity or were released on the eve of Guatemala's first civilian election in three decades, when the government was eager to bend to foreign demands in exchange for the promise of economic assistance.

Although the army denied any connection to the death squads, no one believed it. Even in Guatemala, where the army was infamous for leaving no witnesses or written accounts of its actions ("We're not Argentina, we leave no survivors," boasted former Army Public Relations Director, Col. Edgar D'Jalma Dominguez, in 1984), it was occasionally indiscreet. When the wife of a trade unionist sought news of her disappeared husband, she was directed to an obscure corner office in the National Palace, where a *judicial* with a black hood over his face recited the details of the kidnapping and torture. (See **due process**.)

Deportation

By Roy Gutman

D

The eighteen-car passenger train drew into the small station at Palic, northern Serbia, halted with a screech, then disgorged the eighteen hundred men, women, and children who had been confined to it for four days. They were inhabitants of the village of Kozluk in eastern Bosnia.

The Serbian government chartered this eighteen-car train to take the Muslim inhabitants of Kuzluk to Austria, which refused to accept them. Kept on board for four days, most of them finally ended up deported to Austria—but alive.

Late in June 1992, two Yugoslav Army tanks rolled into the village center and pointed menacingly at the comfortable houses there. Villagers were offered the choice: leave or have their village destroyed from under them. After signing away their property to Serb authorities, many walked across the nearby Drina bridge into neighboring Serbia, where border guards told them they could not return to Bosnia. Others boarded buses to the Serbian town of Samac, where they were transferred to the train. The government of Serbian President Slobodan Milosevic had provided the trains of the Yugoslav state railways with the intention of deporting the Kozluk residents to Austria, but so few had travel documents that Hungary refused to allow them transit through to Austria.

Individual or mass deportations are war crimes and **crimes against humanity** as defined at the Nuremberg Tribunals following World War II, and war crimes under the 1949 Geneva Conventions. If there is enormous loss of life, deportation may constitute **genocide**, namely the intent to kill or injure, in whole or in part, a national, ethnic, racial, or religious group, according to legal scholar Alfred de Zayas of Rutgers University.

Deportation was not explicitly banned prior to World War II. The 1907 Hague Conventions omitted mention, because mass expulsions were "generally rejected as falling below the minimum standard of civilization and, therefore, not requiring express prohibition," wrote legal scholar Georg Schwarzenberger.

Hitler's Nazi regime had expelled over 100,000 French from Alsace-Lorraine into Vichy France, and over 1 million Poles from western parts of occupied Poland into the German-run "Government-General of Poland." Germany also deported as many as 12 million non-Germans to work for the German war economy as compulsory labor.

The Nuremberg Tribunal repeatedly condemned the practice of "Germanizing" occupied or annexed territories, that is, transferring in part of the German population, as well as deporting civilians from one occupied region to another or to Germany. It stated that deportations into Germany for purposes of slave labor was "not only in defiance of well-established rules of international law, but in complete disregard of the elementary dictates of humanity."

But the victorious Allies in States taken over by the Communists—Czechoslovakia, Hungary, Romania, Yugoslavia, and East Germany—adopted Nazi practices and expelled some 15 million ethnic Germans to the West after World War II. An estimated 2 to 3 million died as a result.

The Fourth Geneva Convention of 1949 explicitly forbids deportations in conditions of war. "Individual or mass forcible transfers, as well as deportations of protected persons from occupied territory to the territory of the Occupying Power or to that of any other country, occupied or not, are prohibited, regardless of their motive." Also forbidden is the common practice of the occupying power deporting or transferring parts of its own civilian population into the territory it occupies. The convention allows the "total or partial evacuation" of any area where either "the security of the population or imperative military reasons" require, even outside the occupied territory, "when for material reasons it is impossible to avoid such displacement," but the evacuated civilians must be returned to their homes "as soon as hostilities in the area have ceased."

Iraq's deportation of Kuwaitis into Iraq and resettlement of Iraqis in Kuwait was singled out for condemnation by the UN Security Council. Serb "ethnic cleansing" in Bosnia from 1992–1995 also qualifies as a crime against humanity and a war crime. Israel's deportation of Palestinians from occupied territories also violates the Geneva Conventions, in the view of the United States, the UN Security Council and General Assembly, and the International Committee of the Red Cross (ICRC). Israel says the convention has no legal bearing on its conduct in the territories but that it has voluntarily applied the "humanitarian provisions" of its own free will, although without specifying which provisions it has in mind.

The five thousand residents of Kozluk were among the most fortunate of all Bosnian Muslims, for most survived their expulsion. Many families finally made it to Austria where they lived as refugees, and the men returned to fight on the side of the Bosnian government.Their departure was never intended to be a "temporary evacuation." As of mid-1998, none had returned to their homes in Kozluk.

(See **internal displacement**; **refoulement**; **refugees**; **transfer of civilians**.)

Disappearances

By Corinne Dufka

The call came around noon on Sunday. "What do you mean, Tita's missing? Who was the last person to see her? Who was she with? Did she go to work on Saturday? What exactly did she tell her mother?" Establishing facts is always a good way to hold back one's feelings in a time of personal crisis.

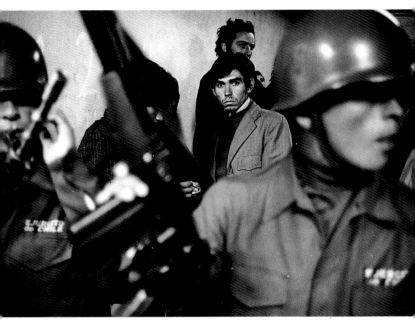

Civilians in Santiago were rounded up and held inside the National Stadium, countless numbers later disappeared. Chile, 1973.

These were the facts. Tita was Margarita Guzman. Salvadoran citizen. Age: 27. Height: 5'5". Weight: 140 pounds. Hair: Black. Eyes: Brown. No distinguishing marks. Single mother of two. Employed as a secretary with a social service organization. Last seen wearing blue jeans, a light blue blouse with small flowers, and black pumps, leaving her office at 1:15 P.M. on Saturday morning, May 4, and heading up Avenida Pablo Segundo.

These things happened. They happened to the poor, to the rich, to the faithful, and it had just happened to my friend Tita. She would never see her children grow big, never light up a room with her sense of humor, never hold her boyfriend again, and never walk the streets of San Salvador as a city at peace. She had disappeared . . . or rather, "been disappeared."

When used as a transitive verb, to disappear means to arrest someone secretly, to imprison and/or to kill them. It has become such a common occurrence in dirty wars ranging from El Salvador and Argentina to Kurdistan and Kuwait that the word seems almost self-explanatory. In international humanitarian law, however, disappearance is complicated for it involves the commission of several separate war crimes including unlawful confinement, failure to allow **due process**, and failure to allow communication between the arrested person and the outside world. It often involves torture and cruel and inhuman treatment, and too commonly it involves murder.

The first stage of a disappearance is capture. Humanitarian law states that State authorities may not make arbitrary arrests, and they must have sound legal bases for taking a person into custody and holding them against their will. The second stage is imprisonment. Additional Protocol II to the Geneva Conventions states that once in custody, a person has the right to humane treatment; the right not to be tortured or otherwise cruelly treated; the right to send and receive letters; the right to due process, including being informed of what he or she stands charged with. A person being detained is presumed innocent, must be granted all the necessary rights and means of mounting a defense—presenting evidence, calling witnesses, and the like—and may not be forced into a confession.

The last stage in a disappearance is murder, or what is sometimes euphemistically referred to as **extrajudicial execution**. Passing and carrying out of a death sentence without the sanction of a regularly constituted court is obviously illegal. The question, though, as in all cases of disappearance and presumed murder is establishing State responsibility. That is both the essence of the task that confronts investigators and the essence of the issue in international law. Not surprisingly, it is the most difficult task as well.

Most disappearances, however, occur in situations other than in international armed conflict—either in internal wars or situations that do not rise to the level of internal conflicts, i.e., disturbances or police actions. Both examples are dealt with in human rights law and the former is addressed in Article 3 common to the four Geneva Conventions. Additionally, the Statute of the International Criminal Court adopted in Rome in 1998 explicitly cites "enforced disappearances . . . by or with the authorization, support or acquiescence of a State or a political organization" as a **crime against humanity** if committed in a widespread or systematic manner.

Try as we did, we never found Tita, nor did we establish with any certainty who had abducted her. We did learn something of her fate, though. Near the Lempa River, outside San Salvador, an old woman stared at her photo for a long time before shaking her head and telling us she was sorry. We tried not to imagine what had happened, but we could not. We'd seen enough of the bodies dumped, sometimes headless and almost always with the clear marks of torture on them, in conspicuous places where passers-by could not avoid seeing them. Rumors from informants who had seen Tita in the hands of the Policia Nacional came and went. But we never found her body, and eventually all of us stopped asking questions except for her little boys, who kept asking why their mother never came home.

Due Process

By Gideon Levy

D

Tarek Burkan is a well-dressed, light-haired Palestinian boy from Hebron, his first mustache growing in. Most of the time I spent with him, he was quiet and seemed calm. Only when I asked him about the circumstances of his detention did he respond openly and aggressively: "Ask the Shabak [Hebrew acronym for General Security Service]. Next time I'll throw stones and then at least I'll understand why I'm detained." There is nothing apparently psychotic in this anger of his, just as there is not in the anger of all the administrative detainees, jailed for months and years in Israel without a trial or an explanation.

They are all residents of the territories conquered by Israel in 1967. During the Intifada, Israel detained thousands; at the time of writing there are more than a hundred. The number varies from time to time, but it is not the number that is significant.

The question is one of principle and it touches on two basic issues: Israel's position among the family of nations and Israel's internal position as a country of law and order in its own right. But the boy Tarek is far removed from all that. I find it hard to believe that he ever heard of the Geneva Conventions, or any other body of humanitarian or international law. He is a mentally ill boy whom I met in his cell in the Megiddo prison in northern Israel, inside the Green Line. It is a military prison more like a camp than a prison, but its fences are well guarded. Until recently it housed most of the Palestinian administrative detainees held by Israel. Early in 1998 Israel started transferring them to civilian prisons, also inside the Green Line, where they are detained together with criminal prisoners. Most of the administrative detainees whom I know preferred the cold winters and hot summers in the Megiddo prison tents and the relative measure of freedom and autonomy there over the crowded conditions of civilian prisons.

Getting back to the boy, Tarek: several weeks prior to our prison meeting, there was a bad stretch in his illness and he started to be dangerous to himself and his surroundings. He is sixteen years old, was orphaned from his father when he was one, and hospitalized in the past in a Bethlehem hospital for the mentally ill. Child and adolescent psychiatry expert, Dr. Fahum Tarek, of the Mental Health Center in Tirat Hacarmel, Israel, who examined him at the request of the prison authorities wrote in his statement: "It is almost certain that he suffered [in the past] from paranoid schizophrenia . . . also during his detention, a psychotic condition with delusional thoughts was suspected." The prison commander admitted that this boy did not belong in Megiddo prison.

Many of the other administrative detainees in Israel do not belong in prison. Among them are young and old, poets and laborers, men and women, Hamas members and left-front members. By no standard, Israeli or international, were any of them given a fair trial—or due process, to use the common law term. Israel is a party to both the Fourth Geneva Convention and the International Covenant on Civil and Political Rights, which lay out several requirements for trials of enemy civilians (see sidebar). These requirements include: the right to be informed of charges; to be tried without undue

127

delay; to prepare and present a defense; to be assisted by counsel; the right not to be forced to confess, and to be presumed innocent until proven guilty. They are also part of Common Article 3 of the Geneva Conventions of 1949, which applies to noninternational armed conflict and forbids "the passing of sentences and the carrying out of executions without previous judgement pronounced by a regularly constituted court, affording all the judicial guarantees which are recognized as indispensable by civilized peoples."

Neither the detainees nor their lawyers have any idea what the charges against them are—everything is privileged and confidential. No witnesses testify against them, evidence is presented by a Shabak representative to the judge alone. They have no idea when they will be released: every six months they can expect notice that their detention has been extended without any explanation. Their detention is carried out on the basis of an administrative order, signed by a military commander, but the real responsibility for it lies with the Shabak, the omnipotent Israeli security organization. All of this is done without any judicial decision, indictment, or trial. Detainees can appeal, but even the appeal process does not meet the minimal standard of due process. For over a year, most of them boycotted the appeal process because of the way it is set up, and only recently have they decided to test it again. Some have been released recently, but it is still too early to tell whether this is the start of a welcome change or merely a coincidence. In the meantime, there are still some whose detention has already been extended nine to ten times, and the majority have been jailed for over two years. There are some who served court sentences only to find that on the day of their release they were put in administrative detention. Since the signing of the Oslo accords, it seems that some are in detention due to their opposition to the accords, or in other words, due to their opposition activity. They are therefore political detainees, even if Israel does not accept the definition.

A report by B'tselem—the Israeli Information Center for Human Rights in the Occupied Territories—stated that "despite the declarations of official spokesmen and judges, whereby Israel adheres to the principles of international law, Israel is de facto very seriously violating each and every one of them." Administrative detentions in the West Bank are carried out under order 1229 of 1988. This authorizes military commanders to detain a person for a maximum of six months when there is "a reasonable basis to assume that reasons of regional security or public safety require that a certain person be held in detention." The order fixes no maximum cumulative time, and therefore detention can be extended repeatedly and indefinitely. Even the meaning of the magic words "regional security" and "public safety" is left to the exclusive discretion of the regional military commanders.

The situation is contrary to the natural principles of justice and to several international conventions to which Israel is a party. Israel ratified the International Covenant on Civil and Political Rights in 1991. Its Article 9 states: "no person shall be detained or arbitrarily imprisoned." Although Israel holds that at the time of and ever since ratification it has been in "a state of general emergency as described in Article 4 of the Covenant," this same Article 4 is not an unrestricted clause. Even during emergency situations, the state is required to protect basic human rights as much as possible and every move against them must pass the test of need and proportionality. Indeed, the European Court of Human Rights emphasized the need for judicial review of detention during emergency situations. Administrative detention, when carried out contrary to the rules of international law, that is when it is done for extended periods or serves as an alternative to criminal

A Palestinian prisoner in solitary confinement cell. Beer Sheba, 1971.

proceedings, is also contrary to Article 14 of the Covenant on Civil and Political Rights, which sets minimum standards for a trial.

Administrative detention in the territories is also subject to the guidelines of international humanitarian law, primarily the Fourth Geneva Convention of 1949. Israel claims that its use of administrative detention is legal, according to Article 78 of the Geneva Convention, which permits detentions due to security requirements. However, in this context, the B'tselem report mentions the International Committee of the Red Cross (ICRC) Commentary to the Geneva Conventions, which states that this article refers only to vital security needs. The commentary notes that according to Article 49, moving detainees to detention sites outside the occupied territories (as Israel does) is prohibited. It is doubtful that Article 78 even applies to the territories. Article 6 of the Fourth Geneva Convention states that the section's application will cease "one year after the general end of the military operations."

The boy, Tarek, has not heard about any of this. In his cell, he is irate about his detention and, primarily, about the lack of information he has about any of the charges against him. Many comrades with the same fate, mentally healthier than him, are no less irate. Nonetheless, the real anger and frustration should have been in the State of Israel: in the final historical reckoning, the end result of administrative detention will be that it will affect the jailers more than the detainees. Tarek Burkan was released after serving six months of detention without a trial. His friends will also be released one day.

Due Process Rights

Under the Third and Fourth Geneva Conventions of 1949, dealing with prisoners of war and civilians respectively, the defendant has the right (items in italics do not apply in internal conflicts):

to be told—early on and in a language he understands—what he is accused of;
to be presumed innocent until proven guilty;
to be tried without undue delay;
to be heard before an impartial decision maker;
to be tried in a "regularly constituted court" *(if the accused is a POW, it may be a military court)*;
to prepare and present a defense;
to present witnesses;
not to be required to testify against himself or to confess guilt;
to be tried in his presence;
to be convicted only of a crime that he himself committed;
not to be punished more than once for the same act;
to be convicted only for what was a crime at the time of the act in question;
to have a sentence no more severe than the law allowed at the time of the act in question;
to be told of his rights of appeal and what time limits there are;
to appeal and ask for pardon or reprieve;
to have any death sentence stayed until six months after notification of the Protecting Power.

Environmental Warfare

By Mark Perry and Ed Miles

E **The testimony of George Claxton, a Vietnam veteran who served in Southeast Asia in 1967, reveals just how widely the United States used Agent Orange. "I took showers in the stuff," he says. "We had wooden stalls with a tub overhead filled with rainwater that was tinged slightly orange. We would pull the string hanging in the shower and bathe in it. We knew it was Agent Orange because we saw the planes spraying it on the jungle every day. We didn't think anything of it really and at first we thought, 'Hell, the army is spraying for mosquitoes.' "**

Claxton's experience was not unusual. Between 1965 and 1975, the U.S. military sprayed millions of tons of Agent Orange on the jungles of Vietnam in "ADMs"—airborne "area denial missions" intended to deny cover to the Vietcong and North Vietnamese Army. The strategy worked: large areas of Quang Tri Province along the 38th Parallel and a swath of land in the "iron triangle" of Tay Ninh Province west of Saigon were stripped of all vegetation.

In the wake of Vietnam, there was worldwide concern about the environmental damage caused by U.S. military operations in Southeast Asia. Shortly after the end of the Vietnam War, in 1975, it began to become clear that a disproportionate number of Vietnam veterans were coming down with non-Hogkins lymphoma and skin sarcomas. The Centers for Disease Control would later determine that the cause of these cancers was the dioxins contained in Agent Orange. The extent of the damage to the natural environment of Vietnam as a result of the spraying was also becoming apparent. While no systematic survey of defoliated areas of Southeast Asia has been conducted, the anecdotal evidence is enormous. Huge portions of Quang Tri and Tay Ninh provinces "look like a moonscape" and remain unsuitable for agricultural use, according to Chuck Searcy, the director of a humanitarian program in Hanoi. And Vietnamese doctors have attested to significant increases in birth defects among people in the affected areas.

The major piece of international humanitarian law prohibiting environmental war was drafted in reaction to what took place in Vietnam, and is contained in two articles of the 1977 Additional Protocol I to the Geneva Conventions. Article 35 states that "it is prohibited to employ methods or means of warfare which are intended, or may be expected, to cause widespread, long-term and severe damage to the environment." This prohibition is spelled out in detail in two sections of Article 55.

The first of these sections involves the protection of the natural environment. "Care shall be taken in warfare," it states, "to protect the natural environment against widespread, long-term and severe damage. This protection includes a prohibition against the use of means of warfare which are intended or may be expected to cause such damage to the natural environment and thereby prejudice the health or survival of the population." The second provision declares that "attacks against the natural environment by way of **reprisals** are prohibited."

Unfortunately, these provisions are more unclear and more ambiguous legally than at least some commentators and activists might have wished. While they impose the obligation to take precautions, they fall far short of a blanket interdiction against certain methods of warfare that may harm the environment. The use of the expression "long-term" is understood to mean decades, not years, so a considerable degree of environmental harm seems to be tolerable under international humanitarian law.

Some further limitations on the ravages of environmental war were secured by the Convention on the Prohibition of Military or Any Other Hostile Use of Environmental Modification Techniques (ENMOD), which was opened for signature in 1977—again, largely in response to the American use of defoliants in Vietnam—and was ratified by the United States in 1980. This convention is now accepted, along with Articles 35 and 55 of Additional Protocol I, as the clearest expression of international humanitarian law in the field of environmental warfare.

By the terms of the ENMOD, States agree not to "engage in military or

A Vietnamese mother with her two blind daughters, 1980. Their father had been a truck driver on the Ho Chi Minh Trail and had often been soaked by Agent Orange.

other hostile use of environmental modification techniques having widespread, long-lasting or severe effects as the means of destruction, damage or injury." In practice, it remains to be seen whether enough ambiguity has been removed from the law to make these provisions serve as an effective way of preventing the most extreme kinds of environmental attacks. These provisions were not in effect at the time of the Vietnam War, so, obviously, they cannot be applied retroactively to what took place then. Some have argued that the Iraqi government's decision, in the waning days of its occupation of Kuwait in 1991, to set fire to the Kuwaiti oil fields and to purposely dump millions of tons of oil into the Persian Gulf was an instance of such a crime. But since no Iraqi officers were ever indicted or tried for these offenses, the practical impact of the provisions remain unclear.

Kuwaiti Oil Wells

By Robert Block

Dante would have at been at home in Kuwait in 1991. A desert paradise had been transformed into an environmental inferno by a spiteful Iraqi leader.

Across the land more than six hundred oil wells ignited by Iraqi soldiers spewed out orange and red fireballs and roared like untamed beasts. The smoke was so thick and so black that when the winds failed it became midnight at 10:00 A.M. Grease dripped from the skies and soot fell like snowflakes from hell. Everything whose natural color should have been white was a charcoal gray: cats, sheep, and the carcasses of slender-billed seagulls who dropped from the heavens while overflying the country.

The burning oil fields on the Kuwait skyline is perhaps the most enduring image to survive the Gulf War and is also one of the greatest environmental crimes ever perpetrated.

It was Saddam Hussein's final defiant gesture. Defeated but unbowed after the Gulf War, his troops placed explosive charges next to every well they could reach in the Ahmadi, Dharif, Umm Quadir, Wafra, Minagish, and Rawdatayn oil fields. If the entire dispute that led to Iraq's invasion of Kuwait was over oil, then Saddam's attitude appeared to be, "If I can't have it, neither can you."

During the war, the Pentagon issued exaggerated assessments of the oil fires and the deliberate oil spills the Iraqis unleashed, putting Saddam Hussein's acts of ecoterrorism in the worst possible light. Nevertheless the horror of the fires and the ecological damage to the Gulf's fragile flora and fauna from what locals called "Saddam's memorial cloud" was very real.

At the time, John Walsh, a biologist with the World Society for the Protection of Animals, was particularly concerned about dozens of species of migratory birds from Central Asia which traveled over the Gulf. He would brave the heat and the smoke from the burning wells and collect dead birds. After picking up one dead gull, he surveyed the spectacle and wondered aloud: "Is this what the end of the world looks like?"

The Greater Burhan Oil Fields, set afire by the retreating Iraqi troops in 1991, evoke apocalyptic imagery.

Ethnic Cleansing

By Roger Cohen

The life of Hiba Mehmedovic, a Bosnian Muslim, came apart on May 31, 1992, soon after the war in Bosnia began. Three Serbs armed with automatic weapons broke into her home and took away her two sons, Kemal and Nedzad, whom she never saw again. A few weeks later, she herself was forced at gunpoint onto a bus, driven to the front line west of her home town of Vlasenica, and abandoned.

She trudged into government-held territory. When I found her, sprawled on the floor of a kindergarten in the town of Kladanj, she was a broken figure emblematic of the war: tearful and terrified, part of a dark tide of Muslims driven from their homes, human flotsam scattered across the floors of empty buildings. Her unseeing eyes spoke of an existence emptied. There were 18,699 Muslims in Vlasenica before the war, about 60 percent of the population; there are none today.

Ethnic cleansing—the use of force or intimidation to remove people of a certain ethnic or religious group from an area—was the central fact of the wars of Yugoslavia's destruction. The practice has a method: **terror**. It has a smell: the fetid misery of refugees. It has an appearance: the ruins of ravaged homes. Its purpose is to ensure—through killing, destruction, threat, and humiliation—that no return is possible.

Yugoslavia, and its Bosnian heart, were bridges. But over four years of war, places of mingling became places of bleak ethnic homogeneity as more than 1.5 million people were shifted in the name of racist ideologies. The single most devastating burst of violence, between April and August 1992, saw Serbs driving more than 700,000 Muslims from an area covering 70 percent of Bosnia.

Such mass **deportation** was not new in this century of ethnic engineering. Greeks out of Turkey; Turks out of Greece; Serbs out of the Fascist Croatia of 1941–1945; Jews out of Hitler's Europe; ethnic Germans out of postwar Czechoslovakia; Palestinians from occupied territories. The waves of forced evictions of ethnic and religious groups have been repetitive, often combining physical removal with devastating violence, or, as in the case of the Jews, genocide.

Ethnic cleansing is a blanket term, and no specific crime goes by that name, but the practice covers a host of criminal offenses. The United Nations Commission of Experts, in a January 1993 report to the Security Council, defined "ethnic cleansing" as "rendering an area ethnically homogenous by using force or intimidation to remove persons of given groups from the area." It said ethnic cleansing was carried out in the former Yugoslavia by means of murder, **torture**, arbitrary arrest and detention, **extrajudicial executions**, **rape** and sexual assault, confinement of the civilian population, deliberate military attacks or threats of attacks on civilians and civilian areas, and wanton destruction of property. The Commission's final report in May 1994 added these crimes: mass murder, mistreatment of civilian prisoners and prisoners or war, use of civilians as human **shields**, destruction of **cultural property**,

A toppled minaret makes an ironic backdrop for a makeshift morgue where the bodies of victims are washed before burial. Bosnia, May 1993.

robbery of personal property, and attacks on **hospitals, medical personnel**, and locations with the **Red Cross/Red Crescent emblem.**

Perpetrators of such crimes are subject to individual criminal responsibility, and military and political leaders who participated in making and implementing the policy "are also susceptible to charges of **genocide** and **crimes against humanity**, in addition to grave breaches of the Geneva Conventions and other violations of international humanitarian law," the 1994 report said.

International law took up the question of the systematic expulsion of civilians, and the barbaric practices associated with it, after World War II. Article 49 of the Fourth Geneva Convention of 1949 forbids "individual or mass forcible **transfers**, as well as deportations of protected persons from occupied territory to the territory of the Occupying Power or to that of any other country." The actions are grave breaches of the Fourth Convention— war crimes of particular seriousness.

Only the security of the civilian population or "imperative military reasons" may justify **evacuation** of civilians in occupied territory, according to the Fourth Geneva Convention. Additional Protocol II of 1977 extends this rule to civilians in internal armed conflicts. In Bosnia, where the Serbs initially enjoyed overwhelming military superiority, there is no evidence that the forced movement of Muslim men, women, and children was driven by such a consideration. As Pero Popovic, a Serb guard at the Susica concentration camp in Vlasenica once told me, "Our aim was simply to get rid of the Muslims."

Article 49 applies to international conflict. I traveled with enough Serb forces crossing Serbia's border with Bosnia to have no doubt that this was a war organized, financed, and directed from Belgrade. But even if the Bosnian War is viewed as a civil war between Serbs, Muslims, and Croats of the country, the forced expulsions contravene Article 3 common to the four Geneva Conventions, which applies to "conflict not of an international character."

This article states that "people taking no active part in the hostilities" shall always "be treated humanely, without any adverse distinction founded on race, color, religion or faith, birth or wealth." It prohibits "humiliating and degrading treatment" and "violence to life and person, in particular murder of all kinds, mutilation, cruel treatment, and torture."

There is also the Nuremberg Charter to consider. Article 6 defined "crimes against humanity" as including "murder, extermination, enslavement, deportation, and other inhuman acts committed against any civilian population, before or during a war." And Nuremberg made it clear that population transfer is a war crime.

Mrs. Mehmedovic's most precious possession was two photographs of her sons, aged twenty-seven and twenty-five when they were dragged from her house. I took the photographs to Popovic, the Serb guard in Vlasenica, who had recanted. His look of recognition was unmistakable. He told me the two boys had been executed at the Susica camp.

(See **Bosnia; internal displacement; refugees; siege; starvation.**)

Evacuation of Civilians from the Battlefield

By H. Wayne Elliott

The battlefield is not a place most people want to be. Soldiers are there because of the mission and their duty. Civilians who find themselves on the battlefield are, in most cases, there by accident or at least unintentionally. Wounds, death, and destruction accompany combat. People will be wounded and perhaps killed. Buildings and personal property will be destroyed. What duty is owed by soldiers to those civilians who find themselves caught up in the fight?

A civilian can be defined by who he is not. Generally, a civilian is a person who is not a combatant and does not take a direct part in the hostilities. On the battlefield the soldier is concerned with whether those present are legitimate military objectives, most often called "lawful targets." If they are true civilians, they should not be participating in the fight. If they choose to do so they are subject to being targeted and, if captured, might be brought before a judicial tribunal as an unlawful **combatant**.

Suppose a commander knows there are true civilians in the battlefield area. What obligations are placed on that commander? Must an effort be made to evacuate the civilians? There is no obligation to evacuate civilians from the battle area. At the same time, deliberately endangering noncombatants is a violation of the laws of war. In practice, commanders often avoid the problem of civilians in the battle area by simply giving a warning. This might be accomplished by dropping leaflets, or by making announcements over loudspeakers or radio. At first glance, such a practice might seem unlikely or even blissful. But, as a military matter such warnings make sense (unless, of course, surprise is a factor). First, the commander giving the warning is making a demonstrable effort to avoid harming noncombatants. Second, as a military matter, a warning to civilians that they should remove themselves from the area has the propaganda effect of reminding them that their own military force may be unable to stem the advancing forces. Third, most civilians will move toward their own forces and not their enemy. When that occurs, their own forces may well be presented with a major logistical and tactical problem.

The law actually places the burden of protecting civilians most heavily on the force that has some real control over the civilians. Thus, while an attacking force can not deliberately target civilians, neither can a defending force use civilians as some sort of a shield against legitimate attacks.

Suppose that the civilian noncombatants are inside a besieged area, such as Sarajevo during the Bosnian War. Article 17 of the Fourth Geneva Convention does provide that the "Parties to the conflict shall endeavor to conclude local agreements for the removal from besieged or encircled areas" of noncombatants. The word "endeavor" clearly shows that such evacuation is not compulsory. In fact, the commander of the besieged place will tend to want to evacuate the civilian noncombatants because they consume supplies and rations. At the same time, and for the same reason, the commander of a besieging force is not likely to agree that persons who are a drain on enemy resources should be permitted to leave. Whether an agreement is reached or not, civilians cannot be specifically targeted. During the siege of Sarajevo snipers killed individuals who were clearly civilians (school-age children, old people, sick, etc.). In the case of some of those killed at Sarajevo, war crimes were committed—not because the civilians were not evacuated, but because civilians were targeted.

As the force advances, the more general obligations under the Fourth Geneva Convention concerning the occupation of enemy territory might be triggered. When an advancing force becomes an occupying force, the law places that force in the position of an interim government. As such, its responsibilities to the civilian population are much greater and more defined.

The burden when it comes to protecting civilians from the combat effects of war falls on three distinct parties: First, the advancing force, which must make every effort to avoid unnecessary harm to civilians. Second, the defending force, which may well have the best chance at removing civilians

Farewell Sarajevo: Five centuries ago, Jews fleeing the Spanish Inquisition set up home in Sarajevo. In 1993, the remnants of the ancient community are bused out of range of Serb shells and snipers.

from the area before it actually becomes the scene of combat. Third, and most important, the civilians themselves. They must avoid participating in the fight. In fact, they should simply avoid, if possible, being in the area where the fighting occurs.

(See **collateral damage; ethnic cleansing; internal displacement; siege; transfer of civilians.**)

Executions, Extrajudicial

By Don Oberdorfer

Accompanied by a sudden artillery and mortar barrage and flares casting a metallic glow, two North Vietnamese battalions stormed across lightly defended bridges and lotus-choked moats into the former Vietnamese imperial capital of Hue before dawn on January 31, 1968.

It was part of nearly simultaneous surprise attacks by Communist military forces against nearly every significant city or town in South Vietnam during the lunar new year, or Tet, holiday. The Tet Offensive, as the nationwide attacks would become known, shocked the U.S. government and public into reconsidering and eventually terminating the U.S. military effort in Vietnam.

Hue was occupied for twenty-five days before the North Vietnamese were ousted. During that time, the troops and the political officers who came with them ruled over large parts of the city. One of the central objectives of the occupation, according to a written plan prepared in advance, was to "destroy and disorganize" the administrative machinery that the South Vietnamese regime had established since Vietnam was divided by international agreement in 1954. The effort to root out "enemy" functionaries, according to the plan, was to extend "from the province and district levels to city wards, streets and wharves." The political officers arrived with a carefully prepared "target list" of 196 places, organized on a block-by-block basis, to be given priority attention, including U.S. and South Vietnamese offices and the homes of the officials who worked there, as well as the homes of those who were deemed to be leading or cooperating with their efforts, including foreigners. Once in charge, the occupation forces set about expanding its target lists with the assistance of local sympathizers.

So many were killed. Le Van Rot, the owner of the most popular Chinese soup restaurant in the city, was the government block chief of his area. Four armed men, two from Hue and two from North Vietnam, came to his shop and arrested him, accusing him of being a spy. They bound his arms behind his back with wire and began to tug him toward the door. When he resisted, one of them put a bullet through his head.

Then there was Pham Van Tuong. He worked part-time as a janitor at the government information office. Four men in black pajamas came to his house, calling on him by name to come out of the bunker where he and his family had taken refuge. But when he did come out, along with his five-year-old son, his three-year-old daughter, and two of his nephews, there was a burst of gunfire. All five were shot to death.

Dr. Horst Gunther Krainick was a German pediatrician and professor of internal medicine who had worked for seven years with teams of Germans and Vietnamese to establish a medical school at Hue University. Krainick stayed in his university apartment after the fall of the city, believing he and his wife would not be harmed. Unknown to them, they were on the original target list. On the fifth day of the occupation, an armed squad arrived and put the Krainicks and two other German doctors into a commandeered Volkswagen bus. Their bodies were found later in a potato field, all victims of

South Vietnamese police chief Colonel Nguyen Ngoc Loan executes a suspected Viet Cong officer during the Tet offensive in 1968.

an executioner's bullets.

The same day, North Vietnamese troops came in force to the Roman Catholic cathedral, where many people had taken refuge from the fighting. Four hundred men were ordered out, some by name and others apparently because they were of military age or prosperous appearance. When the group was assembled, the political officer on the scene told people not to fear; the men were merely being taken away temporarily for political indoctrination. Nineteen months later, three defectors led U.S. soldiers to a creekbed in a double canopy jungle ten miles from Hue where the skulls and bones of those who had been taken away had lain ever since. Those killed included South Vietnamese servicemen, civil servants, students, and ordinary citizens. The skulls revealed they had been shot or brained with blunt instruments.

Altogether, South Vietnamese authorities counted about twenty-eight hundred victims of deliberate slaughter during the Tet Offensive in Hue. The fate of some was known immediately. The bodies of others emerged later from mass graves in nearby jungles or the coastal salt flats. Like those taken from the cathedral, they had been shot to death, bludgeoned, or buried alive.

After Hue was retaken, the South Vietnamese authorities were reported to be guilty of some of the same practices. I learned from a U.S. team that "black teams" of South Vietnamese assassins were sent in to eliminate those who were believed to have aided the enemy during the occupation. On March 14, three weeks after South Vietnam regained control, more than twenty prisoners, including some women and schoolboys, were brought to provincial military headquarters with burlap bags covering their heads and hands tightly wired behind their backs. After being taken into a stone building that was reputed to be a place of execution, all the prisoners disappeared.

It is, of course, unlawful to execute an accused person without giving him a fair trial first. Two bodies of law apply—humanitarian law, which applies in an armed conflict, and human rights law, which applies even where the laws of war do not.

Under international humanitarian law, the sorts of killings that took place in Hue are usually termed "willful killing without judicial process." If the victims are enemy prisoners of war (including accredited journalists and civilian suppliers and contractors attached to enemy armed forces), or medical or religious personnel attached to the armed services, such executions are grave breaches under the Third Geneva Convention. If they are enemy civilians, it is a grave breach of the Fourth Geneva Convention.

The requirements for fair trials of military personnel and civilians are similar. Each accused person has rights: against self-incrimination, against being convicted on the basis of an *ex post facto* law, for being advised of his or her rights, of having the right to counsel, to be told the particulars of the charge, to prepare a defense, to call witnesses, to have an interpreter, and to appeal. "As it is prohibited to kill protected persons during an international armed conflict, so it is prohibited to kill those taking no active part in hostilities which constitute an internal armed conflict," the International Criminal Tribunal for the Former Yugoslavia said in November 1998. The key element is "the death of the victim as a result of the actions of the accused." Even when it is unclear whether a situation is an armed conflict, human rights law forbids extrajudicial executions.
(See **death squads; disappearances; due process.**)

The Camera as Witness

By Alex Levac

On April 13, 1984, four young Palestinians commandeered bus number 300 as it made its way from Tel Aviv to the southern city of Ashkelon, and forced it to Dir el-Ballah, a small town in the northern Gaza Strip which at the time was under Israeli occupation. There the bus was surrounded by soldiers and police. Just before sunrise, after an all-night standoff, crack troops stormed the bus, turning the silent pre-dawn into a delirium of screaming, gunfire, and explosions that lasted several minutes.

With other photographers and reporters who had evaded police road-blocks to get to the scene, I ran toward the noise in the near total darkness. Suddenly, I found myself confronting two men who alternated between drag-ging and propping up a third person. Convinced that he was one of the many passengers rescued from the bus, I snapped just one picture. The two men were on me instantly, demanding that I surrender the film from my camera. With a sleight of hand, I managed to give them an unused roll, and they were on their way.

On the journey back to Tel Aviv, I heard the army spokesman telling Israeli radio that one passenger had been killed, a few had been wounded, and the rest rescued unharmed. He said that two of the Palestinian hijackers had died in the raid and that two others had been captured when the troops stormed the bus. However, an hour later, the next news broadcast reported

A young Palestinian hijacker led away by two Shin Bet officers, who crushed his skull with a rock. The official report read that he was shot during the operation to rescue the bus passengers he was holding hostage. Images of police have been distorted on demand of Israeli censor.

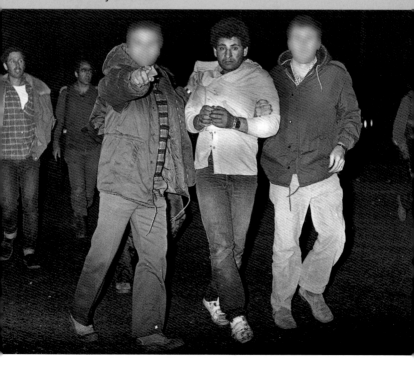

that all four hijackers had died when the troops stormed the bus. And that version became the official government line.

It wasn't until I developed the film that I realized why the men in the picture, members of the Shin Bet—the domestic security service—wanted my film. The man they were dragging off, I discovered to my astonishment, wasn't a passenger at all. He was one of the hijackers—young, handcuffed to his captors, and very much alive. At least one of the Palestinians had survived the raid. The picture was proof that the security officials had lied. The truth peered out from the eyes of this young Palestinian, bound but living. Here was a man who only a short time earlier had been terrorizing a bus full of passengers and striking fear in the hearts of all Israelis.

The more I looked, the more complete his transformation had become from an abhorrent figure to a pitiful one—a man in need of protection from the two Shin Bet agents guarding him. Moments earlier the agents had been heroes rescuing passengers on a bus. Now, standing on either side of their captive, they were the bad guys. Does the knowledge of impending death shape our judgment? From the moment of his death, the Palestinian became a reflection of our own mortal image. Are we to erase him from our collective memory and let him disappear under a mound of earth, or do we raise his ghost and grapple with his right to live, to be tried, to be a human being?

Every photojournalist wants to make an impact, wants his picture to be worth a thousand words. The power of my photograph of the Palestinian hijacker escorted to his death by his Shin Bet captors is drawn from what the observer does not see but is compelled to imagine—the moment the agents crush the Palestinian's skull with a stone, the moment of death.
(See **hostages**.)

Forced Labor

By John Ryle

Forced labor, like slavery, involves the deprivation of liberty, but differs from slavery in that no claim of permanent right of ownership is made over a person subject to it. International agreements put strict limits on the use of forced labor by the State and prohibit its use by non-State bodies and individuals, but they do not ban it outright.

Forced labor is a common feature of modern wars. In Burma (Myanmar), for example, conscription of civilians as unpaid labor for the military authorities is widespread. Typical duties include the construction of roads, barracks, and railways, and porterage for army contingents. Such projects often involve large-scale relocation of populations. In the worst instances, civilians from ethnic minorities in areas of rebel activity have been forced to march ahead of troops as a human shield against landmines.

In the former Yugoslavia, between 1993 and 1996, forced labor was used by all sides, but most systematically in the Serb-controlled areas of northern Bosnia, where non-Serb minorities under Bosnian Serb control were subject to a "work obligation." Forced labor details were assigned to the front line of conflict; they were also put to work in factories and mines; the work obligation was used as a means of public humiliation for prominent members of minority ethnic groups.

All these practices involve infringements of one or other of the various international agreements that touch on the issue of forced labor. Article 3 common to the four Geneva Conventions of 1949 applies in internal conflicts and requires humane treatment to those who do not take part in hostilities and arguably limits forced labor by imposing minimum standards on it. The Fourth Geneva Convention specifies that, in occupied territory, civilians cannot be compelled to join the armed forces of an occupying power, or to engage in certain kinds of war-related work, such as the production of munitions, and if under age eighteen they may not be forced to work at all.

F

Chechens accused of collaborating with Russians are forced to labor at digging trenches around Grozny, 1996.

Civilians under military occupation, both in wars between States and, as specified in Additional Protocol II of 1977, in internal conflicts, cannot be required to work longer hours or under conditions worse than the local norm. Civilian internees in a war between States cannot be compelled to work, unless they are medical personnel (who can be required to attend fellow internees) or are employed in administrative, kitchen, civil defense, or other work on behalf of other internees. Enforced prostitution is specifically prohibited in Article 27 of the Fourth Convention.

There are detailed rules in international law for the treatment of **prisoners of war** set out in the Third Geneva Convention of 1949. Most of the restrictions on civilian employment detailed above also apply to them; beyond this, the Geneva Conventions specify that POWs forced to work must be paid a wage, unless their work involves only the maintenance or administration of their place of detention. They cannot be forced to do degrading, unhealthy, or dangerous work. Military officers cannot be forced to work.

In order to determine whether a particular case of forced labor contravenes any or all of the international norms specified above, it will be useful to know the following. First, who is being forced to work: whether they are prisoners of war, women, under the age of eighteen or over forty-five, or members of an ethnic or other minority. Second, the nature of the work and working conditions: who the work is for, the hours and days worked, the distances from home, whether the work is war-related, whether the products are exported, and whether or not they are paid.

Forced labor is also addressed by two conventions of the International Labor Organization (ILO), a constituent organization of the UN. ILO Convention 29 (1930), which was an attempt to tackle the issue of forced labor in European colonies in Africa and Asia, restricts forced labor duties to able-bodied males between eighteen and forty-five, and to those whose absence "will not affect family life in the community." Another ILO Convention (105) forbids parties from using forced labor as a punishment for expressing political views or as a means to economic development.

The applicability of the ILO Conventions in wartime is limited by the exemption they make for emergencies (including war). But they have nevertheless proved effective in drawing attention to abuses in countries where there are undeclared internal conflicts, such as Burma (which has ratified ILO Convention 29, but not Convention 105). Signatories to ILO Conventions are obliged to submit reports, which are considered by meetings of experts at the International Labor Conference. Outside bodies cannot make official representations at these meetings, but information from human rights reports may be put on the record and governments involved can be asked to respond. Some Western countries have laws banning the import of products manufactured using a conscript labor force. This constraint on trade may be the most effective sanction against many forms of forced labor.

Other international agreements that touch on the issue of forced labor include the UN Convention on the Rights of the Child and the UN Declaration of Human Rights. The UN International Covenant on Civil and Political Rights reiterates the ban on the use of forced labor as a punishment for holding political views, as a means of economic development, or as a form of discrimination against a social group.

(See **compelling military service; sexual violence: enslavement and forced prostitution.**)

Free Fire Zones

By Lewis M. Simons

In the mid-1960s, when I was covering the war in Vietnam for the Associated Press, U.S. commanders were issued wallet-size cards bearing the warning to "use your firepower with care and discrimination, particularly in populated areas." Often, these cards ended up in a pocket of a pair of tropical fatigues, where they remained, ignored, for the duration of the bearer's tour of duty.

F

The U.S. Eleventh Armored Cavalry Regiment spray the area in an exercise they call "Mad Minute." Cambodia, 1970.

The intention of the Department of Defense in issuing the cards was to help prevent jittery U.S. soldiers from mistakenly, or intentionally, declaring a suspect village a "free fire zone," then destroying it and its residents. All too often, postmortem investigations revealed that such zones had been peaceful and should not have been assaulted. This type of incident with its attendant hostile publicity—My Lai was perhaps the most infamous, if not necessarily the most egregious—was a recurring nightmare of the military high command and a succession of U.S. administrations.

But the cards only served to accent official naiveté. In reality, U.S. troops in Vietnam seldom knew with any certainty which villages were friendly, siding with the Americans and their Saigon-based allies, and which supported the Hanoi-backed Viet Cong Communist guerrillas.

The practice of establishing free fire zones was instituted because many villages in what was then South Vietnam willingly provided safe haven to Viet Cong fighters. Some, by contrast, were forcibly occupied by marauding bands of guerrillas, who used the villages for cover. Many more were devoted-

151

ly anti-Communist. Yet, the American forces often had fundamental difficulty in distinguishing among any of these villagers. The fact that the guerrillas commonly dressed in black cotton pajama-style outfits, like those worn by most Vietnamese peasants, served only to heighten the confusion.

But despite the GIs' confusion, international law enjoins armies to avoid targeting any but military objectives and assures protection to civilians, in almost any circumstance. Free fire zones as defined by Department of Defense doctrine and the rules of engagement are a severe violation of the laws of war for two reasons. First, they violate the rule against direct attack of civilians by presuming that after civilians are warned to vacate a zone, then anyone still present may lawfully be attacked. The rule prohibiting direct attacks on civilians provides no basis for a party to a conflict to shift the burden by declaring a whole zone to be "civilian free." And second, they violate the rule against **indiscriminate attack** by presuming without justification in the law that warning civilians to leave eliminates the legal requirements to discriminate in targeting its weapons.

Where the protection of the Geneva Conventions does not provide a mantle to civilians is when they take "a direct part in hostilities." There were, of course, occasions when Vietnamese civilians directly attacked U.S. troops, but those which drew the attention of news reporters were overwhelmingly those in which a village was labeled a free fire zone and innocent lives were taken in outbursts of indiscriminate fire and brutality.

Faced with this negative coverage and with severe difficulty in enforcing international laws limiting the imposition of free fire zones, as well as other elements of the rules of engagement, the Pentagon over time added more directives to its pocket cards: a village could not be bombed without warning even if American troops had received fire from within it; a village known to be Communist could be attacked only if its inhabitants were warned in advance; only once civilians had been removed could a village be declared a free fire zone and shelled at will.

According to an article by Maj. Mark S. Martens of the U.S. Army's Judge Advocate-General's Corps and a distinguished graduate of the U.S. Military Academy, Oxford University, and Harvard Law School, all these rules were "radically ineffective." Often they were simply ignored. In some cases, illiterate peasants couldn't understand leaflets dropped to warn them that their villages would soon become a free fire zone. In other cases, hurried, forcible evacuations left large numbers of defenseless civilians behind, to be killed by bombing, shelling, small arms assaults, or burning. "The only good village," went one bit of cynical GI wisdom, "is a burned village."

Ineffective efforts to rein in the GIs' propensity to create free fire zones in Vietnam resulted in a sense among many Vietnamese as well as Americans that U.S. forces were undisciplined. More important, perhaps, the widely touted grand plan to capture the "hearts and minds" of the Vietnamese was immeasurably diminished by the perception—let alone the outbreaks of reality—that Americans did not value Vietnamese lives.

Toward the end of the 1960s, the term *free fire zone* itself was dropped from the U.S. military lexicon in no small part because that doctrine embraced actions that the United States today would regard as illegal. Subsequent U.S. military manuals and rules of engagement, whether for ground, air, or naval forces, tend to track quite closely with the central principle of international humanitarian law on **civilian immunity** and the prohibition on the targeting of civilians.

(See **civilians, illegal targeting of**; **immunity**.)

Genocide

By Diane F. Orentlicher

Invoked with a frequency, familiarity, and reverence rarely associated with instruments of law, the 1948 Convention on the Prevention and Punishment of the Crime of Genocide has come to embody the conscience of humanity.

Its moral force is surely ironic. For the record of the Genocide Convention since its adoption has been notable above all for States' nearly wholesale failure to enforce its terms.

Although the treaty envisages (but does not require) the creation of an international court to punish genocide, forty-five years passed before the first international criminal tribunal was established. Its jurisdiction was limited to crimes, including genocide, committed in the former Yugoslavia since 1991. A similar, more circumscribed, tribunal was created for Rwanda one year later. It was not until September 2, 1998—a half-century after the United Nations General Assembly adopted the Genocide Convention—that the first verdict interpreting the convention was rendered by an international tribunal following a trial (one other defendant had previously pleaded guilty to genocide). On that day the Rwanda Tribunal found Jean-Paul Akayesu guilty on nine counts for his role in the 1994 Rwandan genocide.

Nor did any State bring a case under the Genocide Convention to the World Court until 1993, and this was scarcely a milestone in international enforcement efforts. The case was brought by a State that had endured genocidal crimes—Bosnia-Herzegovina—against a State allegedly responsible—the former Yugoslavia—and not by other States determined to enforce the law of universal conscience on behalf of desperate victims beyond their borders.

To the contrary, when those same crimes were being committed—and gruesomely portrayed in the daily media—legal experts in the U.S. government were asked, in the words of a former State Department lawyer, "to perform legal gymnastics to avoid calling this genocide." And as Rwandan Hutus slaughtered hundreds of thousands of Tutsis, the Clinton administration instructed its spokespeople not to describe what was happening as genocide lest this "inflame public calls for action," according to the New York Times. Instead, the State Department and National Security Council reportedly drafted guidelines instructing government spokespeople to say that "acts of genocide may have occurred" in **Rwanda**.

Five decades of nonenforcement have left the Genocide Convention's core terms shrouded in considerable ambiguity, making it that much easier for recalcitrant politicians to equivocate. (Such equivocations nonetheless fly in the face of the convention, which requires States parties not only to punish genocide—a measure that does demand legal certainty—but also to prevent and repress the crime—action that by its nature must not await the certain knowledge that genocide has occurred.)

The definition of genocide set forth in the Genocide Convention is authoritative and has been incorporated verbatim in the statutes of the Yugoslavia and Rwanda tribunals as well as that of a permanent International Criminal Court (ICC) that will be created after sixty states have ratified the statute adopted in Rome in July 1998. After affirming that genocide is a crime under international law whether committed in time of peace or war,

the 1948 convention defines genocide as "any of the following acts committed with intent to destroy, in whole or in part, a national, ethnical, racial or
religious group, as such: killing members of the group; causing serious bodily
or mental harm to members of the group; deliberately inflicting on the group
conditions of life calculated to bring about its physical destruction in whole
or in part; imposing measures intended to prevent births within the group;
forcibly transferring children of the group to another group."

In the 1948 convention, then, the crime of genocide has both a physical
element—comprising certain enumerated acts, such as killing members of a
racial group—and a mental element—those acts must have been committed
with the intent to destroy, in whole or in part, a national, ethnic, racial, or
religious group "as such." In its verdict in the Akayesu case, the Rwanda
Tribunal found that the systematic rape of Tutsi women in Taba Province constituted the genocidal act of "causing serious bodily or mental harm to
members of the [targeted] group."

In addition to the crime of genocide itself, the 1948 convention provides that the following acts shall be punishable: conspiracy to commit

*Genocide on trial. Left-right: The genocide trial of a Hutu, Jean-Paul Akayesu, is
delayed in 1996; judges file in at the Hague International Tribunal for the Former
Yugoslavia in 1995; the scene at Nuremberg; war crimes trial defendants Hermann
Goring and Rudolf Hess in the dock at Nuremberg.*

genocide, direct and public incitement to commit genocide, attempt to commit genocide, and complicity in genocide.

What was left out of the convention is as important as what was included. Although earlier drafts of the convention listed political groups among
those covered by the intent requirement, this category was omitted during
final drafting stages. Too many governments, it seemed, would be vulnerable
to the charge of genocide if deliberate destruction of political groups fell
within the crime's compass.

Also excluded was the concept of cultural genocide—destroying a group
through forcible assimilation into the dominant culture. The drafting history
makes clear that the 1948 convention was meant to cover physical destruction of a people; the sole echo of efforts to include the notion of cultural
extermination is the convention's reference to forcibly transferring children
of a targeted group to another group.

In this and other respects the conventional definition of genocide is
narrower than the conception of Polish scholar Raphael Lemkin, who first
proposed at an international conference in 1933 that a treaty be created to
make attacks on national, religious, and ethnic groups an international
crime. Lemkin, who served in the U.S. War Department, fashioned the term
genocide from the Greek word *genos*, meaning race or tribe, and the Latin
term for killing, *cide*. (In his 1944 book, *Axis Rule in Occupied Europe*,
Lemkin noted that the same idea could also come from the term "*ethnocide*,

consisting of the Greek word 'ethnos'—nation—and the Latin word 'cide.' ")

Although Lemkin's conception included the physical extermination of targeted groups, this was, in his view, only the most extreme technique of genocide:

"By 'genocide' we mean the destruction of an ethnic group . . . . Generally speaking, genocide does not necessarily mean the immediate destruction of a nation, except when accomplished by mass killings of all members of a nation. It is intended rather to signify a coordinated plan of different actions aiming at the destruction of essential foundations of the life of national groups, with the aim of annihilating the groups themselves. The objectives of such a plan would be disintegration of the political and social institutions, of culture, language, national feelings, religion, and the economic existence of national groups, and the destruction of the personal security, liberty, health, dignity, and even the lives of the individuals belonging to such groups . . . .

"Genocide has two phases: one, destruction of the national pattern of the oppressed group; the other, the imposition of the national pattern

G

of the oppressor. This imposition, in turn, may be made upon the oppressed population which is allowed to remain, or upon the territory alone, after removal of the population and colonization of the area by the oppressor's own nationals."

Four years would pass before Lemkin's crime was recognized in an international treaty, but the legal foundation was laid during the 1945 Nuremberg and other postwar prosecutions. Although the Nuremberg Charter did not use the term *genocide*, its definition of **crimes against humanity** overlapped significantly with Lemkin's conception of *genocide*. The term *genocide* was used in the indictment against major war criminals tried at Nuremberg, who were accused of having "conducted deliberate and systematic genocide, viz., the extermination of racial and national groups, against the civilian populations of certain occupied territories in order to destroy particular races and classes of people and national, racial or religious groups." Nuremberg prosecutors also invoked the term in their closing arguments, and it also appeared in the judgments of several U.S. military tribunals operating in Nuremberg.

Shortly after the trial of major war criminals at Nuremberg, the UN General Assembly adopted a resolution affirming that genocide is a "crime under international law." In its preamble, the 1946 resolution termed genocide "a denial of the right of existence of entire human groups, as homicide is the denial of the right to live of individual human beings."

The comparatively narrow terms of the 1948 convention—in particular, its exclusion of political groups and its restrictive intent requirement—have enabled political leaders to raise doubts about whether probable genocides satisfy the convention's stringent criteria. Did the authors of the Anfal campaigns of 1988, in which at least fifty thousand Iraqi Kurds are estimated to have been massacred, intend to kill Kurds "as such" or, in the words of one leading scholar, was their aim to eliminate "the Kurdish movement as a political problem?" Did Serb perpetrators of **ethnic cleansing** in Bosnia intend to destroy Muslims and Croats "as such," or did they "merely" seek to establish homogeneous Serb control over coveted territory?

As these questions suggest, a key source of ambiguity is the meaning of the 1948 convention's intent requirement. Although the drafting history is somewhat ambiguous, I believe that it is a mistake to treat the convention's use of the term *intent* as though it were synonymous with *motive*. That Serb perpetrators of ethnic cleansing may have slaughtered Muslims so that they could obtain control over territory does not negate their intent to destroy Muslims "as such" in order to achieve their ultimate goal.

The Genocide Convention imposes a general duty on States parties "to prevent and to punish" genocide. Those charged with genocide are to be tried either in the State where the crime occurred or "by such international penal tribunal as may have jurisdiction with respect to those Contracting Parties which shall have accepted its jurisdiction." Although the convention does not mention a third possibility—prosecution in a third State—it is now well established that any State can assert jurisdiction over crimes of genocide, wherever the crimes occurred and whatever the nationality of the perpetrators and victims.

In addition to individual criminal responsibility for genocide, the convention also establishes State responsibility—that is, international legal responsibility of the State itself for breaching its obligations under the convention. Parties to the convention can bring a case before the International Court of Justice alleging that another State party is responsible for genocide. As noted above, the first case of this sort was brought against Yugoslavia by Bosnia-Herzegovina in 1993 and is still pending.

Article 8 of the convention contemplates measures not only to punish genocide, but also to stop it in its tracks: "Any Contracting Party may call upon the competent organs of the United Nations to take such action under the Charter of the United Nations as they consider appropriate for the prevention and suppression of acts of genocide or any of the other acts enumerated in article 3." States that are parties to the convention could, for example, seek Security Council authorization to use military force to stop genocide being committed in another country.

Finally, although treaties themselves are binding only on States that are parties to the treaties, in a 1951 advisory opinion the International Court of Justice observed that the principles underlying the Genocide Convention are part of customary international law, which binds all states.

Genocide in History
Although Lemkin implied that Nazi crimes were fundamentally different from any previously committed, Hitler's "Final Solution" was not the first campaign of extermination that would meet Lemkin's definition of genocide. The systematic extermination of Armenians by the Young Turks beginning in April 1915 was the first genocide in this century. Emboldened by the world's acquiescence in the slaughter of Armenians—over 1 million are estimated to have been put to death—Hitler is famously reported to have reassured doubters in his ranks by asking, "Who after all is today speaking of the Armenians?"

Among more recent episodes of wholesale slaughter, at least some scholars have concluded that the Turkish massacre of Kurds in the district of Dersim in 1937–1938, the massacre of Hutus by Tutsi perpetrators in Burundi in 1972, the Khmer Rouge campaign of extermination in the mid-1970s, and the 1988 Anfal campaign against Iraqi Kurds meet the legal definition of genocide.

Among these cases, perhaps none better illustrates the complexities of the 1948 convention's definition of genocide than the case of **Cambodia**. In view of the magnitude of the carnage there—1.5 million out of Cambodia's 7 million citizens are believed to have died as a result of Khmer Rouge policies—there has been a keen desire to affix the term *genocide* to their crimes. Since, however, both the perpetrators and the majority of victims were Khmer, reaching this conclusion has required agile legal reasoning. Some scholars have invoked the concept of *auto-genocide*, arguing that it is possible to satisfy the 1948 convention's definition even when the perpetrators sought to kill a substantial portion of their own ethnic/national group. Others, more conservatively, have conceded that the vast majority of victims were killed for reasons that may be broadly termed political, but note that certain minority groups, such as the Muslim Cham and Khmer Buddhists, were specially targeted for destruction and argue that at least the crimes against these groups were genocidal.

While some campaigns of extermination more clearly qualify as genocide than others—the Holocaust and the 1994 Rwandan genocide are instances— the truth is that plausible arguments can be raised with respect to most cases of possible genocide. In the absence of judicial resolution or political resolve, virtually any case of genocide can be questioned. The first defendant tried before the Rwanda Tribunal argued, for example, that the massacres in Rwanda were politically motivated, a gruesome manner of waging civil war. In response the tribunal concluded that, "alongside the conflict . . . genocide was committed in Rwanda in 1994 against the Tutsi as a group." That the execution of this genocide "was probably facilitated by the conflict" did not negate the fact that genocide occurred.

The dearth of precedents enforcing the convention—a grim testament to the international community's failure of will—has for decades left experts able to do little more than argue knowledgeably about whether well-known candidates for the label "genocide" meet the legal definition. The ambiguities built into the Genocide Convention can finally be resolved only when States are willing to acknowledge forthrightly that genocide has occurred and to enforce the law of conscience.

G

Gray Areas in International Humanitarian Law

By Ewen Allison and Robert K. Goldman

A conflict between government forces and rebels can be governed by three sets of rules, and the problem for observers is to determine which applies. Gray areas in humanitarian law revolve around whether a given situation is an armed conflict, and if it is, whether it is internal or international.

One concern is how to classify an internal situation falling in the gray zone between peace and war. The line separating particularly violent internal tensions and disturbances from low-level armed conflict may sometimes be blurred and not easily determined. Such situations typically involve riots, isolated and sporadic acts of violence resulting in mass arrests, the use of police, and, sometimes, the armed forces to restore order. The foregoing do not amount to what humanitarian law would call an armed conflict. Instead, they are governed by domestic and human rights law. A gray-zone conflict would actually be internal armed conflict if, at a minimum, it was protracted and involved armed clashes between government forces and relatively organized armed groups. Determining what counts as protracted and well organized requires a case-specific analysis of the facts.

Another form of internal conflict involves determining if, because of the disintegration of the State, there is any government entity with armed forces capable of quelling civil strife between armed groups from different clans, religions, tribal, or ethnic groups. In a truly anarchic situation with minimal levels of organization, the applicable internal law is Common Article 3, which also applies to government clashes with armed insurgent groups. If, however, there is a conflict between a government and dissident armed forces, and the dissident group is organized under responsible command and exercises territorial control, then Common Article 3 is supplemented by Protocol II. To apply Protocol II, at least one of the parties to the conflict must be a government, defined as a generally recognized regime that has a right and duty to exert authority over a population and provide for its needs.

Another gray area involves whether a conflict is internal or international. History has shown that this internal/international distinction is often artificial. For example, troops from a foreign country may fight alongside rebels or government troops involved in internal hostilities. Where such foreign intervention occurs, it may be unclear whether the hostilites are governed by the internal or international armed conflict rules. Such a conflict is called an "internationalized internal conflict." The recent hostilities in Bosnia and Angola are examples of such mixed armed conflicts.

This question is less significant now, thanks to a decision by the International Criminal Tribunal for the former Yugoslavia. In the Dusko Tadic case, the Appeals Chamber found that leading principles of international humanitarian law apply to both sorts of conflicts. Yet these specific principles and rules for *international* armed confict are not transposed word-for-word into the laws of *internal* armed conflict. It is, therefore, unclear whether certain provisions apply to both. Generally, the more basic a principle is, the more likely it is to apply across the board.

(See **international vs. internal armed conflict**.)

Guerrillas

By Jon Lee Anderson

In 1982, I was standing in a village in Guatemala's central highlands when a unit of armed government troops appeared, pulling two frightened-looking Indian men in civilian clothes held by rope nooses around their necks.

I asked one of them who the men were. "They are subversives," he replied. I asked how he knew that, and the soldier said that the men had been carrying a hunting rifle, and had tried to run away when they were spotted. He drew his fingers across the front of his throat in a slashing motion. The other soldiers watching our exchange broke out laughing, while the condemned men, seemingly lost in thought, looked fixedly at the ground.

G

Clearly, no mercy was going to be shown to these men. Whether they were guerrillas or not, however, their treatment was a clear violation of the international laws of war. The Guatemalan Army considered Indians to be subversives, and subversives to be guerrillas; it drew no distinction between civilians and **combatants**. Under international humanitarian law (IHL), guerrillas are included in the category of irregular forces—defined more specifically as fighters who use unconventional methods of warfare, such as sabotage, ambushes, and sniping. There are, however, protections for captured guerrilla fighters even in an internal conflict.

Guerrilla warfare *per se* is not illegal under IHL, but guerrillas must follow the same laws that apply to all regular armed forces.

Like all fighters, guerrillas have different rights depending upon whether the armed conflict is international or internal. Under the Geneva Conventions of 1949, a person fighting in irregular forces, often the kind of fighter we today would regard as a guerrilla, is considered a lawful combatant in an international armed conflict provided that he fights under certain specified conditions. The importance of being a lawful combatant is twofold. First, if captured by opposing international forces (not by his government), he may not be prosecuted or punished for taking part in combat. Second, he must be treated as a prisoner of war under applicable international rules.

In order to be granted the privilege of being a lawful combatant, the fighter must, however, observe four rules:

1. Be commanded by a person responsible for his subordinates; this requirement is intended to ensure that irregular forces have a structure of command and discipline capable of following the laws of war.

2. Wear a distinctive sign or article of clothing visible at a distance in order to indicate that he is a combatant and a potential target who may lawfully be attacked by opposing forces; this provision is for the protection of noncombatant civilians.

3. Carry his weapon openly to indicate his combatant status and to distinguish fighters from the civilian population.

4. Observe the laws of war.

Additional Protocol I to the Geneva Conventions attempted to take into account the realities of guerrilla warfare, in particular the routine practice of concealment among the general population. In a controversial rule, the protocol requires only that a guerrilla combatant in an international armed conflict carry his arms openly just before an attack. The United States has, for a variety of reasons, not ratified the protocol. In this particular instance, the United States believes it represents a step backward in the protection of civilians since it increases the legal ability of guerrilla fighters to expose civilians to greater risk.

Guerrillas in internal armed conflicts are covered by Article 3 common to the four Geneva Conventions of 1949, and more controversially, by Additional Protocol II of 1977, which has not received wide acceptance. To qualify as combatants under Common Article 3, guerrillas must meet the requirements under customary law, chiefly to conduct themselves with the discipline necessary to show that they adhere to the laws of war. Thus, insurgents must give humane treatment to captured civilians and government soldiers. Insurgents, too, can punish their detainees only after giving them fair trials.

One More River: Contras in the Chontales Department of Nicaragua, 1987.

Even if they observe all the rules, guerrillas, in internal conflicts, benefit only from a very limited combatant's privilege. They are fully liable, if captured by their government, to be tried for rebellion, sedition, and for acts, undertaken as guerrillas, such as murder or destruction of property. If a country's domestic law permits, they may be executed provided they are tried and sentenced "by a regularly constituted court, affording all the judicial guarantees which are recognized as indispensable by civilized peoples."

In 1985, I was in Nicaragua traveling with a unit of the CIA-backed Contra guerrillas, who were fighting a campaign against the leftist Sandanista government. "Tigrillo," the commander, had a girlfriend called Marta. One day, I talked to Marta on her own, and she revealed tearfully that she had only joined the Contras after being abducted by Tigrillo's band, along with several civilian men from her village. Accused of being government sympathizers, the men had been hacked to death in front of her; Marta had been spared because Tigrillo found her attractive.

In this case, the Contra guerrillas had violated IHL. Not only had they kidnapped and murdered civilians, they also had kept Marta with them as an unwilling hostage.

Two years later, in the countryside outside the eastern Sri Lankan town of Batticaloa, I visited a base of the Tamil Tigers, a guerrilla group fighting against the predominately ethnic Sinhalese government for an independent Tamil state. During an interview, the Tiger commander, Kumarrappa, ordered his troops to produce a captured "spy." Soon, a tiny, terrified woman with bedraggled hair was produced. Her name was Athuma. Kumarrappa explained that she was to be blown up alive after being tied to a lamppost with explosive wire. Hearing this, Athuma began begging for her life. Kumarrappa listened briefly, smiling, then silenced her by declaring that she would be killed anyway. He waved his hand, and Athuma was led away.

Here, as in Nicaragua, the Sri Lankan guerrillas were in flagrant violation of the laws of war. The civilian woman, Athuma, was to be executed after having been terrorized and mistreated, without benefit of a fair trial. But the Tigers' brutality was matched by the Sri Lankan Army, which roamed the area, torturing and shooting Tamil civilians at will. Tamil suspects who ended up in the local detention camp were often executed and their bodies burned to eliminate evidence. Thus, terror breeds terror.

As these stories illustrate, visits by an outsider to areas where guerrilla wars and counterinsurgency campaigns are being waged can become bewildering, traumatic experiences. In each place mentioned, I was present as a nonpartisan journalist, but found myself unexpectedly faced with situations where I felt a moral obligation to try to save lives. I had no primer like this one, where the laws are clearly outlined, to help me formulate my arguments more convincingly. It is difficult to know whether men who feel themselves to be above the law can be persuaded by legal arguments, but it is certainly worth a try. In guerrilla wars, where the combatants usually impose their own cruel codes of legality, arguments based on international law probably carry more weight than appeals for compassion.

(See **international vs. internal armed conflict; irregulars; paramilitaries; soldiers, rights of.**)

Attitudes toward international humanitarian norms and law by the belligerents in the Gulf War could not have been more distinct. The U.S.-led coalition commander, Gen. Norman Schwarzkopf, frequently consulted with law of war experts, including members of the International Committee of the Red Cross (ICRC), to ensure that specific military operations would not be seen later as violations. In fact, Schwarzkopf's aides requested so much guidance from the ICRC that its representatives eventually stopped providing it, protesting that they were not legal counsel for the coalition. Iraqi President Saddam Hussein, on the other hand, declined to meet with ICRC representatives.

Of course, the Gulf War was a conventional conflict, and U.S.-led coalition forces enjoyed a great advantage of superior firepower. Though they arguably committed some laws of war violations that contributed to needless civilian deaths, allied forces were able to fight a relatively clean campaign and still win. Saddam Hussein's forces, on the other hand, committed many violations including grave breaches of the 1949 Geneva Conventions and the 1977 Additional Protocol I. Similarly, during the civil uprisings inside Iraq that immediately followed the Gulf War, Saddam disregarded humanitarian norms in crushing them.

U.S. and Iraqi leaders were responding to different considerations in their attitude toward international humanitarian law (IHL). U.S. commanders feared that any perceived violations by coalition troops might undermine the strong support for the war being expressed back home. Elsewhere, they feared that such violations might break up the U.S.-led coalition of twenty-seven countries against Iraq, and, in particular, compel Arab States to withdraw from it. U.S. leaders feared as well that any coalition intervention during Iraq's civil uprisings might also split the coalition. Saddam, meanwhile, has never demonstrated much concern for Iraqi public opinion, though, during the Gulf War, he did try to appeal to Pan-Arab sentiments.

On the road from Samarah and Nasariyah, one of the ubiquitous portraits of Saddam Hussein toppled by the bombing of the warehouse behind. Iraq, 1991.

Saddam's targeting of civilian population centers in Israel, in particular, was designed to bring Israel into the Gulf War and then, hopefully, split Arab States from the U.S.-led alliance.

Each side in the Gulf War has been accused of violations of IHL; in some cases, the violation is legally clear-cut, while in others experts still debate.

Allied forces destroyed many electrical power stations in Iraq. The attacks adversely affected Iraq's civilian population, as they rendered sewage plants in many civilian areas inoperable and left many hospitals without power. This led some observers like Human Rights Watch (HRW), a private monitoring organization based in New York, to ask whether the attacks violated IHL and its provisions against attacks on civilian objects. In particular, was the subsequent civilian toll excessive in relation to the concrete and direct military advantage anticipated from the attack? Other observers, however, including the ICRC, saw the same attacks differently. While concerned about the civilian suffering they created, the ICRC nonetheless recognized that electrical power stations can be, and traditionally have been, legitimate military targets.

Coalition forces also launched attacks that killed many civilians, raising questions about **indiscriminate attacks** involving needless civilian casualties. On February 14, for example, a British plane fired a laser-guided missile at a bridge in the Al-Fallujah neighborhood west of Baghdad. It missed and hit a residential area, killing up to 130 civilians. Some observers, including former U.S. Attorney General Ramsey Clark, claim that all such coalition attacks that resulted in Iraqi civilian casualties constitute war crimes. But without evidence that the neighborhood was intentionally, or negligently, targeted or that it was part of a broader pattern of indiscriminate attacks, this incident does not stand either as a grave breach or as a serious violation of the Geneva Conventions.

Another tragedy had occurred the day before, when a U.S. cruise missile penetrated the Ameriyaa air-raid shelter in Baghdad, killing up to three hundred civilians, including at least ninety-one children. CNN broadcast the carnage. U.S. Brig. Gen. Richard Neal in Riyadh later admitted that allied forces had intentionally targeted the shelter. He also said that coalition commanders knew that the shelter had been previously used by civilians in the mid-1980s during the Iran-Iraq War, but that it had since been converted to "a hardened shelter used for [military] command and control." HRW refers to Neal's statements to argue that the attack on the shelter was a laws of war violation. Before they fired at it, allied forces, according to HRW, were obligated, to first warn Iraq that they now considered the former civilian shelter a legitimate military target. HRW added that, in its view, the evidence of the shelter's alleged conversion to a military purpose was insufficient to overcome the presumption that it was still being used by civilians. Other observers, however, including lawyers for coalition forces, disagree. They point out that the shelter had been used solely for civilian purposes several years previously in the Iran-Iraq War, so allied commanders were not obligated to warn Iraq that they now considered the shelter to be a legitimate military target in the Gulf War. Coalition partners, however, have yet to make their evidence public about the shelter's alleged conversion to military use.

U.S.-led forces also killed many civilians when coalition planes, including B-52 bombers, launched heavy strikes in and around the port of Basra. Coalition forces sought to destroy several specific military targets there. Some critics claim coalition forces had resorted to the kind of **carpet bombing** often seen in World War II, constituting indiscriminate attack, by treating a whole area containing several targets as a single target, in violation of Article 51 of Additional Protocol I. No one disputes that the attacks killed many civilians (though no reliable figures are known) living in residential areas around the port. The question is whether such attacks violated IHL. A U.S. Army spokesman in Riyadh later described Basra as a "military town," which was quartering, among other forces, a strong contingent of elite Republican Guard troops. Lawyers for coalition forces blame Iraq for the subsequent civilian toll. They point out that Iraq was legally obligated to separate military forces from civilians and not to use the latter as a **shield**, and that the presence of civilians around military targets does not render such targets immune from attack. Nonetheless, coalition forces, critics argue, could have used more precise arms, such as cruise missiles or laser-guided weaponry, that might have accomplished the same objective with less

An Iraqi soldier burnt to death as he drove his truck near the Euphrates River near An Nasiriya. Iraq, 1991.

collateral damage to civilians. U.S. military lawyers have noted in response, however, that the obligation to use more precise weapons systems is qualified by considerations of **military necessity**, including availability and need for their deployment in missions against other **military objectives**. Both HRW and the ICRC concluded the resort to saturation strikes claimed needless civilian lives and damage, but the controversy continues.

Another controversial incident involving coalition forces occurred on the last day of the ground campaign, as an entire column of Iraqi troops was retreating from Kuwait. These troops had not surrendered, making them legitimate military targets. Yet, they put up only minimal resistance, while coalition aircraft dropped Rockeye fragmentation bombs and other antipersonnel arms, killing thousands. The ICRC concluded that the attacks "cause[d] unnecessary suffering and superfluous injury," and that they were tantamount to "a denial of quarter." Many other observers, however, counter that the concept of denial of quarter does not apply to forces that have not surrendered.

The ICRC also singled out some U.S.-led coalition partners for not devoting enough resources to properly register all their Iraqi prisoners with the ICRC or any other "central tracing agency." Saudi Arabia, for one, registered none of its prisoners.

Other forces associated with the U.S.-led coalition as well violated humanitarian norms, though it remains unclear whether the violations took place within the context of an internal or international conflict, and which international norms or laws, therefore, would apply. Following the Gulf War, Kuwaiti authorities committed many human rights violations upon their repatriation. Mobs acting with the blessing of authorities harassed, detained, tortured, and sometimes summarily executed thousands, including Palestinians and others suspected of having supported the Iraqi occupation.

Nevertheless, Iraq is responsible for far more violations of humanitarian norms and laws, as its forces entirely disregarded them throughout the Gulf War and its aftermath. On many occasions, Iraq intentionally targeted civilians, which is a grave breach of the Geneva Conventions. During its occupation of Kuwait, Iraqi troops also harassed, tortured, and sometimes summarily executed thousands of Kuwaitis. Other Iraqi abuses also stand as clear rules-of-war violations. Before the Gulf War, Iraq used civilians, typically foreign nationals, as human shields to seek to protect military targets in both Kuwait and Iraq. In Kuwait, this practice was clearly a war crime under Article 51 of Additional Protocol I, because a state of war and occupation clearly existed with respect to Kuwait. Using foreign nationals as human shields within Iraq before the opening of hostilities between Iraq and the coalition forces is a less clear-cut case. In an unmistakable violation, Iraq, during the war, failed to register coalition prisoners of war with the ICRC. Iraq as well humiliated and tortured some coalition prisoners. (Though one U.S. soldier who was a prisoner of war later admitted that he had abused himself to avoid being shown on Iraqi television.)

Iraqi forces also fired Scud missiles that hit civilian population centers in Saudi Arabia and Israel, an act which some claim was the war crime of directly targeting civilians or indiscriminately attacking population centers. Nonetheless, for these attacks to constitute war crimes, it must first be proven either that Iraq intentionally targeted the civilian centers in order to attack civilians directly or else failed to take measures to insure that military objectives were targeted. Though some of the thirty-seven missiles directed into Saudi Arabia appear to have been aimed at military targets, others appear to have been aimed at cities like Riyadh, the Saudi capital. Most of the thirty-nine Scud missiles fired into Israel and the occupied West Bank seem to have been aimed at cities like Tel Aviv, the Israeli capital. Three questions remain open. Could the missiles Iraq fired at population centers reasonably be shown to have been aimed at legitimate military targets in those cities within the limits of Iraqi technological capabilities? Did anticipated specific and concrete military benefit of such attacks for Iraq outweigh civilian costs (excluding from the calculation the illegal military advantage gained from terror attacks on civilians themselves)? On the other hand, did coalition authorities violate their IHL duties by commingling civilians with military targets in Saudi Arabia? It would appear in fact as difficult to prove illegality in the Scud attacks on Saudi Arabia as it would the coalition attacks on Basra and Baghdad.

But the Scud attacks on Israel would appear to be the most difficult for Iraq to justify, given that coalition forces were not present in Israel, nor was Israel a party to the conflict. Absent some substantial evidence showing that Israel was about to enter the war against Iraq, thus justifying a preemptive military strike against legitimate military targets, the Scud attacks against Israel would appear to have been terror attacks directed against civilians. It is widely acknowledged that Iraq's aim was to draw Israel into the conflict by attacks on its civilian population; although IHL is silent with respect to how a war starts or spreads, Iraq's method appears in this case illegal.

Iraq also committed several acts of **environmental warfare** as part of its military strategy. The ecological impact of the attacks, which provided Iraq with perhaps a slight and only fleeting military advantage, will no doubt be felt for years. During the Gulf War, Iraq released millions of liters of crude oil into the Persian Gulf in an attempt to undermine seawater desalination plants that were being used by coalition forces. Toward the end of the war, Iraq set fire to as many as 950 oil wells, which discharged tons of toxic gases into the atmosphere. To be considered a violation of IHL, such acts must

A Pillar of Fire: Kuwaiti oil fields burning after the Iraqi retreat in 1991.

cause the environment widespread, long-term, and severe damage. Experts still disagree whether the above acts meet this threshold.

Iraqi forces committed human rights violations against many of its own citizens, principally in the Shia- and Kurdish-led insurgencies immediately after the end of the coalition-led campaign, which is at least inconsistent with international humanitarian norms. Here U.S. President George Bush also played a key role. On March 1, Bush called upon Iraqis "to put [Saddam] aside" and bring Iraq "back into the family of peace-loving nations." The same day, Shias in southern Iraq began calling for insurrection, while Kurds in northern Iraq rebelled two weeks later; coalition forces stood by as Iraqi troops, backed by tanks and helicopter gunships, decimated the insurgents through scorched-earth campaigns. In many of these attacks, Iraqi forces appear to have made no attempt to distinguish between civilian and military targets. On March 20, in As-Samawah in southern Iraq, Iraqi units advanced behind a human shield of captured Shia women, as they shot Shia men on sight. On March 28, in Kirkuk in northern Iraq, Iraqi helicopter gunships and multiple-rocket launchers dropped a blanket of fire on fleeing Kurdish guerrillas and civilians, again without appearing to distinguish between them. Iraqi Army Special Forces, which led the assault, also summarily executed many Kurdish combatants (as well as *Newsweek* freelance photographer Gad Gross) after capture.

Iraq further violated humanitarian norms and human rights in its treatment of foreign detainees at the Abu Ghraib prison west of Baghdad, where captured journalists were also held. Though captured journalists were treated as prisoners of war, in accordance with Article 4 of the Third Geneva Convention, Iraq generally failed to acknowledge holding them until their release, in violation of the rules of war. At least one journalist, CBS News correspondent Bob Simon, was physically tortured.

Iraq as well violated the human rights of many Iraqi detainees in Abu Ghraib prison. I was detained there along with photojournalist Alain Buu for two weeks beginning about one month after the end of the Gulf War. Though we were not physically harmed, we saw and heard many Iraqis being tortured by prison authorities: hitting a man on the buttocks with a flat board intermittently all night long, while making him crow like a rooster; hosing down a stripped prisoner outside on a cold day, and then stunning him repeatedly with an electroshock weapon; and beating a sixteen-year-old boy, accused of sedition, with rubber hoses. Sometimes we just heard, coming from another cellblock in the prison, the long screams of men in extreme, sustained pain. Some of the violence was perpetrated capriciously by guards; other acts were executed under orders from higher authorities to extract information.

The Gulf War and its aftermath demonstrate the strengths and gaps of international humanitarian norms and law. Though the U.S.-led coalition in some cases at least encroached upon the rules of war, the allies in most cases did make a conscious effort to adhere to them. Saddam Hussein chose to ignore them nearly altogether. The international community has yet to make any party accountable, in any form, for any Gulf War–related violation. (See **civilians, illegal targeting of**.)

Health Care System

By Eric Stover

War directs scarce resources away from health and other human services, and often destroys the infrastructure of these services; it also facilitates the spread of disease. Since the early 1970s, another major threat has emerged for health care systems. Military attacks on medical personnel and medical facilities, though prohibited under international humanitarian law, have reached alarming proportions throughout the world.

One recent example occurred in Kosovo during the Yugoslav government's offensive against ethnic Albanian rebels in the summer and fall of 1998, when troops destroyed tens of thousands of buildings, including health clinics, and displaced hundreds of thousands of civilians who sought shelter in the surrounding mountains and forests. Aid officials estimated that about twenty doctors were arrested by Serbian special police or fled the country and that hundreds of civilians may have died because of the collapse of the health care system. After the assuault, a climate of fear descended on the few health care workers who remained in the war zone. Several doctors said that, in spite of their ethical obligations to treat all those in need, they were afraid to provide medical care because it could serve as a pretext for government police to arrest them.

Attacks on medical facilities are prohibited under the Geneva Conventions of 1949 and the 1977 Additional Protocols. These instruments provide that warring factions have an obligation to protect civilians, the **sick and wounded**, combatants who are *hors de combat*, and medical and religious personnel. All sides in a conflict must protect certain objects from damage, including **hospitals** and other medical facilities, ambulances, and equipment bearing the **Red Cross** or **Red Crescent** symbol that have removed wounded from the field; transport and facilities used by humanitarian and relief agencies; and objects indispensable to the survival of the civilian population, such as crops, livestock, and drinking **water installations**.

But the reality is very different. In contemporary conflict, **medical personnel** and patients are assaulted, abducted, tortured, or murdered. Ambulances can become the target of mortar and sniper fire. **Medical transports** carrying vital medical supplies and food may be shelled or prevented from reaching towns and cities under **siege**. All of these acts may be considered grave breaches of the Geneva Conventions and Additional Protocol I or crimes against humanity. As **refugees** flee to safety, they congregate in makeshift camps where the combination of fatigue, malnutrition, unsanitary conditions, and overcrowding often sends diseases like cholera and measles on a killing spree.

During the 1994 genocide in Rwanda, military and militias known as *Interahamwe* (those who attack together) entered dozens of hospitals and clinics, murdering and maiming patients and staff. One of the most horrific incidents took place in the university town of Butare, where machete-wielding militiamen slaughtered twenty-one children who had been evacuated to a Red Cross orphanage.

During the 1980s, Mozambique National Resistance (RENAMO) guerrillas in Mozambique ransacked over one thousand primary health centers, representing 48 percent of the national total, leaving 2 million people without access to health care.

In Bosnia-Herzegovina, where armed conflict was marked by almost every conceivable violation of medical neutrality, Sarajevo's main medical center, the Kosevo Hospital, was struck by at least 172 mortar shells in 1992 and early 1993. The most flagrant attack on the hospital complex took place in May 1992, when Bosnian Serb forces, at close range, repeatedly shelled the Children's Clinic and the adjoining Obstetrical and Gynecological Hospital, forcing staff to evacuate seventeen newborns (many removed from their incubators and without supplemental oxygen) and thirty-three older children. Nine of the babies later died for want of heat and oxygen.

Even without coming under direct attack, health care systems have to cope with an enormous burden in wartime. Hospitals in or near war zones are usually understaffed and have few, if any, orthopedic surgeons, let alone general surgeons with extensive experience treating blast-related injuries. Patients with mine blast injuries often require twice as much blood as patients wounded by other munitions. Many—if not most—mine amputees will need to be fitted with some kind of prosthetic, which will need to be replaced every three to five years. And after the fighting stops, the pressures continue. Antipersonnel **mines** place a tremendous burden on the health care systems in postwar countries. Victims of mine blasts are more likely to require amputation and remain in the hospital longer that those wounded by other munitions. Unexploded ordinance and small antipersonnel mines strewn along footpaths, rice paddies, riverbeds, and around villages continue to maim and kill the children and grandchildren of the soldiers who laid them.

The other threat to health care systems is disease. Throughout history, conquering armies have not only killed and maimed their enemies, they have brought with them communicable diseases, such as the bubonic plague, tuberculosis, measles, smallpox, chicken pox, whooping cough, mumps, and influenzas, which, when invading a human population without any previous exposure to them, are likely to kill a high proportion of those who fall sick. In the early 1500s, during the conquest of Mexico, millions of Aztec Indians died of chicken pox introduced by Hernan Cortés and his men. Two centuries later, British troops in the American colonies on at least one occasion during the Indian uprising of 1763, known as Pontiac's Rebellion, deliberately sent blankets infected with smallpox to Shawnee and Delaware Indians. During the Revolutionary War, American troops also accused the British of spreading smallpox by forcing infected people out of cities with the design of spreading the disease among American soldiers.

Hors de Combat

By Kurt Schork

Iraqi Army troops and Kurdish peshmerga fought several days of pitched battles in and around the city of Sulaymaniyah in October of 1991. By the afternoon of the third day Iraqi resistance in Sulaymaniyah had been reduced to a complex of buildings at the southwest edge of the city. Hundreds of Kurdish irregulars gathered for a final push against the Iraqis, which I witnessed.

Left: Kurdish Pehsmerga guerrillas guard disarmed Iraqi prisoners, October 11, 1991, in the north of Iraq. Right: The Kurds slaughtered the prisoners, ignoring the doomed Iraqi's plea.

After an hour or so of small arms, rocket, and mortar exchanges Kurdish forces mounted an infantry charge across several hundred meters of open field and captured the first line of buildings in the Iraqi position. As the Kurds advanced uphill toward the final cluster of buildings they topped a small rise in the ground, beyond which numbers of Iraqi soldiers lay dead and wounded. Other Iraqi soldiers in that area of open ground made clear they were surrendering by laying down their weapons, kneeling on the ground, and locking their hands behind their heads. Many were crying "Allahu Akbar" (God is Great), pleading for mercy. No further shots were fired from the main building at the top of the rise, where most of the remainder of the Iraqi soldiers were located. In effect, the battle was over.

The Iraqi soldiers I could see were *hors de combat*, that is, "out of combat" and therefore entitled to be protected, not attacked, and treated humanely according to the provisions of international humanitarian law. Article 3 common to the Geneva Conventions of 1949, which governs "conflict not of an international character" such as the Kurdish rebellion in northern Iraq, states: "Persons taking no active part in the hostilities, including members of armed forces who have laid down their arms and those placed *hors de combat* by sickness, wounds, detention, or any other cause, shall in all circumstances be treated humanely."

For those deemed *hors de combat*, the article prohibits "violence to life and person, in particular murder, mutilation, cruel treatment and torture." The ban is absolute. As the International Committee of the Red Cross Commentary to Common Article 3 makes clear: "No possible loophole is left; there can be no excuse, no attenuating circumstances." In an international conflict, violation of this principle constitutes a grave breach.

Instead of accepting the surrender of the Iraqi soldiers, as required by law and as had been the practice in recent fighting around Sulaymaniyah, the Kurds executed them. An Iraqi soldier with no weapon, and with his

hands in the air, was shot and killed a few steps from me. Seven unarmed prisoners kneeling on the ground nearby were shot to death moments later. Individually and in small groups, every Iraqi soldier I saw outside the main building was executed. None had weapons, nor were they resisting or trying to escape.

By the time I reached the main building at least seventy-five Iraqi soldiers had been herded into a large room. None was armed or resisting and many appeared to have been wounded in the fighting before it stopped. These prisoners were also shot and killed. Kurds with Kalashnikovs emptied magazine after magazine into what became a blood-soaked pile of bodies. Some Kurdish noncombatants joined in the slaughter, using blocks of concrete to crush the heads of the Iraqi soldiers who had not yet died of their wounds. Within thirty minutes, all Iraqi soldiers at the location—probably about 125—were dead.

The murder of these Iraqi soldiers was a war crime, judged by even the narrowest definitions of international humanitarian law. Once a combatant "falls into the power of an adversary," is incapacitated, attempts to surrender, or is captured, he is entitled to protection.
(See **quarter, giving no.**)

Hospitals

By Charles Lane

"The guerrillas blew up the hospital."

I still vividly remember the scorching hot day in November 1989 when I heard those words and instantly recognized that there might be a story behind them. I was working as Central America correspondent for *Newsweek*. El Salvador was in the middle of a ferocious nationwide offensive by a Marxist guerrilla group known as the Farabundo Marti National Liberation Front (FMLN). The FMLN had surprised the Salvadoran Army with large-scale coordinated attacks on the capital, San Salvador, and all the major provincial towns across the tiny, Massachusetts-size country. One of the towns they hit was Zacatecoluca, a provincial capital near the country's international airport. Amid the ensuing chaos, both sides charged each other with horrific human rights violations. It was in that atmosphere that I heard the first report of a guerrilla assault on the hospital in Zacatecoluca.

Hospitals, of course, enjoy a special protected status under international humanitarian law. It is a war crime deliberately to attack a hospital or other medical unit, whether civilian or military. It is also unlawful to use a hospital in direct support of a military operation—to convert one wing of the hospital into an ammo dump, for example. (Indeed, hospitals that are misused in this manner lose their legal protection.) Medical personnel in general may not be attacked; but at the same time it is unlawful to use medical facilities, or related equipment such as ambulances, as camouflage or protection for military personnel, or as a shield for military forces.

International humanitarian law is not, however, completely inflexible in how it evaluates **collateral damage** to hospitals that may result from attacks on **legitimate military targets** nearby. The rule of thumb is that if the damage to the hospital is not excessive in view of the direct and concrete military advantages to be gained from attacking the nearby target, then the damage may be considered lawful.

To go back to that hot day in El Salvador nine years ago. I clambered into my beat-up Mitsubishi Montero Jeep and took off down the road for

Sandbags protect the patients of the Gaza Hospital, Sabra-Chatila, during the Israeli invasion of Lebanon in 1982.

Zacatecoluca. I will never forget the shock I felt when, without warning, a huge explosion erupted from what seemed like only two inches from my right ear. Temporarily deafened, I recovered my other senses enough to realize that an army artillery piece had just been fired from about twenty-five yards away; the Salvadoran military was pouring shells into the hills around Zacatecoluca, in a desultory attempt to deal with the retreating guerrillas.

When I reached the town, I made immediately for the large, modern public hospital not far from the main square. Once inside, I did indeed find that the pediatric ward had been blown to smithereens. Windows were broken, the elevator destroyed, bits of bedding lay strewn about on the floor. And the hospital personnel confirmed to us that the damage had been caused when a guerrilla unit detonated a large bomb in the ward.

End of story? Not quite. The destruction was heavy, but not entirely wanton. There had been heavy fighting that day between the army and the guerrillas. Neither side occupied the hospital or attempted to do so, but as the fighting raged among the narrow cobblestoned streets of the town, a few Salvadoran Army soldiers had become separated from their unit and attempted to flee onto the roof of the hospital. The FMLN forces cornered the government soldiers, and, in an attempt to flush them out, decided to detonate an explosive charge in the pediatric ward, the spot nearest to the soldiers' rooftop hideout.

Hence, two crucial legal questions arise: First, were the soldiers a legitimate target for the FMLN? Almost certainly yes. (It could even be argued that the hospital lost its protected status because the soldiers chose to hide themselves there, but their flight onto the hospital roof seemed less calculated than a decision made amid the heat and panic of battle, with no cooperation from the hospital staff, and it would seem perverse to make the hospital pay for that.)

Second, were the FMLN troops within their rights to use an explosive to attack the soldiers, knowing that to detonate it would cause substantial damage to the wing of the hospital where civilian children were treated? I think that in this instance, the answer is also yes—especially in view of the fact that hospital personnel told us that the guerrillas gave them ample warning and permitted them to evacuate all the patients and medical personnel before they set off their bomb.

But it is a qualified yes. The answer, under international law, would ultimately hinge on the question of whether killing or capturing a handful of already fleeing enemy troops really warranted the eminently foreseeable damage to a hospital facility. And that damage was extensive; not total destruction of the entire building, to be sure, but serious enough to force dozens of sick and injured people into a makeshift outdoor clinic. It might reasonably be argued that this level of damage was unwarranted, notwithstanding the FMLN's laudable effort to evacuate the building first. In fact, the FMLN never did capture or kill the soldiers. If humanitarian law was violated, the FMLN theoretically might be required to pay reparations for the damage caused. But there was no evidence of **willfulness** in the legal sense required to constitute individually culpable war crimes.

So I went back to San Salvador and incorporated the Zacatecoluca hospital incident into that week's article. It was true, as I initially heard, that the guerrillas had blown up the hospital. But a close investigation of all the factors that led them to take that action, and of the manner in which they took it, showed that, tragic as it was, the assault may well have fallen into the category of a questionable but lawful military action, rather than that of a major violation of human rights or an individually culpable war crime.

Hostages

By Sean Maguire

"If the bombing starts again we've been told we will die." The chilling words of the unarmed Canadian officer radioed to United Nations headquarters in Sarajevo, just hours after NATO jets had struck a Bosnian Serb ammunition dump to punish noncompliance with UN resolutions.

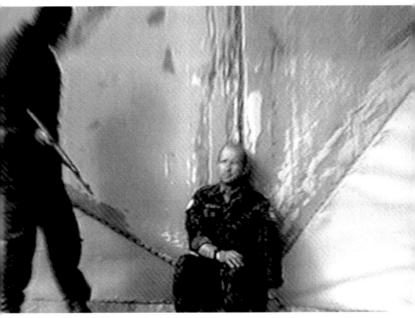

A hooded Serb soldier guards chained UN peacekeeper held hostage. Bosnia, 1995.

Now the officer and his colleagues were held by the Bosnian Serbs as human shields. The threat to their lives was obvious, though whether they would die at the hands of their captors or as casualties of bombing was unclear. Television pictures showed them chained to the door of a munitions facility and being forced to drive their car to and fro across the air-raid rubble to prevent the planes returning. A forlorn Polish officer was handcuffed outside a radar site while two masked Serb soldiers stood by, shotguns balanced on their hips. The black hoods, which made the guards look like executioners, were to conceal their identities.

Those two Serbs were taking warranted precautions. Indictments for war crimes had already been handed down by the Hague Tribunal, and the Bosnian Serbs knew their actions would be closely scrutinized. Since 1949, the taking of hostages has been forbidden by the four Geneva Conventions. Using prisoners of war or detainees as human shields has been outlawed either specifically or implicitly by clauses that forbid a party from harming those "not actively taking part in hostilities" in its control.

Common Article 3 of the conventions bans the taking of hostages in internal conflicts while the Fourth Convention forbids civilians being taken hostage during times of war. Ignoring these prohibitions during an international conflict is a grave breach of humanitarian law, leaving those responsible liable to international pursuit and prosecution. The conventions also decree that both prisoners of war and civilians should not be "used to render certain points or areas immune from military operations." Civilians get further protection from the 1977 Additional Protocol to the Geneva Conventions dealing with internal conflicts. It, too, bans hostage taking.

The practice of taking hostages in war has a long pedigree. In the past, it was used to secure the obedience of an occupied people or adherence to the terms of a treaty. The practice was specifically outlawed in 1949 because of the finding at the Nuremberg Trials that existing laws appeared to permit reprisal executions. Under certain conditions an army is still allowed to take **reprisals** for an illegal act by an adversary, but cannot use "excessive" force or execute prisoners of war or civilians.

The International Committee of the Red Cross (ICRC) defines hostages as "persons who find themselves, willingly or unwillingly, in the power of the enemy and who answer with their freedom or their life for compliance with the orders of the latter (the enemy) and for upholding the security of its armed forces."

Disputes about the nature of modern conflicts make it difficult to judge if and how the protections of the Geneva Conventions apply. Should you be hijacked on an international flight, your abductors would not be contravening the Geneva Conventions, which deal with hostages taken by "an authority," but the 1979 International Convention Against the Taking of Hostages, which explicitly outlaws such cross-border criminality.

"Hostages" was the description the UN gave to the four hundred peacekeepers the Bosnian Serbs rounded up from depots and garrisons at the end of May 1995. The ICRC, however, disagreed. It argued that since the UN had ordered air strikes it had become involved in the Bosnian conflict and its personnel were therefore prisoners of war. The ICRC did make plain its horror that once they were forced to serve as human **shields** they were being used as hostages and not treated as prisoners of war. The Hague Tribunal subsequently indicted Bosnian Serb leaders Radovan Karadzic and Ratko Mladic for the hostage-taking campaign and for using UN personnel as human shields.

At the time, unfortunately but unsurprisingly, the Bosnian Serb tactic worked. "I was a kind of insurance policy against NATO threatening to bomb again," said Capt. José Mendez after his release. The Spanish officer spent ten days sitting in the middle of a runway at the main Bosnian Serb air base hoping that NATO would not call the Serb bluff. It did not. The next NATO bombing campaign, which led to the Dayton peace agreement, took place when UN soldiers were no longer vulnerable to capture.

(See **reprisal killings**.)

Humanitarian Aid, Blocking of

By David Rieff

The aid workers who trucked relief supplies from Metkovic in Croatia to the ruined towns and villages of central Bosnia and on to Sarajevo knew they were engaged in a game of humanitarian Russian roulette.

For the fighters, the humanitarian convoys were resupplying their enemies. That made the aid workers enemies as well. "You say you are helping women and children," I heard a Croat fighter say bitterly to an official of the Danish Refugee Council at an improvised checkpoint in western Herzegovina. "You are doing nothing of the sort. You are helping the Muslims."

The Danish official only shook her head. "You're quite wrong," she said. "We are taking no sides; our aid is neutral." The Croat soldier's only response was a bitter laugh.

We waited at the checkpoint for a long time. We would wait for just as long at half a dozen others before we finally arrived in the town of Travnik, controlled by the Bosnian government. The Croats stopped us along the road. The Serbs shelled us from the hills. That was what pushing a humanitarian convoy through was usually like. At the checkpoints, the law counted for little. As the Danish official put it to me, "In this war, not only do the fighters not obey the law, they don't even know what we're talking about when we speak of humanitarian requirements."

And yet the need for **humanitarian interventions** to alleviate the worst of consequences on civilians is one of the few questions about which almost all people outside Bosnia could agree. There was no consensus about the rights or wrongs of the conflict, let alone how to resolve it. But there was real determination to see that humanitarian aid got through, and real indignation when it could not. When the Serbs closed the Sarajevo airport, or convoys were blocked, all outside parties were outraged. Humanitarian aid was supposed to be beyond the politics of the war, beyond all questions of military or psychological advantage. It was something that was unarguably good, and, as such, something that must not be interfered with.

The legal bases for this view were already powerful with the passage of the Fourth Geneva Convention of 1949. It imposed on all its parties the obligation to allow "the free passage of all consignments of medical and hospital stores" and of "all consignments of essential foodstuffs, clothing and tonics intended for children under fifteen, expectant mothers and maternity cases" even to its military adversaries. The 1977 Additional Protocols to the Geneva Conventions further cemented both the obligations of belligerents and the rights of noncombatants. Article 69 imposes on occupying powers the obligation to provide relief supplies to the population of its adversary "without any adverse distinction," to ensure that population's physical survival (it also called for the provision of articles necessary for religious worship). Article 70 requires belligerents to treat offers of relief not as interference in the conflict, so long as the relief effort was "humanitarian and impartial in character," but as a duty imposed by international humanitarian law (IHL).

On the ground, and not only in **Bosnia**, things have been more complicated. In a war of **ethnic cleansing**, the last things fighters want to do is make it possible for the civilian populations of their adversary to remain, let alone be decently housed and fed, or be allowed to worship freely. In so many cases, the violation of IHL was the norm, and respect for it the exception. In northern Bosnia, the Serbs did not provide articles of Muslim religious worship, they systematically blew up mosques. And the more convoys they blocked, the likelier it was that the Muslim population would flee, bringing about the ethnic cleansing that had been the goal of the war in the first place.

The bitter truth was that to stand for international laws governing the free movement of humanitarian aid was to stand against the war aims of the Bosnian Serbs and, to a lesser extent, the Bosnian Croats, and their respective masters in Belgrade and Zagreb as well. For the fighters of the Croatian Defense Council (HVO) to allow a humanitarian convoy into Bosnian government–controlled East Mostar, for example, was to sanction the continued physical presence of Muslims in that part of Bosnia-Herzegovina. And all the killing and destruction had been undertaken precisely with the opposite goal in mind. In this sense, when we who accompanied the aid convoys watched representatives of the United Nations High Commissioner for Refugees (UNHCR) or the private aid groups plead for access, all of us—the aid workers, the fighters at the checkpoints, the civilian beneficiaries, and, of course, the journalists—understood that what was really at stake was the continuation of the war itself. In other words, what in IHL often constitutes a war crime was, for the fighters, the essential tactic of their fight.

But even on strictly legal grounds, the situation was not always clear in a place like Bosnia. The Fourth Geneva Convention and the 1977 Additional Protocols are encrusted with exceptions on the subject of blocking humanitarian aid. That is because the Bosnian conflict is not at all the kind of war either the framers of the convention or the additional protocols had anticipated. Article 23 of the Fourth Geneva Convention states that an army must be satisfied that there are no "serious reasons" for fearing that relief supplies will be diverted from their intended destination and recipients, or that control over distribution will not be effective, or that the enemy will not derive some substantial benefit to its war effort or have its economy shored up. Article 18 of Additional Protocol II emphasizes the "exclusively humanitarian and impartial nature" of all appropriate relief efforts. The guarantee of access comes with the right of belligerents to inspect convoys to see that the aid is what it purports to be and is destined for populations that are entitled to it.

In wars that pit not armies but armed populations against each other, such guarantees are almost impossible to ensure. Fighters on all sides use humanitarian relief supplies for their own purposes, and the laws do not adequately come to grips with the problem of a war in which the distinction between soldier and civilian is unclear, if it exists at all.

It will be a long time before such questions are resolved, for ultimately they are political and moral as much as they are legal. In the Bosnian context, the loopholes in the law making the blocking of aid a war crime could easily be exploited to prevent aid convoys from getting to where the needs are greatest. None of this, of course, is of much comfort to the civilian populations trapped in wars of ethnic cleansing for whom humanitarian aid remains almost the only hope.

Humanitarian Intervention

By David Rieff

At the height of the siege of Sarajevo, when hundreds of shells were hitting the Bosnian capital every day, many there believed they would not survive. The United Nations airlift, which provided food for many who would otherwise have starved, was constantly being interrupted as Serb forces repeatedly shelled the airport runway. As the months turned into years and the siege was not lifted, it seemed, both to Sarejevans and to many sympathetic foreigners, that either the city would be destroyed or some kind of outside intervention would have to take place.

H

"How can you in the West allow this to go on?" an actress at Sarajevo's National Theater asked me in January of 1993. "My teeth are falling out, I'm covered in eczema, I haven't had a bath in months, and I'm a privileged person by the standards of this town. I know no one outside really understands what is going on here; you all think we're savage Balkan people pursuing our ancient ethnic bloodlusts. It's utter nonsense, of course. But even if that's what you think, even if you won't come help us because we have right on our side, why can't you help us for humanitarian reasons? Why can't you just stop the siege?"

Overhead, as if it had been choreographed, a jet screamed through the afternoon sky. It was a NATO fighter on a routine reconnaissance. The actress smiled. "Good timing, wasn't it?" she said. "If it would dive down and drop some bombs, I could have a bath."

She was right about the befuddlement afflicting most people in the U.S. and in western Europe when they thought about Bosnia. Those who believed that the Bosnian government should be aided because it was in the right were always in a small minority, even among those who thought force needed to be used to bring the ethnic cleansing and the siege of Sarajevo to an end. It was more common to hear the argument that what was happening was so horrible that it simply had to be stopped, and that if military means were needed then military means had to be employed. In other words, what was most credible to the vast majority of those who paid attention to Bosnia— even at the height of the slaughter, a small percentage of the Western public—was not a political intervention but an intervention that needed to be undertaken solely on humanitarian grounds.

In the end, when the mass murder of more than seven thousand Muslim men and boys at Srebrenica finally forced the Western powers to act, they did so not out of a political determination to restore a unified Bosnian state but instead out of a version of a humanitarian impulse. The bloodshed and the slaughter, Western leaders finally concluded, could not be allowed to go on.

Humanitarian intervention is at once an immensely powerful and a terribly imprecise idea. No formal legal definition of it exists, but its fundamental premise is that outside powers have the right and, perhaps, under some circumstances, the duty to intervene to protect people in other countries who are being victimized, even if what is taking place is a conflict within a State. Whereas classical interventions are political in character and involve one State either imposing its will by force on another or coming to the aid of another (and thus in no sense challenging the long-standing notion that

State sovereignty should be for all practical purposes inviolable), humanitarian interventions offer a direct challenge to such notions of sovereignty. This is especially true for those interventions directly into the internal affairs of a single State. In a deep sense, they also sidestep considerations of the political rights and wrongs of a given conflict. What matters, from the perspective of the State or group of States contemplating a humanitarian intervention, is the effect a conflict has on civilians.

An example of this kind of thinking was the debate in 1996 over a Canadian proposal for a humanitarian intervention in what was then eastern Zaire to protect the millions of Hutu refugees who were at risk from both the attacks of Tutsi-led Rwandan forces and from the ebb and flow of the Zairean civil war. The Canadians argued that the rights of a civilian population at risk outweighed any other consideration, including the effect that such a humanitarian deployment might have on the political struggle then taking place in Zaire. Those who argued against the deployment in effect were saying that

UN peacekeepers support a wounded woman during a Serb shelling. Sarajevo, 1994.

humanitarian needs alone could not justify such outside interference. Many also made the cautionary argument that forecasting the long-term effect of humanitarian military intervention was itself fraught with uncertainty.

As a matter of international law, humanitarian intervention remains purely a matter of the political preferences of the person making the argument. It seems generally accepted that the Security Council can declare anything it likes to be a "threat to international peace and security," subject not to any genuinely objective constraints of law but only to the political vetoes of its permanent members. Its determinations are shaped by public opinion, international activists, CNN, and the political considerations of Security Council members, as well as by broader, and more principled policies and laws. Within international humanitarian law (IHL), the leap from provisions providing for the delivery of humanitarian relief to military intervention is a long one, but not too long for those politically motivated to do so.

In practice, humanitarian intervention has often served as a justification for States to act in conflicts where there is no domestic support for more straightforward political interventions. The public in North America and western Europe has, for all the talk of compassion fatigue, proved remarkably sympathetic to the use of force to avert or bring to an end a humanitarian disaster. On the other hand, humanitarian intervention has also been a justification for other political motivations. In Rwanda, in 1994, it was commonly assumed that the French humanitarian intervention dubbed Operation Turquoise used the humanitarian imperative as a cover for France's decision to continue to try to influence events in the Great Lakes region of Africa with military force and, more specifically, to save the French-supported, but genocidal, government. And historically, many of the imperial campaigns launched by the European colonial powers in the nineteenth century were justified on humanitarian grounds.

Today, humanitarian interventions have been largely the brainchildren of UN bureaucrats and of humanitarian relief organizations who are unable to operate safely in conflict zones. These groups have become some of the most fervent interventionists. A French humanitarian official, Bernard Kouchner, even popularized the legal theory of the French scholar Mario Bettati of the "right of intervention." Of course, whether people would react in the same way if the price in the lives of soldiers and in money grew too high is another question entirely. This is in part due to the fact that Western politicians routinely, but often improbably, describe humanitarian interventions as safe. When, as with the U.S.-led United Nations Operation in Somalia (UNOSOM II), this turns out to be false, pressures to abort humanitarian interventions mount quickly and usually become politically irresistible.

In international law, the tug of war between State sovereignty and the obligation of other countries to maintain international peace and security continues to rage. In practice, the idea, at least in the case of so-called failed States, that the principle of State sovereignty is simply irrelevant and the needs of persons preeminent has been gaining favor and is becoming a common starting point for discussions of what to do about situations where there is immense human suffering and little prospect of immediate relief. That was the way the U.S. intervention in Somalia was presented to the American public, and how the Canadians made the case for their proposed deployment in eastern Zaire. As the costs of humanitarian interventions mount, the willingness of outside States to intervene to protect people from systematic violations of internationally recognized human rights or provide them with relief is an open question. But humanitarian intervention remains an immensely attractive idea to many, and in the absence, after the end of the Cold War, of either any real system of international security or any real transfer of authority to supranational institutions like the UN, it is likely to remain an enduring, if half-hearted, one.

Identification

By H. Wayne Elliott

During the American Civil War soldiers rarely wore any sort of identifying disk. Before battle most soldiers would write their name and unit on a slip of paper and pin it to their backs. That simple battlefield expedient sometimes worked. A few soldiers bought ornate engraved pins or metal identification tags from sutlers. The tags had the soldier's name and unit and, sometimes, his hometown. Neither government issued identification disks. The haphazard way in which soldiers were identified probably explains why almost half the Civil War graves in national cemeteries are marked "unknown."

Only a few years later, in the Franco-Prussian War, the Prussian Army issued not only identification disks but required each Prussian soldier to carry an identification card. These cards were called the soldier's *grabstein* (his "tombstone"). Today, the laws of war require that soldiers be identified. In the not-too-distant future we can expect to find electronic disks that would contain a great deal of information about the soldier. DNA coding may mean that there simply will be no more "unknown soldiers." Regardless of the methods used, identification as a lawful combatant and a member of the armed forces is crucial to determining the treatment to be afforded—whether sick, wounded, dead, or captured; whether a soldier, medic, or civilian.

While the military uniform may be circumstantial evidence that the person in it is a lawful **combatant**, the laws of war do not recognize the uniform alone as absolute proof that a person is a member of the military. Status as a member of the military is important. A person who participates in hostilities without being authorized to do so by proper authorities runs the risk of being charged as an unlawful combatant and prosecuted as such. Perhaps more important, a party to the conflict is not obligated to extend **prisoner of war** status to persons who are not lawful combatants. For this reason, armies make every effort to identify those who serve it in combat.

In most armies today soldiers carry identity disks (often referred to as dog tags in the U.S. forces). The disks are referred to in the First Geneva Convention of 1949 in connection with the duty to identify the wounded and the dead. However, the conventions themselves do not mandate that such tags be issued or that the soldier actually carry them. The disks generally have the soldier's name, identifying number, blood type, and religion. These facts would be important considerations in providing proper care in case the soldier is wounded or killed. The disks are primarily intended as a means to aid in the identification of the soldier who, because of wounds or death, otherwise might be unidentified.

Article 17 of the Third Geneva Convention requires that each party to a conflict issue an identity card to persons who are liable to become prisoners of war. The card must include the person's name, rank, identifying number, and date of birth. The card can also include other information as well as the person's signature, fingerprints, and a photograph. The card must be shown by the prisoner on demand, but it cannot be taken away from him. The drafters of the convention required only information that would have no real intelligence value so the captor would have no reason to take the card from the prisoner. If the prisoner has lost the card, Article 18 requires that the detaining (i.e., the capturing) power provide him with another similar card.

The identification card is also important in determining the treatment to be afforded the prisoner of war. The rank of the prisoner of war at the time of capture is on the card and will determine whether the captive is to be treated as an officer or enlisted person. The duties expected of prisoners of war vary with rank, so the card is quite important.

Related to the requirements governing the identification card are the general rules concerning prisoner interrogation. The captive is "bound" to give only his name, rank, date of birth, and serial number when questioned. This requirement is often misunderstood. The Third Geneva Convention, in Article 17, requires that this information be given. The same information is on the identification card, and that card must be shown upon demand. Hence, there is no reason not to provide it when questioned. While this is all the prisoner is bound to give, the captor might ask for more information, including militarily sensitive data. Nonetheless, the POW need not respond with anything more than the four items set out in the Third Geneva Convention and may not be punished or mistreated for failing to do so.

Those who are given an opportunity to observe or talk with prisoners of war should ask to see the identification documents. Not only is the card evidence of the person's status under the laws of war, its absence is evidence that the captor is not in full compliance with the same laws. The presence of the identity disks and the identification card is a ready, and visible means of determining some minimal level of compliance with the laws of war concerning prisoners.

(See **dead and wounded**.)

Illegal or Prohibited Acts

By Ewen Allison and Robert K. Goldman

Illegal or prohibited acts are categorized either according to the body of humanitarian law they violate or consequences for the perpetrator. Some acts involve prohibited means or methods of warfare ("Hague law," that is, the law arising from the Hague Conventions of 1899 and 1907). Other acts harm **protected persons—sick and wounded**, shipwrecked, or **civilians** ("Geneva law," that is, the law arising from the Geneva Conventions).

The most serious of illegal acts are grave breaches of the Geneva Conventions of 1949. Illegal acts, other than grave breaches, are known as serious violations and, unlike grave breaches, are not subject to universal **jurisdiction**, although they may and often will be subject to prosecution in different courts, including international tribunals.

Illegal acts include: use of prohibited means and methods of warfare, including poison or other **weapons** calculated to cause unnecessary suffering; **perfidious** attacks not involving the abuse of protective emblems or emblems or uniforms of neutral countries; failure to wear a uniform to identify oneself as a legal **combatant**; **pillage**; **terrorism**; interference with **humanitarian aid** shipments; nonextensive, unjustified destruction of **property**; attack or bombardment of **undefended towns**, dwellings, or buildings; seizure of or willful damage done to certain **cultural** institutions, e.g., those dedicated to religion, education, charity, arts, sciences, or historic monuments and works of art; **reprisals** against protected persons or objects; and any breach of an **armistice**.

For its own purposes, the International Criminal Tribunal for the Former Yugoslavia defined a serious violation as one that has grave consequences for its victim and which breaks a rule protecting important values. Unnecessarily burning a village's crop is serious; stealing a loaf of bread is not.

Regardless of whether an individual must be punished, parties to a conflict are responsible for all violations of international humanitarian law. (See **war crimes**.)

Immunity from Attack

By Emma Daly

Our friend lay in bed, plucking nervously at the gray, bloodstained sheets, her eyes covered by a bandage, her face patterned with glass cuts. "I want to go home," she said vehemently. "I'm terrified of staying in this building."

Man having shrapnel removed from his leg in the corridor of the Trauma Clinic at Kosevo Hospital. Sarajevo, Bosnia, 1993.

We could understand her concern: the concrete blocks and curved facades of the Kosevo hospital complex in Sarajevo were scarred by shrapnel marks, bullet marks, and shell craters. Two weeks earlier, two patients had been killed when a shell hit their ward. We could hear the sounds of bombardment in the distance, and, suspiciously close to the **hospital**, the hollow sound of outgoing mortar fire. Hospitals are generally immune from attack under the Geneva Conventions, which grant civilians and civilian objects a high level of theoretical protection in times of war. The **siege** of Sarajevo, however, made a mockery of the humanitarian ideal that the dangers of war should be limited, as far as possible, to the armed forces engaged in the fighting.

The concept of immunity, the rule that certain people and places should be "protected and respected" during wartime, can be dated back at least to 1582, when a Spanish judge suggested that "intentional killing of innocent persons, for example, women and children, is not allowable in war." The Geneva Conventions of 1949 confirmed immunity for civilians, hospitals, and medical staff, and the 1977 Additional Protocols to the conventions state: "The civilian population and individual civilians shall enjoy general protec-

189

tion against the dangers arising from military operations."

The absolute rule is that civilians must not be directly targeted for military attack. Furthermore, some individuals considered especially vulnerable —children under fifteen, the elderly, pregnant women, and mothers of children under seven—are granted special protection and may, for example, be moved to safe zones exempt from attack by agreement of the warring parties. The wounded, sick, or shipwrecked, military personnel who are considered to be *hors de combat*, are protected, as are **prisoners of war**.

Hospitals, both fixed and mobile, ambulances, hospital ships, medical aircraft, and **medical personnel**—whether civilian or military—are also entitled to protection from hostile fire under the Geneva Conventions, provided that structures are marked with a **red cross or red crescent** and not used improperly or near military objectives, and staff are properly protected. Staff include not only doctors, nurses, and orderlies, but the drivers, cleaners, cooks, crews of hospital ships—in short, all those who help a medical unit to function. Some aid workers—for example, Red Cross volunteers treating the sick and wounded on the battlefield—are also covered, as are military chaplains. Other than hospitals, certain other buildings cannot be attacked. Places of worship and historic monuments are protected, as are civilian structures like schools and other objects that are not being used to support military activities. Under the 1954 Convention on Cultural Property important places of worship, historic sites, works of art, and other cultural treasures are likewise protected from attack.

There are exceptions. A school, for example, becomes a **legitimate military target** if soldiers are based there. With hospitals, the situation is more complicated since they are permitted to keep armed guards on their grounds. But immunity from attack can be lost if the people or objects are used to commit acts that are harmful to one side in a conflict. If the Bosnian Serbs besieging Sarajevo had concluded that government forces were firing weapons from within the Kosevo hospital complex, they would have had the right to fire back—but only if they had first asked the Bosnian government to stop using the hospital as a **shield** and had given them a reasonable period to comply.

Causing harm to an innocent person or object is not always illegal. Civilian deaths and damage are allowed as the result of an attack on a military target, but only if the attack is likely to confer a definite military advantage. Damage to people or objects who are in principle deemed to be immune under international humanitarian law must not be excessive in relation to the expected military gain. For example, breaking the windows of a hospital during an attack on an arms dump five hundred meters away would not be illegal since the civilian damage would be far outweighed by the military gain.

But keeping legitimate military targets separate from protected civilian sites is hard to do on the ground. Under international humanitarian law, the parties to a conflict are obliged to separate their military from their civilians as much as possible. But the reality is that this can be difficult. In Sarajevo, for example, the territory under siege was so small that to do so was all but impossible. That said, in Sarajevo, as in many towns across Bosnia-Herzegovina, it seemed clear that the besiegers' primary target was civilians. That was one of the reasons why Radovan Karadzic and Ratko Mladic, the civilian and military leaders of the secessionist Bosnian Serbs, were charged with war crimes by the International Criminal Tribunal in The Hague.

(See **civilian immunity**; **civilians, illegal targeting of**; **medical transports**; **proportionality**; **protected persons**.)

Imprisonment of Civilian Population

By Ewen Allison and Robert K. Goldman

When the World War II Allies began preparing the Nuremberg Trials to prosecute Axis war criminals, they faced the problem that the existing laws of
armed conflict did not address crimes against one's own nationals. The Nazis,
for example, had arrested and deported millions of civilians to **concentration
camps** where they were held without trial, abused, and executed. To address
the war's atrocities, the Nuremberg Charter for the first time codified **crimes
against humanity**, that is, crimes which may have been committed before or
during a war and against one's own population. It included "murder, extermination, enslavement, deportation, and other inhumane acts done against any
civilian population, or persecutions on political, racial, or religious grounds."

I

   In their verdicts, the Nuremberg judges repeatedly referred to "acts of
imprisonment" as being among the crimes against humanity, and subsequently it has been recognized as such in customary law.

   The statutes of the UN International Criminal Tribunals for Rwanda and
the former Yugoslavia, established by the UN Security Council, both list
imprisonment as a crime against humanity. The charter of the International
Criminal Court of 1998, in an article approved by UN member-States without
dissent, says that "imprisonment or other severe deprivation of physical liberty in violation of fundamental rules of international law," if carried out as a
widespread or systematic attack on any civilian population, is a crime
against humanity.
(See **unlawful confinement**.)

Incitement to Genocide

By Colette Braeckman

"You have to work harder, the graves are not full," urged the voice on the radio. In April 1994, when the genocide started in Rwanda, ordinary people were glued to their receivers. In a part of the world where most people do not have electricity, that's the way information gets disseminated. But in Rwanda that spring the popular radio stations seemed to have only one aim: to incite the Hutu masses to exterminate their Tutsi neighbors.

The most popular station of all was RTLM (Radio Televison des Milles Collines), the Thousand Hills Radio Television. It was known for having the best disc jockeys in Rwanda and for its attractive mix of African music, news programming, and political analysis. Founded in 1993 and owned by family members and friends of President Habyarimana, the station preached an extremist message of Hutu supremacy, but many apolitical Rwandans became listeners because of the music it played. In fact, their hearts and minds were being prepared for genocide. When the killing was unleashed on April 6, it became clear what the owners and managers of the station had created— an infernal pulpit from which the message to kill could be disseminated throughout Rwanda.

The incident that triggered the mayhem was the downing of Habyarimana's plane by a missile. Within minutes of the crash, RTLM journalists accused Belgian troops in Rwanda on a UN peacekeeping mission of shooting down the plane. The next morning, ten Belgian soldiers were brutally killed, and UN forces withdrew. It was RTLM that gave the signal to begin the massacre of Tutsis and moderate Hutus.

RTLM on April 7 and April 8: "You have to kill [the Tutsis], they are cockroaches . . . " May 13: "All those who are listening to us, arise so that we can all fight for our Rwanda. . . .Fight with the weapons you have at your disposal, those of you who have arrows, with arrows, those of you who have spears with spears. . . . Take your traditional tools. . . . We must all fight [the Tutsis]; we must finish with them, exterminate them, sweep them from the whole country. . . . There must be no refuge for them, none at all." And on July 2: "I do not know whether God will help us exterminate [the Tutsis] . . . but we must rise up to exterminate this race of bad people. . . . They must be exterminated because there is no other way."

The message worked. By July of 1994, when the victory of the Tutsi-led Rwandan Patriotic Front (RPF) put an end to the genocide, up to 1 million Rwandans—mostly Tutsis, but also Hutus belonging to the democratic parties in Rwanda—had been slaughtered. The radios had been all too successful in inciting the genocide.

What they did, which was both to prepare the ground for the killing and encourage listeners to go on killing once the genocide had begun, was, of course, utterly illegal under international humanitarian law, which does not recognize an absolute right to free expression. By definition, most of those killed were civilians, that is, "persons taking no active part in the hostilities." In an internal conflict, as stated in Article 3 common to the four

Hutus accused of genocide crowd the yard of Kigali prison. Rwanda, 1994.

193

Geneva Conventions of 1949, civilians "shall in all circumstances be treated humanely without any adverse distinction founded on race, color, religion, sex, birth, or wealth."

As the rampage spread, the key document became the Genocide Convention of 1948, to which Rwanda became a party in 1975. The convention defines the crime of genocide as "acts committed with intent to destroy, in whole or in part, a national, ethnical, racial or religious group as such." The acts include killing members of the group, causing serious bodily or mental harm, and deliberately inflicting on the group conditions of life calculated to bring about its physical destruction in whole or in part. The convention not only makes genocide itself an international crime but states in Article 3 that "direct and public incitement to commit genocide" is punishable. And in September 1998, an ad hoc International Criminal Tribunal for Rwanda (the ICTR), sitting in Arusha, Tanzania, sentenced Jean Kambanda, the former prime minister, for direct and public incitement to commit genocide, in part for encouraging RTLM to continue its calls to massacre the Tutsis. That same month, the court convicted Jean-Paul Akayesu, the leading civilian in Taba commune, on charges that included the direct and public incitement to commit genocide.

The prohibitions set forward by the Genocide Convention and the precedent set by the ICTR were affirmed in the statute of the International Criminal Court (ICC), which was adopted on July 17, 1998. One hundred and twenty nations approved the Rome Statute, which laid the ground rules for the first international criminal court in history; Article 5 of the statute listed genocide first among the crimes over which the court had jurisdiction.

The hate-mongering journalists of RTLM stayed on the air until the very last moment of the Rwandan genocide. In July 1994, when the RPF—the Tutsi army that came from neighboring Uganda—defeated the Rwandan army and put an end to the genocide, the RTLM staff took a mobile transmitter and fled to Zaire, together with Hutu refugees. Ferdinand Nahimana, a well-known historian who served as RTLM's director, fled to Cameroon. There he was arrested and delivered to the Arusha tribunal, where he will have to answer to a very special charge: incitement to genocide.

The new Tutsi-led government closed RTLM, but the message continued when Hutus launched another clandestine radio station in Kivu, Zaire, to incite hatred against Tutsis in Burundi, using the same slogans.

Indiscriminate Attack

By Roy Gutman and Daoud Kuttab

As Western air forces bombarded Iraqi military targets at the start of the Gulf War, Iraq repeatedly fired SS-1 (Scud) missiles into Israel. Scuds never were known for their precision, but they became even less accurate as a result of Iraq's earlier decision during the Iran-Iraq War to triple the range to 560 miles.

The margin of error was at least two thousand yards, making the missile almost useless for hitting military targets but highly effective in terrorizing the population in an urban area. Of the eleven attacks on Israeli targets, many landed in densely populated residential areas in Tel Aviv or Haifa or in open fields; others were intercepted by U.S.-supplied Patriot antimissile missiles and never came anywhere close to the target. There is no evidence that Iraq made any attempt to aim the Scud missiles at military targets.

The Scud assaults exemplify indiscriminate attack, a defined war crime under the 1977 Additional Protocol I to the 1949 Geneva Conventions. An indiscriminate attack is one in which the attacker does not take measures to avoid hitting non-military objectives, that is, civilians and civilian objects. Protocol I states: "Parties to the conflict shall at all times distinguish between the civilian population and combatants and between civilian objects and military objectives and accordingly shall direct their operations only against military objectives."

An indiscriminate attack also includes using means and methods that, like the Scud, cannot be directed at specific military objectives or whose effects cannot be limited.

Military objectives are limited to "those objects which by their nature, location, purpose or use make an effective contribution to military action and whose total or partial destruction, capture or neutralization, in the circumstances ruling at the time, offers a definite military advantage." Although every instance of indiscriminate attack violates the law of armed conflict, it is equally the case where attacking a military target may cause collateral damage to civilians or civilian objects. If the harm to civilians is proportionate to the military advantage expected, the attack, other things being equal, is a legal act of war. If the harm is "excessive in relation to the concrete and direct military advantage anticipated," the attack is prohibited, whether or not indiscriminate. (Concrete means perceivable by the senses; direct means having no intervening factor.)

Although the United States and several other countries have not ratified Additional Protocol I, this provision is considered to be part of customary law and therefore binding upon all parties to a conflict. Indiscriminate attack has never been specifically banned in internal conflicts, yet this principle carries over as a matter of customary law.

Nearly every army has at some point carried out what today would be described as an indiscriminate attack. Examples include Germany's V-II rocket attacks during World War II, the Allied "strategic bombing" and firebombing of Dresden and Hamburg, as well as the U.S. **carpet-bombing** during the Vietnam War. To curb the practice, Additional Protocol I prohibits an attack "by bombardment which treats as a single military objective a number of mil-

itary objectives located in a city, town, village, or other area containing a similar concentration of civilians or civilian objects."

The point of this provision is to prevent an attacker from treating a whole city that contains not only civilians but also military targets as a single military target. The individual military objectives may still be targeted, with the possibility of **collateral damage** to civilians, but weapons must be aimed individually. What counts as sufficiently discriminate targeting is an important question of interpretation, in light of the physical constraints of weapons systems and the inability even with "smart" weapons to achieve perfect targeting. For that matter, there is not even a requirement that only smart weapons be used.

Even after the protocol came into effect, some of the world's most advanced armies violated the law. Human Rights Watch (HRW) in *Civilian Pawns: Laws of War Violations and the Use of Weapons on the Israel-Lebanon Border* (1996) documented repeated examples of indiscriminate attack during Israel's long-running conflict with the Hizbollah in southern Lebanon. During the 1993 Operation Accountability, the Israeli army targeted Hizbollah members—whether civilians or military—as well as sympathizers and relatives and also shelled whole villages without distinction of specific military objectives. (It should be noted that Israel is not a party to the 1977 Protocol I.)

There were direct attacks on purely civilian targets such as Sidon's wholesale vegetable market, and at one stage Israel warned it would fire on any means of transportation in about twenty villages, turning the region into a **free fire zone**. But Hizbollah, in the period before the Israeli operation, had also fired Katyusha rockets at Israel, hitting no military installations but causing the civilian population to flee south. This, too, was a clear violation of the ban on indiscriminate attacks. Also, Hizbollah issued no warnings and it used weaponry with obvious inaccuracy. In addition, HRW concluded, Hizbollah, in not directing its weapons at military targets, had used weapons to terrorize the civilian population. In essence, what may have started as indiscriminate attack resulted in direct attack, aimed at civilians—also clearly a war crime. The excuse used by Hizbollah, that it was firing in retaliation, made clear that it was attacking civilians by way of **reprisal**.

In 1995 and 1996, Israel and the Hizbollah again attacked each others' civilian targets. In Operation Grapes of Wrath in April 1996, there was evidence that Israel had carried out "indiscriminate and disproportionate attacks against civilians in what had become virtual 'free-fire' zones across large swaths of the south" of Lebanon, culminating in the shelling of a makeshift refugee compound at a UN post south of Tyre in which more than one hundred displaced civilians were killed. Israel said Hizbollah had fired mortars and Katyusha rockets from a position three hundred meters from the UN post. Locating military objectives near a concentration of civilians, known as shielding, is also a war crime, and the laws of armed conflict are clear that an attacker is not precluded from attacking a legitimate military target by the proximity of civilians or civilian objects. While acts of shielding did not render the zone immune from attack, neither did they "give Israel license to fire *indiscriminately* into a wide area that includes a UN base and concentrations of civilians," Human Rights Watch correctly noted (emphasis added). The International Committee of the Red Cross (ICRC) one day later issued a statement in which it "firmly condemned" the Israeli shelling at Qana and reiterated there was an "absolute ban" on indiscriminate attacks. However, a senior ICRC official said after an investigation that the real problem here was the fact that the Israeli system was designed to automatically

Hanoi residents in their blast shelters. Vietnam, March 1967.

fire back on the source of the original attack. Therefore Israel did not take sufficient precautions in their attack to ensure that it would not result in disproportionate civilian deaths. The UN's military advisor concluded in a May 1996 report that it was "unlikely that gross technical and/or procedural errors led to the shelling of the United Nations Compound." However, he added "it cannot be ruled out completely."

(See **civilian immunity; civilians, illegal targeting of; legitimate military targets; military necessity; proportionality; shields.**)

Types of Indiscriminate Attack

1. An attack that is not targeted at military objectives. (Damage to civilian property that is actually intended is known as **wanton destruction**, especially if it is wide-scale.)

2. Use of weapons that are not able to be properly targeted.

3. Use of weapons that have uncontrollable effects.

4. An attack that treats an area with similar concentrations of military and civilian objectives as a single military objective.

5. An attack that may be expected to cause harm to civilians or civilian objectives in excess of the concrete and direct military advantage anticipated.

Internal Displacement

By Maud S. Beelman

From a distance, the line of cars and buses that snaked along the rural stretch of northwest Bosnian roadway looked like a traffic jam on that languid August afternoon, as girls in summer white bicycled past fields of cornflower blue. Up close, the terror in the eyes of the people of Sanski Most, the belongings stuffed into satchels and plastic bags, and the police riding shotgun told the real story.

More than fifteen hundred Slavic Muslims were being forced from their homes that day in mid-August 1992 by ethnic Serbs trying to purge northern Bosnia of their neighbor-turned-enemy. The Serbs had even provided city buses to transport those without cars, though the generosity was soon to degrade into a terrifying all-night trek over blood, body parts, and across the front lines. Four months into the war, the UN High Commissioner for Refugees had begun to realize that the mass movement of civilians in Bosnia was not the chaotic happenstance of war, but rather a calculated, orchestrated transfer of populations aimed at creating ethnically pure areas.

Europe had not seen this kind of mass expulsion of civilians since World War II. Hitler's atrocities across the continent had given rise to the 1949 Geneva Conventions, which include specific protections for civilians. Article 49 of the Fourth Geneva Convention declares that "individual or mass forcible transfers . . . are prohibited, regardless of their motive."

Those in the Sanski Most convoy, by virtue of being moved to another location in the same country, are regarded under international humanitarian law as internally displaced persons (IDPs). If sent across an international border, it would be a **deportation** and they would be treated as **refugees**.

Additional Protocol II of 1977, which applies in internal conflicts, provides that forced civilian displacement may be undertaken legally only when civilians' very safety or "imperative military reasons" require it. In addition, Article 17 says that civilians cannot be forced from their "whole territory" for reasons connected with the conflict. The article does not say unambiguously what is meant by "territory." The International Committee of the Red Cross (ICRC) Commentary to the Additional Protocols states that the intent here is to minimize civilian displacement that is politically motivated.

The standard is the same for international or internal conflicts: if civilians have to be moved for either of those two reasons—safety or military imperatives—their evacuations are to be under protected, hygienic, and humane conditions, and as short-lived as possible. None of that applied in the case of Sanski Most, which fell under Bosnian Serb control in the earliest days of the war and saw no fighting for three years until autumn 1995.

International law, therefore, was unambiguous. Article 49 of the Fourth Geneva Convention prohibits the mass transfer of Bosnia's civilians and Article 17 of Additional Protocol II prohibits the expulsions.

Despite IHL, here they were. The daylong journey had descended into the heart of darkness as the convoy turned from the main road onto isolated country paths and made its way through an increasingly hostile gauntlet of Serb soldiers and civilians shouting, "Butcher them, butcher them!" As the sun set, the worst was yet to come. With guns stuck in their faces, the peo-

199

ple of Sanski Most were ordered from the buses and their cars, most of which were seized. With what belongings they could carry, they were sent on foot into the darkness through a no-man's land separating two armies. I went with them.

Old and young, fit and feeble, we trekked along a mountain road that was cratered by mortar impacts, mined on one side, and covered by snipers. In places, the blood was so thick our shoes stuck momentarily to the road, and we stumbled onto chunks of human flesh and other remnants—teddy bears, backpacks, slippers—of those who had gone before. At the front line—a high wall of boulders dynamited from the mountainside—a crippled man was carried over, his wheelchair passed after him. Babies were handed to their mothers. Old men and women, stooped with age, struggled over the rocks to the government-controlled side. The foot journey lasted six hours and covered twelve miles.

By December 1995, just after the Dayton peace accord, at least 1.2 million Bosnians had been internally displaced. Three years later, only a fraction had returned home. "Civilians, not soldiers, were the principal and often intentional victims in the Bosnian conflict. Forced displacement was not just a by-product but an objective of military action and persecution," Sadako Ogata, the UN High Commissioner for Refugees, said at the time.

But three years later, it happened again in the Serbian province of Kosovo, where Serb troops spent much of 1998 crushing an uprising by the 90 percent ethnic Albanian population. As many as 350,000 people had been displaced by September 1998. The majority were women and children.

Not all internal displacements are **ethnic cleansing**. In **Colombia**, both sides in the government-rebel conflict have forcibly relocated civilian populations to gain political or economic advantage. Worldwide, there were an estimated 20 to 25 million IDPs in 1998, compared to about 13 million refugees, that is, those forced across international borders.

Legal and humanitarian experts concede existing law is insufficient and weakened by a lack of political will. Interpretations of "imperative military reasons" vary widely, and governments also worry about getting involved in what may be considered the internal affairs of another State. According to Francis Deng, the UN's top representative on IDPs, "Lack of political will is ultimately the issue. Even if you had fine principles, fine laws, but you don't have the will to enforce them, then it's as good as a dead letter." (See **evacuation of civilians**.)

I

Internally displaced Bosnian Muslims driven out of Banja Luka by the Serbs make their way to refuge with all they can carry.

International Committee of the Red Cross (ICRC)

By Michael Ignatieff

The International Committee of the Red Cross (ICRC) was founded in 1863, the brainchild of Jean-Henri Dunant, a Swiss businessman who had witnessed the Battle of Solferino between France and Austria in 1859 and was shocked by the carnage that resulted from the neglect of the wounded.

Dunant campaigned throughout Europe for a new principle, that wounded enemy soldiers deserved the same medical treatment as troops of one's own nation. Five Geneva notables set up a committee in 1863 with Dunant as its secretary, the nucleus of what was to become the International Committee of the Red Cross, and in 1864, the Swiss government hosted a sixteen-nation international conference to recommend improvements in medical services on the battlefield. Parties to this first Geneva Convention agreed that hospitals, ambulances, and medical staff should be viewed as neutral in conflict and adopted the red cross as the symbol of the medical corps.

From its inception, the ICRC has had a unique and intimate relationship to the Geneva Conventions. Under the 1949 Geneva Conventions and the Additional Protocols of 1977, the ICRC has the mandate to: (a) visit and register prisoners of war, and to deliver mail and food parcels; (b) deliver emergency humanitarian aid to civilians in the midst of armed conflicts; (c) trace missing persons, civilian and military, and reunite them with their families; (d) train armed forces to respect international humanitarian law; (e) extend and develop the Geneva Conventions; and (f) act as go-betweens to secure prisoner exchanges, repatriations, and release of hostages.

The ICRC now has delegations in over fifty countries, just under half of them in Africa. Its annual budget is just over $550 million, most of which comes from governments, chiefly the United States, the European Union, Scandinavian countries, and Switzerland. Its executive committee is entirely Swiss, most of its delegates are still Swiss—though they are recruiting non-Swiss nationals.

ICRC representatives, known as "delegates" work with national Red Cross and Red Crescent societies in the field, and most of their local field workers come from the national societies. Institutionally, however, the ICRC looks on the national societies warily, believing that some of their leaderships are either corrupt or excessively partial to the policies of the local ruling elites.

The ICRC is a unique organization in terms of its legal status under international law, its role in establishing and upholding the Geneva Conventions, and its history and role in bringing relief impartially to civilian victims and the wounded of all nations. These different roles give rise to a unique moral dilemma, whether to denounce publicly the violators of the laws that the ICRC seeks to uphold and develop and that provide the organization its special status, or operate discreetly in order to preserve its ability to cross battle lines, gain access to prisoners, and monitor their treatment. Put more simply, the question is whether the ICRC should speak out—and risk losing access to victims—or keep silent and become complicit in evil.

It is a difficult call, and through most of its history the ICRC has chosen to remain publicly silent. The organization is haunted by its failures. Despite securing initial access to German concentration camps as early as 1935, and despite acquiring unrivaled intelligence about Nazi plans to exterminate the Jews, the ICRC leadership in Geneva failed either to reveal what it knew or to make any public protest. Courageous delegates did save Jews in Hungary and Greece, but the organization did not secure access to the camps until 1945, when it was too late.

This dilemma recurred in July 1992, when ICRC delegates became aware of Serb detention camps in central Bosnia where Muslim prisoners were being starved, tortured, and subjected to summary execution. This time, while maintaining public silence on the matter, local ICRC delegates provided off-the-record corroboration of information journalists had secured from other

Homeward bound: International Committee of the Red Cross plane returns injured child after treatment. Afghanistan, 1990.

sources, and thus helped to break the story of the camps. There are times that the ICRC denounces gross human rights violations, but officially the organization is still unwilling to take public stands, for fear of compromising its reputation for neutrality and impartiality.

As an organization dating back to the middle of the nineteenth century, the ICRC has an immense institutional memory. It visited and transmitted Red Cross messages and parcels for millions of POWs in two world wars; its tracing agency helped reunite hundreds of thousands of refugee families; its delegates have been eyewitnesses to every major armed conflict since 1864, and its expertise in negotiating access to all sides of a conflict is unrivaled.

Independence is its watchword. Officially, its representatives keep their distance from other nongovernmental organizations (NGOs) in the field and from the UN. During the Bosnian War, they fought tenaciously to keep their operation separate from UN agencies, refusing convoy escorts from UN peacekeepers, for example, on the grounds that it would compromise their neutrality.

It is an organization which goes by the book—the Geneva Conventions, their clauses and subclauses. This legalistic bias gives their work precision and discipline, but there are other humanitarian organizations (Médecins sans Frontières, for example) that are critical of their cautious, lawyerly neutrality. But the ICRC, like its crusading founder, also plays a central role in campaigns to "civilize" warfare, such as banning blinding laser **weapons** and antipersonnel land **mines**.

Since its creation, the ICRC has been trying to stay true to its mission of being "first in and last out" of any war zone. In the increasingly crowded and competitive field of international humanitarian relief, that helps it stand apart. This has sometimes paid off. During the NATO air strikes in Bosnian Serb territory in August 1995, all the NGOs from NATO countries were evacuated. The ICRC remained and was able to provide humanitarian assistance to the hundreds of thousands of Serb civilians forcibly cleared from the Krajinas by Croat and Muslim forces.

In August 1998, Tomahawk missiles slammed into an Afghan facility the U.S. government said was a terrorist training camp. In the streets of the Afghan capital, Kabul, crowds tried to take over the American embassy; shots were fired at foreigners and two aid workers were killed. The UN evacuated all its personnel from Afghanistan to nearby Pakistan. So did all the NGOs. Only the ICRC remained. Thirty of its delegates stayed on, feeding the war widows of Kabul, keeping the military hospitals open, fitting prosthetic limbs on child amputees, and trying to keep their lines of communication open to all of the factions in Afghanistan's brutal civil war.

The ICRC sometimes pays the price for its staying on. On December 17, 1996, in an ICRC hospital near Grozny, Chechnya, masked assailants scaled the wall of the compound and using pistols fitted with silencers executed six Red Cross personnel in their sleep. But the ICRC still refuses to post armed guards inside hospitals or as escorts for their convoys.
(See **Red Cross/Red Crescent emblem**; **training in international humanitarian law**.)

International Humanitarian Fact-Finding Commission

By Frits Kalshoven

The International Humanitarian Fact-Finding Commission (IHFFC) is an independent, permanent body that owes its existence to Article 90 of Additional Protocol I of 1977. In place since 1991, with its seat and secretariat at Berne, it is at the disposition of parties to armed conflicts that suspect, or are suspected of, serious violations of international humanitarian law (IHL). Although originally created for international armed conflicts, it holds itself capable to function in an internal armed conflict as well; a stance to which no government has objected. The IHFFC considers that it can offer its services to parties to a conflict without having been invited to do so but it will take such a step only if it appears prudent.

I

It is competent to: (1) inquire into alleged serious violations of IHL; (2) facilitate, through its good offices, the restoration of respect for IHL. The IHFFC regards the two functions as not necessarily linked, enabling it to carry out its good offices function independent of any inquiry (and vice versa). This does justice to their somewhat different orientations: while an inquiry into alleged violations may point in the direction of criminal proceedings, good offices may be conducive not just to the restoration of an attitude of respect for IHL but for the other party as well.

States may accept the competence of the IHFFC in relation to other States doing the same, by depositing a declaration to that effect with the Swiss authorities. At the moment of writing, fifty-three States have made such declarations—many of them European (including from the former Eastern bloc), and one of the UN Security Council's permanent five, Russia. (Another, the United Kingdom, has announced its intention to do so soon.) A State's acceptance of IHFFC competence does not bind that State in relation to its opponent or opponents in an internal armed conflict within its territory. The fifteen IHFFC members "of high moral standing and acknowledged impartiality" are elected for five-year terms by the States that have made such declarations. Since the 1996 elections it is composed of eleven Europeans (one from Russia) and four from other continents with the exception of Asia.

For the IHFFC to carry out its functions impartially and effectively requires the consent of the parties involved. This indispensable requirement may at the same time be one of the factors why to this day the IHFFC has remained largely unused.

Frits Kalshoven is President of the IHFFC.

International vs. Internal Armed Conflict

By Steven R. Ratner

"The division of world society into national and international is an arbitrary one," in the words of the political scientist John Burton, but a division nonetheless clung to by much of international humanitarian law.

Because the traditional laws of war—and laws of war crimes—concerned only conflicts between States, States accusing each other of violating them or of committing war crimes needed to characterize a conflict as truly international and not internal. Thus, the Geneva Conventions and Additional Protocol I address in nearly all their aspects international conflicts only. They apply in the event of "declared war or or of any other armed conflict [between States] even if the state of war is not recognized by one of them," as well as "all cases of partial or total occupation of the territory of a [State], even if the said occupation meets with no armed resistance." The easy cases involve invasion, assault, artillery bombardment, or air raid by one State against another; but the harder cases turn upon the perspectives of the belligerents and States observing the situation.

One such hard case, all too typical these days, is a **civil war** with foreign involvement or provocation, but without the foreign State's resort to the classic acts of war. What level of such involvement in a case like **Bosnia** or Zaire is enough to trigger the Geneva Conventions? International law offers no precise answers to this question. The International Court of Justice has held that a foreign State is responsible for the conduct of a faction in a civil war if (a) the faction is a *de facto* agent of the foreign State or (b) the foreign State otherwise orders it to commit certain acts. The UN's Yugoslavia Tribunal held in the Tadic case in 1997 that the *de facto* agent standard applied to trigger the Geneva Conventions; it went on to find that the Bosnian Serb army in that particular case was not a *de facto* agent of Serbia, that Serbia was thus not a party to the conflict, and that the conventions did not apply. The International Committee of the Red Cross Commentary to the Geneva Conventions suggests a lower standard, focusing on who had made the decision leading to the illegal acts. The issue remains unresolved.

The legal consequences of characterizing a conflict as solely internal have been quite significant. First, the Geneva Conventions provide only very basic protections in the event of civil wars through Article 3 common to the conventions. That article prohibits certain flagrant violations of human dignity like murder, torture, ill-treatment, and taking of hostages. Second, Additional Protocol II of 1977, which specifically addresses internal conflicts, provides fewer protections during such conflicts than the Geneva Conventions do for international conflicts. Third, for prosecution of **war crimes**, the conventions create criminal liability only for violations committed in international armed conflicts.

Nevertheless, recent developments have shown the possibility of prosecuting war crimes in internal conflicts without having to find some sort of linkage to an international war, through reliance on special statutes and customary international law. First, the Rwanda Tribunal statute explicitly gives that court jurisdiction over serious violations of Common Article 3 and

Additional Protocol II; second, the Yugoslavia Tribunal has interpreted its Statute to allow for jurisdiction over serious violations of Common Article 3 and other serious violations of the laws and customs of war in internal conflicts; and third, the statute of the International Criminal Court specifically provides for criminality over many acts committed in internal conflicts. (See **gray areas in international humanitarian law; guerrillas; paramilitaries.**)

Article 3 Common to the Four Geneva Conventions of August 12, 1949

Article 3, whose text is repeated in all four Geneva Conventions, is the only part of the conventions that applies explicitly to internal armed conflicts. It has been called a "treaty in miniature," and sets forth the minimum protections and standards of conduct to which the State and its armed opponents must adhere. Additional Protocol II of 1977 also covers internal conflicts, but it is less widely accepted among States than the 1949 Conventions. The protections it spells out are at the core of international humanitarian law.

In the case of armed conflict not of an international character occurring in the territory of one of the High Contracting Parties, each Party to the conflict shall be bound to apply, as a minimum, the following provisions:

1. Persons taking no active part in the hostilities, including members of armed forces who have laid down their arms and those placed *hors de combat* by sickness, wounds, detention, or any other cause, shall in all circumstances be treated humanely, without any adverse distinction founded on race, color, religion or faith, sex, birth or wealth, or any other similar criteria.

To this end the following acts are and shall remain prohibited at any time and in any place whatsoever with respect to the above-mentioned persons: (a) violence to life and person, in particular murder of all kinds, mutilation, cruel treatment and torture; (b) taking of hostages; (c) outrages upon personal dignity, in particular humiliating and degrading treatment; (d) the passing of sentences and the carrying out of executions without previous judgment pronounced by a regularly constituted court, affording all the judicial guarantees which are recognized as indispensable by civilized peoples.

2. The wounded and sick shall be collected and cared for.

An impartial humanitarian body, such as the International Committee of the Red Cross, may offer its services to the Parties to the conflict.

The Parties to the conflict should further endeavor to bring into force, by means of special agreements, all or part of the other provisions of the present Convention.

The application of the preceding provisions shall not affect the legal status of the Parties to the conflict.

Iran-Iraq War Jonathan C. Randal

Under the cover of realpolitik, studied international indifference to the horrors of the long Iran-Iraq War in the 1980s contributed to the belligerents' sense of impunity by wittingly tolerating massive violations of humanitarian law, war crimes, and even probable genocide. A decade after the fighting stopped, that rankling legacy still poisons relations between Iran and Iraq and has set dangerous precedents for future conflicts.

Such great power accommodation with evil still is hard to stomach, if easily understandable. Enmity between the two Gulf regional powers existed long before Tehran's Islamic firebrands' threats to export their revolution prompted Iraq's preemptive invasion and eventual international fears of Iranian victory. Strained relations between the neighbors stretch back at least to early Islam's split between mainstream Sunni Baghdad and Shia dissidents in

In the decades preceding the war Washington outfitted the Shah of Iran with state-of-the-art weapons, military bases, and technicians and anointed him *de facto* gendarme of the Gulf. The Soviets, with smaller British and French inputs, similarly overarmed Iraq. Cold War rivalries dovetailed neatly with arms sales generating easy hard currency earnings to pay for oil. The Gulf then accounted for two-thirds of "free world" imports of crude.

Yet even for this bloodstained century, the conflict that lasted from September 1980 to July 1988 staked out new ground in horror, including the first widespread use of chemical weapons by a government against its own citizens and a meticulously documented campaign of genocide against Iraqi Kurds.

In this, the most lethal war of the past fifty years, as many as 750,000 Iranian soldiers and perhaps a third that number of Iraqi troops died on the battlefield. The fighting also provided staggering evidence illustrating systematic disregard for what passes for the rules of warfare—and not just by the belligerents.

Iranian women in chadoors practice with pistols in a war little covered by the Western media despite its horrendous casualties. Iran, 1986.

For much of its duration, the conflict was construed in many foreign eyes as a curious throwback to World War I's murderous trench warfare, complicated by ideological zeal indecipherable to those unversed in the Middle East's ancient, bloody, and unforgiving history. Initially the West found the belligerents so equally menacing and unattractive that cynics, personified by former U.S. Secretary of State Henry Kissinger, delighted in both regimes' progressive debilitation.

The "best" outcome was deemed the mutual exhaustion of Ayatollah Ruhollah Khomeini's Iranian Islamic Republic, which was bent on spreading revolution across the Muslim world, and of Saddam Hussein's secular, imitation-Prussian regime in Iraq notorious for bullying its own citizens and the smaller Gulf Arab oil sheikhdoms. This patronizing attitude provided the five permanent members of the United Nations Security Council with ethically

Iranian soldiers celebrate an advance in the Faw peninsula in 1980. By the time the war was finished, approximately one million Iraqis and Iranians had been slaughtered.

questionable justification for inaction despite binding obligations in the face of repeated and manifest violations of international treaties to which Iran and Iraq and, of course, they were signatories.

The International Committee of the Red Cross (ICRC), neutral guarantor of acceptable warfare's rules known as international humanitarian law, was reduced repeatedly to breaking its customary silence to express explicit exasperation with the belligerents' misbehavior and implicit criticism of the great powers' indulgent complicity with such violations.

This moral abdication in the century's last classic international war soon was taken on board by players in the series of internecine conflicts in Rwanda, Somalia, Liberia, Bosnia, and elsewhere that ushered in the immediate aftermath of the Cold War. That planetary struggle was well into its death throes even as Khomeini "drank the poisoned chalice" and in the summer of 1988 finally accepted the Security Council's cease-fire terms that he had spurned the previous year.

But achieving that outcome required the great powers to abandon the initial splendid isolation of their "plague-on-both-your-houses" approach. Forcing the change were unmistakable signs of Iraqi collapse, which prompted them to provide just enough military aid to keep Iran at bay—and Saddam in the fight. Iraq's brief initial success after invading Iran had quickly crumbled in the face of increasingly resolute Iranian resistance paid for in casualties unacceptable by any but a revolutionary regime.

Eventually backed by all the permanent Security Council members except China, a major international exercise in realpolitik was set in motion after Iran drove the Iraqis back across the international border in 1982 and spurned a multibillion-dollar reparation package in exchange for ending hostilities. That international community's pro-Iraq tilt successfully denied Khomeini's dream of an Islamic Republic in Iraq and of spreading his

An Iraqi colonel captured by Iranians, near Khoramshahr, September, 1982. More than ten years after the end of the war, both sides still hold thousands of POWs.

revolution further afield. Involved was crucial military aid, sometimes overt, more often clandestine, ranging from openly "loaned" French Super Etendard fighter-bombers to covert American jamming of Tehran's radar and furnishing of spy-satellite photographs that pinpointed Iranian targets. Even so, Iraq barely outlasted Iran. Far from "behaving," just two years after the war an unchastened Saddam invaded Kuwait.

Creating the stalemate to save Saddam from his own folly was not without terrible human cost. The war's free-wheeling cycle of human rights violations multiplied with ever more deadly innovative twists and turns. These violations were regularly denounced by human rights organizations, but to no avail.

Over the years one side or the other, sometimes both, violated the 1949 Geneva Conventions and Additional Protocols of 1977 prohibiting the targeting of civilians and civilian objectives, forbidding the use of children in combat, and protecting prisoners of war, as well as the 1925 Protocol banning the use of chemical weapons.

211

Countless waves of untrained Iranian boy-soldiers armed only with plastic keys purportedly guaranteeing entry to heaven blew themselves up by the tens of thousands clearing mine fields or died charging into artillery barrages worthy of Verdun or Stalingrad. Iraqi missiles crashed through the night to spread terror among Iranian city dwellers hundreds of miles from the front. Relentless Iraqi and Iranian shelling destroyed each other's cities and towns near the international border.

Particularly troublesome for the ICRC was both sides' penchant for interfering in its usually cut-and-dried procedures. Both Iran and Iraq frustrated the ICRC's tracing of **prisoners of war** and the identification of the missing and dead, thus enormously complicating postwar efforts to sort out who had survived and delaying repatriation.

Iraq repeatedly complained its prisoners of war were "liquidated," kept incommunicado, or, in the case of Shia soldiers, brainwashed and compelled to join the "Badr Brigade's" special turncoat military units organized at Iranian instigation to fight one day for an Islamic Republic in their motherland. The ICRC had trouble with Iran in registering prisoners and persuading Tehran to allow prisoner interviews without witnesses.

Tehran protested that its prisoners in Iraq were prevented from praying together, which Baghdad justified on security grounds. Iraq prevented the ICRC from visiting some twenty thousand Iranians captured starting in 1987.

Even after the fighting ended in 1988, no significant prisoner repatriation took place for two more years despite the cease-fire's provisions for their immediate return and persistent ICRC prodding. (In 1990 Saddam relented to improve relations with Iran as Iraq braced for the U.S.-led coalition to wrest back Kuwait.) When finally some forty thousand men from each side were sent home, the exchanges violated ICRC regulations against such one-for-one prisoner releases.

A decade after the war's last shot was fired, all prisoners were still not back home. But in April 1998 Iran, in a fresh bid to improve relations with the Arab world and break out of two decades of isolation, repatriated some six thousand Iraqi prisoners of war. ICRC officials who visited prisoners of war in Iran reported many of the remaining twelve thousand official detainees looked twenty years older than their actual age. Many had long since joined the Badr Brigade and feared that going home would entail reprisal.

Underpinning Iranian refusal to observe ICRC obligations was not ignorance, as was initially true with Iraq, but the Islamic revolution's rejection of any undertakings by the Shah and his Pahlavi dynasty, which Khomeini had overthrown eighteen months before Iraq started its preemptive war. The ICRC, its rules, regulations, and persistent officials with their claims of objective behavior were all suspect as Western and Christian and disregarded as nonbinding on a revolution burning with its own militantly self-righteous vision of universality.

No such ideological explanation easily springs to mind in trying to understand Saddam's rationale for breaking the taboo against using **chemical weapons**, first against Iranian troops, then against his Kurdish fellow citizens. But his decision was in keeping with his long established penchant for the jugular in punishing anyone who dared cross him. (Gassing Kurds—or the reprisal killing of eight thousand civilian members of Kurdish guerrilla leader Massoud Barzani's tribe in 1983—was all the same to Saddam.) He shrewdly gambled the outside world would tolerate almost anything to stop Khomeini.

After all, during the war Western companies wittingly sold Iraq "dual use" chemicals and equipment for purported "fertilizer" plants, which they knew full well could produce a variety of treaty-banned gases and nerve agents. These weapons still cause problems for UN inspectors now tasked with removing them from Saddam's arsenal. It strains credulity to believe Western governments were not aware of the dangers of such chemicals before Iraq's occupation of Kuwait in 1990.

But it was only then—with pressure on to demonize Saddam and with their own troops exposed to his chemical weapons—that Western governments overcame their amnesia and started denouncing Iraq's use of these proscribed arms. To this day the UN is shielding the Western firms involved. Rolf Ekeus, the former chief UN arms inspector in Iraq, has confirmed privately that the Security Council cut a deal in 1993 with UN inspectors, Baghdad, and the International Atomic Energy Agency not to reveal the companies' identities.

The desire to avoid responsibility is understandable given the damage

Wounded Iranian soldiers waiting for evacuation to hospitals behind the front line, during an Iranian offensive which caused fifty thousand dead and many more wounded in its opening days of April 1992. Shalamche, Iran.

those weapons caused. The most publicized example concerned the Iraqi Kurdish village of Halabjah near the Iranian border. Furious that Kurdish guerrillas allied with Iranian revolutionary guards had captured the town, on March 15, 1988, Saddam had it attacked by waves of war planes.

They dropped mustard gas, a World War I favorite, as well as tabun and sarin, both nerve agents developed by the Nazis but never before deployed, and VX, which Iraq was testing for the first time. At least three thousand Kurdish civilians died.

For once the obscene effects of chemical weapons were graphically recorded. Iranian helicopters ferried in foreign correspondents, television teams, and photographers. Their reports, and especially images of corpses frozen in Pompeii-like poses in Halabjah streets, shocked the world.

Halabjah should not have come as the surprise it did. In November 1983 Tehran lodged the first of several complaints with the UN charging Baghdad with using chemical weapons to stop Iranian human-wave infantry attacks.

Iraq refused a UN proposal to send experts to both belligerents for on-site investigations.

The 1984 UN report dealing solely with findings on Iranian soil agreed that Iraq had used mustard gas and tabun. But without film and photographic illustration it had little impact. The Security Council issued a wishy-washy resolution that refrained from naming Iraq. The council's rotating chairman condemned the use of chemical weapons in a separate, little-noticed declaration issued in his own name. The council scarcely could have done less.

But even the outcry over Halabjah did not stop Iraq from again using chemical weapons against its Kurds (technically not even a violation of the 1925 Geneva Protocol on chemical weapons, whose virtually toothless provisions had not foreseen wartime use by signatory governments against their own citizens). Indeed Halabjah was not an isolated case. Iraqi documents

Unknown soldier: In Iran the long conflict brought back all the horrors of the trench war warfare from World War I.

among millions captured by the Kurds in 1991 establish that in 1987 and 1988 Saddam, in a campaign code-named Al Anfal, used chemical weapons at least sixty times against Kurdish villages.

Iraqi and Kurdish officials agree at least sixty thousand Kurds died in Al Anfal. Saddam continued gassing Kurds even after the 1988 cease-fire. His atrocities against the Kurds were "so grave," noted a UN report, and "of such massive nature that since the Second World War few parallels can be found."

So damning are the Al Anfal documents that human rights lawyers are convinced they constitute a strong case against Saddam for genocide, defined by the UN as the "intent to destroy in whole or in part national, ethnic, racial or religious groups, as such." Human Rights Watch went to enormous effort and expense sifting through 4 million documents and publishing a book marshaling seemingly irrefutable evidence. "It's ridiculous how much there is," remarked a knowledgeable lawyer.

But only governments can bring genocide charges. So far no State—or coalition of States—has volunteered to do so, apparently for fear of retaliation or of compromising chances for lucrative contracts with Baghdad. The United States has blown hot and cold, convincing some human rights lawyers that Washington only evinces interest when it exhausts other arguments against Saddam.

Nothing so illustrates the impunity displayed by Saddam as the assessment of his cousin Ali Hassan Majid, who commanded the Al Anfal operations. In 1989 the man Kurds call Ali Chemical justified his repeated use of poison gas by boasting: "Who is going to say anything? The international community? Fuck them!"

So far the only positive result to emerge from the Iran-Iraq War's massive violations of human rights law is the revised Chemical Weapons Convention signed in Paris in January 1993. It outlawed use of such weapons, their storage, development, manufacture, transfer, sale, or gift and ordered destruction of existing stocks.

However laudable, the convention came too late for those gassed to death or Halabjah's abandoned and forgotten survivors. British geneticist Christine Gosden visited Halabjah ten years after the attack. Forensic evidence she gathered showed survivors suffering from horrifying genetic defects, skin lesions, respiratory ailments, unusually high rates of aggressive cancers and miscarriages, birth deformities such as cleft palates and harelips, lung disorders, and heart disease.

(See **poisonous weapons**.)

I

Irregulars

By Ewen Allison

The term *irregular* is often used to describe a combatant who belongs to a paramilitary group, militia, volunteer corps, organized resistance movement, or rebel force. Irregulars are frequently part-time combatants who do not wear a uniform or carry arms openly when on active duty. However, irregulars can also be part of a country's armed forces, as they are in Switzerland, where the army is composed almost entirely of uniformed militias.

Irregular is not necessarily a synonym for **guerrilla**. Guerrillas are fighters distinguished by their use of tactics such as ambushes, sniping, and sabotage. Irregulars might not use such tactics at all, while regular armed forces often do.

In internal armed conflicts, the most important characteristic of irregulars is that they prefer to blend into the civilian population and thus, often, endanger civilians as government forces will destroy or otherwise punish entire villages or towns in an attempt to neutralize rebel irregulars.

Partisan is commonly used to describe irregulars who resist the occupation of a country by a foreign power—for example, French Maquis in World War II. Partisans might operate inside or outside occupied territory.

In international conflicts, irregulars may be considered lawful combatants, entitled to prisoner of war status if they adhere to certain standards. These include that they: distinguish themselves from the civilian population (i.e., look like combatants); carry weapons openly during engagements or deployments; be commanded by a responsible officer and, generally, be expected to comply with international rules relating to armed conflict. Failure to meet these standards can lead to trial and punishment for hostile acts. (**Mercenaries,** within the legal definition set forth under the 1977 Additional Protocol I, are not entitled to prisoner of war status.)

In internal armed conflict there is no prisoner of war status and the government is free to try its armed enemies for treason or other violent acts. Each trial, however, must be in a "regularly constituted court, affording all the judicial guarantees which are recognized as indispensible by civilized people" according to Article 3 common to the Geneva Conventions of 1949.

Journalists, Protection of

By William A. Orme, Jr.

In the vicious civil conflicts and undeclared cross-border battles that are increasingly the norm for full-blown shooting wars, few combatants are aware that the Geneva Conventions afford special protections to journalists. It might be prudent for a reporter in such situations to keep a Kevlar-coated copy of the Geneva Conventions in the left breast pocket since the protective powers of international treaties are based on the assumption that the combatants will observe international law.

The laws of armed conflict stipulate that journalists play a unique and essential role in wartime. A century ago war correspondents ran the risk of being shot as spies. Though this can still happen today—the 1998 killing of an Iranian journalist by Taliban militiamen being just one recent case in point—the executioners at least now face the possibility of internationally sanctioned punishment.

The spirit and the letter of international humanitarian law are clear. When accredited by and accompanying an army, journalists are legally part of that military entourage, whether they see themselves that way or not. This has been the legal practice at least since the early nineteenth century. If captured by opposing forces, they can expect to be treated as prisoners of war. The Geneva Conventions say so quite unambiguously: equating war correspondents with "civilian members of military aircraft crews" and other integral, albeit nonuniformed, participants in the greater military enterprise. Absent evidence of atrocities outside their roles as war correspondents, they are not to be treated as spies.

Journalists are legally entitled to greater autonomy than most other civilian noncombatants: reporters can be detained only for "imperative reasons of security," and even then are entitled to be held with the same legal protections as a prisoner of war, including the right not to respond to interrogation (though notebooks and film may legally be confiscated by military personnel).

The 1949 Geneva Convention regulations were tailored for the accredited uniformed war correspondent, who could be viewed by the enemy as part of the military entourage. Though clearly not a soldier, the correspondent was still performing an officially sanctioned role in an organized military force. To the extent that tradition or prudence dictated by-the-books treatment of noncombatants or prisoners of war, the correspondent presumably benefited.

Those days are largely gone. The fear of being taken prisoner can still be quite real in Iraq or Chechnya or the Afghan highlands, but the potential captors might well not be conversant with international humanitarian law. Being held hostage by guerrilla forces or a renegade pariah regime in the 1990s is a qualitatively different (and usually more frightening) experience than being an Axis or Allied prisoner of war in the 1940s. In the early 1960s many correspondents and combat photographers still wore army-issue fatigues. A decade later the Vietnam press corps stood conspicuously apart from the fighting force in dress, political perspective, and even national loyalties. (Indeed, since the 1977 adoption of Additional Protocol I, journalists are now advised that the protections they are afforded under the Geneva Conventions may not apply if their clothing too closely resembles that of combat personnel.) Article 79 of Protocol I in addition to reiterating the rights of journalists accredited to armed forces provides for an "identity card" issued by a government attesting to their status as a journalist.

The camera of Japanese photographer Taizo Ichinose is preserved as a relic in a family shrine in Kyushu, Japan, 1996. Ichinose escaped injury when he lost this camera in an ambush.

The rights most journalists enjoy in wartime today were won in their respective national political cultures. In the final analysis, field commanders tolerate the presence of the press because of the political power and legal protections the press has acquired in their own local arenas. Some reporters may feel that to demand special protection under international humanitarian law is to invite special regulation under such law. Regardless, the protection is explicitly stated in law. In many instances accreditation comes with the territory: it is the only way to get access to the military transportation needed to cover the conflict, or to the official briefings (where it is often explained that what has just been seen firsthand may not have in fact happened and the real story is what was not seen by reporters).

But journalists roaming around the wilder conflicts of the world are forced to live instead by the Dylan dictum: to live outside the law you must be honest. Never pretend to be what you are not or deny being what you are unless your life depends on it. Carry a camera, but never a gun. And keep that dog-eared copy of the Geneva Conventions in your breast pocket until after the shooting stops.

(See **civilian immunity**; **protected person**.)

J

Journalists in Peril

By Frank Smyth

Three weeks after the Gulf War ended, we entered northern Iraq with Kurdish guerrillas who were fighting Saddam Hussein and traveled 150 miles south to Kirkuk on the front line between rebel and government forces. Though writers working for dailies and network crews had already come to Kirkuk and left, I and two photographers working for weeklies, Alain Buu and Gad Gross, along with our armed Kurdish guide, Bakhtiar Muhammed Abd-al-rahman Askari, elected to stay. We all naively thought Saddam would soon be overthrown.

Everything changed on March 28, just after dawn. Thousands of Kurds—guerrillas and civilians—were still in the city. Incoming artillery and tank shells shook the ground, first claiming the life of a young girl on her bicycle. "This is Saddam Hussein!" yelled one man who knew her. "Mr. Bush must know." Soon several small helicopters broke the sky. They opened up with machine guns, as the guerrillas returned fire with antiaircraft guns. I saw Kurdish guerrillas carrying two surface-to-air missiles. The incoming shells were becoming more accurate, and tanks were closing in on the town. By about noon, the smaller helicopters were joined by four or five helicopter gunships. Glistening like angry hornets, they fired machine guns and unloaded seemingly endless volleys of exploding rockets. The gunships provided crucial air cover for dozens of advancing tanks. Several multiple-rocket launchers dropped a blanket of fire on fleeing guerrillas and civilians.

The four of us took shelter behind a wall of bulldozed earth. My bravado began crumbling like dirt. A tank appeared over a hill. Gad and Bakhtiar ran toward some small houses. Alain and I dove into a ditch. We were separated through the night while Iraqi soldiers camped around us. We heard them talking, walking, peeing—even opening cans of food. I turned off the alarm on my watch and tried to control my breathing. When I get nervous, I take quick, short breaths. But Alain's blood pressure dropped from the stress, and he soon began sleeping. I woke him to stop his snoring. The temperature, too, dropped in the night. We couldn't allow our teeth to chatter, either.

Embracing each other like lovers to stay warm, we stayed in the ditch for over eighteen hours. I watched an ant colony at work below, and envied each bird passing above. Shortly after sunrise, Alain and I heard a commotion coming from the houses. It sounded like some people had been captured. Within minutes, we heard one short automatic rifle burst. It was followed by a scream, and then broken by another burst that ended in silence. A blanket of terror descended upon us. We both feared that it had been Gad screaming.

I began to silently panic, as my imagination went back in time. I felt like a small boy who had agreed to play a deadly game of hide-and-seek with some of the bigger kids in the neighborhood. But they had severe rules, which I had foolishly agreed to in advance: "If we catch you, we kill you." I never thought I'd get caught. Now . . . I imagined myself, still as a kid, trying to talk my way out of it, and, according to my own reasoning, failing every time.

From within the ditch, Alain and I looked out in opposite directions, hoping that if we were seen, we might have a chance to surrender. An hour later, Alain jumped up with his hands held high and yelled "Sahafi" (journalist). "What are you doing?" I said, though it was already too late. Alain said that a soldier had seen him. I forced myself up and followed him. Soldiers with raised rifles threatened to kill us. One drew his finger sardonically across his neck. But a military intelligence officer, who seemed to be newly arrived on the scene, intervened. He reassured us that we would not be killed, even as he ripped a pendant of the Virgin Mary off Alain's neck.

He brought us to some other military officers with different uniforms who were army special forces commanders. They told us about Gad. He had "killed himself," said one, because "he had a gun." Another officer showed us Gad's camera bag and press tags, which were stained with blood. We were certain then that Gad and probably Bakhtiar had been summarily executed after being captured. The army commanders said in both English and Arabic that they wanted to kill us, too. But the military intelligence officer insisted that we be transferred to a military intelligence unit for interrogation. He saved us.

We underwent many blindfolded interrogations, and were later brought to Baghdad and imprisoned. During one particularly severe interrogation, I was accused of being a CIA agent, while Alain was later accused of being a French intelligence agent. Though treating us as prisoners of war, Iraq failed to report our captures to the International Committee of the Red Cross. Nevertheless, after eighteen days, on the last night of the Muslim holy period of Ramadan, Saddam released us. But Iraqi authorities kept Gad's camera bag. His remains have yet to be recovered.

Jurisdiction, Universal

By Françoise Hampson

Can an American be tried before American courts for speeding on the roads of France? When considering whether someone can be convicted, it is necessary to consider not only the conduct in question, but also which courts have jurisdiction. The most common basis of jurisdiction is territorial (i.e., the courts of the place where the action took place), but some legal systems, mainly civil law ones, also recognize jurisdiction based on nationality (i.e., French courts can try French citizens in some cases for criminal conduct outside France). International law also permits a State, in some circumstances, to exercise criminal jurisdiction on other bases. In some cases, the courts of any State may try an individual. This is called universal jurisdiction.

In October 1998, Gen. August Pinochet, the former Chilean dictator, was arrested by British authorities at the request of a Spanish prosecutor. This case may potentially say important things about the scope of universal jurisdiction, but at this writing, the outcome is unknown.

Only the most serious offences are, in international law, subject to universal jurisdiction. A State has primary jurisdiction over these offenses, but whether or not an individual will be tried depends, among other things, on whether the *domestic* law of the State allows for trial of such crimes. The most serious offenses subject to universal jurisdiction include serious violations of the laws and customs of war, **crimes against humanity,** and, since the ruling of the International Criminal Tribunal for the Former Yugoslavia (ICTY) in the case of Tadic, violations of Article 3 common to the four Geneva Conventions of 1949, applicable in noninternational armed conflicts.

In addition, certain treaties provide for universal jurisdiction, such as the UN Convention against Torture. Surprisingly, the **Genocide** Convention is not in this list, though any State may assert universal jurisdiction. It provides for territorial jurisdiction or jurisdiction to be exercised by an international penal tribunal. Generally, treaties which provide for universal jurisdiction require the State to try the suspect or to extradite him/her to stand trial elsewhere.

One category of behavior is subject to a special regime. Grave breaches of the Geneva Conventions 1949 and Additional Protocol I of 1977 are defined within the treaties and can only occur in international armed conflicts. Every State bound by the treaties is under the legal obligation to search for and prosecute those in their territory suspected of having committed grave breaches, irrespective of the nationality of the suspect or victim or the place where the act was allegedly committed. The State may hand the suspect over to another State or an international tribunal for trial. Where domestic law does not allow for the exercise of universal jurisdiction, a State must introduce the necessary domestic legislative provisions before it can do so. That is not enough; the State must actually exercise jurisdiction, unless it hands over the suspect to another country or international tribunal.

(See **civilian immunity; international vs. internal armed conflict; protected persons.**)

Jus ad Bellum/Jus in Bello

By Karma Nabulsi

Under international law, there are two distinct ways of looking at war—the reasons you fight and how you fight. In theory, it is possible to break all the rules while fighting a just war or to be engaged in an unjust war while adhering to the laws of armed conflict. For this reason, the two branches of law are completely independent of one another.

Jus (or *ius*) *ad bellum* is the title given to the branch of law that defines the legitimate reasons a state may engage in war and focuses on certain criteria that render a war *just*. The principal modern legal source of *jus ad bellum* derives from the Charter of the United Nations, which declares in Article 2: "All members shall refrain in their international relations from the threat or the use of force against the territorial integrity or political independence of any state, or in any other manner inconsistent with the purposes of the United Nations"; and in Article 51: "Nothing in the present Charter shall impair the inherent right of individual or collective self-defense if an armed attack occurs against a Member of the United Nations."

Jus in bello, by contrast, is the set of laws that come into effect once a war has begun. Its purpose is to regulate how wars are fought, without prejudice to the reasons of how or why they had begun. So a party engaged in a war that could easily be defined as unjust (for example, Iraq's aggressive invasion of Kuwait in 1990) would still have to adhere to certain rules during the prosecution of the war, as would the side committed to righting the initial injustice. This branch of law relies on customary law, based on recognized practices of war, as well as treaty laws (such as the Hague Regulations of 1899 and 1907), which set out the rules for conduct of hostilities. Other principal documents include the four Geneva Conventions of 1949, which protect war victims—the sick and wounded (First); the shipwrecked (Second); prisoners of war (Third); and civilians in the hands of an adverse party and, to a limited extent, all civilians in the territories of the countries in conflict (Fourth)—and the Additional Protocols of 1977, which define key terms such as *combatants*, contain detailed provisions to protect noncombatants, medical transports, and civil defense, and prohibit practices such as indiscriminate attack.

There is no agreement on what to call *jus in bello* in everyday language. The International Committee of the Red Cross (ICRC) and many scholars, preferring to stress the positive, call it international humanitarian law (IHL) to emphasize their goal of mitigating the excesses of war and protecting civilians and other noncombatants. But military thinkers, backed by other scholars, emphasize that the laws of war are drawn directly from the customs and practices of war itself, and are intended to serve State armies. They commonly use the more traditional rubric, the laws and customs of armed conflict or more simply, the laws of war.

(See **aggression; crimes against peace; just and unjust war; war crimes**.)

Just and Unjust War

By Karma Nabulsi

Doctrines of what constitutes a just war developed out of Roman law, religious encyclicals, military theory and practice, modern political theory and philosophy, as well as international law and jurisprudence. The roots in Western thought can be traced to classical moral, legal, and historical sources and include the scholastic tradition as well as the medieval notions of chivalry and honor. A critical debate in the United States over participation and conduct in the Vietnam War revived just war theory in the West among secular philosophers and Christian thinkers.

The debate was an attempt to determine whether U.S. participation in the war was unjust in origin or in the way it was being fought. Distinctly different but significant notions of just and unjust war arose in Communist theories on the "people's" war against fascism in the 1930s and 1940s, "national liberation" struggles against colonial powers after World War II, and "holy war" in modern Islam, for example, during the Iran-Iraq war. "Jihad" has become a cliché for the struggle of radical Muslim forces against mostly Western powers.

The criteria for engaging in a just war, first summed up by Dutch philosopher Hugo Grotius in the seventeenth century and drawing on older, medieval Catholic theologians, consists of seven elements: (1) that there be a *just cause*; (2) that there is a *right authority* (legitimate sovereign) to initiate the war; (3) a *right intention* on the part of the parties using force; (4) that the resort to force be *proportional*; (5) that force be a *last resort*; (6) that war is undertaken with *peace as its goal* (not for its own sake); (7) and that there be a reasonable *hope of success*.

More recently, the term *just war* has been largely replaced by the term *legitimate use of force*. The principles of just war today are contained in the United Nations Charter, which reaffirms the inadmissability of the acquisition of territory by force. Although conquest was legally prohibited in Europe in the mid-nineteenth century, European powers compensated by engaging in conquests abroad. Within Europe there remained a branch of thought, largely Prussian, which continued to argue that the principle of conquest—might is right—provided ample cause for a just war. This school of thought lost all legitimacy as a result of World War II.

Today, a just war is commonly understood to mean one that is fought in self-defense, as authorized in Article 51 of the UN Charter. This is the one principle that has been clearly defined and consistently emphasized throughout the history of just war theory. The United Nations General Assembly also has set out a comprehensive and strict definition of illegal **aggression** and justified self-defense.

A non-Western, indeed predominantly anti-Western, school of thought on just war thinking—the doctrine of national self-determination—arose out of the struggles for colonial emancipation. The United Nations went some way toward endorsing this doctrine through General Assembly resolutions of the 1960s. The justification for launching military action in the Gulf War, conveyed in the preambles to numerous Security Council resolutions, also relied upon principles of just war as espoused in the UN Charter.
(See **crimes against peace**; **jus ad bellum/jus in bello.**)

Legitimate Military Targets

By Gaby Rado

Six months before it ended, the war in Bosnia was brought home to the foreign television journalists in the form of an enormous rocket that exploded in the courtyard of the Sarajevo television building. Fired from a Bosnian Serb stronghold, the explosive—actually a gravity bomb strapped to rockets—destroyed the offices of two international television agencies as well as the European Broadcasting Union. Most of the wounded were foreign journalists.

Faridoun Hemani, a Canadian friend employed by Worldwide Television News, was filmed walking around with blood pouring down his face, trying to guide others out of the building. "We heard something hit the TV station, but it didn't sound like a big deal. Then suddenly, everything came falling down on us," recalled Margaret Moth, a brave CNN camerawoman who had lost most of her jaw in a sniper assault two years earlier and had gone back to work in Sarajevo.

Unbeknownst to most television reporters, customary law long ago deemed radio and television stations to be **military objectives** as are other military-industrial, military research, infrastructure, communications, and energy targets. The logic is that they can usually be put to military use and are essential for the functioning of any modern military in time of conflict. Journalists *per se* are not a legitimate target, but if they are wounded while visiting or working in a legitimate target, it is considered **collateral damage**.

The definition of a legitimate target is central to the laws of armed conflict. Additional Protocol I, Article 52, defines a legitimate military target as one "which by [its] nature, location, purpose, or use makes an effective contribution to military action and whose total or partial destruction, capture or neutralization, in the circumstances ruling at the time, offers a definite military advantage." Any attack requires that it be justified, in the first place, by

Only the central tower survives the persistent Serb shelling of the offices of Oslobodjene, *an independent Sarajevo newspaper that continued publishing from a bunker underneath the ruins.*

L

military necessity. However, no object may be attacked if damage to civilians and civilian objects would be excessive when compared to that advantage. And if there are doubts whether a normally civilian facility is contributing to military action, the object is presumed to be civilian.

Legitimate military targets include: armed forces and persons who take part in the fighting; positions or installations occupied by armed forces as well as objectives that are directly contested in battle; military installations such as barracks, war ministries, munitions or fuel dumps, storage yards for vehicles, airfields, rocket launch ramps, and naval bases.

Legitimate infrastructure targets include lines and means of communication, command, and control—railway lines, roads, bridges, tunnels, and canals—that are of fundamental military importance.

Legitimate communications targets include broadcasting and television stations, and telephone and telegraph exchanges of fundamental military importance.

Legitimate military-industrial targets include factories producing arms, transport, and communications equipment for the military; metallurgical, engineering, and chemicals industries whose nature or purpose is essentially military; and the storage and transport installations serving such industries.

Legitimate military research targets include experimental research centers for the development of weapons and war matériel.

Legitimate energy targets include installations providing energy mainly for national defense, such as coal and other fuels, and plants producing gas or electricity mainly for military consumption. Attacks on nuclear power stations and hydroelectric dams are generally, but not always, prohibited by the laws of war.

One of the major problems in differentiating legal from illegal or criminal acts of war concerns apparently civilian objectives that may have a use by the military. Most buildings used by civilians in peacetime are protected under international law. Article 52 of Additional Protocol I states, "In case of doubt whether an object which is normally dedicated to civilian purposes, such as a place of worship, a house, or other dwelling or a school, is being used to make an effective contribution to military action, it shall be presumed not to be so used."

It is a **war crime** to attack willfully anything that is not a legitimate military target. On the other hand, incidentally causing damage to a protected person or object is not always a war crime. Although the categories listed above indicate facilities typically regarded in customary law as legitimate targets, attacking forces are still obliged to meet the test of whether predictable harm would be **proportional** to the military advantage. Given that it is a balancing test which must often be performed under condition of imperfect information, commanders customarily have latitude to exercise their judgment. Still, if the harm is "excessive in relation to the concrete and direct military advantage anticipated," it is a war crime.

Levée en Masse

By Karma Nabulsi

The *levée en masse*, or mass uprising, has acquired something of a mythical status in the history of war. The Red Cross representative at the negotiations that produced the Geneva Conventions of 1949 said that they had "practically never occurred"; whereas in countries such as Poland, popular and long-lasting national uprisings took place with great regularity throughout the nineteenth century. Napoleon made increasing use of *leveés* as a means of national defense when the combined armies of the Allies entered French soil. Warsaw in the early days of the Nazi invasion during World War II is a more modern example.

The term *levée en masse*, which first became an international legal term at the Brussels Conference in 1874, must be distinguished under the laws of war from an insurrection by a people against its own national government. The *levée en masse* is defined as taking place against foreign troops either invading or occupying a country, restricting the definition to one involving national self-defense. It refers especially to situations in which the populace spontaneously takes up what weapons it has and, without having time to organize, resists the invasion.

Those who join in a *levée* may under certain circumstances claim the **combatant**'s privilege, that is, the right to fight the enemy. Captors may not prosecute combatants for their hostile acts but must grant them **prisoner of war** status upon capture. (They may be prosecuted, however, for other crimes and for disciplinary infractions.) The privilege is normally reserved for members of a country's armed forces, including partisans.

There are several conditions for obtaining the combatant's privilege. The *levée en masse* may be undertaken against foreign troops only when and where they invade the country. Participants must carry their weapons openly and respect the laws and customs of war. Once territory has become occupied, civilian resisters can be punished by the occupying power.

Even after effective occupation of territory, members of the armed forces who have not surrendered, organized resistance movements, and genuine national liberation movements may resist the occupation, but they must distinguish themselves from the civilian population, or at least carry their weapons openly during attacks and deployments. Any direct involvement by civilians in these hostilities would be unlawful.

Indirect support to the resistance movement, such as providing information or nonmilitary supplies, would be lawful under international law but is likely to contravene security laws passed by the occupying power, in which case those responsible would be liable to trial and punishment or to undergo restrictions on their freedom of movement. Even in that event, they would be entitled to the protection of the Fourth Geneva Convention, and collective action against them would be unlawful.
(See **soldiers, rights of**.)

L

Liberia Mark Huband

Legal protection played absolutely no part in the Liberian conflict. No side considered establishing camps for holding prisoners of war. Instead, all perceived enemies, soldiers and civilians alike, were executed—many after having been tortured. Indeed, from the point of view of simple morality, not to mention international humanitarian law, the Liberian civil war of 1990–1997 was a horror story pure and simple, a conflict in which the law was ignored and every possible act of brutality was committed.

Still, however anarchic events in Liberia seemed to outsiders and however barbarous they were, the country's collapse into civil war during the early months of 1990 was not an unavoidable event, the man-made equivalent of a natural disaster. Instead, it was the culmination of years of political crisis.

For, in reality, Liberia had lost its way long before the rebels led by Charles Taylor launched the war that left their nation in ruins.

Outside actors, particularly the United States, played a central role in the Liberian catastrophe. For the Americans, Liberia had had an historic relationship with them and had been a useful Cold War ally, and they were unwilling to oppose any regime that came to power in the Liberian capital, Monrovia. The decision of the United States to support the 1980 coup of an obscure Liberian army master sergeant, Samuel K. Doe, and, subsequently, to bolster Doe's corrupt and chaotic dictatorship for the decade that it lasted, led ineluctably to the disaster of the civil war. For if the war to overthrow Doe soon became a grotesque story of horror, greed, and atrocity in which every tenet of humanitarian law was broken on a daily basis by all sides, the seeds had been sown in the period of Doe's rule.

Once the fighting began in earnest, though, it was clear that the factions had no intention of even paying lip service to the laws of war, nor to the laws governing the protection of civilians during wartime. All the factions acted with a sense of complete impunity, and they were not wrong in sensing that the outside world cared little about what was going on in

An NPFL fighter carries a wounded comrade to safety. Liberia, 1996.

L

Liberia and certainly would do nothing to prevent the atrocities that were taking place there. At no time, for example, was there any talk, as in Rwanda after the 1994 genocide, of setting up an international tribunal to try the worst offenders. And this impunity gave the slaughter a further momentum.

But the collapse of Liberia's State structures was at the root of the descent into savagery. As the government forces lost territory to the approaching rebel force led by Charles Taylor, its administrative authority rapidly collapsed. The Armed Forces of Liberia (AFL) effectively took over, imposing military rule. But by this time the military itself could no longer be considered a national institution. Doe's tribal allies within the army hierarchy first isolated and then began killing troops from other tribes, whom they assumed to be sympathetic to Taylor's National Patriotic Front of Liberia (NPFL).

No quarter: A militiaman from Charles Taylor's National Patriotic Front shoots a prone, unarmed prisoner. Liberia, 1997.

Before very long, a combination of the AFL's inherent indiscipline and ineffectiveness as a fighting force, and the failure of the government to rally tribes other than Doe's Krahn to its side, transformed the government army into just one more warring faction. This loss of legitimacy was itself a major factor in furthering the violence, since AFL soldiers came to regard the war as a fight for personal survival. The burning of villages and the slaughter of their inhabitants came to characterize the AFL's strategy. And as rebel forces drew closer to Monrovia, the AFL unleashed a reign of terror on the capital. Civilian disappearances became commonplace, and bodies began to pile up in the streets.

Predictably, it was civilians from tribes associated with the NPFL who were the most vulnerable. One of the worst of these massacres occurred in Monrovia's St. Peter's Church on July 29, 1990. A survivor recounted what had happened: "The soldiers shot the door open, and took all the food they could see inside, and they killed the woman who had the key to the [church's] warehouse, after raping her. Guards stood at the gate and we stayed inside. Nobody could leave, and then it got dark, and the soldiers came back the same night. . . . There were around 200 [AFL] soldiers who came in. And they began cutting a boy with a knife, and they cut and cut everybody with their knives and machetes."

The night of terror left six hundred people dead. Neither senior AFL officers nor government officials ever denied responsibility. The church was unprotected and had a large Red Cross flag on its gate. The leader of the massacre, Michael Tilly, had committed numerous acts of grotesque violence before and enjoyed the protection of individuals within the AFL and the government.

Obviously, such attacks on civilians by troops under the command of a government are totally prohibited by international law. Additional Protocol II to the Geneva Conventions imposes on military units the obligation to pro-

Nigerian members of the West African peacekeeping force protect frightened civilians. Monrovia, Liberia, 1997.

tect civilians, and to distinguish in their operations between combatants and civilians. Noncombatants are **protected persons** in civil wars as they are in wars between States.

This does not mean there was no purpose to massacres like the one perpetrated at St. Peter's Church. The AFL's victimization and murders of civilians was ostensibly meant to discourage recruitment to the NPFL. But pressure of this kind is also illegal under international humanitarian law. The AFL's attacks on what it perceived as "enemy tribes" might be regarded as attempted **genocide** as defined by the 1948 Convention for the Prevention and Punishment of the Crime of Genocide. For although genocide was not the declared aim of the AFL, their attacks on the Gio and Mano tribes arguably amounted to an attempt at extermination of all or part of those peoples.

Predictably, AFL atrocities were matched by those of the NPFL led by Charles Taylor, whose election as president of Liberia in 1997 marked an end to the war, as well as by those of the breakaway Independent National Patriotic Front of Liberia (INPFL), led by Prince Johnson. The direct testimo-

A Krahn catches and stabs a suspected NPFL member.

ny of countless rebel fighters attests to this. As an NPFL soldier named El
McCarthy told me, "I wear a ring and two fetishes on rope around my nec
you are my enemy, the ring will burn me. If somebody is my enemy I will
him on one side. People beg. They say: 'Please don't kill me.' But I don't t
them. I have killed fifty people. I cut off their heads or shot them. They
begged for their lives. But I didn't trust them."

As life in Monrovia became intolerable, and refugees fled into NPFL-c
trolled territory, the sight of fleeing government officials being executed
NPFL checkpoints became almost routine. And it was not only governmen
officials. Numerous NPFL fighters, most of them teenagers, admitted to rc
tinely killing civilians to whom they took a dislike. To talk about the
protections afforded by the Geneva Conventions may seem almost bizarre
the circumstances, but the 1949 Conventions demand protection for civil
and aliens. Yet foreigners, in particular Nigerians, were routinely killed, in

part as a message to the Nigerian government that it should not send a peacekeeping force to end the conflict. The 1992 murder of five American nuns living in rebel territory may also have been intended as a warning.

At one point, Prince Johnson ordered his INPFL fighters to hold forty-eight foreigners hostage, apparently in an effort to draw the world's attention to Liberia. Such hostage taking is specifically prohibited by Article 4 of the 1977 Additional Protocol II to the Geneva Conventions. But then, that violation was perhaps the least of Johnson's offenses against international law. It was Johnson who captured and tortured Doe to death in 1990. He had the deposed president's ears cut off and then ate them while the entire event was captured on film. Paradoxically, Johnson's troops were probably less guilty of violence against civilians than the other belligerents.

Such acts of physical mutilation, however, were a hallmark of the Liberian conflict, and ritualistic killings were committed by all sides. That they are prohibited by Common Article 3 of the four Geneva Conventions, of Additional Protocol II, and further contravened the customary principles stated in the the articles of the Brussels Conference of 1874, the Hague Conventions on land warfare of 1899 and 1907, and the Geneva Convention of 1929 governing the treatment of prisoners of war, was always obvious, and, alas, totally irrelevant. Perhaps, if there had been, as in Rwanda in the aftermath of the genocide of 1994, the expectation of a tribunal to try the worst offenders the situation might have been different. But there was not. The result is that, just as they were during the war, the criminals who survived are still very much on the loose, and one of them now occupies the presidential palace in Monrovia.

L

Limited War

By Peter Rowe

A State may make it clear, by what its leaders say or by its actions, including unilateral declarations or bilateral agreements, that it is fighting a limited war. By this it may mean that it wishes to engage its enemy only within certain defined territory, or that it does not seek to persuade any other State to take part in the conflict as an ally, or that it does not intend to use certain weapons at its disposal, or that it intends only to destroy a certain type of military infrastructure, such as radar installations.

The armed conflict between Great Britain and Argentina in 1982 could be described as a limited war in the sense that Britain had the capability to strike at mainland Argentina but chose not to do so. No other State was involved and Britain for its part limited the conflict to the Falkland/Malvinas Islands and a belligerency zone that Britain declared around it, the purpose being to distinguish neutrals from enemy combatants. Had a Royal Navy warship come across an Argentinian warship in the Pacific during the time of the conflict it would probably not have attacked it.

International humanitarian law (IHL) applies as soon as an armed conflict occurs, even if a state of war is not recognized by any of the combatant nations. Thus, once an armed conflict occurs, the intensity or the scope of the conflict is irrelevant. The same obligations are owed by the combatants engaged in it as are owed in any other form of armed conflict between States. It follows that the concept of limited war, like **total war**, although of great importance for understanding the behavior of parties in wartime, is not a legal term within IHL.

In practice, however, a limited war may be intended to be of short duration. As a result it may be considered impracticable to build prisoner of war camps. Prisoners of war may therefore be repatriated during the conflict, an event which took place during the Falkland conflict in 1982. With modern weapon systems a State may have the capacity to strike with very accurate weapons at prime **military objectives** without any other military action being necessary. The capability of the attacked State to respond may, in consequence, be nonexistent or very limited, and the object of keeping the conflict limited can be achieved.

In all of these situations, IHL applies.

Mass Graves

By Elizabeth Neuffer

You could smell the mass grave at Cerska long before you could see it.

The sickly, sweet smell of the bodies came wafting through the trees lining the dirt track up to the grave. The killers had chosen their spot well, an obscure rise off a rutted road few needed to travel.

Investigators with the International Criminal Tribunal for the Former Yugoslavia (ICTY) had discovered the grave. And the stench that hovered in the air indicated they were exhuming it, collecting evidence for war crimes cases.

The corpses were dressed in civilian clothes. They had gunshot wounds to the back of their heads. Their decaying hands were bound behind their back. These men and boys, forensic experts at the scene said, had been gunned down in cold blood.

The Cerska grave is one of several exhumed in Bosnia that help explain the fate of approximately seven thousand Bosnian Muslim men and boys from Srebrenica, who disappeared after Bosnian Serb forces overran the UN safe area in July 1995. Bosnian Serb leaders asserted that Srebrenica's men, wielding arms, were killed in combat.

The grave proved otherwise.

Individual and mass graves provide vital evidence to war crimes prosecutions, especially those involving **extrajudicial executions** and targeting of civilians. Forensic experts over the last twenty years have worked to exhume and examine graves in Argentina, Guatemala, El Salvador, Honduras, Ethiopia, Mexico, and Iraqi Kurdistan. Exhumations in Argentina, for example, helped show that many of the thousands of civilians who disappeared during the juntas had been executed; that forensic evidence was presented during the 1985 trial of nine Argentine generals, five of whom were later convicted.

In recent years, forensic teams have exhumed mass graves in Rwanda and the former Yugoslavia, some of the largest graves yet discovered. Evidence from the exhumations will be a key part of upcoming war crimes cases. For example, evidence from graves like Cerska, combined with witness testimony, would be part of the case against former Bosnian Serb leader Radovan Karadzic and army commander Gen. Ratko Mladic. Both men have been charged with **war crimes**, **genocide**, and **crimes against humanity**.

To prove genocide or crimes against humanity in the case of Srebrenica, prosecutors would have to show that Bosnian Muslims were deliberately targeted for mass executions. Forensic evidence will help establish that the dead in a mass grave are Bosnian Muslim civilians and that they were executed.

Mass graves themselves can be a violation of international law. The Third and Fourth Geneva Conventions and Additional Protocol I contain provisions governing the proper burial, identification, and registration of those killed in war. Prisoners of war, for example, must be "honorably buried" in

From top to bottom, victims of the fall of Srebrenica in the mass grave at Pilice Collective Farm; view of the mass grave at Ovcara where the Serbs murdered patients and staff from the hospital in Vukovar; forensic scientists Dr. Clyde Snow and Bill Haglund and their team examine the mass grave at Ovcara.

…aves that bear information about them.

But the right to exhume a mass grave or to halt tampering with a g… s not clear under international law. UN General Assembly resolution 307… dopted in 1973, calls for States to cooperate in war crimes investigatio… rticles 32 and 33 of Additional Protocol I require parties to search for m… ng persons after hostilities end, and otherwise assist in finding out thei… ate. But an individual country does not have to allow suspected mass gr… o be examined.

Not all mass graves contain victims of war crimes or atrocities. Some… ay hold the bodies of hurriedly buried combatants. Witnesses and surviv… ill help identify which grave is which. Even then, the mass grave may n… e obvious.

Experts often comb through a field or forest to find a mass grave. Th… ill look for abrupt changes in vegetation to indicate recent burial activi… r changes in the texture and color of earth. Depressions or mounds are… nother sign digging has recently taken place.

Reporters who come across what they believe to be a mass grave sh… ot interfere with it. Mass graves are often mined or strewn with unexplo… rdinance. Disturbing a grave might also compromise the evidence it con… ains. Do not try to excavate, or collect anything protruding from the gra… nly photograph the grave and mark its location on a map.

Mass graves can be easily tampered with and the evidence they cont… st forever. It is important to exercise judgment about whom is notified… uspected mass grave. Two starting points are the International Committe… he Red Cross (ICRC) and the UN High Commissioner for Human Rights. Th… oston-based Physicans for Human Rights, which sends forensic teams to… xamine graves around the world, is another. Once forensic experts arrive… he scene, they will conduct their search with an archaeologist's precisio… ach part of the human skeleton—some two hundred bones and thirty-tw… eeth—has its tale to tell.

A forensic team will begin by probing the grave, often with a metal … eeking to test its consistency and detect the smell of dead bodies. Once… vestigators have dug down to the level of bodies, they will sift the eart… or shreds of evidence and dust off each body. Bodies are carefully exami… efore being removed. Valuable evidence can include blindfolds, bullets, … onds that will indicate how a victim was killed. Jewelry or papers help w… dentification.

The science of determining the cause of death is complex. An expert … xamining a bullet wound can determine where a person was shot, the ra… f the shooting, and the angle at which the bullet entered—all clues to … hether someone was executed or not. Identification is the next step. … xperts rely on witnesses, who may know who is in which grave. Accurate… ental records help make a match between a body and a missing person. … sting can also be used to help identify victims.

Success varies. In Rwanda, identification is almost impossible, due t… ck of records and the vast size of graves. But experts are optimistic the… ill be able to identify most of the two hundred bodies exhumed from … vcara, Croatia, thanks to a list of who was in the grave. They are less op… istic about the Cerska grave, given how many people have gone missing…

But grieving mothers and wives still hope they will succeed. "Bring … ody to me," said Hatidza Hren, a Bosnian Muslim searching for her husba… I will recognize his bones."

See **disappearances; medico-legal investigations**.)

Medical Experiments on POWs

By Sheldon H. Harris

According to the Hippocratic oath, it is the duty of medical personnel not only to heal the sick and offer comfort to those beyond healing but also to do nothing knowingly harmful to a patient. But beginning in the 1930s and continuing throughout World War II, the Japanese medical profession as a whole, and, most particularly, medical staff attached to the Japanese military routinely committed atrocities, subjecting prisoners of war, noncombatants, and political and common criminals alike to hideous medical experiments.

Although the Imperial government had pledged to treat prisoners of war (POWs) with care and respect, prisoners were treated brutally while medical treatment for sick prisoners was either nonexistent, or, at best, primitive, apathetic, or indifferent. The consequences of this policy of mistreatment are revealed by a comparison of mortality rates in Japanese POW camps with those in Europe. The death rate in Japanese camps was at least 27 percent. In Europe the figure was roughly 4 percent.

Graver still was the decision on the part of the Japanese medical establishment as Japan's army conquered a wide swath of territory in the Pacific and on the mainland of Asia in 1942 to treat POWs and conquered peoples as prime candidates for human experimentation, as well as substitutes for the animals traditionally used for medical training purposes. Captives, both military and civilian, were strapped to gurneys, vivisected without anesthesia, injected with scores of different pathogens, or used in demonstrations of surgery techniques.

In one instance in the Philippines, several prisoners were used to teach neophyte Japanese physicians the art of surgery. A number of healthy males were taken into a field, forced to lie down on a sheet, had masks placed over their noses, and were anesthetized. The victims were then cut open as the senior surgeon demonstrated "proper" techniques to his students. When the lesson was over, one of the surgeons would shoot the patients, since they were no longer useful for teaching purposes.

In another incident in China in 1942, a senior surgeon conducted an "operation exercise" for the benefit of the young doctors and other medical personnel attached to his unit. This surgeon injected an anesthetic into the lumbar region of a healthy patient. When one of the observers questioned the surgeon as to whether he was going to disinfect the needle he was using for the injection, the surgeon replied, "What are you talking about? We are going to kill him."

Captured American airmen were frequently subjected to vivisection experiments. In July of 1944 on Dublon Island in the South Pacific, a surgeon used American POWs for a particularly ghastly experiment. Eight POWs were subjected to tests in which tourniquets were applied to their arms and legs for periods up to seven and eight hours. Two of the men died from shock when the tourniquets were removed. They were then dissected and their body parts were tested for various maladies. Their skulls were saved as souvenirs by the principal surgeon. In another episode in May and June of 1945, eight American airmen were vivisected at Kyushu Imperial University, one of Japan's most prestigious medical schools. Lungs were removed from two of the prisoners. Other victims had their hearts, livers, and stomachs removed. Still others, their brains and gall bladders. Of course, none of the eight survived.

These are only a few examples from what was a systematic pattern of medical atrocities. From 1942 until Japan's surrender in mid-August of 1945, Japanese physicians and support staff performed hundreds of similar experiments. Many hundreds, if not thousands, of test subjects died. But few of the perpetrators were ever brought to justice, and many enjoyed distinguished careers in postwar democratic Japan.

No Japanese government has ever acknowledged the guilt of these physicians, although the laws of armed conflict completely prohibit such crimes and did so during World War II, even before the passage of the 1949 Geneva Conventions. The 1906 Hague Convention, which Japan had ratified before hostilities broke out, provides that "officers, soldiers, and other persons officially attached to armies, who are sick or wounded, shall be respected and cared for, without distinction of nationality, by the belligerent in whose power they are."

At the Nuremberg Tribunals following World War II, medical experiments were declared a crime against humanity. The Geneva Conventions of 1949 defined medical experiments on POWs and protected persons—that is, civilians under the control of an occupying force—as a grave breach, and the 1998 Rome Statute of the International Criminal Court stated that medical experiments are war crimes, whether they occur in an international armed conflict or an internal one. It defined the crime as: "Subjecting persons who are in the power of an adverse party to physical mutilation or to medical or scientific experiments of any kind which are neither justified by the medical, dental or hospital treatment of the person concerned nor carried out in his or her interest, and which cause death to or seriously endanger the health of such person or persons."

(See **biological experiments**.)

Medical Transports

By Michael Ignatieff

When is a helicopter an ambulance and when is it a gunship? The line is sometimes not as clear as it seems.

The Russian-built Mi-17 helicopter shuttling through the ground-fire above Freetown in 1997 made up to fifteen sorties a day. Sometimes it was airlifting troops, ammunition, fuel, and food to the Nigerian troops who were dislodging Sierra Leone's military junta and reinstating Tejan Kabbah, the country's elected president. But sometimes, it was also carrying doctors and medics, plus "casvacs"—casualty evacuations. It came under continuous fire. Is firing on a casvac a violation of the Geneva Conventions? If the Mi-17 had been downed and the casualties killed, would that constitute a violation of international humanitarian law (IHL)?

According to the Geneva Conventions, the mere fact that transports are carrying casualties does not entitle them to protection. It all depends whether the helicopter carries a clear **Red Cross** or **Red Crescent emblem** and whether, when flying over enemy territory, the pilots file a flight plan beforehand with the combatants and keep to the altitudes, departure, and arrival times stipulated on the plan. If these conditions are not followed, or if the chopper is used for hostile purposes, it is a legitimate target, whether or not there are wounded on board.

It's not hard to see why. How are ground troops supposed to tell the difference between the Mi-17's resupply and its casvac sorties? In the Sierra Leone case, the Mi-17 didn't carry a Red Cross marking. In any case, if it had done so, it would have contravened the provisions of the Geneva Conventions outlawing the use of aircraft for the transport of weapons and matériel.

Detailed rules applying to aircraft are spelled out in Articles 24 to 31 of the 1977 Additional Protocol I on International Armed Conflict. This prohibits the use of medical aircraft to gain any military advantage over an adverse party and allows the adverse party to the conflict to force the plane to land for inspection. If the aircraft is in conformity with the rules, it should fly on "without delay." In the event of a violation, it may be seized, although the sick, the wounded, and medical or religious personnel among its occupants are to be treated as protected persons. Medical air transports are allowed only to carry light weapons for self-defense as well as the small arms and ammunition of the sick or wounded. They cannot be used to collect or transmit intelligence data or carry equipment for such purposes or even to conduct searches except by prior permission.

The rules applying to ambulances or other ground vehicles are straightforward. Like **medical personnel**, they "may in no circumstances be attacked," but must be "respected and protected," according to Articles 35 and 19 of the First Geneva Convention of 1949. They also should be marked with the Red Cross or Red Crescent emblem. They are subject to inspection and lose their protection, subject to a prior warning and a reasonable time limit, if they are used to commit acts harmful to the enemy that are outside their humanitarian duties.

Whether the niceties of the convention *can* apply in messy cases like Sierra Leone is another question. The convention implies that States, military

M

hierarchies, and chains of command have clear lines of responsibility. None of these were present in Sierra Leone. The Mi-17 wasn't owned by a State, but by a private British company—Sandline International—providing **mercenary** aid, on a cash basis, to President Kabbah, with the British government allowing it to be refueled and serviced on British warships in Freetown's harbor, while hiding behind official denials of involvement.

Sierra Leone belongs to a family of ethnic conflicts where the Geneva Conventions are honored more in the breach than in the observance. Even when medical transports *are* clearly marked with a Red Cross and are obviously carrying only casualties and medical personnel, they are often attacked. The worst recent case was in Rwanda in 1994, during the genocide, when gangs pulled victims out of Red Cross ambulances and finished them off.

Journalists traveling in Red Cross ambulances, hospital ships, and medevac helicopters cannot be sure that they will be protected. In theory, Additional Protocol I, Article 79, requires that journalists be treated as civilians. In theory, journalists can hitch a ride in Red Cross and ICRC vehicles, providing, of course, they do not carry weapons, and they are prepared to sign an insurance waiver. In practice, nonmedical personnel often attract suspicion at inspections and checkpoints. Are they spies? Are they military personnel in disguise? Military inspection of Red Cross transports is allowed and the presence of nonmedical personnel can be used as an excuse to impound, seize, or attack. Indeed, the presence of anyone other than the sick, the wounded, or the medical or religious personnel tending them is prohibited on medical aircraft. The rule of thumb is to get authorization on paper from the ICRC or from local combatants to travel. Also remember the insurance waiver. Anyone who climbs on board their Land Cruiser should make sure someone back home has arranged insurance coverage—if they can find a company willing to write a policy!

Medical Personnel

By Eric Stover

International Humanitarian Law specifically prohibits military attacks on medical personnel and units. The Fourth Geneva Convention specifies in Article 20 that "Persons regularly and solely engaged in the operation and administration of civilian hospitals . . . shall be respected and protected." Other articles forbid the destruction, closure (whether temporary or permanent), or knowing interruption of the supply of food, water, medicines, or electricity to civilian hospitals and clinics. Article 19 notes that protection of civilian hospitals and mobile or permanent units may be forfeited if "they are used to commit, outside their humanitarian duties, acts harmful to the enemy."

Physicians and other health workers remain protected under IHL so long as they identify themselves as medical personnel; respect principles of medical ethics, including medical confidentiality; provide care to all victims on the basis of need, without discrimination of any kind; and do not bear arms, with the exception of light weapons for self-defense. A physician or health worker who undertakes nonmedical functions during an armed conflict cannot claim the protection of the rules of war. Dr. Che Guevara, in his political and combatant roles in Bolivia during the 1960s, could make no claims to any of the protections defined by medical neutrality. Nor could the Bosnian Serb leader Radovan Karadzic, a psychiatrist.

Medico-Legal Investigations of War Crimes

By David Rohde

As a dozen photographers and reporters anxiously awaited the team's first move, John Gerns, a forensic investigator, calmly hoisted a six-foot long, T-shaped iron rod from a pickup truck. Gerns and a team of investigators from the International Criminal Tribunal for the Former Yugoslavia (ICTY) had finally arrived in a pastoral meadow in Lazete, Bosnia.

Hurem Suljic, a fifty-two-year-old Bosnian Muslim, had told investigators he had narrowly survived the mass execution of hundreds of Bosnian Muslims here by Bosnian Serb soldiers in July 1995. Nine months after the executions allegedly occurred, a kaleidoscope of wildflowers had sprouted above what Suljic said was a **mass grave**.

Standing at the edge of the meadow, Gerns used his body weight to slowly drive the prod into the ground. Pausing a moment to catch his breath, he gently pulled the stake from the earth and did something that baffled many of the journalists. Gerns sniffed the tip of it. The forensic investigator, the journalists were later told, was checking the soil for the smell of decomposing human flesh.

The Lazete exhumation was the final stage of a medico-legal investigation, an inquiry into a death that can be carried out in peacetime or war. In most criminal justice systems, when an individual succumbs to a violent or suspicious or unattended death, a medico-legal investigation is conducted to probe the circumstances surrounding their demise.

The investigation begins with the accumulation of ante- and post-mortem evidence. When it is completed, a legal document is produced, mainly a death certificate that identifies the deceased and, as far as possible, the cause and manner of death.

Medico-legal investigations can also be inquiries into the possible use of torture or chemical weapons. Experts may examine former prisoners or detainees for signs of torture or refugees who have survived chemical weapons attacks.

In Lazete, the deceptively placid meadow presented war crimes investigators with an opportunity to triangulate different types of evidence—in this case, to prove whether or not the commander of the Bosnian Serb Army was responsible for a mass execution.

Hurem Suljic, who survived the massacre by hiding under the body of a fellow prisoner, had given investigators a sworn statement that he had witnessed Bosnian Serb Army commander Gen. Ratko Mladic overseeing the Lazete executions. Investigators found landmarks near the meadow, such as a school and railroad tracks, that matched Suljic's statement. But investigators needed to find bodies and determine the victims' cause of death to corroborate his account.

William Haglund, an American forensic anthropologist, led the team that day. The investigators, as with most peacetime medical inquiries, included experts from various disciplines such as pathology, radiology, anthropology, archaeology, and odontology.

As the exhumation began, journalists quickly grew tired of its slow, painstaking pace. Investigators first mapped out the meadow and photographed it before digging. Whenever a bullet casing, bone, or body was found it was carefully labeled, photographed, and placed in a plastic bag. Just as in a civilian murder investigation, evidence, no matter how overwhelming, can be thrown out or discredited in court if collected improperly.

Investigators, if they are conducting a proper inquiry, should follow the "Manual on the Effective Prevention and Investigation of Extra-Legal, Arbitrary and Summary Executions," also known as the "Minnesota Protocol," adopted by the UN in 1992. The manual details how every step of a medicolegal investigation, from gathering antemortem evidence, such as medical records and X-rays, to conducting autopsies, should be carried out.

The findings in Lazete and other mass graves in the hills surrounding Srbrenica proved damning. One hundred and sixty-four bodies were exhumed from the graves. Many of the victims had their hands tied behind their backs

M

The clothes of a murdered Bosnian from Srebrenica laid out in the temporary morgue in Kalesija. Bosnia, 1996.

and wore blindfolds. Religious artifacts and other objects found on their bodies indicated they were Bosnian Muslims. By late 1997, one of the bodies had been identified based on DNA analysis as one of the men who had fled Srbrenica in the summer of 1995.

Suljic's account had been corroborated, but the most chilling piece of evidence was a snapshot found in the shirt pocket of one of the victims. A smiling woman, apparently the victim's wife or girlfriend, stared out from the tattered photo. A bullet had torn through the center of it.

Mercenaries

By Elizabeth Rubin

Colonel Roelf was an Afrikaner who as a soldier and trained assassin spent his adult life suppressing black African liberation movements for the apartheid-era South African defense forces. Yet when I met him in the spring of 1996 in Sierra Leone, the black African civilians whose homes he had liberated in the midst of a brutal civil war said they regarded him as their savior.

Roelf was in Sierra Leone with Executive Outcomes (EO), a private mercenary army composed of former South African soldiers, which had been hired by the government to end the war. "We want to help African countries to neutralize their rebel wars and not depend on the UN to solve their problems," Roelf told me one afternoon in the remote diamond region where he and his fellow mercenaries had set up their hilltop military base. "We are something like the UN of Africa, only with a smaller budget." When some Sierra Leonian women stopped by to request protection for a soccer game down by the river because rebels were still roaming the bush, Roelf promised to help. "I am the ombudsman here," he said. Roelf was in fact more of an independent marshal hoping to enlarge his bank account with diamonds. And he was clearly attempting to dress up his mercenary operation with the language of international peacekeeping. But the village chiefs didn't care whether Roelf was a mercenary, an Afrikaner, a UN peacekeeper, or what, so long as he continued to protect the people with his soldiers and helicopter gunships.

Between 1991 and 1995 Sierra Leone descended into a state of violent anarchy with both rebels and renegade government soldiers waging a war of terror against civilians—torching villages, hacking people to death, or chopping off their hands, feet, and genitals. The international community had little inclination to get involved. The United Nations had seen enough humiliation with Somalis dragging dead American peacekeepers through the streets of Mogadishu, the Bosnian Serb Army taking United Nations peacekeepers hostage, and Rwandan *genocidaires* killing Belgian blue helmets. So the young Sierra Leonian military president turned to the international market and hired Executive Outcomes. They agreed to destroy the rebels and restore law and order in return for 15 million dollars and diamond mining concessions. Within a year EO stabilized the country enough for the population to line up for its first presidential elections in twenty-eight years.

EO belongs to the burgeoning industry of private security companies that have entered the theater of war in the last decade offering to do what the United Nations cannot—take sides, deploy overwhelming force, and fire preemptively for a hefty fee. As Roelf's corporate employer back in South Africa stresses, unlike the mercenaries of yore, the company will only work for "legitimate governments." Nevertheless, EO also fits Additional Prorocol I's definition of mercenaries—any person who is not a national of a party to the conflict and who is promised material compensation in excess of that paid to his employer's armed forces.

International laws concerning the status of mercenaries and the use of them by warring parties are extremely murky due to the changing political atmosphere in which they have been drafted. Mercenarism is perhaps the second-oldest profession. Back in the days of Italian city-states even the Pope contracted *condottieri* to hire outside soldiers for defense. In the seventeenth and eighteenth centuries the Swiss were renowned for their free standing battalions hired out to other European countries. It was not until this century, during the turbulent period of decolonization in Africa, that mercenaries gained notoriety as bloodthirsty dogs of war wreaking havoc with the sovereignty of weak, newly independent African States. Such freelance guns-for-hire are accountable to no nation-state and no international laws. They will work for the highest bidder regardless of the cause and are rightly regarded as destabilizing agents. After all, they have no stake in the country's future and as long as war continues, so do their salaries.

So, in 1968, the United Nations General Assembly and the Organization for African Unity established laws against mercenaries, making the use of

Belgian mercernary Marc Goosens, killed in an attack on a Nigerian bunker, is carried away by Ibo soldiers. Biafra, 1968.

them against movements for national liberation and independence punishable as a criminal act. In 1977, the Security Council adopted a resolution condemning the recruitment of mercenaries to overthrow governments of UN member-States. The 1977 Additional Protocol I to the Geneva Conventions, in Article 47, stripped mercenaries of the right to claim combatant or prisoner of war status, thus leaving them vulnerable to trials as common criminals in the offended State. It also left the definition of mercenaries, in the view of many critics, dangerously subjective and partly dependent upon judging a person's reasons for fighting.

The United Nations Charter, however, also declares that nothing shall impair the inherent right of individual or collective self-defense if an armed attack occurs against a UN member. With the proliferation of low-intensity internal conflicts around the globe and the reluctance on the part of member-States to intervene militarily, States and even humanitarian operations may, in the future, rely more on private security companies. So did Sierra Leone violate the laws against the use of mercenaries? Or was it practicing its right to defend against State collapse?

Depending on how you tally the gains for Sierra Leone, there was some truth to Roelf's claims. EO's intervention allowed over 300,000 refugees to return home. To keep the same number of people in squalid refugee camps in neighboring Guinea was costing the international aid community about $60 million a year. Furthermore, the civilians trusted EO much more than they'd ever trust their own unreliable soldiers to keep order. On the other hand, the new civilian government owed millions to a company of South African mercenaries and was wholly dependent upon them to stay in power. As it turns out, the World Bank ordered the bankrupt civilian government to terminate their contract with EO. With no reliable national army or peacekeeping force, the country slid back into violent disarray. A year later, rebels and rapacious government soldiers overthrew the government and ruled by terror. The cycle didn't end there. About eight months later, a British company related to EO launched an assault with a Nigerian force and threw out the junta, causing a tremendous political scandal in London. In the end, where have all these private armies left Sierra Leone? At the time of writing, the weak civilian president is back, the mercenaries are gone, and angry rebels are still cutting off the hands and arms of Sierra Leonians far away from the capital.

At the heart of the debate about mercenaries and security companies is the question of whether it is possible to make a distinction, in legal terms, between good and bad mercenaries. Would Sierra Leone have been better off if EO were employed on a semipermanent basis? What to make of the Serb and Croat soldiers—formerly enemies—who were hired by Zaire's dictator, Mobutu Sese Seko, to stanch a popular revolution? Or the Romanian and South African snipers paid by the Bosnian Serbs to kill Bosnian civilians during the siege of Sarajevo? Perhaps the time has come to modify the laws and the definition of mercenaries. International law experts have suggested that by affording mercenaries the status and hence the rights of **combatants**, they would be more likely to abide by their obligations as combatants. Perhaps. Perhaps not. Others suggest a law requiring security companies to be registered with national governments. This would at least make the companies accountable to a government licensing body, which would require such companies to abide by international laws. Despite the fact that states are likely to use these private companies as covers to engage in unpopular foreign policy, this may be the best possible means of control.

While Executive Outcomes is not the most savory form of crisis intervention, it was hard to argue with the words of Sam Norma, the Sierra Leonian deputy defense minister, who said to me back in April of 1996, "Our people have died, lost their limbs, lost their eyes and their properties for these elections. If we employ a service to protect our hard-won democracy, why should it be viewed negatively?" Given the abominable condition of Sierra Leone today, and the fact that no legitimate force has come to the rescue, perhaps Sierra Leonians could keep their limbs if the international community let them keep their mercenaries.

Military Necessity

By Françoise Hampson

Military necessity is a legal concept used in international humanitarian law (IHL) as part of the legal justification for attacks on **legitimate military targets** that may have adverse, even terrible, consequences for civilians and civilian objects. It means that military forces in planning military actions are permitted to take into account the practical requirements of a military situation at any given moment and the imperatives of winning. The concept of military necessity acknowledges that even under the laws of war, winning the war or battle is a legitimate consideration, though it must be put alongside other considerations of IHL.

It would be overly simplistic to say that military necessity gives armed forces a free hand to take action that would otherwise be impermissible, for it is always balanced against other humanitarian requirements of IHL. There are three constraints upon the free exercise of military necessity. First, any attack must be intended and tend toward the military defeat of the enemy; attacks not so intended cannot be justified by military necessity because they would have no military purpose. Second, even an attack aimed at the military weakening of the enemy must not cause harm to civilians or civilian objects that is excessive in relation to the concrete and direct military advantage anticipated. Third, military necessity cannot justify violation of the other rules of IHL.

Moreover, the action in question has to be in furtherance of a military, not a political, goal. This poses obvious problems of characterization. Is persuading the enemy to surrender a military or political goal? Is "persuading" the enemy to surrender by aerial bombardment a military or political goal?

What constitutes a military objective will change during the course of a conflict. As some military objectives are destroyed, the enemy will use other installations for the same purpose, thereby making them military objectives and their attack justifiable under military necessity. There is a similarly variable effect on the determination of **proportionality**. The greater the military advantage anticipated, the larger the amount of **collateral damage**—often civilian casualties—which will be "justified" or "necessary." This flexibility also appears with regard to the prohibition of the use of weapons that cause "superfluous injury or unnecessary suffering." The greater the necessity, the more suffering appears to be justified. Thus, even in the Advisory Opinion on the Legality of the Use of Nuclear Weapons the majority of judges in the International Court of Justice in The Hague left open the possibility that a State might be able to justify its use of **nuclear weapons** where the very survival of the State was under serious threat.

State practice recognizes that judgments about military necessity often require subjective evaluations with incomplete information on the battlefield and imperfect knowledge of where the failure to take action might lead. For this reason, great discretion has always been attached to commanders' judgments, especially those made under battlefield conditions. Rarely, if ever, is the judgement of a field commander in battle—balancing military necessity and advantage—subject to legal challenge, let alone criminal sanction. An exception would be when the method of warfare used by the commander was illegal per se, and therefore not covered by the claim of military necessity.

M

In some cases, there is a presumption that certain actions are unlawful; it was not possible to prohibit them in absolute terms but they are unlawful unless justified by "imperative military necessity." This qualification of "absolutely necessary" or "for reasons of imperative military necessity" puts a significant burden of proof on those invoking the exception. Examples include the Fourth Geneva Convention, which restricts the internment of protected persons and the transfer or deportation from an area of occupied territory; Additional Protocol I, which would normally prohibit a scorched-earth policy but which allows it in exceptional circumstances in national territory; and Additional Protocol II, which normally prohibits the **internal displacement** of the civilian population.

In the course of hostilities, these rules impose significant restraints on the conduct of law-abiding forces, but those forces may be able lawfully to invoke military necessity where their very survival or the requirements of winning the conflict are at stake.

(See **civilian immunity**; **civilians, illegal targeting of**; **immunity**; **indiscriminate attack**; **military objectives**; **property**; **willfulness**.)

M

Military Objectives

By Hamilton DeSaussure

The term *military objective* is often used to describe the overall plan of a given mission: to take a certain hill, to reach a river, or to bring back hostages. In the more narrow sense, a military objective can refer to a specific target for neutralization or destruction. The laws of war use the term in the latter sense: to identify and attack a locality, facility, or enemy personnel that under the circumstances constitutes a **legitimate military target**. Certain potential objects or individuals clearly are unlawful targets. For example, any direct attack upon the civilian population, or upon any places, localities, or objects used solely for humanitarian, cultural, or religious purposes such as hospitals, churches, mosques, schools, or museums are immune. On the other hand, such **immunity** is lost if they are used or employed for enemy military purposes. There is always a presumption in favor of the immunity. Additional Protocol I to the Geneva Conventions of 1949 provides "in case of doubt whether an object which is normally dedicated to civilian purposes, such as a place of worship, a house or other dwelling or a school, is being used to make an effective contribution to military action, it shall be presumed not to be so used."

At one time, over a century ago, the laws of war set forth a simple rule as to what constituted a military objective. It was a fort or fortified place and adjacent towns assisting in their defense. This definition soon became obsolete at the beginning of the twentieth century as firepower increased the range of destruction and aircraft became an instrument of war that penetrated deep into enemy territory. The concept of the "defended place" was substituted for forts and fortified places at the two Hague Peace Conferences, which codified the laws of armed warfare just prior to World War I. Of course, what constituted a defended place was far more indefinite and variable than what qualified as a fort or fortress. The average person can identify a fort, but when is a town or city defended? Is it defended if it contains no military installations or armed forces and has no strategic military value but remains within the protective zone of an air defense unit which covers hundreds of miles of territory? The term defended place became as outmoded as the so-called fortified place with the advent of World War II and the increased capabilities of aerial and artillery firepower to attack the industrial infrastructure of war.

There was an intergovernmental attempt after World War I to specify what constituted legitimate military objectives by enumerating categories of legitimate targets. The rules proved too restrictive and no belligerent nation cited them as precedent in subsequent conflict. It became easier to list those categories of personnel and places that were not legitimate objects of attack than to define those that were. However, the wholesale destruction and killing wrought by mass aerial bombing in World War II made it imperative to redefine the scope of the military objective. The systematic destruction of urban areas city block by city block and the attack on the morale of the enemy population, which was sanctioned by both Allied and Axis bomber forces, brought forth many outcries for more humane rules of armed conflict. The destruction of the city of Dresden, killing as many as 100,000 civilians in one coordinated attack by British and U.S. bombers in two days in February

1945 reflected the lack of any meaningful definition of the military objective. In the Far East, firebomb attacks alone in the space of a few months killed eighty-four thousand civilians and destroyed many homes and urban facilities. This was before the holocaust of the atom bomb. While these events occurred in a high-intensity, global conflict they demonstrated the urgent need to update and codify the laws of armed conflict and clearly state what could and could not be a legitimate target for hostile attack.

The contemporary rule defining military objects is found in the Additional Protocol I of 1977. Article 52 limits attacks to places, localities, facilities, structures, and "objects which . . . make an effective contribution to military action *and* whose total or partial destruction, capture or neutralization, in the circumstances ruling at the time, offers a definite military advantage." However, the rules provide specific immunity for certain individuals and localities. First, the civilian population must never be the object of attack, making it clear that morale or terror-bombing tactics are clearly a war crime today. Civilian objects used for peaceful purposes, are also protected. But the new rules go further by providing that in cases of doubt whether certain objects normally used for civilian purposes are being used to help the military mission, thereby losing their protection from attack, a presumption shall be made that it is not so used. Second, Protocol I also outlaws **carpet or area bombing** tactics. It provides that it is unlawful to bomb "as a single military objective a number of clearly separated and distinct military objectives located in a city, town, village, or other area containing a similar concentration of civilians or civilian objects." This is a useful and humane rule that eliminates the territorial or mass-bombing attacks so frequently resorted to in World War II, and to a lesser degree in the Vietnam conflict.

The enormous fire-raising attacks by U.S. forces over large urban areas in Japan in 1945 and the devastation wreaked city by city in Europe throughout World War II would be regarded today as flagrant violations of the modern rules and clearly prohibited by the Additional Protocols regardless of the nature or intensity of the conflict. Many contemporary writers of the laws of war consider that the size and scope of the conflict affect the scope of the military objective—that is, as nations devote more of their resources to the war effort and become more heavily committed to a successful conclusion, economic activities such as transportation, supply, and communications normally used only for civilian purposes may become legitimate targets. This is true but still would never today justify expansion of the legitimate target to include the civilian population or civilian areas as such.

Third, Protocol I also provides that any loss of civilian life incidental to the attack on legitimate military targets must be reduced to what is absolutely necessary to accomplish the mission. It would be indiscriminate and unlawful to cause civilian casualties that are excessive under the circumstances. The military target itself always must be identified and individually singled out for attack within the limits of available technology and weapons. Precision guided munitions (PGMs) were used in successful Vietnam air campaigns, such as Linebacker I and II, and made a critical impact on the United States's successful prosecution in Operation Desert Storm. Where there is a high concentration of civilians, it is imperative to use PGMs, as opposed to "dumb bombs," when available and subject to military necessity.

Military operations in the Gulf War in 1991 demonstrated the precision with which military targets could be hit without injury or disruption of the civilian population. Tomahawk cruise missiles disabled power plants and missile sites and destroyed military headquarters in Baghdad with minimum loss to civilians and civilian structures. F-117 stealth fighters and F-111 fighter-bombers were able to "thread" laser land-guided bombs through areas as small as doorways and air vents with surgical accuracy. The introduction of PGMs and high technology systems for spotting targets make it even more necessary to isolate the target from the civilian population and dwellings. One air force writer has pointed out that while it would often take forty-five hundred sorties dropping nine thousand gravity bombs (presumably weighing about two thousand pounds each) to destroy a target in 1940–1945, one F-117 on one sortie could take out a precision target with the use of a PGM in the Gulf War. The circular error probable (CEP) or range of the possible hit is now measured in feet, rather than in miles.

Of course PGMs are expensive, not always available for certain missions even to the technologically superior force, and often should be conserved for a later phase of the battle. However the operational decisions on their use cannot obscure the fact that state-of-the-art military combat has forever changed what and how much civilian loss is permissible. An operational decision to use gravity-driven weapons when more precise munitions are available can make the attack excessive and unlawful if civilians are killed who would have been spared with the use of more accurate weapons.

Therefore, the loss of civilians, even deliberately located in and around a military target must clearly be shown to be absolutely necessary. Additional Protocol I specifically stipulates that feasible precautions in minimizing civilian loss includes the choice of weapons as well as the means and methods of attack. For example, bombing a military headquarters facility in a densely populated city would never justify the use of unguided bombs if PGMs were available to the striking force and if it appears that innocent civilians within the vicinity would be injured or killed. However, the defending force cannot deliberately use civilians as a shield for their own military operations, such as moving them into a critical command and control center. An example of this principle is Iraq's use of the Amirya bomb shelter during the **Gulf War**. The United States attacked it, killing between two hundred and four hundred civilians, causing some to allege a violation of the laws of war. The fact that civilians are used as a shield does not cause them to lose their normal protection. This means that the attacking forces should nonetheless make particular efforts to avoid or at least minimize their injury or death.

In armed conflicts between two States where only one armed force has high-technology weapons systems the humanitarian rules do not change. Each force is judged by the capabilities it possesses to defend itself or launch an attack. The high technology State cannot rely on the lack of PGMs by its enemy to justify its own resort to less than its own state-of-the-art weaponry. At the same time, the defending force must use all means available to avoid attacks on, or excessive incidental damage to, the civilians when it launches its own defense or attack.

The military commander planning or executing the attack cannot be the final arbiter of whether the loss of civilian life and property is reasonably proportionate to the attacks military advantage. Only by the independent assessment of nonparticipating entities or organizations can the strict rules for the limitation of unnecessary suffering and destruction be upheld.

In the final analysis, the loss of any civilian life or property as a result of an armed attack, regardless of the level of the war, or the intensity of the particular planned mission, must clearly be shown to have been unavoidable with the use of the most precise weapons available to the attacking force. (See **proportionality; military necessity**.)

M

Mines

By John Ryle

**The use of landmines—both antipersonnel and antitank mines—is
governed, in principle, by Protocol II of the Conventional Weapons
Convention of 1980 (Prohibitions or Restrictions on the Use of Certain
Conventional Weapons That May Be Deemed to Be Excessively Injurious
or to Have Indiscriminate Effects).**

Israeli reinforcements pass a minefield. Sinai, 1973.

The provisions of Protocol II are widely agreed to be vague and unenforce-
able. "Preplanned" minefields, it stipulates, must be recorded and civilians
are to be given warning of remotely delivered mines "unless circumstances
do not permit." Some legal specialists argue that mines are unlawful under
international customary law, which prohibits the use of **weapons** that are by
their nature indiscriminate. Neither customary law nor the Conventional
Weapons Convention have had any perceptible effect in controlling the
growth of mine use, which has become widespread in the post–Cold War era,
particularly in internal conflicts.

In 1997, after a worldwide campaign, a new agreement covering antipersonnel mines was concluded in Ottawa. The Ottawa Treaty, signed by over
125 countries and ratified, as of September 1998, by 41, is due to enter into
force in 1999. It prohibits the production, stockpiling, transfer, and use of
antipersonnel mines. It further obliges States party to it to clear mines they
have laid and to make provisions for victims of mines. But major mine pro-
ducers such as the United States, Russia, China, India, and Pakistan have not
signed the Ottawa convention; it does not cover antitank mines; and non-
State actors—rebels and insurgent groups—cannot be party to it.

NATO and the Geneva Conventions

By Roy Gutman

Ten months after NATO troops took charge of security in Bosnia-Herzegovina under the Dayton peace accords, a reporter for the *Boston Globe* toured northern Bosnia in search of indictees charged by the Hague War Crimes Tribunal.

In the British-controlled northwest sector, the former commander of the notorious Omarska concentration camp was employed as deputy police chief in Omarska, and three other Hague indictees were on the roster as policemen. In Bosanski Samac, in the American sector, an indictee sat down for an interview in his office where he worked as the town's top official. That was October 1996. In the weeks that followed, reporters visiting Foca, southern Bosnia, in the French zone, spotted Bosnian Serbs indicted for systematic rape making the rounds of cafés and bars; others visiting Vitez, central Bosnia, a Dutch-controlled area, sighted Bosnian Croats indicted for massacres of civilians in free circulation.

Moreover, the two top Serb leaders, military commander Ratko Mladic and political leader Radovan Karadzic, traveled freely on roads patrolled by American and French troops. Both were indicted for genocide, the most heinous crime in the lexicon.

The tolerance of impunity by leading world powers illustrates the central problem of the laws of armed conflict: their implementation relies entirely on the will of political leaders. And none of them, starting with the United States, chose in the first nine months of their deployment to risk a life to impose the laws which their predecessors had drafted, signed, and ratified. Subsequently, they arrested at least a half dozen indictees, while allowing Karadzic to go into seclusion and then hiding.

All four of the 1949 Geneva Conventions oblige States to search for and try those suspected of grave breaches, regardless of the suspect's home country or the site of the crime. "Each High Contracting Party shall be under the obligation to search for persons alleged to have committed, or to have ordered to have committed, such grave breaches, and shall bring such persons, regardless of their nationality, before its own courts," or hand them over "to another High Contracting Party concerned." The International Committee of the Red Cross (ICRC) Commentary states that the suspect can be handed over to an international criminal tribunal.

The United States, Britain, and France signed and ratified the conventions, as did every other participant in the U.S.-led "Implementation Force" (IFOR) and later "Stabilization Force" (SFOR). All States are also obliged under UN Security Council resolution 827 to cooperate with the tribunal and "take any measures necessary under their domestic law" to comply with orders or requests for assistance from the tribunal. NATO, however, devised, and later reinterpreted at its convenience, its own rule for troops: IFOR troops will detain war criminals "only when they confront them in the normal course of their assigned mission." When challenged, top NATO authorities said States' obligations under the Geneva Conventions were not their responsibility and might break the consensus underlying the deployment.

Neither NATO, nor SHAPE (the Supreme Headquarters of the Allied Powers in Europe), nor IFOR, as an entity, "is a party to the 1949 Geneva Conventions or Protocol I thereto," Max Johnson, the legal adviser to the supreme allied commander in Europe, wrote Amnesty International in March 1996. He added that IFOR, as a multinational force under the operational command and control of NATO, "should not be equated to a State in terms of international obligations." IFOR, moreover, was "not an army of occupation" that was "free to do anything it pleases." NATO's reluctance to arrest war criminals reflected "the political realities in the region" and the fear that a more aggressive posture "might not achieve consensus" among IFOR's thirty troop-contributors.

It was the same "not my department" attitude of the United Nations. "We go by the mandate. We are not authorized to enforce law and order," Gen. Manfred Eisele, Assistant Secretary-General for Planning in the Department of Peacekeeping Operations, said in a 1998 interview. "The real responsibility for the apprehension of indicted war criminals lies with the local authorities."

By such logic, the deputy chief of police in Omarska should arrest himself.

In a sense, the arrival of NATO in Bosnia to replace the failed UN mission gave the indictees a new lease on freedom. IFOR, under its mandate to separate military forces, effectively prevented either Bosnian political entity from arresting any indictee outside its jurisdiction. Thus NATO, in effect, took on the role of shielding indictees.

At the heart of NATO's stance was the reluctance of the U.S. executive branch to risk the lives of U.S. ground troops. "There are obviously political considerations involved in this issue [of whether IFOR was obliged to arrest]," Judith A. Miller, the Pentagon's general counsel stated in September 1996. But then she went on to reinterpret the Geneva Conventions, ignoring universal **jurisdiction** against grave breaches. "We read these provisions as applying to the territory of the United States, not as a universal obligation or carte blanche to search for alleged war criminals in the sovereign territory of foreign countries," she told the American Bar Association.

The U.S. and NATO attitudes raise profound questions. Amnesty International concluded that Miller's arguments "constitute nothing short of a calculated policy of evasion of legal obligations imposed by international law." Professor Diane Orentlicher of American University noted that according to the logic stated by NATO official Johnson, "any State could violate the Geneva Conventions with impunity merely by joining other countries in a military alliance."

In fact, the legal case is only an excuse. "It's all political decisions dressed up in legal rhetoric," said a knowledgeable Pentagon official. (See **United Nations and the Geneva Conventions**.)

Nuclear Weapons

By Burrus M. Carnahan

For over fifty years, the legality of nuclear weapons has been one of the most emotional and intellectually divisive issues in the laws of war. Eminent experts in international law can be found on both sides of the question.

Those supporting the legality of nuclear weapons argue that such **weapons** can be used in accordance with the laws of war. The United States government, for example, has for thirty years claimed that it recognizes the following legal principles as applying to the use of nuclear weapons: that the right of the parties to a conflict to adopt means of injuring the enemy is not unlimited; that it is prohibited to launch attacks against the civilian population as such; and that distinction must be made at all times between persons taking part in hostilities and members of the civilian population to the effect that the latter be spared as much as possible.

Supporters of nuclear weapons argue that the actual practice of States is a more primary source of international law than theoretical legal principles. They note that the five original nuclear powers (United States, Soviet Union/Russia, United Kingdom, France, and China) have deployed nuclear weapons for decades, and have openly claimed the legal right to use these weapons in self-defense. (In 1998, India and Pakistan also openly claimed the right to nuclear weapons.) It has also been pointed out that the 1968 Treaty on the Non-Proliferation of Nuclear Weapons (the NPT) expressly recognizes the legal right of the five original nuclear powers to possess nuclear weapons. Over 170 countries are parties to the NPT.

Those opposing the legality of these weapons include a number of nongovernmental organizations (NGOs), such as the International Committee of the Red Cross (ICRC), which expressed reservations, as well as some governments. They tend to base their arguments on the general humanitarian principles underlying the laws of war. For opponents, the vast destructive power of nuclear weapons makes a mockery of efforts to protect hospitals,

A photo of the ruins of Hiroshima, signed by men of the Enola Gay's crew: Pilot Colonel Paul Tibbets Jr., Bombardier Major Thomas W Ferebee, and Navigator Captain Theodore J. Van Kirk.

the sick and wounded, civilians, and others as required by these humanitarian principles. Civilians may be spared "as much as possible" in a nuclear war, but in practice, they believe, it will be possible to spare very few. The civilian casualties and environmental damage will inevitably be disproportionate to the value of the military targets that nuclear weapons destroy.

In 1994, several NGOs opposed to the use of nuclear weapons convinced a majority of the United Nations General Assembly to ask the International Court of Justice at The Hague for an advisory opinion on the legality of nuclear weapons and their use. Under the UN Charter, the General Assembly is authorized to request such an opinion from the court on any legal question. (The United States opposed adoption of the resolution but was outvoted.) The court's opinion, delivered on July 8, 1996, illustrates how deeply divided the international legal community is on this issue. The fourteen judges then sitting on the court split evenly on whether nuclear weapons could ever be lawfully used in accordance with the laws of war. In that situation, the president of the court is allowed to cast a second vote to break the tie. By this procedure, the court gave the General Assembly the following ambiguous advice:

> "[T]he threat or use of nuclear weapons would generally be contrary to the rules of international law applicable in armed conflict, and in particular the principles and rules of humanitarian law;

> "However, in view of the current state of international law, and of the elements of fact at its disposal, the Court cannot conclude definitively whether the threat or use of nuclear weapons would be lawful or unlawful in an extreme circumstance of self-defense, in which the very survival of a State would be at stake."

(See **indiscriminate attack; military necessity; proportionality**.)

Occupation of Territory

By Caryle Murphy

I never met Asrar Qabandi, but it's safe to say she shared my shock as we awakened in Kuwait on August 2, 1990, to discover that Iraq had invaded the tiny Gulf emirate under the cover of darkness.

As a correspondent for *The Washington Post*, I set out to report on the chaotic scene unfolding under the sullen, gray skies of early morning. Tanks were rolling by the hotel and a fierce artillery battle was going on just blocks away. Qabandi, meanwhile, set off on a far more daring and dangerous venture.

The thirty-one-year-old Kuwaiti, who had gotten a master's degree in computer science in Colorado, left her father's home, adopted a bogus identity, and joined the Kuwaiti resistance. Using a hidden satellite telephone, she faxed information to exiled Kuwaiti leaders and gave interviews to CNN. She transported guns and money to Kuwaiti fighters, hid Westerners from Iraqi troops, picked up injured fighters in ambulances, and smuggled government documents out of Kuwait. The sixth of ten children, Qabandi was forthright, outspoken, and determined.

But the Iraqis discovered her and in November she was arrested at a checkpoint. For the next two months, she was held at Meshatil agricultural research station, which the Iraqis had turned into a detention and torture center. She was beaten, then chained to a desk for the first seventeen days of her captivity. On January 14, 1991, just three days before the war to free Kuwait began, Qabandi's body was dumped outside her family home. She had four bullets in her stomach and one between her eyes. The right side of her face had been sliced with an ax. Her hands were tied with plastic tubing.

Qabandi's death was murder. It was also a war crime because it violated the 1949 Fourth Geneva Convention which in Section III sets out the rules on the belligerent occupation of a foreign territory. Under the laws of war, territory is considered occupied when a foreign power actually controls it.

Iraq justified its invasion of Kuwait by claiming that it originally belonged to Iraq and then annexed it as its "nineteenth province." No other State accepted that claim. The international community held Iraq to its obligations under the Fourth Geneva Convention as an occupying power, specifically, to respect the rights of **protected persons** under its control.

It is true that in Qabandi's case, the Iraqi government might have tried to cite provisions in Section III that allow occupying powers to arrest and punish resisters. In fact, occupying powers can repeal or suspend local laws where they are a threat to its security or that block implementation of the Fourth Geneva Convention. An occupying power may even institute provisions for maintaining "the orderly government of the territory" and protecting the property and lines of communication of the occupying army or administration. But this right is subject to wide-ranging conditions which state that: an accused has the right to a lawyer and a regular trial, where he or she can present and call witnesses and has the right to appeal the verdict; the occupying power must respect and apply the provisions of local laws which it does not suspend or repeal; while an occupier has the right to bring offenders before its own military courts, those courts must sit in the occupied territory and be nonpolitical. In other words, their aim cannot be political persecution; a death sentence may be imposed only for serious crimes, including espionage and sabotage resulting in death, and only after the court takes into account that an accused, not being a national of the occupying power, has no duty to be loyal to it. If imposed, the death sentence may not be carried out until at least six months after the occupying power has notified an outside government charged with protecting the civilians of the occupied territory.

Apart from these restrictions, the convention specifically prohibits torture, murder, corporal punishments, mutilation, and "any other measures of brutality."

Iraq violated Section III of the convention in other ways as well: Iraq barred the departure of foreign nationals, including Americans, Europeans, Thais, Indians, and Filipinos, among others. The convention says that foreign nationals have the right to leave occupied territory, though the occupying power can object to this when its national interests make it absolutely necessary. Iraq's national interests did not appear to threatened by the departure of foreign nationals from Kuwait; hundreds of Kuwaitis were arrested during the occupation and transferred to prisons in Iraq. In the last days of the occupation, about fifteen hundred men were rounded up and taken to Iraq, presumably as hostages of war. These actions violated several provisions of the conventions that ban the deportation of civilians from the occupied territory, the taking of hostages, and the physical or moral coercion of civilians, particularly to obtain information; Iraq encouraged its citizens to move to Kuwait and settle there. Although this did not occur on a large scale, it violated the conventions, one of whose provisions states that the occupying power shall not transfer its civilian population into occupied territory. Other Iraqi violations of the conventions included the failure to allow Kuwaitis access to humanitarian relief and to the International Committee of the Red Cross facilities for tracking prisoners; the withholding of normal medical care from Kuwaitis in some hospitals; the theft of State and personal property, including the transfer of thousands of automobiles from showrooms and private garages and the plundering of university libraries and scientific laboratories.

Pillage is forbidden by the conventions, yet Iraq destroyed or set ablaze royal palaces, the National Assembly, the Foreign Ministry, some museums, and hundreds of oil wells.

None of the Iraq's violations of Section III on occupied territories described here—all of which appear to meet the legal definition of violations of international humanitarian law—have been judicially addressed by any international tribunal. The Western powers that led the international effort to reverse Iraq's occupation of Kuwait have made no serious effort to prosecute any Iraqi official for these alleged war crimes, in part because they do not have any of these officials in custody or any reasonable expectation for the moment of apprehending them.

Still, the record of these violations of international humanitarian law and war crimes is there in the statements of Kuwaitis taken by journalists, human rights workers, and others. This will not help Asrar Qabandi and the scores of other Kuwaitis who, like her, were illegally executed and deposited on their families' doorsteps. But it ensures that what happened is no longer secret. In Qabandi's case this is especially poignant because her first name, Asrar, means "secrets."

(See **due process**; **unlawful confinement**.)

Paramilitaries

By Christiane Amanpour

In April 1992, Zeljko Raznatovic (a.k.a. "Arkan") arrived with his uniformed militia in the east Bosnian town of Bijeljina to begin a campaign that came to be known as "ethnic cleansing."

The town was practically undefended, and his forces set up roadblocks, arrested civilians, and went house to house seizing others. One witness saw three people get their throats slit at a checkpoint. Another saw a woman shot as she was eating burek, a cheese pastry. When Arkan was done, twenty thousand Muslims had either fled, been transported to camps, or were slaughtered.

Arkan headed a paramilitary group called the Serbian Volunteer Guard, later known as Arkan's Tigers. A paramilitary force is a legal armed formation

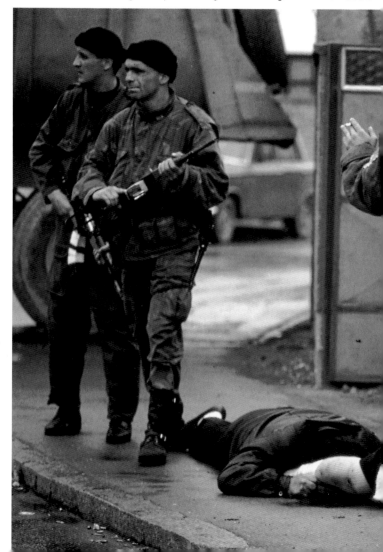

P

that is not integrated into a regular armed force. The term *paramilitary,* which is not a legal term, covers militias, volunteer corps, and even police units taking part in armed conflict. They are lawful **combatants** under international law. This means they must be under responsible command, carry distinctive signs, carry arms openly, and obey the laws and customs of war.

Like other legal combatants, paramilitaries, if fighting in an international conflict and captured, are to receive the protections of the Geneva Conventions accorded to all prisoners of war. They are to be treated decently like anyone else detained because of the conflict, that is, protected from the dangers of war, given all the food and medical care needed, and allowed outside contact through the International Committee of the Red Cross (ICRC). Like any other force, they cannot be tried for the mere act of taking part in hostilities as combatants, but can be interned as POWs until the conflict stops. But paramilitaries, like anyone else, may be tried for war crimes they commit.

Notwithstanding their often legitimate military functions, paramilitaries are routinely deployed by governments to preserve plausible deniability and

One of Arkan's "Tigers" kicks the head of one of two women they have just shot. The women had run to the aid of the dead man also murdered by the paramilitaries.

P

to cloud the issue of command and control. Too often, paramilitaries provide a cover for governments intent on violating international law. They also protect political leaders from direct responsibility for war crimes. But their activities are sometimes controlled under public law, and they often operate in subordination to the regular army.

In the former Yugoslavia, paramilitary forces were the primary agent of criminal violence, murdering unarmed men, women, and children, raping and pillaging, and instituting a campaign of terror with the goal of forcing all non-Serbs out of territories that historically were ethnically mixed. As officially recognized armed formations, they are indisputably subject to international law for their role in alleged war crimes, crimes against humanity, and genocide.

A series of decrees established the role of paramilitary troops as the former Yugoslavia began to disintegrate. In August 1991, Serbia issued a decree regulating the enlistment of volunteers in the territorial defense, a paramilitary formation, which allowed volunteers to take part in maneuvers and training, thereby acquiring arms. In December 1991, the rump Yugoslav government established "volunteer" forces as an adjunct to the Federal Army. Arkan, a soccer promoter and café owner, was a close political associate of Serbian strongman Slobodan Milosevic. Already by that autumn, Arkan, with the help of a recruitment campaign in the state-owned media, had begun rallying unemployed soccer hooligans and criminals and training them at army facilities.

Arkan thus did not operate as a free agent; on more than one occasion he even took command. UN investigators determined that Arkan's forces worked in coordination with the Federal Army in eleven municipalities in Bosnia, and in three of those municipalities, including Bijeljina, Arkan was reported to be the leader of the joint operation to seize cities and expel their native populations. In Zvornik, at the start of April 1992, Arkan issued the ultimatum to surrender and then called in the army to begin the shelling. His trained army of killers and commandos moved into town in Federal Army vehicles. In black woolen caps and black gloves cut off at the fingers, they combed the city with prepared lists and assassinated leading Muslims.

Three years later, Milosevic referred to the volunteers as "bandits and killers." He said in an interview they amounted to "only a couple thousand" troops, and "were totally marginal in that war." The UN Commission of Experts said upward of twenty thousand paramilitary troops took part in the war and played a central role in the mayhem.
(See **civil patrols**; **guerrillas**; **irregulars**.)

Parlementaires

By Ewen Allison

In late July 1995, after pounding the town of Zepa for days with artillery, rockets, and machine guns, Gen. Ratko Mladic, commander of the attacking Bosnian Serb forces, accepted the town's surrender. Mladic had earlier demanded that the town surrender all men of fighting age as prisoners of war, and promised to escort all women, children, and elderly to government lines and safety. Despite the pleas of Zepa's mayor, Mehmed Hajric, NATO and UN forces refused to intervene. Finally, Mayor Hajric took a white flag in hand and went to Mladic to negotiate the surrender of Zepa. He and three companions were seized by the Serbs and imprisoned in the neighboring town of Rogatica. Shortly thereafter the Bosnian forces took Zepa.

After fifteen days of imprisonment, Hajric managed to escape. However, according to the Hague Conventions on Land Warfare of 1899 and 1907, which remain in force and are considered part of conventional international humanitarian law, Hajric enjoyed a special protection. He had the status of parlementaire and could not, without reason, be arrested and detained.

A parlementaire is a person who is authorized by one party to a conflict to speak with another party to the conflict, and who travels under a white flag. Hajric met both requirements—he had the authority to appoint himself as negotiator, and did, in fact, carry a white flag.

Although the rules on parlementaires evolved during earlier centuries and were codified in the Hague Conventions, they apply today. A parlementaire may be accompanied by a flag bearer, an interpreter, and a trumpeter or drummer. The commanding officer to whom a parlementaire is sent is not required to meet him and may take measures to prevent the parlementaire from spying.

Significantly for Hajric's case, a parlementaire may not be directly attacked, and almost always has the right not to be arrested, detained, or executed. A parlementaire loses these rights if he abuses his mission—by spying or committing a hostile act. Even if accused of such abuses, he retains the right to a fair trial and humane treatment.

Hajric, however, had done nothing amiss. His detention was unlawful.

P

Perfidy and Treachery

By David Rohde

They had fled from Srebrenica, the world's first UN-declared civilian safe area, after it had fallen to the Bosnian Serbs on July 11, 1995, and the tales several dozen of these Bosnian Muslim men told were chillingly consistent.

The Dutch UN peacekeepers and the NATO jets the UN Security Council had promised would protect Srebrenica had put up scant resistance. The men knew that they were earmarked for death and they had fled, joining a three-mile-long, single-file column of fifteen thousand mostly unarmed men trying to make their way across thirty miles of enemy territory to reach Bosnian government lines. Over and over again along the line of march, hundreds had been killed in a series of well-planned ambushes by Bosnian Serb forces. After that, Bosnian Serb soldiers wearing stolen UN uniforms and driving stolen UN vehicles announced over megaphones that that they were UN peacekeepers and that they were prepared to oversee the Bosnian Muslims' surrender and guarantee they would not be harmed.

Disoriented and exhausted, many Bosnian Muslims fell for the lie. It was only after they had surrendered that they discovered their fatal mistake. For in surrendering, they were going to their deaths. Those whom the Serbs got their hands on were killed by firing squad.

Srebrenica was the worst massacre in Europe since World War II. The shock at what took place there was so great that to separate war crimes from entirely licit military actions seemed, and in many ways still seems, almost obscene. And yet from the point of view of international humanitarian law, the ambushes the Serbs sprang on the fleeing Bosnians were legal ruses soldiers can employ in wartime. Investigators for the International War Crimes Tribunal for the Former Yugoslavia said the fact that many of those in the retreating column were Bosnian government soldiers made the column a military threat and thus a legitimate target. In legal terms, the Bosnian Serb ambushes did not lull the Bosnian Muslims into a false sense of protection under international law, rather they led them to miscalculate the nature of the threat.

What was entirely criminal was the Bosnian Serbs' use of UN emblems and matériel to lure the fleeing Muslims to surrender—a clear example of a war crime. The prohibition in modern times against what is alternatively called "perfidy" and "treachery" goes back to the American Civil War. But the definitive statement banning the kind of deceptions the Bosnian Serbs engaged in on the roads out of Srebrenica can be found in Articles 37, 38, and 39 of the 1977 Additional Protocol I to the Geneva Conventions.

Article 37 of Protocol I states that "acts inviting the confidence of an adversary to lead him to believe that he is entitled to, or is obliged to accord, protection under the rules of international law applicable in armed conflict, with intent to betray that confidence, shall constitute perfidy." And Article 38 explicitly prohibits the use of "the distinctive emblem of the United Nations, except as authorized by that organization." It also prohibits the "improper use of the distinctive emblems of the **red cross**, **red crescent** or red lion," which, if used perfidiously, is a grave breach.

The difference between perfidy and treachery is the difference between wrongful deception and betrayal. Perfidy is making someone believe a falsehood, while betrayal involves an act that actually harms the person. In international law, treachery and perfidy are used interchangeably.

Other examples of perfidy are feigning to negotiate under a flag of truce or surrender, feigning to be incapacitated by wounds or sickness, and feigning of civilian, noncombatant status. Article 39 prohibits the use of flags, military emblems, insignia, or uniforms of the opposing side at the time of an attack in order to protect or impede military operations.

But the protocol states explicitly that ruses of war are not prohibited. A ruse is an act that is intended to mislead an adversary or to "induce him to act recklessly" but which infringe no rule of armed conflict and do not attempt to gain his confidence by assuring protection under law. Camouflage,

The remains of a Bosnian from Srebrenica who may have surrendered to Serbs treacherously disguised as UN Peacekeepers. Pilice, 1996.

decoys, mock operations, and misinformation are all permitted ruses. An example of a legal ruse was when U.S. forces gathered at sea during the Gulf War to trick Iraq into thinking an amphibious assault was imminent; the attack eventually came by land. Another example might be sending a bomber toward barracks in order to draw air defense away from a shipyard.

In the case of the Muslim men of Srebrenica, the textbook definition of perfidy, which is actually extremely narrow, was all too tragically fulfilled. The Bosnian Muslims who surrendered did so because they were tricked by the Serbs into believing they were in the presence of UN peacekeepers. This was not a ruse, which is legal in warfare, but treachery pure and simple, and it cost thousands of people their lives.

The killing of all those who surrendered, who were ***hors de combat***, is, of course, the gravest breach of all.

Persecutions on Political, Racial, or Religious Grounds

By William Shawcross

Just before Christmas 1975, I drove east from Bangkok a couple of hundred miles to Thailand's border with Cambodia. It was some eight months since the Khmer Rouge Communists had won power in Cambodia, defeating the U.S.-backed government of Gen. Lon Nol.

Since then the Khmer Rouge had expelled all Westerners (and most other foreigners), emptied all the towns of people, and embarked on a radical Maoist experiment to return the country to an autarchic preindustrial age.

The only witnesses of the terror which this plan involved were those refugees who had managed to make it to the Thai border. (Those who

P

reached Vietnam were kept silent by the Vietnamese Communists, still at that stage allied to the Khmer Rouge.)

The refugees I met in a United Nations High Commissioner for Refugees (UNHCR) camp at the border town of Aranyaprathet all had horrible tales to tell. They spoke of Khmer Rouge cadres beating babies to death against trees, of any adult suspected of ties to the old regime being clubbed to death or shot, of starvation and total lack of medical care, of men with glasses being killed because they were "intellectuals." It was absolutely clear to me that these refugees were telling the truth. History shows that refugees usually do. Less clear at that time was why the Khmer Rouge were behaving in such an atrocious way.

The killing continued and even intensified over the next three-and-a-half years. No intervention was attempted to stop it. When U.S. Senator George McGovern proposed a military intervention in the name of protecting humanity, he was mocked.

At the end of 1978, after perhaps 1.5 to 2 million of the 7 million people in Cambodia had died, the Khmer Rouge were overthrown by their

A reclining Buddha overlooks the skeletal remains of murdered Cambodians discovered near a temple by the Vietnamese when they occupied Sisophon in 1980.

P

erstwhile Vietnamese allies. Hanoi installed instead a client Communist regime. Its policies can in no way be compared to those of the Khmer Rouge, but it was a brutal one-party system nonetheless.

In 1980 I visited Cambodia and was taken to a mass grave outside Phnom Penh where victims of the Khmer Rouge terror were buried. These people had been clubbed to death; their hands were still tied, the skulls were bashed in, and some of the bones still had putrid flesh clinging to them.

I had heard about such mass graves since childhood—my father was the chief British prosecutor at Nuremberg and one of my earliest memories is of listening to recordings of his speeches for the prosecution. In one he quoted the terrible atrocities seen at a grave in a place called Dubno. The images of families of all ages herded towards pits where SS men smoking cigarettes were waiting to shoot them made a lifelong impression on me. Obviously I had hoped never to see such sights myself. But in Cambodia I did.

Since the overthrow of the Khmer Rouge no real effort has been made to bring the Khmer Rouge leaders to justice. In summer 1979 the Vietnamese staged a show trial of the leaders in absentia—it was a farce. Since then there has been no successful effort to bring the Khmer Rouge to justice, in part for political reasons.

The question is with what precise crimes they should be charged. Since the majority of their victims were other Cambodians, the Genocide Convention on its face probably does not apply to the majority of these killings, and this has been the predominant view within the international legal community until recently. However, there is *prima facie* evidence that they assaulted in particular such ethnic and religious groups as the Cham, the Vietnamese, and the Buddhist monkhood. These attacks would probably meet the standard in the Genocide Convention of action with an "intent to destroy in whole or in part" these groups.

Crimes against humanity have been linked to armed conflict, whether internal or international, but there is an expanding body of opinion which suggests that under international law this need not always be so and that large-scale killings can constitute crimes against humanity even in the absence of armed conflict. The International Tribunal for the Former Yugoslavia has ruled that crimes against humanity need have no link to armed conflict, and the 1998 Rome Statute of the International Criminal Court makes no reference to a link. A State Department study in 1995 concluded that the Khmer Rouge could be tried for crimes against humanity, and the United States and other governments attempted unsuccessfully in 1998 to bring Pol Pot to trial shortly before his death.

The Khmer Rouge's systematic murder, extermination, unacceptable forced labor, torture, forcible transfers of population—all provide *prima facie* evidence of massive persecutions. A prosecution of the Khmer Rouge for crimes against humanity would likely feature charges of persecution as well as extermination and murder at its center. Nuremberg and subsequent tribunals determined the following acts to constitute elements in persecution: deprivations of the rights of citizenship, to teach, to practice professions, to obtain education, and to marry freely; arrest and confinement, beatings, mutilation, torture, confiscation of property; deportation to ghettos, slave labor, and extermination; plunder and destruction of businesses as a means of terror or related to other violence; deprivation of fair trial rights; a collective fine, seizure of assets, creation of ghettos, forcing the wearing of yellow stars, boycott of businesses, preaching hatred, and incitement to murder and extermination.

The 1998 Rome Statute for the International Criminal Court includes persecution among listed crimes against humanity and defines it as "the intentional and severe deprivation of fundamental rights contrary to international law by reason of the identity of the group or collectivity." The statute proscribes "persecution against any identifiable group or collectivity on political, racial, national, ethnic, cultural, religious, gender, or other grounds that are universally recognized as impermissible under international law, in connection with any other act referred to in this paragraph [on crimes against humanity] or any other crime within the jurisdiction of the court." A crime against humanity, according to the statute, must be committed as part of a "widespread or systematic attack."

Until now there has been no accountability in Cambodia at all. Even though it is almost twenty years since they were overthrown and further abuses have since been committed against the Cambodian people, the crimes of the Khmer Rouge are without parallel. Peace and justice go hand in hand. There is still no real peace in Cambodia; one reason is that a culture of impunity has developed there as a result of the total lack of accountability.

Nuremberg embodied the rhetoric of progress. The judgment of Nuremberg was grasped, in Rebecca West's words, as "a sort of legalistic prayer that the Kingdom of Heaven should be with us."

It was predictable that that prayer would not be fulfilled. But even when the prescriptions laid down at Nuremberg are ignored as cruelly as they have been in the last fifty years, they have not been forgotten. Now, perhaps, with the creation of the international court in Rome, they will be put into practice once again. In Cambodia as well as in Bosnia and Rwanda, the atrocities of the recent past need to be examined.
(See **genocide**.)

P

Pillage

By Thomas Goltz

Pillage has been a feature of nearly every conflict fought since ancient times. But rarely has it been carried out with such ruthless efficiency as in the war between Abkhaz separatists and the new government of Georgia in 1992 and 1993. One reason the conflict exploded into open war was the stunning amount of pillaging carried out by the Mkhedrioni, a quasi-State militia led by warlord Jaba Iouseliani, and the National Guard, commanded by Tengiz Kitovani.

The "White Knights" and National Guard requisitioned entire airplanes to haul their heisted televisions, radios, refrigerators, carpets, and chairs out of the Abkhaz capital of Sukhumi. The Abkhaz paid the Georgians back in spades when they managed to drive not only the Georgia "defense" forces from the territory in late September 1993, but also the vast majority of the Georgian population living in the area. Anything left behind became fair game for seizure—cars, appliances, the contents of kitchen pantries, everything.

Although the practice of pillage in conflict has been prohibited for nearly a century, few countries and cultures are exempt from the charge. The 1907 Hague Convention states: "The pillage of a town or place, even when taken by assault, is prohibited." Prior to the Hague Convention, pillage was widely accepted as justified after assault, to compensate for the risks and losses from that method of conquest. In practice, it was often hard to distinguish between pillage after assault and requisitioning of food from peasants to sustain the army. The advent of new methods of food preservation, including canning in the nineteenth century, meant armies could carry their supplies, allowing limits to be placed on both requisitioning and pillage.

Requisitioning—the taking of "necessities" from a population for the use of an army of occupation—is legal, however. Requisitioning must be ordered by the local commander, must be proportionate to what the area can provide, must take the needs of the population into account, and should be of such a nature as not to require the population to take part in military operations against their own country. Requisitioned goods shall "as far as possible, be paid for in ready money; if not, their receipt shall be acknowledged." However, goods possessed by the enemy's armed forces are "subject to the laws and customs of war," that is, they may be seized as booty.

The 1949 Geneva Conventions reduce the ban to three words: "Pillage is prohibited." The requisitioning of food or medical supplies is permitted only for their use by the occupation forces and administrative personnel, and then "only if the requirements of the civilian population have been taken into account." The conventions also require that fair value be paid for requisitioned goods, and set out specific restrictions on requisitioning medical facilities.

Although the ban on pillage is most often observed in the breach in contemporary conflict, matters were worse before the law was codified; Europe's great museums testify to the grand scale of pillaging during wars of the past centuries. In many of the wars following the end of the Cold War,

American forces caught a column of Iraqi troops and civilians as they beat a retreat north in cars laden with booty. Mutla Ridge, Kuwait, March 1991.

pillaging turned into a principal feature of the conflict. The Iraqi Army pillaged Kuwait as it departed that country under the pressure of Operation Desert Storm in early 1991, and Serb paramilitaries stripped Croatia and Bosnia-Herzegovina of all movable privately owned goods, fencing them in Belgrade and Novi Sad.

Not every expropriation is pillage. Not long after the Azerbaijan Army retook control of northern Karabakh in the summer of 1992 and put down the secession in that part of the Armenian enclave, I watched Azeri oil tankers pull up to the storage vats of brandy in occupied towns, drain the contents into the trucks, and drive away. The drivers told me that the brandy was to be sold for the benefit of widows and orphans, but in fact it was often used to fuel military vehicles. Not far from this scene, horse-drawn carts, piled high with refrigerators, stoves, and diverse plumbing fittings, trundled slowly through the countryside, carrying the contents from smoldering villages toward markets elsewhere.

The fortunes of war shifted, and nine months later, after ethnic Armenians had seized the Azeri province of Kelbajar, a British colleague visiting Stepanakert, the self-proclaimed capital of the breakaway province, came upon a large "used refrigerator and television" market. The Armenians began the systematic removal of window and door frames as they went house to house in occupied Azeri cities such as Agdam, Fizuli, and Zangelan.

Decanting the brandy, especially when it was being used by the fuel-starved Armenians was probably not pillage. Most likely it was public property, and the Azeris could claim to be the State. A State has the right to declare a state of emergency or martial law and requisition goods needed to sustain the civilian population. Indeed, if used in the war effort, as it was to fuel tanks, the seized brandy was legitimate war booty.

The refrigerators and televisions, windows and door frames, on the other hand, are undoubtedly a case of pillage, for they were stolen from private civilian homes and not requisitioned by proper military procedures for any proper military purpose. The rule of thumb is that in an international conflict, any goods seized without proper procedure have been pillaged; in an internal conflict, to determine whether an army has pillaged, it is thus important to find out first whether the goods are private or State property. If the internal party has a claim to being the government of the region, then it has a claim to the goods owned by the State.

Poisonous Weapons

By Gwynne Roberts

Shaho was nine when the Iraqi Kurdish town of Halabja was chemically bombed by the Iraqi Air Force in 1988.

He still vividly remembers the planes overhead, the clouds of gas smelling of fruit, and then fleeing for his life to Iran. Within weeks, Shaho began to suffer back pains and has been unable to stand or walk for the past six years. His condition is known as scoliosis, severe curvature of the spine. He has no doubt what caused it.

"Before the chemical attack, I was perfectly healthy," says Shaho. "I am certain that poison gas caused my illness. My mother lost her sight at the time, and I've got gradually worse ever since." He spends each day at home lying on his mattress, turned every thirty minutes by his devoted sister to avoid bedsores. His family has gone deep into debt to try to find a cure—without success. (Although research into the effects of nerve and mustard gas on the human body is limited, such agents are known to cause disorders in a range of tissues in addition to the brain and spinal cord and may thus be responsible for abnormal growth of cells in bone.)

Nizar, twenty-three, also from Halabja, is hardly able to walk and crumbles to the floor after a few paces. He bursts into tears. "I can't even go to the toilet on my own," he says. "Please help me. I am afraid of ending up in bed forever." He too was gassed and he lay unconscious for two days. The gases, which smelled of apples, attacked his nervous system, and over the years he has gradually lost control of his muscles. Both cases link severe neurological damage to **chemical weapons**.

In one way both were lucky—they, at least, survived the bombardment.

The battle for Halabja began on March 15, 1988, when Kurdish rebels and Iranian Revolutionary Guards, equipped with chemical warfare suits, moved into the town, driving out Iraqi units in heavy fighting. Townspeople were then stopped from fleeing Halabja and forced by the invaders to return to their homes. This tactic was to cost thousands of lives.

The chemical attack began a day later at 6:20 P.M. and continued sporadically over three days. Wave after wave of bombers—seven to eight in each wing—attacked Halabja, a town of eighty thousand, and all roads leading to the surrounding mountains. They dropped a cocktail of poison gases: mustard gas, the nerve agents sarin, tabun, and, according to a well-informed Iraqi military source, VX, the most lethal of all, which Iraq had just begun to manufacture. Clouds of gas hung over the town and the surrounding hills, blotting out the sky and contaminating the fertile plains nearby.

The townspeople had no protection and the chemicals soaked into their clothes, skin, eyes, and lungs. At least five thousand, and probably many more, died within hours. Many were poisoned in the cellars where they had sought refuge—trapped by gases that were heavier than air. It was the largest chemical attack ever launched against a civilian population.

On the road out of the town, an estimated four thousand were killed near the village of Anab as they attempted to flee to Iran. Many flung themselves into a pond to wash off the chemicals but died within minutes. Their corpses lay undisturbed for months, deadly toxins from their bodies seeping into the earth and reportedly contaminating the water table.

Some survivors fled into Iran, where they live to this day. Others who escaped to nearby Kurdish towns returned to Habalja and now live in the very homes where scores of close relatives perished. They say they know that their houses are still contaminated but cannot afford to live anywhere else. They complain that mortar dust still causes skin lesions and eye soreness.

Evidence of the attack still litters the hills around Halabja. Empty chemical shells with Russian markings stand upright in the plowed earth like grotesque mushrooms. Casings are still to be found stacked in local scrapyards, and even used as flowerpots by Halabjans.

The chemicals are also thought to have blighted the lands around Halabja, once the most fertile region in the Middle East. Farmers complain that agricultural output has dropped dramatically, pomegranate orchards

Iraqi forces killed this Kurdish woman and child with poison gas in Halabja, 1988.

have dried out, and other fruit trees have become unproductive.

The chemicals also seem to have caused mutations in plant and animal life. The town has been visited by plagues of locusts for the first time in living memory. According to a local surgeon, snakes and scorpions have become more poisonous since the attack, some twenty people dying from lethal bites during the past year alone, a tenfold increase in the region.

But these chemical weapons have left behind an even more frightening legacy. According to Christine Gosden, professor of medical genetics at Liverpool University, who accompanied me to Halabja in early 1998, these poisons have genetically damaged the local population.

Since the attack, Halabja has been shunned by the outside world and ignored by the international aid agencies. Its inhabitants, however, are living a total nightmare—their health has been irreversibly damaged in the attack, as well as that of their children and their children's children.

During our visit, we were literally overwhelmed by people exhibiting a variety of serious irreversible medical conditions ranging from aggressive cancers, neurological damage, and skin diseases to heart-rending disfigurements and severe psychiatric disorders. Surgeons have grown used to removing bullets from people unsuccessful in their attempts at suicide.

Professor Gosden, working with doctors in the area, compared the Halabja rates of infertility, congenital malformations, and cancers with those of an unexposed population from a city in the same region. She found that, ten years after the attack, the frequency rates were three to four times higher. Most worrisome of all, she discovered that more and more children were dying each year of leukemia and lymphomas. Their tumors were more aggressive than elsewhere, and there is no chemotherapy or radiotherapy available.

"The situation is a genetic time bomb which is exploding into future generations," she said. "It is far worse that I could have ever imagined."

Shaho's case exemplifies the need for further research. Scoliosis may seem an unlikely side-effect of chemical weapons, but Dr. Gosden points out that the human bone structure is not static; in fact our entire skeleton is replaced each year. Other bone disorders such as osteoporosis can lead to the shrinking of the skeleton, while cancer can cause severe Dowager's hump and the weakening and fractures of bone.

There is little doubt that Halabja is a medical catastrophe. There is also little doubt in the minds of Halabjans who is responsible for it: Saddam Hussein. The attack happened during the final stages of the **Iran-Iraq** conflict and the Iraqis were in clear breach of the 1925 Geneva Protocol banning the use of "asphyxiating, poisonous, or other gases, and of all analogous liquids." The attack also violated the 1899 and 1907 Hague Regulations, which ban the use of "poison or poisoned weapons."

Their deployment against civilians, however, puts this crime onto another dimension. Iraq has not ratified the 1977 Addition Protocols to the Geneva Conventions protecting civilians during combat. But in this case, the Hague Regulations of 1907 are applicable. They stipulate that any force bombarding a populated area has to take precautions to minimize incidental damage. It is clear that no such precautions were taken.

There are growing calls in the United States, encouraged by the government, to set up a war crimes tribunal and brand Hussein a war criminal. The Halabja gas attack, and its aftermath, are crucial in the case.

There is one fly in the ointment, however. In 1990, against all the evidence, the U.S. Defense Department alleged that Iran was also responsible for the chemical attack on Halabja. An internal Pentagon study assembled what it claimed was "conclusive intelligence" that Iran was complicit in one of the worst civilian massacres in the Iran-Iraq War. This report, leaked to *The Washington Post*, is being used by Iraqi officials to divert the blame.

Many people are skeptical of the Pentagon evidence, not least the people of Halabja. I talked to many Halabjans during my visit who were present during the 1988 attack, and all agreed that Iraq alone was responsible. The Kurdish guerrilla armies who were allied to Iran at the time and fought in and around Halabja also concur, and that includes the Kurdistan Democratic Party of Masoud Barzani, whose current relations with the Iranians can only be described as hostile. Why would Iranian commanders whose troops were in Halabja at the time use poison gas against their own men? they ask. Their logic seems inescapable.

Yet, the allegation of Iranian complicity in Halabja—never rescinded in Washington—complicates the issue under international law. Iraq will almost certainly claim that Iran used poison gas first, and its response was in retaliation. Issued at a time when the United States supported the Iraqis both politically and materially, this piece of black propaganda has now returned to haunt the current U.S. administration.

Prisoner of War Camps

By H. Wayne Elliott

In the early 1970s a popular television comedy was set in the most unlikely of places—a German prisoner of war (POW) camp. The exploits of *Hogan's Heroes* brought laughter to millions. The bumbling camp commandant, Colonel Klink, never figured out that the POWs were really running the camp. Obviously, the series hardly reflected the reality of life as a World War II POW. But, in at least one respect, it was realistic: in almost every episode there occurs a conversation between the prisoners and the guards in which the requirements of the Geneva Conventions are raised. Even inside the camp, the law, specifically the Third Geneva Convention, must be obeyed. The law sets out the duties, responsibilities, and rights of both the prisoners and the guards. Nonetheless, it is unlikely that a real POW camp would be a place where one would find a lot of frivolity. What considerations go into

P

establishing, and maintaining, a POW camp? What should one really expect to find inside a prisoner of war camp?

Clearly, prisoners of war lose their freedom. But they are not criminals. They are enemy soldiers for whom participation in the war has come to a halt. The Third Geneva Convention is built around the idea that POWs retain their military status and are entitled to humane treatment. The International Committee of the Red Cross (ICRC) is charged, under Article 126, with overseeing the implementation of the treaty requirements, but others might also visit a POW camp—for example, journalists or humanitarian aid workers.

A person visiting a POW camp should have at least a general idea, if not detailed knowledge, of what the Third Geneva Convention or individual regulations concerning camp activities require. Some knowledge of the law should make it more difficult for a capturing power to present the outside world with a facade of compliance while, in reality, it is violating the fundamental precepts of the law.

An initial consideration in evaluating a POW camp is its location. Is the camp located in an area that is unsafe? The camp should be far enough from the combat area so that the POWs are not endangered (Article 19). It should

Suspected Viet Cong are led roped together to a prison camp. Vietnam, 1967.

P

be located in an area where the environment does not threaten the health of the POWs. There is also a general prohibition on housing POWs in penitentiaries (Article 22). The POWs should be housed in such a way as to protect them from the effects of the war, specifically aerial bombardment. If military considerations permit, the camp should be marked with the letters PW or PG (*prisoner de guerre*), which are visible from the air. The buildings in which the POWs are quartered must meet the same general standards as the quarters made available to the forces of the captor. Women prisoners must be separately housed from the men (Article 25).

For the Third Geneva Convention to have any real utility inside the camp, its contents must be known to those inside—prisoners and guards. Article 39 requires that the camp commander have a copy of the convention in his possession. Article 127 takes this somewhat further and requires that the military personnel who have responsibility for POWs must be "specially instructed" in the convention's requirements. At the same time, the POWs must also know their responsibilities. Article 41 requires that the full text of the convention, in the language of the prisoners, be posted in the camp.

If the text of the convention is available and known to the POWs and the guards, what sort of considerations go into evaluating compliance? An initial inquiry concerns who is actually in the camp. If the people held are lawful prisoners of war they should have been given an opportunity to fill out and send a "capture card." The purpose of the card is to let the next of kin know of the capture and provide some general information as to the health of the captive. The format for the card is set out in an annex to the convention. Because the card must be filed within seven days of the arrival in camp of a new prisoner, a legitimate POW camp, properly run, should have a supply of the cards on hand. If the cards are not present, a crucial factor in captivity—letting others know—is missing.

Some evaluation factors are obvious. Medical care must be provided for those who need it. There should be an infirmary in the camp and it should be staffed with qualified medical personnel. That does not necessarily mean medical doctors, but at least people with some medical training. In fact, if medical personnel are among the POWs they should be working in the medical facility (Article 33).

The prisoners must be fed and provided with drinking water, but the convention requires that the normal diet of the POWs should be taken into consideration (Article 26). Thus, it would be improper to force Muslim POWs to eat food forbidden by their religion. The POWs should be properly clothed. In most cases this means the POWs will wear a uniform of some type, either their own or one issued by the captor. If many POWs are in civilian clothes, there might be cause for further inquiry. First, POWs are generally soldiers and should be in uniform. Second, a POW who has civilian clothes is a greater escape risk. So if a large number of the "POWs" are in civilian clothes, the possibility exists that they may be civilians and not real POWs.

POWs are still soldiers and are expected to act like soldiers. POWs are expected to salute their captors who are higher in rank. Every POW, regardless of rank, must salute the camp commander. This might seem silly at first glance. But it actually helps both the POW and those who guard him maintain their military status and dignity. Of course, discipline is enhanced when such military traditions are followed. The absence of basic military courtesy, such as rendering salutes, can also be evidence that the camp is not being properly run.

Generally, POWs can have contact with the outside world. This means the POWs have the right to send and receive letters from home (Article 71).

The POWs are also permitted to receive relief shipments of food, medicine, clothing, etc. (Article 72).

In every camp, there will be problems with discipline. The laws of war recognize the right of the detaining power to maintain discipline in the camp. There is, in the convention, an extensive list of provisions to help ensure that punishment for various infractions is meted out in a fair and humane way. An appropriate question is how violations of camp rules are treated. Generally, the laws of war recognize the right of a POW to attempt to escape and the duty of the detaining power to prevent an escape. Article 42 specifically addresses escapes and the use of force in preventing them. It provides that the use of weapons against POWs is "an extreme measure" and their use "shall always be preceded by warnings appropriate to the circumstances." A relevant question to ask of camp personnel is how attempted escapees are punished. Another area of interest would be the practice of the detaining power regarding POWs suspected of committing war crimes. Are accused war criminals held in the camp? If so, with what offense are they charged? What procedures exist for trial? If a trial is contemplated, has the protecting power been notified in accordance with Article 104 of the convention?

The final stage in the life of a POW is release from captivity and repatriation. The camp should have some procedure in place to accomplish that as quickly and efficiently as possible.

The rules governing POWs are extensive, and the Third Geneva Convention and the ICRC Commentary on the Convention fill a 764-page book. The general rule is that the captives must be treated humanely. By setting a strict regime for the administration of a POW camp, the laws of war provide many benchmarks by which the standard of humane treatment can be measured.

(See **combatant status; due process; prisoners of war, non-repatriation of; soldiers, rights of; willful killing.**)

P

Prisoners of War, Non-repatriation of

By Mark Huband

Mustapha Sirji swayed from one foot to the other. The towering mud walls of the Martyr Mohammed Lasyad Prison rose around us out of the Algerian desert.

Forgotten by the country that had sent him to war, he had spent twenty-one years locked in a desert jail which echoes with the sound of prayers as the burning sun sinks beneath the barren Sahara outside.

"I ask the others if I am a human being here, or if I am an animal," he says, his eyes glazed. "We are Muslims. We believe in God. We pray. We are not rocks. We are living in this inferno. We are the forgotten victims of this drama. We have our lives to live. I have lost my youth. We have lost our families. Every time we receive letters somebody has died. How long is this going to go on? Please, will somebody notice us?"

Mustapha Sirji and his comrades are among twenty-three hundred Moroccan soldiers taken prisoner by the Polisario Front, a guerrilla army that fought for more than fifteen years to establish an independent state in the former Spanish colony of Spanish Sahara. Spain actually granted independence in 1975, but within days neighboring Morocco occupied the mineral-rich region. And the war that cost Mustapha Sirji his freedom began.

That conflict has now reached a stalemate, and there is no more fighting. Instead, all sides are awaiting the results of a UN-brokered effort to organize a referendum on the future of what is now known as Western Sahara. The people of the area, most of whom belong to the nomadic Sahrawi tribe, will be asked whether they wish to gain full independence or become part of Morocco. As preparations for this vote drag on, the Polisario has withdrawn to small strips of territory along Western Sahara's eastern and southern borders, and across the border, in neighboring Algeria. But they have taken their Moroccan prisoners with them, and all efforts to arrange their release, despite the fact that hostilities have stopped, have so far been unavailing.

Five prisons in the Tindouf region of Algeria are home to the Moroccan POWs. The Mohamed Lasyad Prison, said to be the most decent of the five, is a large sandy courtyard surrounded on three sides by a twenty-foot wall. On the fourth side is a rocky outcrop. Dome-shaped huts line the wall, built by the prisoners themselves. The courtyard is where the five hundred men do what they have been doing every day for twenty years: praying and playing football.

"Nobody really wants to talk with you," Mustapha Sirji told me. "We have had a few visitors before—some people brought food—but they leave and we never hear from them again. They all say they will raise our case with the outside world. But they never do, and so we are left alone again. Forgotten again."

Under international humanitarian law, the continued imprisonment of Mustapha Sirji and his comrades is a grave breach, that is, a war crime. Article 118 of the Third Geneva Convention of 1949 states that prisoners "shall be released and repatriated without delay after the cessation of active hostilities." The obligation is restated in the 1977 Additional Protocol I, which lists the "unjustifiable delay in the repatriation of prisoners of war or civilians" as a grave breach; this means there is **universal jurisdiction** over violations. The obligation on any side holding prisoners to arrange for their prompt release and repatriation does not depend on a formal peace treaty having been signed, although a belligerent is entitled to make sure that its adversary has genuinely stopped fighting and does not intend to resume the conflict; otherwise, repatriating prisoners would be analogous to reinforcing the enemy's army. If that risk is not present, under international law the duty to repatriate is clear. Prisoners, however, do have the right, in the view of the International Committee of the Red Cross (ICRC), to refuse forcible repatriations. Such situations arise where a change of government in the POW's home State might make return dangerous.

That is not the situation of the Moroccan POWs. They are desperate to go home. And yet, despite the fact that a cease-fire between Morocco and the Polisario Front was agreed to in September 1991, the Moroccan prisoners of the Polisario continue to languish in camps like Martyr Mohammed Lasyad Prison, just as Iranian prisoners spent years in detention in Iraq after the end of the Iran-Iraq war. Representatives of the Polisario claim they would gladly free the detainees, but the Moroccans have refused because, as a roving ambassador of the Polisario put it, "that would mean they would have to give us the Polisario POWs they are holding. But they won't, because they don't want to recognize Polisario or admit that this is a war."

The result for men like Mustapha Sirji, most of whom were taken prisoner in their twenties, is that while they are alive (the prisoners do not complain of ill-treatment), they have have had their youth stolen from them. Illegally detained and now entering their forties, they must face the prospect of having their middle age stolen from them as well.

P

Property: Civilian, Destruction of

By Amira Hass

Three architectural styles of buildings and two types of ruins dip among plump, round-cheeked cactuses and elegant almond trees, densely filling a mellow valley before climbing, scattered, over the hill slopes. These buildings tell the story of Beit Mirsim, a Palestinian village just touching the southern part of the Green Line (the 1948 armistice border between the West Bank/Jordan and Israel). They tell not only the story of destruction by the victorious Israeli Army, but also of the continuing effects of the Six-Day War of 1967 on people's lives.

There is also a subtext to be read here: that of the persistent Israeli urge to

P

"clear" Palestinians away, to make them "move eastward," and leave forever their childhood landscapes. And there is the other side of this coin: Palestinian resilience.

During the Six-Day War, an Israeli Army unit ordered the villagers of Beit Mirsim to evacuate their homes, which were situated hard by the Jordanian border. Half of the village's agricultural lands had already been lost to Israel after the war of 1948, and this time the villagers had refused to leave the hills overlooking the village. To this day, the villagers can recall clearly how, in a matter of hours, the valley was filled with the heart-breaking sounds and scenes of explosives tearing away their homes made of big, heavy stones, with arched windows and doors. Israel's Defense Forces (IDF) destroyed houses in several villages adjacent to the Green Line or in the eastern Jordan Valley. Only in Beit Mirsim and a neighboring village did people return.

The laws of armed conflict permit the deliberate destruction of property under certain circumstances. Article 52 of the 1977 Additional Protocol I to the Geneva Conventions sanctions such attacks, but only on "those objects

Destroyed home of suicide bomber, Sufyan Jabarin, responsible for the August 1995 bus bombing in Ramat Ash Kol, Jerusalem, leaving 59 dead. Dharirya village, West Bank, 1996.

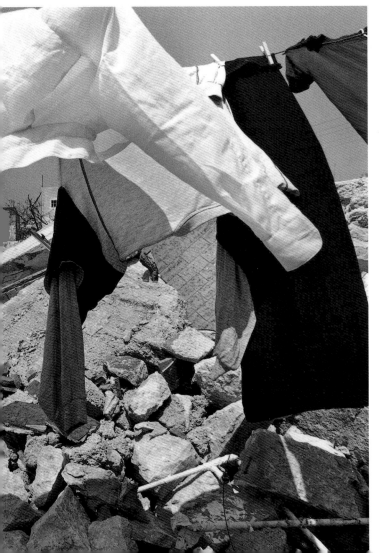

P

which by their nature, location, purpose or use make an effective contribution to military action and whose total or partial destruction, capture or neutralization, in the circumstances ruling at the time, offers a definite military advantage." This provision addresses the situation of military forces making a direct attack on civilian objects and property for the purpose of destroying it.

In the view of the villagers of Beit Mirsim, their homes neither offered the IDF's Jordanian adversaries definite military advantages nor impeded Israel's own military plans in that particular sector. In their view, the destruction of their homes had little to do with concrete military advantages at the time. They believe their homes were destroyed in order to cause them to leave the zone permanently, not by the exigencies of battle. The destruction of homes in order to persuade the civilian population to flee permanently violates the laws of armed conflict.

It is not known whether Israeli commanders at the time of the destruction would have agreed that it served no concrete military purpose. As a general rule, however, under battlefield circumstances, in which concrete military advantages must be weighed against **collateral damage**, under conditions of uncertainty and imperfect information, and often with great speed, there has been great hesitation to second-guess the judgment of commanders who must make this determination.

Since it is anything but clear that the destruction of Beit Mirsim offered definite military advantage to Israeli forces, it can be argued that what the Israelis did was a grave breach of the Geneva Conventions and Additional Protocol I. According to the Hague Conventions of 1899 and 1907—which the Israeli Supreme Court has ruled applies to the West Bank and the Gaza Strip—it is illegal "to destroy or seize the enemy's property, unless such destruction or seizure be imperatively demanded by the necessities of war." They also state that "private property . . . must be respected."

Provisions of the laws of armed conflict also govern the conditions under which property may be destroyed as collateral damage. It may not exceed the threshold of **military necessity**, and may not be wanton.

Another legal basis for evaluating the destruction of houses at Beit Mirsim is the Fourth Geneva Convention, which expressly forbids destruction of civilian property under conditions of occupation except as justified by military necessity. Israel states that the *de jure* applicability of the Fourth Convention is "doubtful" and since 1967 it applies the "humanitarian provisions" of the Fourth Convention to the occupied territories, without specifying which provisions. No other country recognizes Israel's selective interpretation of the 1949 Conventions. The Fourth Convention holds that "extensive destruction and appropriation of property, not justified by military necessity and carried out unlawfully and wantonly" is a grave breach.

Nonetheless, the issue at Beit Mirsim, as in any instance of what seems at first glance like a possible case of destruction, is that of military necessity. And because commanders can always make such a claim that the exigencies of war compelled them to act as they did, enforcing prohibitions against destruction of enemy property will always be problematic, and their claims of military necessity, or, for that matter, their entirely legal wish to pursue military advantage, will be difficult to refute.

Military necessity or no military necessity, the people of Beit Mirsim are tenacious about their homes and village. They were so persistent about staying there that in 1967 Defense Minister Moshe Dayan personally went to negotiate with them. "General Dayan came to speak with us," recalled Abu Sherif, now seventy. "At last he agreed that we build one room, in place of each demolished house. We told him: 'But General Dayan, one room is not enough for a family of ten.' And he replied, 'We hope that things will improve and that with the course of time you will be able to build more.'" The second architectural generation was then born: tiny one-room constructions, made of smaller stones.

After the 1993 Oslo agreement between the Palestine Liberation Organization and the Israeli government, villagers began building once again—without waiting for redeployment of Israeli troops or Israeli building permits which never come. They built a third generation of houses, spacious, ugly-looking, made of naked concrete. In the course of 1997, fifteen of the thirty families still living there received orders to stop "illegal" construction and demolish their own houses. One was blown up—smashed, gray concrete blocks, a broken tap, cramped and twisted black iron bars which crawl upward out of the rubble. Construction has now stopped.

(See **military objective**.)

P

Property:
Wanton Destruction

By Victoria Brittain

Nothing could prepare a visitor for the sight of Cuito, a town in Angola's central highlands that Jonas Savimbi's National Union for the Total Independence of Angola (UNITA) forces besieged for most of 1993 and 1994.

Not a building was left standing on the main street, which became the front line of defense for Angolan government forces. No roof or window remained intact, and many apartment blocks were collapsed into heaps. The pink walls of the grandiose old Portuguese colonial government buildings were scarred by tens of thousands of rifle rounds. Only one wall and the bell tower of the cathedral were left standing. And, of course, the electrical and water systems were destroyed.

Even buildings that enjoyed special protection under international humanitarian law were not spared. The large regional **hospital** had to be abandoned. But after the staff moved the surgical equipment and medical equipment to a small shop in a government-held part of town, the attacks continued. A UNITA shell eventually found its mark and destroyed the shop. The government, too, showed little respect for protected spaces. Later in the fighting, government war planes bombed the central hospital, perhaps not illegally, as it was a UNITA military position.

A Human Rights Watch study said that by July of 1993, UNITA was raining some one thousand heavy artillery shells on Cuito every day, and the rebel force "had clearly made little attempt to target precisely its shelling." It concluded that as many as thirty thousand people, mostly civilians, had died during the **siege**, almost a third of those who perished during the Angolan civil war. The damage to property, while not as tragic, was vast. The siege of Cuito was the occasion for massive violations of the Geneva Conventions and their protocols, among them **indiscriminate attack** and **wanton destruction**.

In a strictly geographical sense, the conflict was internal and many of the protections for property therefore would not apply; but as a conflict that from a very early stage had outside participants and support—Cuba, South Africa, and Zaire among them—many experts, including the International Committee of the Red Cross (ICRC) treated it as an "internationalized" conflict, for which the full body of law governing international armed conflict would apply.

Under the laws of armed conflict, civilian property may not be targeted as such, simply for the sake of destroying it. It must constitute a **legitimate military target** or **military objective**. Its destruction must be required by **military necessity**. A party to a conflict may damage or destroy civilian property only if damage would not be excessive compared to the military advantage to be gained. This prohibition was stated in the 1907 Hague Conventions and is now viewed as part of **customary law**. Destruction or seizure of property is prohibited unless it is "imperatively demanded by the necessities of war." The 1977 Additional Protocol I to the Geneva

Conventions states explicitly that "civilian objects shall not be the object of attack or reprisals, and objects or installations ordinarily of civilian use are presumed to be civilian unless determined to be otherwise." The 1998 Rome Statute for the International Criminal Court lists "extensive destruction and appropriation of property, not justified by military necessity and carried out unlawfully and wantonly" as a grave breach.

To determine whether this devastation and seizure constituted a war crime—individually culpable violations of the laws and customs of war—or instead were legal acts, an outsider arriving after the battle would have to know how the government force defended the town, the location or shifting locations of military installations and infrastructure used in their support, and whether any of the protected religious, cultural, or medical buildings were being used for military purposes, or as shields by one side or the other.

In the Angolan case, both sides were often at fault. The bishopric building in Cuito, for example, in which dozens of refugees had taken shelter, was destroyed after having been attacked three times. Normally it should have **immunity** from attack as a civilian structure, but particularly as a building used for religious, cultural, or medical purposes, protected by rules on **cultural property**. UNITA captured the building in 1993. Government forces recaptured it the following month, and then, after a fierce battle lasting seven days, UNITA retook it. Both sides had used it as a shield; both sides were partly responsible for its destruction. The level of the damage to the building and the way it came about suggests it was the target for indiscriminate attack—that is, there was no attempt to distinguish this building from any others.

Such devastation was a hallmark of the Angolan civil war. For a while, it was the deadliest conflict on earth, with one thousand people dying daily not only from the fighting itself, but also from starvation and disease. The devastation was so rampant that the ICRC, citing its role under the Geneva Conventions as the custodian and promoter of international humanitarian law, issued a rare public rebuke to both sides in the conflict.

"Military forces," the ICRC declared in June of 1994, "do not have an unlimited right regarding the choice of methods and means of warfare; a clear distinction must be made in all circumstances between civilians and civilian objects on the one hand and combatants and military objectives on the other." The prohibitions include: attacks on civilian objects, acts or threats of violence whose main purpose is to spread terror among the civilian population, and "all attacks directed indiscriminately at military and civilian objectives and those which may be expected to cause incidental loss of human life, injury to civilians or damage to civilian objects which would be excessive in relation to the concrete and direct military advantage anticipated." Furthermore, the ICRC said pointedly, hospitals, ambulances, and any other object bearing the Red Cross are not to be attacked or used for military purposes, and are to be "respected in all circumstances." (See **civilian immunity**.)

Proportionality, Principle of

By Horst Fischer

The principle of proportionality is embedded in almost every national legal system and underlies the international legal order. Its function in domestic law is to relate means to ends. In armed conflict, the principle is used to judge first, the lawfulness in *jus ad bellum* of the strategic goals in the use of force for self-defense, and second, the lawfulness in *jus in bello* of any armed attack that causes civilian casualties. In the Gulf War, allied forces acted in individual and collective self-defense against Iraq under Article 51 of the UN Charter, but they disagreed whether the principle of proportionality permitted them to occupy Iraqi territory or oust Saddam Hussein. Many States felt that only the liberation of Kuwait was a permitted goal.

In the conduct of war, when a party commits a lawful attack against a **military objective**, the principle of proportionality also comes into play whenever there is **collateral damage**, that is, civilian casualties or damage to a nonmilitary objective. The U.S. attack on the Amiriyah bunker in Baghdad in 1991, which was aimed to destroy a military target but cost many civilian lives, is a case in point. If it was a military objective in which civilians were sheltering, an attack on the bunker would be lawful, subject to the principle of proportionality.

As formulated in Additional Protocol I of 1977, attacks are prohibited if they cause incidental loss of civilian life, injury to civilians, or damage to civilian objects that is excessive in relation to the anticipated concrete and direct military advantage of the attack. This creates a permanent obligation for military commanders to consider the results of the attack compared to the advantage anticipated. The target list has to be continuously updated as the conflict develops with special attention given to the safe movement of civilians. The attack on the Amiriyah bunker might have been illegal, if—which has never been proved—the United States did not follow carefully enough the movement of the civilians seeking shelter in Baghdad.

Some states ratifying Protocol I have stated that the concrete and direct military advantage anticipated from an attack can only be considered as a whole and not only from isolated or particular parts of the attack. Article 85 defines an **indiscriminate attack** undertaken in the knowledge that it will cause excessive damage to the civilian population is a grave breach and therefore a war crime. The principle is hard to apply in war, still harder after an attack has occurred. But grossly disproportionate results will be seen as criminal by all belligerent parties and the world community.

"Terror attacks" on the civilian population, or area bombardments that by their nature do not distinguish between military objectives and civilian targets, are prohibited, and the principle does not come into play. If deliberate, the bombing of the Sarajevo market square during shopping hours in 1994, which killed thirty-four civilians, would have been a war crime. The Rome Statute of the International Criminal Court reaffirms this by qualifying in Article 8 as a war crime intentionally directing attacks against the civilian population as such or against individual civilians not taking direct part in hostilities. The use of indiscriminate weapons such as cluster bombs in populated areas is a war crime as well.
(See **civilian immunity**; **legitimate military targets**; **military necessity**.)

Protected Persons

By Heike Spieker

In international humanitarian law, individuals are accorded a range of "protections" from the effects of hostilities. Individuals accorded such
"protections" are called "protected persons" within the specified limits of
protection given them by international humanitarian law. They fall into several distinct categories. Historically the first group of individuals protected
by international treaties were combatants and not civilians. Early treaties
dealt with the treatment of casualties, protections for medical personnel and
facilities, and humane conditions for prisoners of war.

In 1949, the four Geneva Conventions enunciated the first comprehensive set of rules protecting combatants and noncombatants in international
armed conflicts. The first three conventions referred to the protection of
combatants and related personnel—wounded and sick in the field; wounded,
sick, and shipwrecked at sea; and prisoners of war—and the fourth to the
protection of civilians. A combatant in simplest terms is a member of an
armed force—a person who takes an active part in hostilities, who can kill,
and who, in turn, is a lawful military target. A combatant can acquire the
status of a protected person under a number of circumstances—for example,
if captured or wounded.

The four conventions require that protected persons be humanely treated "without any adverse distinction founded on race, color, religion or faith,
sex, birth or wealth, or any other similar criteria." Protected persons may not
be willfully killed, injured, or used for medical experiments. Captured and
detained persons must be given the food, clothing, shelter, and medical and
spiritual care they require. No one may be deprived of the right to a fair trial.
Protected persons may not be tortured, coerced, used as human shields or
face collective punishments.

The conventions do allow for some distinctions. They provide that
"women shall be treated with all the regard due to their sex," and that
female prisoners of war have treatment equal to that given men. The Fourth
Geneva Convention also provides that women be protected against "rape,
enforced prostitution, or any form of indecent assault." Additionally, it
establishes "particular protection and respect" for groups of individuals such
as the wounded and sick, expectant mothers, aged persons, children, minis-
ters of religion, and medical personnel.

The Fourth Geneva Convention further divides protected civilians into
three categories: aliens in the territory of a party to the conflict, persons in
occupied territory, and internees. These three groups are provided with protections that vary according to membership in one group or another, but all
must be given the basic protection codified in Article 27: respect, protection, and humane treatment under all circumstances.

Additional Protocol I of 1977 supplies an ingredient missing from the
Fourth Convention. Specifically, Article 51 states that any civilian "enjoys
general protection against dangers arising from military operations" and forbids direct attacks against them as well as so-called indiscriminate attacks,
which do not distinguish between civilians and combatants. Additional
Protocol I also elaborates on Fourth Convention provisions that relief actions
be undertaken if a civilian population is not adequately provided with the

basic supplies essential to its survival.

Civil Conflicts: The first explicit treaty provision covering protected persons in noninternational armed conflicts—often called internal armed conflicts or civil conflicts—is found in Common Article 3 of the 1949 Geneva Conventions. The basic principle is to require humane treatment without adverse discrimination. It prohibits violence to life and person, the taking of hostages, and outrages upon personal dignity. The article calls for basic judicial and procedural guarantees and an obligation to collect and care for the wounded and sick.

This principle of humane treatment under all circumstances is further developed in the 1977 Additional Protocol II, which extended to internal armed conflict many of the rules found in Protocol I and the 1949 Conventions. Protocol II covers the civilian population, both as a group and as individuals; the essence of the protection is the prohibition against making civilians the object of attack. Attacks are prohibited against dams, dikes, and nuclear power stations if they may result in severe civilian losses. Also banned are attacks on objects necessary for the survival of the civilian population. Additionally, terrorism and starvation of civilians are prohibited as methods of combat. So is forced displacement, unless undertaken for security or imperative military reasons. Relief operations are to be undertaken when the civilian population is suffering "undue hardship." An important caveat is that technically Protocol II applies only to internal armed conflicts in States that have ratified it. Thus Common Article 3 is the applicable law for most instances of noninternational armed conflict.

(See **international vs. internal armed conflict**; **sexual violence**.)

P

Q,R

Quarter, Giving No

By John Burns

The ancient name for Sri Lanka, Serendip, long ago passed into English as the word "serendipity," meaning "the making of pleasant discoveries by accident." Lying off the southeastern coast of India, the island earned its name from European mariners who found on this lush, gentle island a sanctuary from the forbidding vastness of the Indian Ocean.

It has been a harsh irony of the 1980s and 1990s that Sri Lanka, with its white beaches and scented uplands, has become synonymous with one of the world's most violent and merciless conflicts. In two separate civil wars, one still continuing and the other ended by the unremitting harshness of government forces in the early 1990s, at least 100,000 Sri Lankans have died. In a population of 18 million, the losses have been compared to those suffered by France and England in the century's two world wars. Even more horrifying, many thousands of the dead were slaughtered not in battlefield combat, but as a result of a take-no-prisoners tactic adopted by all sides.

In one of the wars, the Sri Lankan forces, representing the island's Sinhalese Buddhist majority, are fighting the Liberation Tigers of Tamil Eelam, who want a separate State in the north and east of the island for the predominantly Hindu Tamil minority. The second conflict, within the Sinhalese community, was between the government and the ultra-leftists of the Janatha Vimukthi Peramuna (JVP), which paralyzed large parts of central and southern Sri Lanka in 1988 and 1989. Prisoners who live to tell the tale have been a rarity in both conflicts.

The war between the government and the Tamil Tigers, with origins that go back to a savage outburst of anti-Tamil rioting that broke out in 1983, reached a cataclysmic moment in the small hours of July 19, 1996, at a remote spot in the northeast of the island in the bloodiest battle of the conflict. Desperate to regain the initiative after the loss six months earlier of their stronghold in the Jaffna Peninsula at the extreme north of the island, the Tamil Tigers attacked a strategic base of the government forces at Mullaitivu, a coastal outpost southeast of the peninsula.

Attacking from sea and land, waves of Tiger fighters, many of them young boys and girls barely into their teens press-ganged into suicide squads known as the Black Tigers, overran the base. By dawn, at least six hundred Tigers were dead, along with thirteen hundred government soldiers, the highest single casualty toll in the history of the conflict. After the Tigers withdrew, a relief column of government forces found not a single government soldier still alive.

The wounds of many of the dead, some clutching white flags of surrender, indicated they had been shot dead or blown apart by grenades at close range; hundreds of others appeared to have been herded together, doused with gasoline, and burned to death. What occurred at Mullaitivu, it seemed, was less a battle, at least in its concluding stages, than a massacre.

A distinguishing feature of the Sri Lankan fighting, and a cause of acute concern to international humanitarian organizations like Amnesty International and the International Committee of the Red Cross (ICRC), has been the rare occasions when the opposing forces have taken—or acknowledged having taken—prisoners. Fighters on both sides who have dared to speak candidly to human rights investigators and reporters have admitted that the rule, sometimes explicit in battle orders, more often understood, was that no enemy combatants were to be left alive.

Where prisoners have been taken, as often as not it has been to serve the ends of propaganda, not humanitarian concern, as when government forces have captured Tiger fighters as young as eleven and twelve and taken them to remand homes in Colombo where foreign television crews have been invited to film them as proof of the Tigers' use of children in combat. At times when they have sought respite from government military pressures, as they did with a six-month cease-fire that they later abrogated in 1994–1995, the Tigers have also held and exchanged prisoners.

But overall, the Sri Lankan fighting has been a chilling demonstration

Funeral for a man shot arbitrarily by army machine-gun fire. Sri Lanka, 1986.

of the survival of a practice going back to the earliest recorded wars—a practice that became known as "giving no quarter" to an enemy (a phrase that literally meant denying shelter, but which came to mean denying the right of survival).

Although ancient history contains examples of generals ordering troops to spare soldiers defeated in battle, and even of attempts by early lawgivers to punish those judged too brutal with the enemy, modern efforts to ensure humane treatment of enemy fighters date back to the American Civil War, when President Lincoln, in 1863, promulgated what became known as the Lieber Code, a codification of the laws of armed conflict, which expressly forbade Union troops to give no quarter.

A conference in Brussels in 1874, attended by European powers in the aftermath of the Franco-Prussian war, eliminated what had been a major loophole in the Lieber Code, the so-called great straits provision, which allowed a soldier or a fighting unit to eliminate survivors of battle when their "own salvation" made taking prisoners impossible.

In 1949, the execution or elimination of defenseless soldiers was defined as one of the grave breaches of the laws of international armed conflict in each of the four Geneva Conventions. In 1977, Additional Protocol I to the Geneva Conventions gave in Article 40 what many legal scholars regard as the most authoritative definition of the principle.

The article provides, among other things, that "a person who is recognized or who, in the circumstances, should be recognized to be ***hors de combat***, shall not be made the object of attack." The article defines *hors de combat* as including those "in the power of an adverse party"; those who clearly express "an intention to surrender"; and those who have been "rendered unconscious or otherwise incapacitated by wounds or sickness" and are therefore incapable of defending themselves. In internal conflict, Article 3 common to the four Geneva Conventions binds parties to treat "humanely" soldiers who have laid down their arms, and those made *hors de combat* by sickness, wounds, detention, or any other cause.

In Sri Lanka, despite numerous assurances over the years, neither the government forces nor the Tamil Tigers seem to have cared that the practice of eliminating defenseless enemy soldiers is a grave war crime. While recent years have provided some examples of the government of President Chandrika Bandaranaike Kumaratunga prosecuting soldiers and policemen for unlawful killings, the Tamil Tigers have remained relentless, killing large numbers of civilians in a series of suicide bombings, and executing government soldiers at will. On the battlefield in Sri Lanka, it seems, there will continue to be no quarter given by either side, until one side or the other prevails in the war. (See **protected persons; soldiers, rights of**.)

Q

Red Cross / Red Crescent Emblem

By Christian Jennings

For the seven Burundian soldiers, the fire instructions and target designation were simple. The ambush party lay in the tall elephant grass at the side of the road in northern Burundi's Cibitoke Province. They were waiting for two white Toyota Land Cruisers, clearly marked on the hood, side panels, roof, and rear doors with the internationally recognized emblem of a red cross on a white background.

Ten minutes and dozens of Kalashnikov rounds later, one of the Land Cruisers was lying bullet-riddled in the ditch, and the three **International Committee of the Red Cross (ICRC)** delegates traveling inside were dead, one of them beheaded; but the second vehicle had managed to escape.

The attack on two vehicles from the ICRC on June 4, 1996, on the road between the Burundian villages of Rugombo and Mugina, was one of the most blatant contemporary violations of the symbol of the Red Cross. Subsequent investigations both by journalists present in Cibitoke that day and by the ICRC have established that the Swiss delegates were targeted specifically.

Article 38 of the First Geneva Convention of 1949 establishes the red cross on a white background as the emblem of the medical services of the armed forces. All permanent medical personnel or chaplains are required to wear it, as a waterproof armband on the left arm, and are entitled to display the flag. It is also the emblem of the Red Cross and Red Crescent Movement, the National Societies, the ICRC, and the International Federation of Red Cross and Red Crescent Societies. Their personnel can use the symbol at all times.

The Red Cross "is the emblem of the Convention, and therefore an emblem of protection. It allows its bearers to venture onto the battlefield to carry out their humanitarian tasks," the ICRC said in its Commentary on the Additional Protocols of 1977. The nature of the symbol as a "protective emblem" means that an attack on vehicles and individuals carrying that emblem is a serious violation of the Geneva Conventions and a war crime.

The protection applies as well in internal conflicts. Additional Protocol II of 1977, which governs internal armed conflict, specifies in Article 12 that the "distinctive emblem shall be respected in all circumstances."

All indications were that the Burundian military specifically targeted the two ICRC vehicles because of the nature of their humanitarian activities in the country: at the time of the incident, the ICRC was the only humanitarian organization working in Cibitoke. Its staff was consequently witness to massive abuses of the civilian population by both the Tutsi military and Hutu rebels, including mass killings, forced displacement and rape. Also, as the army claimed, "they were feeding the rebels."

The incident raises doubt whether the Red Cross or Red Crescent emblem provides any form of protection to its bearer in the complex ethnic and national conflicts running in fifteen African countries. The characteristic of current conflict is a multiplicity of factions, fueled by militias or war lords

R

who show no respect for international humanitarian law. Incidents of abuse of the emblem abound. An ICRC transport plane was fired on in Zaire in 1996 as it brought in a mobile hospital to Uvira. One antiaircraft round actually hit the center of the Red Cross emblem on the fuselage. During the Rwandan genocide of 1994, Tutsis were on occasion dragged from Red Cross ambulances and slaughtered by Hutu extremists.

A different but equally serious war crime is the abuse of the Red Cross emblem. The Geneva Conventions and Additional Protocols state that the emblem "may not be employed" except to protect medical units and establishments, and using it to deceive someone into thinking he is safe and then attacking or capturing him constitutes "perfidious use" and is a grave breach if it is intentional and causes the death of or serious injury to an adversary. Transporting weapons in a vehicle marked with a Red Cross is thus a grave

A wounded person being taken to the hospital in Peshawar. Pakistan, 1981.

breach. In Kosovo in June 1998, refugees fleeing to Albania reported that Serb forces fired at them from helicopters bearing Red Cross markings, also a grave breach.

The ICRC is still struggling over how to address another abuse; when a national Red Cross society takes a lead role in committing war crimes, particularly unrecognized national societies. During the war in Bosnia, Ljiljana Karadzic, the wife of political leader Radovan Karadzic, who has been indicted for genocide, ran the Bosnian Serb Red Cross. That organization—unrecognized by the ICRC—was involved in the ethnic cleansing of non-Serbs and ran at least one concentration camp, at Trnoplje, near Prijedor, where internees were killed, tortured, and raped.

The Red Cross emblem has aroused controversy for almost as long as it has been around. First adopted in the 1864 Geneva Convention, the red cross on a white background was formally described in the 1949 Geneva Conventions as intended to be a "compliment to Switzerland," formed by reversing the Swiss federal colors: a white cross on a red background. Turkey, asserting that Muslim soldiers found the cross offensive, unilaterally began using a red crescent in 1876, and this was accepted in the 1929 update of the Geneva Convention along with the now unused "red lion and sun" for Iran. Israel sought approval of the red shield of David, a six-pointed star, at the 1949 Conference that produced the current Geneva Conventions. ICRC officials feared it would lead to a flood of new national and religious symbols and already had requests for recognition of the red flame, shrine, bow, palm, wheel, trident, cedar, and mosque. One delegate suggested a red heart. All such proposals have been rejected for fear that abandoning a universally recognized symbol would endanger human lives. The ICRC does not officially recognize societies that use unauthorized symbols: from the red shield of David to the green cross of the Cruz Verde, a renegade national society set up in El Salvador in 1980.

The ICRC no longer works in Burundi since the killing of its three delegates; they say they are waiting for a governmental inquiry. The Burundian military led an inquiry, and immediately blamed Hutu extremists. Those who allegedly took part in the ambush say that the Burundian military officer who led the official inquiry also set up the ambush.

No one has been punished or brought to trial. In an effort to take pressure off the Burundian Army, British and American diplomats in Rwanda and Burundi were still claiming a year after the incident that the ambush had been a mistake, and that in reality it had been meant for the correspondent of Reuters News Agency, also present that day in Cibitoke. But the reporter is also given protection as a noncombatant, and would not have been a lawful target either.

(See **perfidy and treachery**.)

R

Refoulement

By David Rieff

"We cannot return to Rwanda," the young man in the sweat-stained Denver Broncos T-shirt told me earnestly. "We are Hutus, you see, and were we to do so we would surely be killed."

It was a hot day in the early fall of 1994, and we were standing on the grounds of the cathedral in the center of Goma in what was then eastern Zaire. So great was the crush of people that it was hard to hear everything he was saying. And his friends constantly interrupted him. "We can't be sent back," one of them declared. "That would be immoral. We would be killed." "Not just immoral," a third young man added, "it would be illegal. A UNHCR [United Nations High Commissioner for Refugees] official told us that only this morning. We cannot be sent back. That would be refoulement."

There was a hush after the word was uttered. It was this prohibition against refoulement, which means the forced return of a person to a country where he or she faces persecution, that provided for these destitute Hutus their only possible protection against being killed. Defeated on the battlefield, decimated by the cholera epidemic that had exacted a fierce toll from them when they had first arrived from Rwanda, they had discovered the saving grace of **refugee** law, and repeated its provisions like a mantra.

"We are refugees. We cannot be made to go back home," the young man said, "Would you be willing to return to Rwanda if you were in our place?"

The answer to that was easy enough, but the reasons were far more complicated than the refugees wanted to admit. Of the more than 2 million people who fled Rwanda in the aftermath of the genocide of the spring and early summer of 1994 in which between 500,000 and 1 million Tutsis and liberal Hutus were killed, tens of thousands (at a conservative estimate) were either soldiers and officials of the defeated Hutu regime. Many thousands more had been caught up in the frenzy of killing and were guilty of murdering their Tutsi neighbors. But hundreds of thousands of others had played no role in the genocide including thousands of children, many born in the UNHCR-administered refugee camps.

Separating those who were not entitled to refugee status from those who were was an impossible task for UNHCR officials, whose experience lay more in trying to secure the protections refugees are entitled to under international law than in separating legitimate refugees from soldiers who had crossed the border, or from criminals who had committed crimes in Rwanda and whose return there would have been an act of justice, not a violation of international law. The United Nations Convention Relating to the Status of Refugees and its 1967 Additional Protocol stipulated that refugees could not be returned to a place where they faced persecution. But surely its architects had never imagined a situation like the one that occurred in Goma.

Previously, most instances of refoulement involved individuals fleeing across an international border, or, in some cases, moving on to a third country, and claiming that, were they sent home, they would face persecution. An Iraqi Kurd arriving at the Frankfurt airport and being sent home, a Haitian making her way to Miami in a leaky boat and being towed back to Port-au-Prince by a U.S. Coast Guard cutter—these are the instances of refoulement over which international law has some intellectual and moral purchase. In this context, it is possible to talk about the requirements for what constitutes "persecution" within the meaning of the refugee convention; in practice, these requirements differ in interpretation from country to country, but in principle any person who can legitimately claim refugee status is protected from refoulement. Only when a person ceases to be a refugee does the rule against refoulement cease to apply. The real debate is when a refugee gets the right. Are illegal aliens covered? Some countries believe they are; others do not. Does a person have to enter a country officially to get refugee status and the accompanying protection against refoulement? Again, the opinions of international lawyers and governments differ.

What became clear in Goma was that in instances of mass migration—where children and murderers arrive in a great mass, and separating them is

Draconian attacks by the Rwandan Tutsi-led military break the stranglehold of the Hutu militia on the camps in the Congo, and a flood of Hutu refugees begins the long journey home to Rwanda, 1997.

neither easy nor safe—the law is very hard to use, and harder still to use appropriately. Nobody in those camps wanted to return to Rwanda; many had killed before, and there was no reason to suppose they would not kill again.

For UNHCR, it was better to err on the side of maintaining its protection mandate and the prohibition against refoulement than to send back people who feared persecution in a Rwanda where power had changed hands; even if doing so meant, in practical terms, allowing mass murderers to claim the rights of innocent refugees. For those who wanted the Rwandan crisis to be brought to a close, and saw in the refugee camps little more than a safe haven for those who had perpetrated the genocide and their dependents, the prohibition against refoulement seemed like madness.

For two years, UNHCR's view prevailed. Then, the Rwandan Army struck at the camps. Most refugees were forced back across the border. It was an unhappy solution to a problem for which legal definitions of refugee status and legal prohibitions against refoulement only serve as poor guides.

Refugees, Rights of

By David Rieff

Two emblematic figures, the exile and the refugee, loom large in our consciousness at century's end. The twentieth century has been a time of vast refugee flows. Part of this can be attributed to the fact that it is easier to cross borders now than it was, say, 150 years ago. People have always wanted to move away from danger zones; today, whatever the risks, they have the means to do so. As a result, when Hurricane Mitch devastated Honduras in 1998, many predicted that within a matter of months Honduran refugees would pour into the United States.

The Honduran refugees are fleeing a natural disaster and, as such, are something of an anomaly, since refugees from natural disasters constitute only a small percentage of the more than 50 million refugees and displaced people

R

in the world. When most people think of refugees they usually think of the victims of political repression, as in East Timor, religious persecution, as in Tibet, or of civilians fleeing a war zone in which they have become the targets, as in a dozen conflicts from the Democratic Republic of the Congo to Kosovo.

Of course, there is nothing new about repression, and the question of whether war has grown more barbarous in the twentieth century remains a controversial one. Those who, in the aftermath of World War II, devised the international humanitarian law (IHL) on refugees seemed to have believed that it had. So do those who have spent time in such killing zones as Bosnia, South Sudan, and the Great Lakes region of Africa. There, civilians are more often than not the preferred targets of the belligerents, and every villager caught in these maelstroms is, when viewed in a certain light, a potential refugee.

Perhaps this is why Sadako Ogata, the United Nations High Commissioner for Refugees, once observed that "refugees are the symptoms of the ills of an age"—our age. In almost every crisis that has plagued or

Carrying her meager household possessions a refugee woman scans the skies for attacking war planes. Tigre, Ethiopia, 1985.

R

baffled us since the end of the Cold War, from Tajikistan to Burundi, the refugee issue has been at the center. There has been no escaping it, and, it seems, no resolving it.

This is not because of an absence of laws, but, rather, a lack of implementation. Indeed, if the political will of the powerful nations of the world matched the legal protections that already exist for refugees, many of the cruelest tragedies of the last part of the twentieth century might have been greatly diminished. A raft of treaties passed in the aftermath of World War II, and, half a century later, the accumulating weight of customary law guarantees refugee rights. Unlike in the case, say, of internally displaced persons (the distinction is that a refugee is a person who crosses an international border), refugees enjoy a wide array of rights and protections including the right to certain kinds of legal aid and material assistance. Compared to what should be, the situation of refugees in the world today is appalling; compared to what it would be without IHL, it is at least not hopeless. The two most important laws concerning refugees are the Fourth Geneva Convention of 1949, the 1977 First Additional Protocol to the Geneva Conventions, and the 1951 UN Convention Relating to the Status of Refugees. The Geneva Conventions required a certain humane standard of treatment for civilians who do not enjoy diplomatic status. The Fourth Convention granted refugees the right not to be returned to the country where they faced danger or could legitimately claim that they would be subject to religious or political persecution. Additional Protocol I extended the standard for civilian protection set in the 1949 Geneva Conventions to include all civilians regardless of their nationality.

The UN Convention Relating to the Status of Refugees defines who refugees are and how they are to be treated. For the most part, the guarantees the convention grants are the basic human rights outlined in other international legal instruments. Refugees are not to be returned to the place where they face persecution, nor, except on grounds of national security, are they to be expelled without due process. They are not to be treated as illegal aliens (a key right, particularly in western Europe and North America where the authorities routinely try to claim that people claiming refugee status are really economic migrants). Their right to move about in their country of asylum is not to be unnecessarily restricted, and they are to be given identity papers if they do not have them.

In a world awash in refugees, where people in rich countries feel overwhelmed by the press of economic migrants, legal and illegal, and where people in poor countries in areas adjacent to conflict zones have neither the resources nor the expertise to deal with vast refugee flows (2 million Rwandan refugees crossed the border into Zaire in less than a week in the summer of 1994), this has meant that where refugees have been concerned, the situation has grown more and more difficult. In particular, the burdens on the main international organization charged with protecting refugees, the Office of the UN High Commissioner for Refugees, have become excruciating. More generally, the gap between the law and realities on the ground is greater in the area of refugee rights than almost any other. Perhaps that gap is an emblem of failure. But many refugee advocates say that it gives us the means actually to make the ideals of refugee protection a reality, whereas if no such body of law existed, and the idea of protection had not been enshrined within it, the situation would be even more dire than it is.
(See **internal displacement**; **refoulement**; **victims, rights of**.)

Reprisal

By Frits Kalshoven

When a belligerent party is hurt by conduct on the part of its adversary that it regards as a grave breach or systematic encroachment of the laws of armed conflict, one possibility is to retaliate by means of an action that itself violates the same body of law. While recourse to such retaliatory action can be arbitrary and in total disregard of any constraints, rules of customary law have developed in the past that provide the limits within which retaliation could be regarded as a legitimate reprisal. The main elements of this customary "right of reprisal" are: subsidiarity (failure of all other available means), notice (formal warning of the planned action), proportionality (the damage and suffering inflicted on the adverse party not to exceed the level of damage and suffering resulting from its unlawful conduct), temporary character (termination of the reprisal when the adversary stops violating the law).

A reprisal may be "in kind" (violating the same or a narrowly related rule of the laws of armed conflict) or "not in kind" (violating a nonrelated rule). In either case, the reprisal need not and usually cannot be directed against those persons on the adverse side who are responsible for the unlawful conduct, and hence tends mainly to affect people who are "innocent" of that conduct. Also, the adversary often regards an alleged reprisal as a plainly unlawful act that in turn justifies reprisals, leading to a spiral of increasingly serious damage and suffering.

These features have led to a trend to ban reprisals wherever possible. As a result, all four Geneva Conventions of 1949 categorically prohibit reprisals against the persons and objects they are designed to protect. Likewise, Article 20, which concludes the part of Additional Protocol I of 1977 on the wounded, sick, and shipwrecked, prohibits reprisals against the persons and objects protected by that part.

While these bans are generally accepted as entirely justified, the provisions in Articles 51 through 55 of Additional Protocol I prohibiting reprisals against civilians and civilian objects are highly controversial, and some States have entered reservations to their treaty ratifications. A recent example of a reserving State is the United Kingdom, which has formulated its reservation in terms that would permit it to undertake customary "in kind" reprisals.

Additional Protocol II of 1977 is silent on the matter of reprisals. This should not however be interpreted as a right for parties to an internal armed conflict to resort to retaliatory action; the better view is that essential requirements of humanity accepted for international armed conflict apply by way of analogy in internal armed conflicts as well.

(See **protected persons; reprisal killings.**)

R

CRIME

Reprisal Killings

By Kenneth Anderson

In 1944, following the Allied landings at Normandy, French resistance partisans began operating openly and on a large scale against German forces. Organized into the French Forces of the Interior (FFI), they were in contact with the Allied command and the Gaullist Provisional Government of France, although they operated under command independent from those forces. By wearing insignia visible at a distance, carrying their arms openly, operating under responsible command, and adhering to the laws of armed conflict, the FFI qualified as combatants as defined by the 1929 Geneva Convention.

The Germans, however, did not recognize the FFI as legal **combatants**. They took the view that, following the 1940 armistice, France was no longer at war with Germany, and so its citizens in the FFI were criminals, not combatants. The FFI for its part claimed that the Franco-German armistice had been breached and hostilities had resumed. By their reasoning, French forces fighting according to the 1929 rules had to be granted combatant rights, including prisoner of war status for captured fighters. Because Germany did not view the FFI as legal combatants, it killed numbers of them out of hand, by summary execution. On the day after the Normandy landings, for example, the Germans shot fifteen partisans captured at Caen.

As the scale of fighting in France increased, the German claim that the armistice and its terms were still legally in place became unsustainable. Nevertheless, the German forces continued to execute FFI fighters, even though Charles de Gaulle's Provisional Government protested on behalf of the FFI and threatened reprisals. By late summer 1944, many German soldiers had surrendered to the FFI, and the FFI was in a position to act. When it became known to the FFI that the Germans had executed eighty partisans and planned to execute more, the FFI announced that it would carry out eighty reprisal executions. The International Committee of the Red Cross (ICRC) sought to intervene and obtained a postponement pending an agreement by the Germans to grant the FFI legal combatant status. After six days without a German response, the FFI executed eighty German prisoners. It appears that no further FFI fighters were executed after that.

Reprisal is a legal term in international humanitarian law (IHL) describing a particular kind of retaliation. To be a reprisal, it must be undertaken for the purpose of forcing, or inducing, enemy forces to cease their own violation of IHL. It is a self-enforcement of the laws of war, for reprisal is undertaken not in retaliation or punishment, but rather to force the other side to stop its violation. For this reason, a reprisal is technically an action that, if done on its own, would constitute a violation of IHL. When, however, it is done for the purpose of forcing an adverse party to cease violating IHL, it may become a legal act, providing all the legal criteria are met. Moreover, an act of reprisal, to be a reprisal and not mere retaliation, must be proportionate to the violation of IHL committed by the other side.

Today, reprisal has almost entirely disappeared from the canon of IHL. Even assuming that the German position on the legality of FFI combatants was wrong, the 1929 Geneva Convention specifically outlawed precisely this kind of reprisal using prisoners of war. Each successive revision of IHL treaties has put additional categories of combatants and civilians beyond the reach of reprisal actions. The 1949 Geneva Conventions extend the prohibition from prisoners of war to those civilians protected by the Fourth Geneva Convention, and Additional Protocol I of 1977 specifically extends the protection to civilians of any kind as well as to "civilian objects." Perhaps the only circumstance in which IHL today still permits reprisal actions, if at all, is as a response to the use of illegal methods or weapons against combatants. The trend, clearly, is to outlaw reprisal under all circumstances.

The FFI killings of the German soldiers, although effective in stopping the German summary executions, were plainly a violation of IHL as then in force, and would certainly be a violation of IHL and a grave breach of the Geneva Conventions and Additional Protocol I today.

German soldiers surrender to free French forces in Paris. August 25, 1944.

(See **protected persons**.)

Rwanda—
The Genocide Mark Huband

The term genocide is used widely and sometimes loosely, but what took place in Rwanda in April and May of 1994 was the third unquestionable genocide of the twentieth century. As defined by the 1948 Convention for the Prevention and Punishment of the Crime of Genocide, it consists of certain acts "committed with an intent to destroy, in whole or in part, a national, ethnical, racial, or religious group as such." In Rwanda, some-where between 500,000 and 1 million Tutsis and moderate Hutus, who fit the convention's definition of a national group, were murdered.

The planning of this **genocide**, which was important legally because it estab-lished the clear intent of its architects to commit the crime, had become known to the United Nations well before it took place. The Rwandan govern-ment's effort in 1993 to carry out a census in which all Rwandans had to state their tribe had been followed by a slaughter of Tutsis in the northern part of the country. This would prove to be a macabre dress rehearsal for the genocide of 1994.

In the interim, the Rwandan president, Juvenal Habyarimana, signed a peace accord in Arusha, Tanzania, with the Tutsi-led Rwandan Patriotic Front (RPF) that was intended to end the country's four-year civil war. Whether President Habyarimana sincerely intended peace, or more likely, viewed it as a pause in which to finalize plans to exterminate the Tutsis, will probably never be answered conclusively. What is clear is that he was restructuring the Hutu-dominated national administration to put extremists in positions of authority—extremists whose main goal was to conspire to launch a final, genocidal strike against the hated Tutsi minority.

On April 6, 1994, President Habyarimana flew back from Tanzania after a meeting on the peace process. As Habyarimana's plane attempted to land in the Rwandan capital, Kigali, it was shot down by extremist members of the president's own party. They were, in any case, quite ready to sacrifice him since they believed he had conceded too much to the RPF in the peace agreement, even if only temporarily.

Habyarimana's death served as the pretext to launch the genocide. Rwanda's national radio as well as a number of private stations relayed instructions to the death squads, the so-called Interahamwe (the name, in Kinyarwanda, means "those who fight together"), and ceaselessly urged the killers to step up their slaughter. The Rwandan armed forces backed up the Interahamwe in those areas where the killers encountered resistance from Tutsi civilians. Prepositioned transport and fuel permitted the death squads to reach even the most isolated Tutsi communities.

Other genocides—the Turkish slaughter of the Armenians, the Nazi extermination of Europe's Jews and Gypsies—took place largely in secret. Rwanda was different. There was a United Nations peacekeeping force on the ground in Rwanda. Its members stood by and watched as the killings took place. The rest of the world watched on television as Rwanda exploded.

Unhallowed ground: A rotting corpse outside the parish church of Nyarabuye offers a grim foretelling of the thousand more slaughtered inside by Hutu militia.

I recall a young woman pleading silently through the terror in her eyes as she was led to her death past French UN troops. The French were guarding foreign evacuees fleeing the Rwandan capital in an open truck, and a government militia had ordered the convoy to halt on a muddy road near the city's airport. The UN troops waited obediently, saying it was "not our mandate" to intervene. Beside them in a compound, two men were kneeling in silence as the militiamen crushed their heads with clubs, then cut their throats. The woman knelt beside them. Within less than a minute her head was all but severed. Then the convoy was allowed to move on.

The world's governments not only knew what was occurring but were complicit. Article 1 of the Genocide Convention binds its signatories to act to prevent as well as to punish genocide. The fact that the UN knew the genocide was being planned and, presumably, communicated this knowledge to member-States, and the fact that once the genocide began nothing was done, makes what took place in Rwanda in 1994 more than a crime. It was an event that shamed humanity.

It is clear by now that far from having been caught unawares, the great powers were intent on obscuring the reality of what was taking place in Rwanda. When the Security Council met, it was decided that the representative of Rwanda—of the government that was committing the genocide— would be allowed to make a statement. For all practical purposes, the council's main concern appears to have been to debate for as long as possible the question of whether a genocide was taking place.

There were thousands of examples of the State's role. At the Nyarubuye Catholic Mission in eastern Rwanda, I happened upon Leoncia Mukandayambaje, a survivor, sitting outside her hut among the trees. She had fled there when the local mayor, Sylvestre Gacumbitsi, had given the local Tutsi population special passes to allow them to reach the large brick complex. After grouping them there, he arranged for two truckloads of murderers to be sent.

In school rooms, in cloisters, in corridors, and in doorways, the 2,620 victims covered the floor in a carpet of rotting death. Leoncia was saved by her baby daughter, whom she held close to her while the murderers hacked both with machetes. Her daughter's blood covered her. The murderers assumed both mother and child were dead.

By the time the UN Security Council had finally concluded what was plain from the start—that a genocide had indeed been taking place—it was too late to do anything for the people of Rwanda. To have admitted otherwise would have bound the parties to the Genocide Convention, among whom were all the permanent members of the Security Council, to intervene and bring the mass murder to a halt. The council, on May 26, did eventually find that a genocide was taking place. By that time, half a million had died. Secretary-General Boutros-Ghali's acknowledgement was too little, too late.

He was still ahead of U.S. Secretary of State Warren Christopher. From the beginning of the slaughter, the U.S. government had prohibited its officials from using the term *genocide*. Finally, on June 10, Christopher relented, reluctantly and with bad grace. "If there is any particular magic in calling it genocide," he conceded, "I have no hesitancy in saying that."

There was magic, all right, in the sense that using the term would have bound the United States and other governments to act. By the time Christopher made his grudging concession to reality, it was too late, which may have been the idea all along.

The complicity of the so-called world community in the Rwandan genocide should not, of course, obscure the fact that the principal responsibility for the crime lies with its Rwandan architects. Apologists for the Rwandan authorities insisted at the time that the killings were unfortunate by-products of a renewal of the civil war. Later, Hutu extremists justified the killings as acts of self-defense against Tutsi aggression. Such arguments stood reality on its head. Almost all the victims in the spring of 1994 were killed as part of a government-inspired campaign of extermination, not as casualties of the subsequent fighting between the Rwandan Army and the RPF.

According to the provisions of the Genocide Convention, the government was guilty on all counts of the Convention's Article 3: genocide, conspiracy to commit genocide, direct and public **incitement** to commit genocide, and complicity in genocide. Members of the government had used its administration to organize the slaughter and, equally grave, incited the Hutu civilian population to kill their Tutsi neighbors and even, for intermarriage was

Hutu refugees, some possibly implicated in genocide themselves, plead with UN Peacekeepers for protection when the Rwandan Army attacks the Kibeho Refugee Camp. Southern Rwanda, April 22, 1995.

R

common in Rwanda, to kill Tutsi spouses and relatives.

After the slaughter was over, an international tribunal was established to bring the guilty to book, to try them under international humanitarian law and under the provisions of the Genocide Convention. Doubtless, such trials are better than nothing. At least, in the Rwandan case, there will not be total impunity. But trials are a poor substitute for prevention, and the one thing that is clear is that the Rwandan genocide could have been prevented had the outside world had the will to do so. The facts were plain. The legal basis for intervention was there. It was courage that was lacking.
(See **United Nations and the Geneva Conventions.**)

Rwanda—Refugees and Genocidaires Lindsey Hilsum

She was a broad-hipped, middle-aged woman in a Virgin Mary blue dress, one of a million Rwandan Hutu refugees. Her job was to trace the families of orphaned and abandoned children in a refugee camp in eastern Zaire.

But Paulina Nyiramasuhuko had a past. In April 1994, when the genocide of Rwanda's Tutsis and opposition-Hutus was under way, peasant farmer Grace Hagenimana saw Nyiramasuhuko address a meeting at a place called Runyinya. "She came to encourage the people to kill. I saw her in a car with gendarmes as escorts. She said, you must start work, you must chase out the enemies. Then people picked up their machetes." Hagenimana's husband was among those killed.

R

Nyiramasuhuko now awaits trial at the International War Crimes Tribunal in Arusha, Tanzania, where she has been charged with **genocide**, complicity in genocide, **crimes against humanity**, and serious violations of Article 3 common to the four Geneva Conventions of 1949, and of Additional Protocol II. Her story exemplifies international ambivalence toward the war criminals who led the 1994 genocide in Rwanda. As minister of women, Nyiramasuhuko was one of the best-known, most easily identifiable members of the government that orchestrated the slaughter. But she escaped to Zaire through the Zone Turquoise, the area controlled by French forces whose aim was supposedly to bring humanitarian relief and protection to the victims. Once in the refugee camp near Bukavu, she was employed by the Spanish chapter of the Catholic relief organization Caritas (Latin for "loving care") as a social services coordinator. For three years, she traveled undisturbed between Zaire and Kenya. She was finally arrested in Nairobi in July 1997 after the current Rwandese government pressured President Moi.

Failure to apply international law at critical moments has prolonged the suffering of the people of central Africa. Huge sums in emergency aid money

This Hutu man was too sympathetic to the Tutsis, according to the Interhamawe militia, who slashed his head with a machete.

R

have been spent, at the expense of rebuilding the region's economy.

The French government, under President François Mitterand, never hid its antipathy to the Anglophone Rwandese Patriotic Front (RPF), the guerrilla army whose military victory ended the genocide. The French allowed dozens of known "genocidaires," including Pauline, to transit the Zone Turquoise, escaping the tightening noose of the RPF.

The killers reinvented themselves as leaders of refugee camps, supported by international aid agencies, under the UN High Commissioner for Refugees (UNHCR). International obligations under the humanitarian law and the Genocide Convention were subjugated to a general desire to save lives. The guilty were fed alongside the thousands of children whose images haunted Western television viewers. The administrative structures that had facilitated the killing in Rwanda were reproduced in the camps.

Those who had fled justice were never separated from those who had not killed. It was never defined whose responsibility such a difficult and dangerous task might be. This failure resulted in a violation of international law. The camps became safe haunts for war criminals, and bases for guerrilla attacks aiming to destabilize Rwanda, where the new Tutsi-led RPF government was trying to consolidate its power.

When Rwandan government soldiers attacked the refugees in November 1996, exercise books detailing terrorist tactics and the Hutu extremist version of history littered the abandoned camps. Faced with the evidence of what they had succored, one senior aid worker said: "We never knew what went on at night."

The violent breakup of the camps forced most refugees back to Rwanda, but several hundred thousand fled deep into the jungles of eastern Zaire, soon to be renamed Congo. The evidence of terrified eyewitnesses suggests that Rwandan government soldiers—many of them relatives of the victims of genocide—massacred thousands. Rwandan government representatives have at times denied the killings and at other times justified them under international law, saying the victims were known "genocidaires," planning to reinvade Rwanda using children and other refugees as a "human shield." But the countenance of survivors, weakened by their odyssey through the bush, suggested that these pathetic, desperate people no longer constituted an actual threat to the well-equipped Rwandan forces. It has been argued that the killings of Hutus in the jungles of Congo were unprovoked attacks on civilians and refugees, therefore war crimes.

Now Hutu extremist rebels mount hit-and-run raids on Tutsis and army installations inside Rwanda, while government soldiers move against Hutus they suspect of supporting the rebels. Rwanda remains a land of fear, mistrust, and death.

So the international failure to move rapidly against war criminals has condemned central Africa to a still unbroken cycle of violence and impunity.

Safety Zones

By Adam Roberts

The sieges or bombardments of Leningrad, Dresden, Hiroshima, Vukovar, Sarajevo, and Srebrenica caused huge civilian losses and suffering. However, most attempts to devise schemes to protect particular places from the horrors of war have had limited success.

Safety zones is an unofficial term covering a wide variety of attempts to declare certain areas off-limits for military targeting. The Fourth Geneva Convention of 1949 and Additional Protocol I provide for three main types: hospital zones, neutralized zones, and demilitarized zones. These treaty arrangements require consent between belligerents, depend on complete demilitarization, and do not specify any arrangements for defending the areas. They have been used only occasionally.

In post–Cold War conflicts, the UN Security Council or other bodies rather than belligerents have proclaimed safety zones ad hoc. Such areas have been variously called "corridors of tranquillity," "humanitarian corridors," "neutral zones," "protected areas," "safe areas," "safe havens," "secure humanitarian areas," "security corridors," and "security zones." Two motivations have been the safety of refugees and the prevention of massive new refugee flows. Military activity has generally continued within the areas. Unlike self-declared "**undefended towns**," safety zones are not envisaged as being open for occupation by the hostile power.

In northern Iraq after the 1991 Gulf War, the Western powers, having encouraged an abortive Kurdish uprising, established a safe haven enabling some 400,000 Kurdish refugees who had fled to the Turkish border to return. UN agencies subsequently took charge.

The UN Security Council established six safe areas in Bosnia-Herzegovina in 1993 to protect the inhabitants of six towns from Bosnian Serb forces besieging them, but it never defined the geographical limits or its commitment to protect them. The Serbs complained the Bosnians were using these zones to launch attacks against them; yet the zones could not have been neutralized because the inhabitants were unwilling to entrust their security to international forces. In July 1995 UN troops watched as Bosnian Serb forces conquered the safe areas of Srebrenica and Zepa and committed appalling atrocities.

Three-quarters of the way through the 1994 genocide in Rwanda, the Security Council decided on the establishment of secure humanitarian areas, but no country provided troops. Instead, when the worst of the killing was over, the council authorized France to establish by force a zone that ultimately provided refuge for Hutus who had organized the genocide, casting further doubt on the idea.

Overall, safety zones have saved many lives, but establishing them, preventing military activity in them, and protecting them from external assault is difficult and demanding. Safety zones rarely provide an enduring haven from the horrors of war.

(See **evacuation of civilians**.)

Sanctions

By Tom Gjelten

Children die because hospitals cannot get the medicines required to treat them. Factories close and unemployment soars because manufacturers cannot import the supplies and materials they need or export their finished products. Basic foodstuffs are so expensive that the average family can no longer afford to eat well. Can the imposition of sanctions against a nation under some circumstances be a war crime?

Had the argument not been made so often by such disreputable world figures as Saddam Hussein and Slobodan Milosevic, the question might be taken more seriously. When a State—or a group of States—refuses to trade with another country, it is the civilian population in the targeted country that suffers the most. Inevitably, sanctions inflict harm on innocent people, and in extreme cases they may violate international humanitarian law (IHL).

Sanctions arise in a variety of ways. Article 41 of the United Nations Charter authorizes the Security Council to decide on "measures not involving the use of armed force . . . to give effect to its decisions. . . . These may include complete or partial interruption of economic relations and of rail, sea, air, postal, telegraphic, radio, and other means of communication, and the severance of diplomatic relations." International embargoes against Rhodesia, Libya, Haiti, Iraq, and Yugoslavia were enacted under this provision. Alternatively, sanctions can be ordered by a regional organization, as the European Union has done in the Yugoslav case. They can also be imposed unilaterally by one country against another, as in the example of the U.S. trade embargo against Cuba.

A more important distinction is whether the sanctions were imposed or enforced during wartime by one or more of the warring parties. IHL does not apply in the absence of armed conflict. This means that "nonbelligerent" sanctions, including those against Cuba, Libya, Haiti, Rhodesia, and Yugoslavia, may be opposed on moral or political terms but normally cannot be considered war crimes. Supporters of economic sanctions may even justify them as an alternative to military action.

In the case of Iraq, the United States and other countries applied sanctions before launching the Gulf War, in an effort to force the Iraqi regime to withdraw from neighboring Kuwait, which it had invaded in August 1990. But the imposing countries, including the United States, continued to enforce the sanctions in wartime, so they had to conform to IHL.

The 1977 Additional Protocols to the 1949 Geneva Conventions prohibit any wartime measure that has the effect of depriving a civilian population of objects indispensable to its survival. Article 70 of Protocol I mandates relief operations to aid a civilian population that is "not adequately provided" with supplies. Article 18 of Protocol II calls for relief operations for a civilian population that suffers "undue hardship owing to a lack of supplies essential for its survival, such as foodstuffs and medical supplies." Such provisions establish the legally permissible limit of sanctions, though their definition is subject to interpretation. The UN embargo against Iraq exempts "humanitarian" aid, but critics say the sanctions still cause excessive suffering.

Other provisions of IHL similarly restrict the scope and bite of economic

S

sanctions. Article 33 of the Fourth Geneva Convention (on the protection of civilians in wartime), for example, prohibits "collective penalties." The International Committee of the Red Cross (ICRC) Commentary on the conventions interpreted this provision as prohibiting "penalties of any kind inflicted on persons or entire groups of persons in defiance of the most elementary principles of humanity, for acts that these persons have not committed."

Supporters of sanctions may defend the measures against this restriction by arguing that they do not constitute **collective punishment** because they target governments, not people, and that **collateral damage** to the civilian population is unintended and unfortunate. In the case of Iraq, however, that argument was undercut when U.S. officials suggested that the sanctions were intended to create hardship conditions in the country and thus encourage the popular overthrow of the government.

Sanctions imposed under nonbelligerent conditions must normally be judged on the basis of moral or political considerations rather than legal ones. The U.S. National Conference of Catholic Bishops has argued that "sanctions can offer a nonmilitary alternative to the terrible options of war or indifference when confronted with aggression or injustice." But some political philosophers disagree, arguing that aggressively applied sanctions, even in the absence of armed conflict, may be considered a form of **siege** and are objectionable on the same grounds. From this perspective, sanctions run the risk of becoming a form of war against civilians, waged by governments unwilling to expend the blood or treasure necessary to attack an enemy regime directly.

S

Sexual Violence

By Thom Shanker

She gave her name as Marijanna, but it really is Mirsada, and she said very little after arriving at the hospital in August of 1992, when the conflict in Bosnia-Herzegovina was only a few months old and the brutality of the shifting front lines still veiled stories of mass rape.

With the passing weeks, though, the pale-skinned, brown-haired girl—half Croat, half Muslim—spoke of being imprisoned with her mother and two dozen other women in the basement of a municipal hall in her home town of Teslic, in north-central Bosnia. Her jailers, Bosnian Serb **irregulars**, raped her and the others and forced them to have sex with uniformed Bosnian Serb troops deploying through the area. She and her mother each had to watch as the other was gang-raped three times a day, every day, for four months. Mirsada was released only when she became visibly pregnant, and her jailer-rapists said: "Go bear our Serbian children." By the time she crossed the front and found medical care in Croatia, the fetus was too developed to be safely aborted. As she sat in the maternity ward of Zagreb's Petrova Hospital, she kept a palm over her stomach. In her womb was ever-growing evidence of the ever-expanding horror of the Bosnian war. Mirsada was seventeen.

Rape as a spoil of combat can be found throughout history, as far back as the oral recounting of Mediterranean warrior-kings attributed to Homer, but today it has become the focus of international law as never before. Through the ages, the practice of seizing women as war booty, hardly different than cattle and corn, may have been superseded by the rise of a Judeo-Christian tradition and the development of **customary laws** of war in the West, but those laws had scant impact on public acceptance of rape as a natural, if unfortunate, by-product when men took up arms against men. This worldwide shrug, in effect saying that rape is an unavoidable part of the battlefield, caused initial stories from Bosnia to be viewed as unremarkable by citizens in the West (who were confused by the war itself) and discounted by politicians in the West (lest public alarm at atrocities force them to action). It was not until victims like Mirsada came forward and foreign correspondents confirmed the archipelago of sex-enslavement camps and uncovered a program of systematic mass rape that the world took notice, and arguments could be raised that the rapes constituted **crimes against humanity** and were elements of a premeditated program of **genocide**.

Rape has been considered a war crime for centuries. In 1474, Sir Peter von Hagenbach was convicted by an international military tribunal on charges of rape during a military occupation. He had been appointed by Duke Charles the Bold of Burgundy to govern the Austrian town of Breisach, and his brutal tools to subdue the town included pillage, murder, and rape. During the American Civil War, the Union Army operated under a general order prepared by Francis Lieber and signed by President Lincoln in 1863 that made rape a capital offense. In this century, rape has been included—in increasingly explicit terms—in various treaties regulating the conduct of war, starting with Article 46 of the regulations annexed to the 1907 Hague Convention. It assures respect for "family honour and rights"; the prosecution relied on this provision when it brought war crimes charges relating to the pandemic rape of Nanking, China, in the postwar trial before the Tokyo Tribunal.

The history of twentieth-century warfare has shown, though, how little formal and customary laws of war have been observed—and how rarely they have been enforced. The Soviet Army raped its way across Prussia and into Berlin in the final days of World War II, yet Moscow's military judges took a victor's place of honor on the bench at Nuremberg. In fact, the founding statute of the International Military Tribunal in Nuremberg made no specific reference to rape, relying on language prohibiting inhumane treatment to encompass rapes committed by Nazis. And the companion tribunal in Tokyo phrased its provision for war crimes jurisdiction in highly general terms, "namely, violations of the laws or customs of war."

From the postwar period, Article 27 of the Fourth Geneva Convention of 1949 clearly states that women shall be protected against any attack on their honor, in particular against rape, enforced prostitution, or any form of

An eighteen-year-old Muslim rape victim one day after aborting her enforced pregnancy. Bosnia, September 1992.

indecent assault. Article 27 only applies to international conflicts, however, and in the early months of the Bosnian War, the world community tied itself in knots arguing whether the conflict was a civil war within a constituent republic that was attempting to illegally secede from Yugoslavia, or whether the conflict was an international war of aggression, inspired and abetted by Belgrade, the capital of Serbia, against the newly sovereign state of Bosnia-Herzegovina.

This debate mattered not to the question of rape as a war crime. Women in noninternational conflicts are protected by Article 3 common to the four Geneva Conventions of 1949. Although rape is not explicitly prohibited, the prosecutor at the International Criminal Tribunal for the Former Yugoslavia brought sexual assault charges under Common Article 3, citing its provisions on cruel treatment, torture, and outrages upon human dignity, in particular, humiliating and degrading treatment. Women in both international and non-international conflicts are given further protection under the 1977 Additional Protocols to the Geneva Conventions. The appeals chamber of the Yugoslavia tribunal has said that the Common Article 3 establishes minimum guarantees for all armed conflicts. Thus, serious violations of its provisions in international, as well as internal, armed conflicts would be considered war crimes.

In the lengthening shadow of the Yugoslav conflict, it must be noted that sexual assault may also be a war crime when committed against men. Dusko Tadic, a Bosnian Serb, was convicted among other things of violating Common Article 3, as incorporated into the statute of the Yugoslav tribunal under the heading "violations of the laws or customs of war," for his role in the incident during which one detainee at Omarska was forced to bite off the testicle of another. The Yugoslav tribunal subsequently reaffirmed rape as a war crime by convicting Anto Furundzija, a Bosnian Croat paramilitary chief who allowed a subordinate to rape a Bosnian Muslim woman. In the Furundzija case, the first United Nations war crimes trial to focus exclusively on rape, the tribunal carefully chose gender-neutral terms in defining the elements of rape committed against "the victim," whether man or woman.

Consensus is mounting in the international community that rape in wartime—as it falls under a definition of torture or inhumane treatment and as an action willfully causing great suffering or serious injury to body or health—can be considered a grave breach under Article 147 of the Fourth Geneva Convention, which sets out crimes for which States can be held accountable.

Whether by custom, conscience, core principles of humanity, or codified by international law, rape is outlawed as an act of war. It achieved its most recent codification in the new statute establishing a permanent International Criminal Court, adopted by the United Nations diplomatic conference in Rome on July 17, 1998. For the first time, forced pregnancy was listed as a crime under international law, and with a definition that suggests it be used to punish ethnic cleansing: "The unlawful confinement, of a woman forcibly made pregnant, with the intent of affecting the ethnic composition of any population or carrying out other grave violations of international law." The court's statutes treat as a crime against humanity acts of rape, sexual slavery, enforced prostitution, forced pregnancy, enforced sterilization, or any other form of sexual violence of comparable gravity, whether during war or peace, if of a widespread or systematic nature. These same acts of sexual violence also may constitute a grave breach of the Geneva Conventions if committed during an international conflict or a serious violation of Common Article 3 if committed during an internal conflict.

In Bosnia, rape was a weapon of combat. After Mirsada gave birth to a healthy, nine-and-one-half-pound girl, she refused to see the baby. The Zagreb maternity staff, mostly Catholics not expert in Muslim names, called the newborn Emina, after a romantic but sad poem by a favorite Bosnian poet. On the second day after the birth, the nurses noticed that Mirsada was not in her room, nor in the ward, nor anywhere on the hospital grounds. She never contacted the hospital again. Mirsada, though, is not seeking justice against her attackers. Her name does not appear on the roles of witnesses to be called at The Hague, nor is she among those who have contacted victims-rights attorneys bringing separate civil lawsuits against the architects of ethnic cleansing and genocide in Bosnia.

Sexual Violence: Systematic Rape

By Alexandra Stiglmayer

Although the phrase "systematic rape" was widely and correctly used to describe certain forms of the sexual crimes committed against women during the war in Bosnia-Herzegovina, there is no specific crime of systematic rape under international law.

But proving that rape is widespread or systematic is important for establishing a **crime against humanity**. The systematic character of rape may also help establish the stringent intent requirement for the charge of **genocide**.

The systematic pattern of rapes might also be relevant in establishing the criminal responsibility of superior officers for sexual assaults committed by subordinates. Under the statute of the Yugoslavia Tribunal, a commander can be prosecuted for rapes committed by his subordinates if he ordered or aided and abetted the rapes, or if he "knew or had reason to know that the subordinate was about to commit such acts or had done so and the superior failed to take the necessary and reasonable measures to prevent such acts or to punish the perpetrators thereof."

Women in Bosnia-Herzegovina were raped to humiliate and demoralize, as part of a program to terrorize, to drive away the unwanted ethnic "other," to boost the military's morale. It was a broad, systematic—even strategic— campaign, and one encouraged by authorities.

In 1993, a European Community commission estimated the number of rape victims in Bosnia-Herzegovina at twenty thousand. The Muslim-led government insisted the number was fifty thousand. A United Nations commission called systematic rape "an instrument for **ethnic cleansing**," and Human Rights Watch dubbed it "a weapon of war."

Commanders of future wars will have to take note of a historic judgment at Arusha. Jean-Paul Akayesu, mayor of Taba commune, had encouraged and even ordered others to commit rape and acts of sexual violence against Tutsi women, as well as to kill Tutsis outright. The court found that the rape of Tutsi women "was systematic and was perpetrated against all Tutsi women and solely against them." The trial chamber concluded that if done with intent to destroy a protected group in whole or in part, "rape and sexual violence constitute genocide in the same way as any other act," and that Akayesu had systematically targeted Tutsi women to contribute to the destruction of the Tutsi group as a whole. On September 2, 1998, Akayesu was convicted of counts relating to rape and sexual violence as genocide.

S

Sexual Violence: Enslavement and Forced Prostitution

By George Rodrigue

In June 1996, the International Criminal Tribunal for the Former Yugoslavia (ICTY) issued indictments against eight Bosnian Serb soldiers for the enslavement and rape of Muslim women in the eastern Bosnian town of Foca during 1992 and 1993. Members of the Serb military police were accused of repeatedly torturing and raping one fifteen-year-old girl over the course of eight months.

The girl's story was all too typical of the kind of practices that went on throughout the Bosnian war. In July 1992, with at least seventy-two other Muslims, she was held captive in the Foca high school. For a time, she was raped every night by one or more soldiers. The attacks continued after she was moved from the school to Foca's Partizan Sports Hall. And after that, when she was taken to a house that served as a Serb military brothel, she was turned into a servant as well as a sex slave, washing the clothes and cleaning for the soldiers who were raping her. According to the indictment, her captors eventually sold her for five hundred deutsche marks to two soldiers from Montenegro.

Victims' statements indicate overwhelmingly that what happened to the girl in Foca was anything but unique. Multiple witnesses, interviewed separately, described "rape camps" throughout Bosnian Serb–controlled territory, as well as a far smaller number of camps run by Croatian and Bosnian government forces.

This was not the first time the world was confronted with systematic enslavement of women. The 100,000 Asian "comfort women" enslaved in Japanese military brothels during World War II provide perhaps the ghastliest twentieth-century example. Other postwar courts convicted soldiers of the war crime of enforced prostitution: a Netherlands tribunal in Batavia convicted Japanese military defendants who had enslaved thirty-five Dutch women and girls in comfort stations for war crimes including rape, coercion to prostitution, abduction of women and girls for forced prostitution, and ill-treatment of prisoners. These principles have been reaffirmed in the 1949 Geneva Conventions and the 1977 Additional Protocols.

Under some conditions, the kinds of practices that took place with the comfort stations during World War II, and with the sex-slave camps in Bosnia, may constitute the **crime against humanity** of enslavement when they are committed as part of a widespread or systematic attack against a civilian population. In the Foca indictment at ICTY, two of the defendants have been charged with committing the crime against humanity of enslavement. It should be noted that **slavery** is an international crime, whether or not it is linked to a combat environment. The 1998 Rome Statute for the creation of a permanent International Criminal Court includes sexual slavery and enforced prostitution under its categories for crimes against humanity and grave breaches of the Geneva Conventions. It defines enslavement as the

*Every Wednesday for the past four years Kim Sun Duck, 76, and other Korean for-
mer comfort women have picketed the Japanese Embassy in Seoul seeking a public
apology and reparations.*

exercise of any or all of the powers attaching to the right of ownership over
a person and includes the exercise of such power in the course of trafficking
in persons, in particular, women and children.

It should be noted that slavery has long been recognized as an international crime in itself, whether or not committed in the course of armed
conflict or as part of a widespread or systematic attack against a civilian
population. But neither the existing nor the proposed international criminal
tribunals has jurisdiction over the crime of slavery as such; instead, they can
prosecute slavery only as a war crime or as a crime against humanity.

The legal basis for prosecuting those responsible for enforced prostitution and sexual slavery has long existed, even if prosecutions have not
always been robust. The post–Cold War environment of ethnic conflict will no
doubt offer more and equally tragic opportunities for these international
judicial frameworks.

Shields

By Robert Block

The world saw human shields on television when in the events preceding the Gulf War, the Iraqi government seized foreign nationals in both Iraq and Kuwait and held them at strategic and military installations. This is a most obvious case of using civilians as hostages or human shields to attempt to prevent an attack.

International humanitarian law (IHL) prohibits parties to conflict from using civilians to shield military objectives or military operations from attack. But armies and irregular forces use innocent civilians as human shields in conflicts all over the world. Often, they do it in a manner that, unlike Iraq's blatant example, is not instantly recognizable.

Two such cases occurred in the aftermath of the **Rwandan genocide** in mid-1994, when more than 1 million people fled to Zaire and lived in the squalor of refugee camps. Some did not go back because of their role in the slaughter by an extreme nationalist Hutu regime of as many as 1 million ethnic Tutsis and moderate Hutus. Others feared that Rwanda's new pro-Tutsi rulers would be unable to distinguish the guilty from the innocent who fled Rwanda in the final days of that country's civil war. But many others wanted to take a chance and go home where they had families and fertile land. They were not allowed to. Although considered **refugees** by the international community, they saw themselves as prisoners of those who ran the camps.

Marie Akizanye was forty-three years old in 1996 at the time she fled the Rwandan refugee camps in Zaire but looked twice her age. Her face was like dried-out leather. What little remained of the hair beneath her scarf was almost white, while her eyes were yellowed and glassy.

"We wanted to come back to Rwanda, but in the camp there were people who stopped us. They had guns and machetes and they threatened us with death if tried to come back," she said. "They told us that one day we would all go back together by force and they set up military bases among us to

A Salvadorian policeman uses an ice cream vendor as a human shield during a skirmish with demonstrators in San Salvador.

S

attack the enemy."

Indeed, between August 1994 and November 1997, the remnants of the armed forces of Rwanda and the dreaded Interahamwe militias still loyal to the defeated extremist regime of President Juvenal Habyarimana used the refugee camps in Zaire as a staging ground and launchpad for attacks into Rwanda. The extremists would stage raids into Rwanda from the camps and then seek refuge back there, using the refugees as shields from counterattacks. When the camps were broken up by a combined force of Rwanda's new Tutsi-dominated army and Zairean rebels, proof emerged of plans for a massive military invasion of Rwanda from the refugee camps.

Under international law, parties to a conflict must keep military assets as far as possible from concentrations of civilians. It is also a crime of war to use any civilians as a human shield. According to Article 51 of the 1977 Additional Protocol I to the 1949 Geneva Conventions: "The presence or movements of the civilian population or individual civilians shall not be used to render certain points or areas immune from military operations, in particular in attempts to shield military objects from attacks or to shield, favor or impede military operations."

The second example occurred in 1997. Zairean rebels fighting to overthrow the government of dictator Mobutu Sese Seko often complained that when they approached groups of Rwandan refugees who were then fleeing Zaire's civil war, they were often fired upon by armed elements hiding among the civilians. This fact was in turn used as an excuse by the rebels to indiscriminately attack refugee areas, often massacring hundreds of women, children, and elderly—clearly illegal under IHL.

Some cases are not so cut-and-dried.

One such incident took place in El Salvador in March 1984. Under attack for its appalling human rights record, and unable to convince the world that it was waging a righteous struggle against Communist insurgents, El Salvador's military was searching for an incident to bolster its case before upcoming elections.

The army's prayers appeared to have been answered one Monday evening outside the small town of San Antonio Grande when rebels of the Farabundo Marti National Liberation Front (FMLN) attacked a train traveling from the town of San Vicente in the west of the country to the capital, San Salvador.

The railway line cut though the heart of guerrilla territory. Trains plying this route were regularly fired upon or blown up. But these were always cargo trains, usually carrying supplies for the military or the businesses of the army's wealthy patrons—clear military objectives. This time, however, the train was full of civilian passengers.

Eight people, including women and children, were killed and dozens wounded. Here at last was the "proof" of what the Salvadoran Army had contended all along: that its enemies were war criminals with no regard for human life. An attack that does not distinguish between **military objectives** and civilians is a war crime.

The foreign press was summoned to the site the next morning by the Salvadoran military. Inside the train, the bodies of two men, four women, and a child were lying in a pool of congealed blood underneath wooden seats on the floor of a railway carriage. They had been left where they fell, untouched for fifteen hours so reporters could broadcast the guerrillas' deed to more dramatic effect.

Outside, a young woman was on her knees, rooted to a spot where she had collapsed. She was bent over the body of a small boy, resting her head on the back of one hand, while the other clutched at her breast as if trying to tear her own heart out. She wailed, pleading to God for her little son's life while damning the guerrillas. Her cries went out over the airwaves as well.

This, an army spokesman announced with enthusiasm, was proof of the barbarity of the guerrillas. But upon talking to survivors another picture, different from what the Salvadoran Army wanted us to believe, began to emerge.

According to the engineer, the rebels had brought the train to a halt after two mines went off on the track. The rebels had then demanded the surrender of a detachment of soldiers and five thousand rounds of ammunition that were in the last car. The soldiers had refused and a firefight ensued. Surviving passengers said that when the FMLN attack intensified the soldiers had taken refuge in their carriage, shooting at the attackers while hiding behind the civilian passengers for protection. It was then that people were killed.

Not wanting the bodies of its troops to be seen lying alongside those of civilians in a passenger carriage, the army removed the soldiers' corpses long before journalists arrived.

Despite the survivors' story it is unclear whether the soldiers had rushed to the passenger area to use civilians as shields—clearly a war crime—or fled that particular car because they thought it was the best place to take cover, thereby committing no violation of law.

Whatever the truth, in the television propaganda war for the hearts and minds of the world, it was the guerrillas of FMLN and not the Salvadoran Army who lost sympathy points that day.
(See **hostages**.)

S

Sick and Wounded

By Eric Stover

The Geneva Conventions of 1949 recognized that "**military necessity**" has its limits and that **combatants**, as well as civilians, who are wounded or held as prisoners of war *hors de combat* should not be military targets and should be treated with dignity at all times. The conventions also specify that both civilians and combatants who are sick and wounded should be treated equally, and that neither should be given differential treatment.

The sick and wounded, Article 12 common to the First and Second Geneva Conventions of 1949 states, "shall be treated humanely and cared for by the Parties to the conflict in whose power they may be, without any adverse distinction founded on sex, race, nationality, religion, political opinions, or any other similar criteria. Any attempts upon their lives, or violence to their persons, shall be strictly prohibited; in particular, they shall not be murdered or exterminated, subject to torture or to biological experiments; they shall not willfully be left without medical assistance and care, nor shall conditions exposing them to contagion or infection be created."

History is replete with the accounts of sick and wounded combatants and civilians who have been physically and psychologically abused by their captors. One of the most horrific accounts of the abuse of prisoners during World War II took place in a Japanese-run germ warfare factory on the Manchurian Plain. Japanese doctors at the secret facility injected captured Chinese and Korean soldiers, many of whom had been wounded in battle, with bubonic plague, cholera, syphilis, and other deadly germs to compare the resistance to disease of various nationalities and races. Hundreds of prisoners of war died as a result of the **biological experiments** and hundreds more were killed by the Japanese when they fled the laboratory.

During the siege of the eastern Croatian city of Vukovar in November 1991, troops with the Yugoslav People's Army (JNA) and Serb irregulars removed hundreds of patients and staff from the municipal hospital and executed them at the end of a ravine on the Ovcara collective farm, nine kilometers south of the city. Five years later, forensic investigators, assembled by Physicians for Human Rights (PHR) and the International Criminal Tribunal for the Former Yugoslavia (ICTY), exhumed two hundred bodies from a **mass grave** on the Ovcara farm. Some of the bodies were dressed in smocks and white clogs, garb common to hospital employees in Europe. Other bodies bore signs of previous injuries: a thigh bandaged in gauze or a broken arm set in a plaster cast and sling. A pair of broken crutches lay on top of one body. Another had a catheter dangling from its pelvis. By May 1998, the forensic scientists had identified ninety-one of the bodies. The ICTY, in the meantime, had indicted the former major of Vukovar, Slavko Dokmanovic, and three JNA officers—Mile Mrksic, Miroslav Radic, and Veselin Sljivancanin—for the massacre on the Ovcara farm.
(See **medical experiments on POWs**.)

A badly burned woman was tagged "VNC," Vietnamese Civilian. Wounded were usually automatically deemed "VCS," Viet Cong Suspect. Vietnam, 1967.

Siege

By Tom Gjelten

For centuries, armies have tried to capture cities by surrounding them, blocking access roads, and then bombarding the encircled territory until the townspeople, or their defenders, give up. Constantinople was besieged at one time or another by the Persians, the Arabs, the Bulgars, and the Russians. The siege of Leningrad (St. Petersburg) during World War II lasted 872 days and resulted in the death of more than a million civilians.

Fifty years later, it was Sarajevo's turn. In May 1992, the Bosnian Serb Army, having failed in an attempt to overrun the city, closed all roads leading in and out of Sarajevo, blocked commerce, and began to pound city neighborhoods with artillery and sniper fire from all directions. Human rights groups,

S

relief agencies, and some governments said the Serb war tactics around Sarajevo subjected the city to a siege, immorally and illegally.

Under international humanitarian law (IHL), siege is not prohibited *per se*. The capture of an enemy-controlled city is a legitimate military aim, and army commanders have often seen siege as less costly than the alternative—fighting house to house, street by street. Historically, a key element of siege warfare has been to reduce a town's defenses and force its surrender by cutting off its vital supplies and leaving the population, civilian and military alike, to starve. Cruel as this tactic is, the laws of war permitted it at least until the end of World War II, under the rationale of **military necessity**.

The last revision of the U.S. Army field manual on the law of land warfare, for example, informed commanders that civilians who are fleeing a besieged city can, as an "extreme measure," be turned around and forced back into the city for the specific purpose of "hastening its surrender." Implicitly, this principle permitted the deliberate **starvation** of the civilian population, if only as a means of demoralizing the city's armed defenders. Under pre–World War II Hague Regulations, "undefended" cities could not be bombarded, but siege tactics are normally used against defended places, so

Serb snipers shoot and kill a sixteen-year-old cyclist. Sarajevo, 1993.

S

this prohibition did not exclude sieges.

The laws pertaining to siege warfare, however, have changed radically in the post–World War II era. Though the word "siege" is never mentioned as a term of law, the 1949 Geneva Conventions and the 1977 Additional Protocols impose restrictions on warfare that, if enforced, would effectively make siege illegal. Besieging forces are not allowed to target civilians or starve them "as a method of combat," and relief agencies are authorized to provide aid to needy populations.

The most specific limitations are the provisions that bar attacks on civilians. Additional Protocol I, applying to international conflicts, requires that parties to a conflict distinguish between the civilian population and combatants and "accordingly shall direct their operations only against military objectives." Additional Protocol II, applying to internal armed conflicts, is less specific but still declares that "the civilian population as such, as well as individual civilians, shall not be the object of attack."

Prohibitions on the deliberate starvation of civilians and the obstruction of **humanitarian aid** are somewhat more ambiguous. The Fourth Geneva Convention stipulates that an army may legally block food or other relief shipments into a besieged city if the aid would result in more goods becoming available to the local military forces. The question for war crime judges is whether that provision is made meaningless by Protocol I, which prohibits the use of starvation tactics as a means of forcing the local population to leave a besieged zone. This provision may require a besieging force to allow relief supplies to enter a besieged city, even if some of the supplies will inevitably be shared with the defenders. Protocol I also prohibits the destruction of "objects indispensable for the survival of the civilian population." A besieging army is thus forbidden, for example, from destroying a city's drinking **water supply**.

In Sarajevo, officials of the United Nations Protection Force (UNPROFOR) questioned whether the city was genuinely besieged, since Serb forces occasionally allowed UN relief convoys to pass into the city. Comdr. Barry Frewer, the UNPROFOR spokesman, summarized the official view while briefing journalists in July 1993: "The Serbs have encircled the city," he acknowledged. "They are in a position to bring force to bear on the city. You call it a siege. We say they are deployed in a tactically advantageous position."

The dispute was both ridiculous and irrelevant. No word other than "siege" as effectively described the city's condition, and in any case the terminology did not resolve the question of whether Serb military actions were lawful. The critical issue was whether the means of Sarajevo's continued encirclement violated IHL. Some parts of the war record leave little doubt. Indiscriminate shelling of residential areas is clearly illegal. Serb army commanders had modern artillery, a clear line of sight toward their Sarajevo targets, and three years of practice. UN military observers regularly reported deliberate civilian targeting by Serb gunners. The attacks on Sarajevo prompted war crime indictments against Serb commanders judged responsible for firing "on civilian gatherings that were of no military significance."

Might some army find a way to besiege a city without violating IHL? The limits have been tested by Taliban forces in Afghanistan, Hutu rebels in central Africa, and by Russian forces in Chechnya. Lawful or not, siege warfare remains as popular as ever.

Slavery

By Pierre Richard

There were 249 black children and women under a mahogany tree, all of them waiting for the white buyers who were supposed to free them after the trade. The traders, two Arabs in blue jellabias, were nervous. The sale would amount to 14 million Sudanese pounds (fourteen thousand dollars) and they were anxious to know if the whites were serious.

Arab traders in Sudan offering to free slaves to Western humanitarian workers.

"For months, we crisscrossed the north of the country to buy back the slaves and to bring them back here," one of the Arabs said.

The job was very dangerous. Sudan's ruling National Islamic Front government in Khartoum did not have enough money to pay the Arab forces serving in the non-Arab and mainly non-Muslim provinces in the south that are seeking self-determination, so it had been allowing the militias it arms as well as its soldiers to take the southern women and children as slaves. When Arab traders came to redeem the slaves, Khartoum security authorities were furious, the traders said.

One of the women spoke. "I have been in the north for seven years," she said, cradling her two-year-old child in her arms. "I had to work on a farm and sometimes my master would take me into his bedroom. This baby I had from him."

In 1996, Gaspar Biro of Hungary, the special UN rapporteur, reported an alarming increase in the number of cases of slavery, servitude, slave trade, and **forced labor**. "The abduction of persons, mainly women and children, belonging to racial, ethnic and religious minorities from southern Sudan, the

Nuba Mountains and the Ingessana Hills areas, their subjection to the slave trade, including traffic in and sale of children and women, slavery, servitude, forced labor, and similar practices . . . are carried out by persons acting under the authority and with the tacit approval of the Government of Sudan," he wrote. And the State Department's annual human rights review in 1998 spoke of credible but unconfirmed reports that women and children are taken to northern Sudan to work as domestic servants, agricultural laborers, and sometimes concubines.

Enslavement of persons captured during conflict has been classified as a war crime for more than a century, going back to the Lieber Code, drafted for the Union Army in the U.S. Civil War. Today, slavery is outlawed by international law both in peacetime and in wartime. The 1977 Additional Protocol II to the Geneva Conventions explicitly extends this prohibition to internal

Slaves awaiting redemption in Sudan: total price $14,000 for 249.

armed conflict. "Slavery and the slave trade in all their forms . . . are and shall remain prohibited at any time and in any place whatsoever," Article 4 states. Even though the United States and a number of other countries did not ratify that protocol, the prohibition against slavery is regarded as a binding rule of customary international law in all conflicts, whether international or internal. Like the Nuremberg Charter, the 1998 Rome Statute calls enslavement a **crime against humanity** when it is part of a widespread or systematic practice against a civilian population. It defines enslavement, in line with the 1926 Slavery Convention, as "the exercise of any or all of the powers attaching to the right of ownership over a person and includes the exercise of such power in the course of trafficking in persons, in particular women and children."

Slavery, according to Article 1 of the 1926 Slavery Convention, "is the status or condition of a person over whom any or all of the powers attaching to the right of ownership are exercised." The convention defines the slave trade as "all acts involved in the capture, acquisition or disposal of a person with intent to reduce him to slavery; all acts involved in the acquisition of a slave with a view to selling or exchanging him; all acts of disposal by sale or exchange of a slave acquired with a view to being sold or exchanged and, in general, every act of trade or transport of slaves."

But slavery comes in a number of guises, and definitions of it can change. Aware that slavery could also be called serfdom, the 1956 United Nations Supplementary Convention on the Abolition of Slavery, the Slave Trade, and Institutions and Practices Similar to Slavery states that if the condition or status of a tenant "is by law, custom or agreement bound to live and labor on land belonging to another person and to render some determinate service to such person, whether for reward or not, and is not free to change his status" such a serf or tenant can be considered a slave.

Another definition of slavery from the 1956 Supplementary Convention revolves around the concept of debt bondage where "the status or conditions arising from a pledge by a debtor of his personal service or of those under his control as security for a debt, if the value of those services as reasonably assessed is not applied toward the liquidation of the debt or the length and nature of those services are not respectively limited or defined."

Sometimes, this debt bondage takes very curious forms. In Sudan, when the slave traders bring back some children to territory controlled by the Dinka rebels, the children's families have no money to pay the dealer. The trader agrees that parents may keep the child with them, but insists that the child is still his property until the family has paid off their debt.

A number of Sudan specialists, such as British writer John Ryle, assert that the organization involved in slave redemption, Christian Solidarity International (CSI) of Zurich, has indirectly encouraged slave trading by making repeated mass payments. John Eibner of CSI replies that government-sponsored raids in which slaves are taken have been going on since the mid-1980s, and the traders who facilitate the redemptions work within the framework of local peace agreements between Dinka chiefs and Arab clan leaders. He states that the price of redeeming slaves remained constant from 1995, when CSI first became active in slave retrieval, through 1998—about fifty thousand Sudanese pounds. Thus, a slave can be purchased for about fifty dollars.

S

Soldiers, Rights of

By Peter Rowe

Soldiers have rights, insofar as they are members of the armed forces, as defined in international humanitarian law (IHL). They are known as **combatants** and have the right to participate directly in hostilities. This means, in practical terms, that combatants are entitled to attack enemy forces, kill or injure them, and destroy property as part of military operations—activities that if done not in wartime or not by combatants would all be criminal behavior. Thus, if captured, combatants must be treated as prisoners of war under the Third Geneva Convention of 1949 rather than as criminals, because as combatants they are legally entitled to fight.

It is up to a State to determine by its own law, however, who is a member of its armed forces. This has particular significance for the determination of when reservists, common in many countries, become members and thus combatants within the meaning of IHL. Once a person is a member of the armed forces of a State it is irrelevant whether that State describes the duties that he/she is to perform as combat or noncombat duties, or whether the members of the armed forces are conscripted or are volunteers. It is also irrelevant whether the State describes those armed forces as special forces, commandos, presidential guards, or by any other name. Where, however, a State incorporates its armed law enforcement agencies (such as its police force) into its armed forces, it must notify the other party to the conflict, for the simple reason that such bodies would not normally be considered to be part of the armed forces of a State, and so not liable to attack as combatants. Certain armed formations in certain states, such as **paramilitaries**, may or may not be members of the armed forces within the meaning of IHL, depending on how the State's own law treats such paramilitary forces.

According to the 1977 Additional Protocol I to the Geneva Conventions, States are under an obligation not to recruit **child soldiers** under the age of fifteen into their armed forces and to take all feasible measures to ensure that children do not take a direct part in hostilities.

The definition of combatants beyond those who fight for the regular armed forces of a State is regulated by IHL.

IHL treats all combatants alike, except for two distinct classifications. One distinction is between officers and other ranks, and is relevant only to certain obligations imposed upon the capturing State in respect to prisoners of war, such as the prohibition against forcing officers to work. The second distinction, between commanders and others, is extremely important since commanders have specific duties placed on them by Additional Protocol I to ensure that their subordinates are aware of their obligations under IHL and to suppress any breaches of these obligations. In addition, commanders are required to prevent any such violation if they have become aware that their subordinates are going to breach IHL. In this way, a commander has **command responsibility** for the actions of his subordinates, even though he may not directly have ordered the violations.

Captured combatants are entitled to be treated as prisoners of war even if it is alleged that they have committed war crimes. In certain conflicts State leaders have declared that captured air crew are "war criminals" and are not to be treated as prisoners of war. This is contrary to IHL, although a

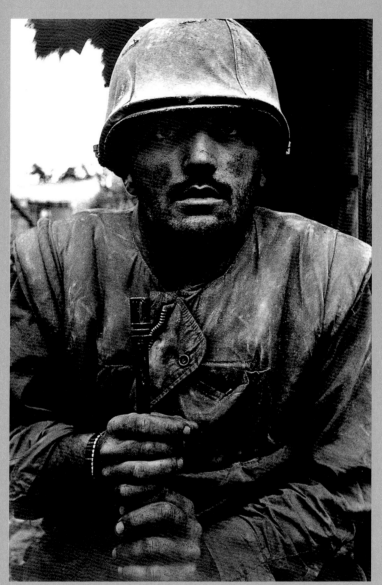

Vietnam combatant.

State is entitled and has the right to investigate war crimes, even those alleged to have taken place among POWs. In internal armed conflict, insurgents are not entitled to POW status under the Third Geneva Convention or Additional Protocol I since the conflict is not international. Accordingly, they may be tried for sedition, treason, rebellion, murder, or other crimes under the domestic law of their State; nonetheless, under Article 3 common to the four Geneva Conventions, and notwithstanding that they may be tried by their State, they retain certain minimal protections under IHL, and in particular, may not be summarily executed and must receive the benefit of a regular trial.

(See **POW camps**; **protected persons**.)

Starvation

By Marita Vihervuori

At the main Serb checkpoint outside Sarajevo, the big Human to Human aid convoy stood stalled in its tracks. Sweating profusely, a uniformed Serb fighter pushed a wheelbarrow full of goods taken from one of the vehicles into the cellar of the house he and his comrades were using as a guardroom. Nearby, other Serb fighters were stacking cartons of the seized aid into a minivan.

Their commander was unapologetic. "According to the orders of the authorities of the Republika Srpska, 30 percent of the supplies in all aid convoys must be turned over to us."

In fact, the Human to Human convoy was one of the few private aid convoys that ever made it to Sarajevo. But not intact. After losing 30 percent of its cargo at the first checkpoint, it was stripped of still more in the Serb-controlled suburb of Ilidza. In the end, only the flour and macaroni made it into the city.

Staff of the United Nations High Commissioner for Refugees (UNHCR) in Sarajevo were well aware that the Serb forces besieging the Bosnian capital were seizing humanitarian aid intended for civilians within the city. They should have been; more often than not, they were allowing the Serbs to take 30 percent of the goods UNHCR itself was bringing in as well. Under international law, the Serbs had every right to inspect all food and medical supplies being brought through their lines into government-controlled territory in order to satisfy themselves that the relief was destined for noncombatants rather than the Bosnian Army. They did not have the right to siphon off the food. **Pillage** is a war crime in an international conflict and a prohibited act in an internal conflict.

Starvation of civilian populations as a method of warfare is prohibited in both international or in internal conflicts, a prohibition stated explicitly in the two 1977 Additional Protocols to the Geneva Conventions. Yet a military force controlling the flow of relief supplies over routes or into territories it controls is under no obligation to do anything to support the military forces arrayed against it. The tension between these two positions has given rise to a complex series of rules that are difficult to implement without the use of force by the international community. The International Committee of the Red Cross (ICRC) takes the position that the fear of diversion to combatants provides no legal justification for refusing passage. But its position is not widely shared.

Humanitarian aid for civilians, under Article 23 of the Fourth Geneva Convention, enjoys the right of free passage through battle lines if intended for "children under fifteen, expectant mothers and maternity cases," and a broader exemption can be made when all or part of the civilian population in occupied territory is "inadequately supplied." Because of a very real military concern that the goods might be used to supply enemy armed forces, "inadequately" is understood in a strict sense.

It is, moreover, prohibited under Article 54 of Additional Protocol I to destroy "objects indispensable to the survival of the civilian population," including foodstuffs and their production, drinking water, and irrigation works, or to undertake actions "which may be expected to leave the civilian population with such inadequate food or water as to cause starvation or force its movement." Whether this prohibition on destruction of such objects extends to a positive obligation to allow their entry to provide for populations at risk of starvation is not clear from Article 54 but might be implied from subsequent provisions on relief operations.

If civilians in a conflict are not adequately provided with supplies, then under Article 70 of Protocol I "relief actions which are humanitarian and impartial in character and conducted without any adverse distinction shall be undertaken, subject to the agreement of the Parties concerned in such relief actions." Short of conditions requiring supplies essential to the survival of the civilian population, relief operations are subject to agreement of the parties.

A victim of an endless civil war where the government was widely accused of using starvation as a weapon. Sudan, 1998.

In an internal armed conflict, if the civilian population is suffering "undue hardship" due to a lack of food or medical supplies "essential to its survival," relief actions "which are of an exclusively humanitarian and impartial nature" and conducted "without any adverse distinction" shall be undertaken subject to the the consent of the State involved.

Although the United States is not a party to Additional Protocols I or II, it supports the prohibition of starvation as a means of warfare.

It was in large measure because of the ambiguity in the law—the tension between **military necessity** and the obligation of all sides in a conflict to allow in articles needed to prevent starvation or the threat of starvation, so as to force civilians to flee their homes—that the United Nations and private relief groups in Bosnia were so vulnerable to the kind of blackmail I witnessed at the Serb checkpoint.

If allowing the Serbs to take 30 percent of the relief supplies meant that they would let in the other 70 percent when, strictly speaking, their obligation to do so was not ironclad, it was better to give in. Or so most aid groups reasoned. The alternative might very well have been to allow the most vulnerable groups—the very old and the very young, in particular—to starve. And more widespread starvation, which the humanitarian effort did manage to stave off in Bosnia, remained a possibility almost to the end of the war.

In Bosnia the signals were far from clear. The UNHCR and other agencies realized early on that it remained open to question whether the Serbs were obligated to allow aid though. Directives from the UN Security Council required as much, but realistically, they also knew they were incapable, as the law required, of preventing some of the aid from flowing to the Bosnian Army. Whatever the legal niceties, in all wars, the army eats first.

These were some of the reasons they acted as they did—another was that there was no will on the part of the UN or the great powers to push the aid through by force. Thus, trying to buy off the fighters seemed preferable to insisting that relief operations had to proceed in an absolutely uncompromising way.

"We could not let all those people die," was the way one UNHCR official in Zagreb put it at the time, "so we closed our eyes to many things." Loopholes in the law as well as realities on the ground had a lot to do with that decision.

(See **humanitarian aid, blocking of**; **siege**; **water supplies and works, destruction of**)

Terrorism

By Rich Mkhondo

When Johannes "Sweet" Sambo was accidentally killed during a police interrogation in the late 1980s, Col. Eugene de Kock, head of the C-10 Unit, a clandestine South African government hit squad, got in touch with his superiors and later ordered his colleagues, including Maj. Chappies Klopper, to remove the body and "Buddha it"—a phrase they had coined, meaning to blow something to smithereens with explosives. His body was taken to a farm, where it was sandwiched between explosives and blown up. The pieces were picked up, thrown on a heap, and blown up again.

This process was repeated until there was nothing left to destroy. Giving evidence in de Kock's trial, in which he was sentenced to spend the rest of life

T

in jail, Klopper said they hoped that whatever remained would be speedily removed by ants. The judge sentenced de Kock to two life-terms and a total of 212 years in prison for his other crimes.

When the facts came out at de Kock's trial, acts carried out by the C-10 unit were widely regarded as having been instances of terrorism under the **apartheid** regime. The term *terrorism* has no universally agreed-upon definition but rather recurring themes including; violence with a political or social purpose, an attempt to intimidate, and directing the act at civilians and other noncombatants. Terrorism is more than simple violence which requires only two parties, an aggressor and a victim. Terrorism needs a third party, who might be intimidated by what happened to the victim.

Acts often described as terrorism have been banned by treaties on international humanitarian law (IHL) and treaties establishing international crimes. These include the Fourth Geneva Convention of 1949 and its two Additional Protocols of 1977. They ban terrorism during international and internal armed conflict, at least insofar as terrorism is understood to mean attacks directed against civilians. Although the term *terrorism* is often under-

A clergyman rescues a suspected police informer from "necklacing," having a rubber tire burned around his neck. Duncan Village, South Africa, 1985.

T

stood to refer to acts by groups that are not part of the State, an important category of terrorist acts is those which may be carried out or sponsored by a State directly or indirectly, or implicitly sanctioned by a State even where its own police or military forces are not involved, such as certain **death squads**.

Various non-IHL treaties also establish categories of crimes for acts generally considered terrorist, outside the context of armed conflict, including, for example, the 1979 International Convention Against the Taking of Hostages, and many conventions on the hijacking of air transport.

What happened in South Africa during the apartheid era was far more than simply the implementation of apartheid, itself a **crime against humanity**. Additional criminal means to defend apartheid were also being used. The extensive powers given to the apartheid State to control the lives of black South Africans and deny them basic rights were not enough; they were supplemented by every species of common law crime, including systematic and organized murder, fraud, kidnaping, and torture.

Many of these crimes were, strictly speaking, simple repression, rather than terrorism in the political sense. Their heinousness as crimes was the same, but only in some instances were they carried out, in accordance with the concept of terrorism, in order to intimidate third parties.

According to human rights organizations, between 1960 and 1990, seventy-three political prisoners were killed in police detention. Official explanations included falling while taking a shower, injuries received from slipping on a piece of soap, fainting and falling against a desk, and falling down stairs. Some were said to have hanged themselves with shoelaces, jeans, and other assorted clothing. During the same period, about 220 political leaders were assassinated by apartheid death squads. Some inquests showed that members of the security forces were able to subvert justice for many years through almost impenetrable conspiracy. At least fifteen thousand people were killed in what the white government said was black-on-black violence, murders antiapartheid groups said were sponsored by the government.

Terrorism is not a legal concept within IHL, despite the fact that many acts often described as terrorist acts are categorically prohibited by IHL. One obvious difficulty with using the term within IHL is that, as has often been pointed out, one man's terrorist is another man's freedom fighter. Apartheid leaders regarded the fight against their policies as terrorism and viewed antiapartheid activists as terrorists. Antiapartheid activists regarded themselves as **guerrillas** fighting an illegitimate regime, something condoned by international law. For example, Brig. Jack Cronje, a member of the Vlakplaas Unit, testified at de Kock's trial that a secret body called the Counterrevolutionary Intelligence Target Center met monthly to select targets for "elimination." "It was necessary to eliminate terrorists and activists, because if they were not eliminated, they would not be permanently neutralized. The strategy was pro-active, striking before they could commit acts of terror," he said.

The African National Congress (ANC), as documented by the South African Truth and Reconciliation Commission, carried out a number of crimes in its fight against apartheid that would accurately be described as terrorist. For example, while the currently ruling ANC targeted government installations, its MK guerrillas also planted bombs in bars, restaurants, and other public places to intimidate or punish supporters of the white government. The ANC has admitted executing suspected apartheid spies and burying them in unmarked graves. It argued that acts such as the blast that killed eighteen people in Pretoria in 1981, could not be classified as terrorism because the bombs were intended to kill members of the military, among others.

In the end, what matters from the legal standpoint is not the characterization of crimes by the ANC or the apartheid regime as terrorism, but the fact of the crimes themselves.
(See **civilians, illegal targeting of**; **indiscriminate attack**.)

Terrorism against Civilians

By Serge Schmemann

The three men stood about twenty-five yards from each other along the Ben Yehuda promenade in Jerusalem, one dressed as a woman. One probably gave a signal, maybe a nod of the head, and all three tripped switches that detonated crude bombs hidden under their clothes—about five pounds of explosives each, packed with nuts and bolts to act as shrapnel.

Already when the first "whump" sounded, many people instinctively knew what it was. Fighter jets routinely break the sound barrier over Jerusalem, but they sound more like a thunderclap. Still, people will freeze until they hear the fading rumble that confirms a jet. The bombs have a different sound, a muffled, nearby thump. People who have heard one recognize it immediately. Even before the second and third explosions sounded on September 4, 1997, many people felt the gruesome familiarity of the sound.

I was on my way to pick my wife up at the school where she worked and had just crossed Ben Yehuda when I heard the blasts. Though I had never heard the sound before, I also knew what it was. In two years in Israel, I had covered the aftermath of nine suicide bombings, and, like everyone else, I was always waiting for the next. I also knew what would happen next. First the cautious pause—terrorists have been known to wait until emergency services congregate to set off another bomb. Then the screams of the wounded and the horrified, the sirens, the chaotic convergence of medics, police, detectives, soldiers, and black-bearded Orthodox Jews who collect every bit of Jewish flesh and bone for a proper burial. Cellular service is overwhelmed, and people search frantically for available phones to reassure their homes.

And everyone there feels that horrible helplessness, that empty rage. "It's almost a sense that this is a fact of life we have to live with," said a young lawyer, Jonathan Shiff, watching the commotion from his window above Ben Yehuda. "It's no way to live, but we do it anyway," interjected a woman standing alongside us.

A suicide bombing is unlike any other act of violence. There is no real defense against an attack that is essentially random, or against a man—all suicide bombers in Israel have been men—so crazed by religion and despair that he is prepared to die. In the communiqués that followed, Hamas, the fundamentalist Islamic movement, described the bombers as martyrs and soldiers. But really, they were only suicides and killers. The twelve-year-old girl slain by their bombs was not a soldier, nor an enemy. Nor were the other victims, a man and two women.

By its very design and purpose, terrorism is a violation of all norms of behavior, law, and combat. Its objective is to demoralize, dehumanize, humiliate, and horrify through acts of random and demonstrative viciousness.

And almost instinctively, the human spirit fights back by reaffirming the very spirit that terror seeks to erode. Within hours the streets were clean of blood and glass, and by morning thousands of Israelis, many from far away, defiantly strolled along Ben Yehuda, filling it with resolve and life.

T

Torture

By Nicole Pope

Ferhat is a broken man. Short and squat, with jet black hair and a bushy mustache, he looks healthy and strong as a bull, yet the life has gone out of his dark eyes.

This young man of thirty-two cannot sleep at night because he is afraid of the dark. He loses his temper when his four young children play loudly, because their screams remind him of the nightly cries he heard from his cell. He speaks in a monotone voice, his rasping accent revealing his Kurdish origins. At times overcome by emotion, he just stops, stares at his shoes, and shakes his head to push back the images that still haunt him, four years after he was tortured in an interrogation center in Istanbul.

Like many others from Turkey's mainly Kurdish southeast, Ferhat (not his real name) was caught up in the conflict that has torn his region since 1984. At least thirty thousand people have died and hundreds of thousands of villagers, Ferhat and his family among them, were forced to leave their homes when they were burned down by the army in an attempt to deny supplies and logistical support to the guerrillas living in remote mountainous areas. Ferhat was not a fighter, but he was a member of a legal pro-Kurdish party that was viewed with great suspicion by the Turkish authorities and has since been closed down by the courts. Arrested on two occasions, in 1993 and in 1994, Ferhat was charged with "aiding and abetting an illegal organization," but refused to confess to a crime he says he did not commit, despite extensive physical and mental pressure. At the end of his first trial, he was acquitted. There was no evidence against him other than a denunciation obtained from another prisoner under similar circumstances.

Ferhat's case takes place in the context of what is considered an internal conflict, even if the Turkish Army often crosses the border into northern Iraq in pursuit of Kurdistan Workers Party (PKK) militants. While a State is entitled to suppress an insurrection as well as detain and sentence rebels, torture is universally prohibited. "No exceptional circumstances whatsoever, whether a state of war or a threat of war, internal political instability or any other public emergency, may be invoked as a justification of torture," states the 1984 Convention for the Prevention of Torture and Inhuman or Degrading Treatment or Punishment.

The convention, to which Turkey is a party, defines torture as "any act by which severe pain or suffering, whether physical or mental, is intentionally inflicted on a person for such purposes as obtaining from him or a third person information or a confession." It may be "inflicted by or at the instigation of or acquiescence of a public official or other person acting in an official capacity." Punishing the detainee for an act he or another person committed, or intimidating him or someone else for reasons based on discrimination, also come under the legal definition of torture.

This is codified in human rights conventions such as the International Covenant on Civil and Political Rights; the Convention on the Rights of the Child; and the European, African, and Inter-American Conventions on Human Rights.

Torture is specifically prohibited in armed conflict, whether international or internal, whether used against soldiers who have laid down their arms, civilians, or even common criminals. The prohibition exists in **customary law** and in treaties. Article 3 common to the four Geneva Conventions of 1949 makes it clear that "violence to life and person, in particular murder of all kinds, mutilation, cruel treatment and torture" as well as "outrages upon personal dignity, in particular humiliating and degrading treatment" are banned under any circumstances. The Hague Regulations of 1907 on customs of war also state in Article 44 that "a belligerent is forbidden to force the inhabitants of territory occupied by it to furnish information about the army of the other belligerent, or about its means of defense."

The law makes a slight distinction between torture, which is often used to force information out of a suspect, and inhumane treatment, which attacks a person's dignity, but the line between the two is often blurred.

Bed used to shackle victims at the Khmer Rouge Torture Center. Phnom Pen, Cambodia, 1998.

Indeed, revenge and hatred, as much as the need to obtain a confession, often drive the torturers to inflict the suffering. Torture is used not just to hurt physically, but also to humiliate the victim, which is why prisoners are often left naked during torture sessions, and rape or pain inflicted on the genitals are among the most commonly used forms of torture. In fact, attacks of a sexual nature are so widespread in time of conflict that Article 27 of the Fourth Geneva Convention specifically refers to the treatment of women who should be defended against "rape, enforced prostitution, or any form of indecent assault." Protecting human dignity in all circumstances is in fact the whole spirit behind the Geneva Conventions.

Turkey, which is also a party to the Geneva Conventions, has accepted the jurisdiction of the European Court of Human Rights, and by mid-1998 lost eight cases over torture. Amnesty International says "torture is routine and systematic" in Turkey and is used in all parts of the country. The U.S. State Department's 1997 report on human rights said "torture remained widespread" and that "police . . . often abused detainees and employed tor-

T

ture during incommunicado detention and interrogation."

Methods appear to differ little from one country to the next. Ferhat shows a network of thin scars on his elbows, left by clamps that kept him painfully hanging for hours while electric cables were attached to his toes and genitals. Cigarette burns dug little round scars on his forearms. "They even burned my mustache," he says. But worse than the physical pain were the days and nights spent in total darkness behind a blindfold, the interrogators' taunts and insults, the death threats, and the click of a pistol while he was waiting for an execution that never came.

Most countries have their own laws banning torture, but the judicial establishment appears at times unwilling to challenge the security forces, and perpetrators go unpunished because of lack of evidence. Victims are often kept in detention until the physical scars subside, making torture difficult to prove. But as Ferhat knows, it leaves indelible marks on the psyche. (See **protected persons**; **sexual violence**; **willful killing.**)

T

Total War

By Peter Rowe

Total war is sometimes used to mean the mobilization of all resources, economic and military, by a society in support of a war effort; this was the American description of its own engagement during World War II. It has also been used to mean a willingness to engage the enemy in any geographic zone, or with any available weaponry, or sometimes a willingness to fight a scorched-earth campaign, even on one's own territory. It has also been used to mean war conducted against an enemy's military and economic infrastructure, across all of its territory, in order to cripple the enemy's ability to wage war; Great Britain used the term in this sense in both World Wars. The term has also been used to mean a willingness to countenance any method or means of warfare, legal or illegal, including, for example, weapons categorically considered illegal, such as **chemical** or **biological weapons**. These extremely varied uses of the term *total war* have radically different legal implications within international humanitarian law (IHL).

The first three meanings of total war need not imply violations of IHL. It is possible, for example, under IHL to mobilize all of a society's resources to war ends. It is also possible to fight lawfully within IHL in any theater or with any legal weapons. It is even possible, although more difficult, to fight a war attacking military-economic infrastructure legally, provided that the attacking forces respect IHL rules regarding indiscriminate attack. Where a party to conflict runs afoul of IHL is the belief that total war permits the suspension of the laws of armed conflict.

IHL applies however intense the armed conflict. Any State that attempted to fight a total war, in the sense that it declared it would not abide by the limitations imposed on its conduct of the conflict by IHL, would be in violation of IHL and presumably would find itself the subject of UN Security Council resolutions.

In addition, it is no defense to individual or State liability for breaches of IHL that one's enemy is fighting a total war. Nor is it a defense to plead **military necessity**; military necessity only justifies actions that are themselves legal. IHL itself gives some latitude to commanders to conduct military operations, but they must act within the limitations of IHL. Nor is it a defense to argue that your breaches of IHL, as part of a total war, are in **reprisal** for the acts of your enemy. There are specific prohibitions in the Geneva Conventions of 1949 and in the 1977 Additional Protocol I of reprisals against those protected by these instruments, such as the civilian population, civilian objects, the wounded and sick, and prisoners of war. (See **legitimate military targets**; **limited war**; **military objectives**.)

T

Training in International Humanitarian Law

By Michael H. Hoffman

Civil and military leaders often claim that their forces always administer and obey international humanitarian law (IHL). How those leaders reply to one simple question can do much to support—or undermine—their claims. What training do your forces receive in IHL?

The 1949 Geneva Conventions contain a provision compelling states to include the "study" of IHL in "programmes of military and, if possible, civil instruction, so that the principles thereof may become known to the entire population, in particular to the armed fighting forces, the medical personnel and chaplains." By extension, insurgents are expected to provide similar instruction to their own forces. Ultimate responsibility for IHL training remains with political authorities and military leaders. The **International Committee of the Red Cross (ICRC)** and national Red Cross and Red Crescent societies also conduct IHL training for civilians in many parts of the world.

Military instruction is, generally, hands-on in nature. Effective IHL training for soldiers usually requires a practical, problem-solving approach. Some armed forces integrate IHL-linked scenarios into their training exercises, others rely more on classroom presentation. In some armed forces IHL training is by military assistance teams from other countries. There are also militaries that offer little or no training, and a few that are not aware that this body of law exists.

Two civilian institutions play an important role in IHL training. The ICRC has a Division for Relations with Armed and Security Forces that conducts IHL training using a multinational faculty composed of retired military officers. The International Institute of Humanitarian Law in San Remo, Italy, attracts military officers from around the world to its intensive IHL courses taught by IHL experts on active duty with their nations' armed forces.

Armed forces that have not yet developed a program of IHL instruction can attain it externally from the military forces of allied nations and/or internationally recognized institutions. There is no real excuse for leaders who fail to train their armed forces in IHL.

(See **command responsibility**; **soldiers, rights of**.)

Transfer of Civilians

By Thomas Goltz

Japarna Miruzeva, twenty-six, lives in the basement of a bombed-out Armenian house with her four children and considers herself lucky to be there.

So do the one hundred or so other ethnic Kurdish families who live in the ruins of about the same number of partially (and sometimes almost totally) destroyed Armenian houses in Shariar, which once, by Soviet standards anyway, was a quaint town famous for its brandy distilleries. The surrounding land is rolling farm country that works its way into the mountains of the so-called Republic of Mountainous Karabakh—the majority-Armenian area that remains legally part of the former Soviet republic of Azerbaijan but that seceded in 1992 and is now a self-proclaimed independent state.

Life in Shariar is bleak at best. Well water is brackish and difficult to get; food is in short supply; there are no doctors; and the surrounding fields have been mined twice—once by the Armenians who used to till them, then by the Azerbaijani Army that will have to defend the town if the Armenians come back to reclaim it.

But Japarna Miruzeva and the other Kurdish families in Shariar believe they have nowhere else to go. They still hope to return to the Kelbajar, the city from which they were expelled by Armenian fighters. And they refuse to join the hundreds of thousands of other **internally displaced** persons (IDPs) in the squalid tent cities, boxcar towns, and multifamily schoolroom domiciles that dot the Azerbaijani countryside. And yet, because Shariar is considered a danger zone by the international organizations charged with dealing with **refugees** and IDPs from the Karabakh conflict (the Office of the United Nations High Commissioner for Refugees considers towns like Shariar too dangerous for its employees and contractors to work in), the Miruzevas can expect little or no help from the international community.

In fact, from an international legal perspective, by allowing the Kurdish refugees to remain in Shariar, the Azerbaijani authorities are violating a whole range of provisions of the Geneva Conventions that prohibit the transferring of one's own population into an occupied zone. The fact that these Kurdish families have no intention of moving and that, in this instance at least, strict adherence to international law and human reality have parted company does not change the legal situation.

The reality is that the Azerbaijani government authorities in Baku find it useful to have Kurds in the ruined towns and villages of the front line with the Armenians of Nagorno-Karabakh. Allowing the Kurds to move into a zone that has been ethnically cleansed runs counter to Geneva Convention law that covers international conflict. "The Occupying power shall not deport or transfer parts of its own civilian population into the territory it occupies," states Article 49 of the Fourth Geneva Convention. "Individual or mass forcible transfers, as well as **deportations** of protected persons from occupied territory" are in fact a grave breach, or war crime. Even in an internal conflict, according to Additional Protocol II of 1977, "displacement of the civilian population shall not be ordered for reasons related to the conflict."

If the security of civilians or "imperative military reasons" such as the movement of a front require it, the population may be temporarily **evacuated,** but they must be returned to their homes when the crisis eases. Article 17 of Protocol II states: "Should such displacements have to be carried out, all possible measures shall be taken in order that the civilian population may be received under satisfactory conditions of shelter, hygiene, safety and nutrition."

The Azerbaijani government has done none of these things, even refusing to allow international organizations like the Halo Trust to clear the mines in the area, a clear violation of the obligation signatories to the Geneva Conventions are under, according to Article 49 of the Fourth Convention, not to detain noncombatants in areas "exposed to the dangers of war."

At the Nuremberg Trials, which preceded the 1949 Geneva Conventions, several Nazi government officials were indicted for the **crime against humanity** of deporting civilians from occupied territory to Germany as slave labor, and transferring German nationals into occupied territory for resettlement. The final judgment against several individual defendants mentioned only deportations, not the resettlement.

The apparent gap in the law today is that in international armed conflict the law does not cover a country transferring its own nationals from refugee or IDP centers in relatively peaceful areas of the country to areas close to front lines. And the problem becomes more acute when the people in question are not being forced to move to such areas but choose to do so.

As one international aid worker put it, "When a family who have been dwelling in a filthy railway car in either Armenia or Azerbaijan decides that the quickest way to end the awful state of refugeehood is to take one's fate into one's own hands and start repairing the wall of someone else's house that now finds itself on the 'friendly' side of the front lines, who is going to tell them to stop? The legal dilemma is punctured by human need."

T

Undefended Towns

By Adam Roberts

Towns or cities that are *undefended* or *open* (the terms are used more or less synonymously) have been the subject of regulation, and confusion, in international law and military practice since at least the late nineteenth century.

The laws of war specify that undefended places should not be attacked. The 1907 Hague Regulations on Land Warfare, still formally in force, state in Article 25: "The attack or bombardment, by whatever means, of towns, villages, dwellings or buildings which are undefended is prohibited." Similar language in the 1907 Hague Convention deals with naval bombardment.

The term *undefended* can be interpreted to encompass all places that are not fortified and do not have an active military presence. In this logic, even a town that is in the interior of a country at war and which has extensive armaments factories or military communications systems could count as undefended. However, the view that such places should be immune from attack has generally been rejected by military planners, especially by airmen, and should not be taken as indicative of prevailing law.

In practice, the words *undefended* and *open* have been defined restrictively, to mean simply places declared to be open for entry and occupation by an adverse party without resistance. In this view, the core meaning of the rule prohibiting attacks on undefended towns is simply that a town in a war zone that has declared itself ready to accept the entry of the adversary's army may not be bombed or subjected to artillery attack. This is widely agreed to be the most persuasive interpretation of the practical meaning and original intention of Article 25 of the 1907 Regulations. This restrictive view has been confirmed in the 1977 Additional Protocol I to the Geneva Conventions, Article 59, which says that a belligerent may declare as a *non-defended locality* "any inhabited place near or in a zone where armed forces are in contact which is open for occupation by an adverse Party."

There have been many cases of towns being declared "open" in this sense. When French forces abandoned Paris in June 1940, the Germans were notified that the city was open for their entry. In June 1944 the German command in Italy asked the Allies to "confirm" the status of Rome as an open city, and then made a unilateral declaration to that effect, followed by surrender of the city to the Allies. Sometimes the concept of open cities has been used differently, to refer to the idea that certain towns should be spared bombardment, even if they are not open to occupation—for example, if they are far from the front line.

Most destructive attacks in modern war have been against cities that were not undefended in the sense of open to occupation by the adversary. This has strengthened the pressure to develop other bases for protecting cities, and their inhabitants, from the ravages of modern war.

The term *open cities* has been used by the UN High Commissioner for Refugees (UNHCR) with a completely different meaning: it refers to an initiative in Bosnia-Herzegovina following the 1995 Dayton peace agreement to reward local authorities who declare their Opstina, or district, open and are committed to the return of minorities to their prewar homes.

(See **legitimate military targets; safety zones**.)

United Nations and the Geneva Conventions

By Roy Gutman

In November 1994, as hundreds of Bosnian and Krajina Serb troops advanced on the UN-declared "safe area" of Bihac, disaster loomed for the municipal hospital, which stood directly in the path of the offensive, and for the nine hundred immobile patients inside. The Canadian commander of UN forces in Bihac was reluctant to intervene. The UN force's civil affairs representative, an American, argued that hospitals have a "sacred" status under the 1949 Geneva Conventions and the UN Protection Force (UNPROFOR) had an obligation to protect this one.

He drafted a memo to this effect, and his superior in Sarajevo, a Russian, issued a formal request. "The Geneva conventions stipulate that hospitals shall not be attacked . . . the support and concurrence of UNPROFOR military will also be needed. Please immediately pursue the plan with the Bihac commanding officer," it said. Acting on the memo, the commander instructed Bangladeshi troops to drive their armored personnel carriers onto the hospital grounds. The Serbs refrained from attacking the hospital, and the ground invasion was halted. Bihac, a town of seventy thousand, was saved.

Two weeks later, the UN's Office of Legal Affairs (OLA), weighed in to ensure that the saving of Bihac did not set a precedent. UN forces, an OLA representative said, are bound only by their Security Council mandate and are not legally obliged to uphold the conventions. "From a strictly legal point of view, obligations (such as the Geneva Conventions) are binding on States. The role of the UN is to carry out the will of the international community as expressed by it in the Security Council," OLA official Stephen Katz said.

The incident illustrates the UN's ambivalent relation to the Geneva Conventions. Nearly every member-State is a legal party to the conventions, and each has undertaken by ratifying them "to respect and to ensure respect" of the provisions. But donning the blue helmets seems to provide States a way to escape their legal obligations.

When States assign troops to peacekeeping duties, the forces answer formally and solely to the Security Council, says the UN. (This is something of a fiction, because in operational terms they are officered, equipped, deployed, moved about, and directed through a national chain of command—at the insistence of the United States and many other countries.) But the United Nations is not a party to the conventions. Sometimes, on the eve of deployments, the Security Council issues a statement reminding States of the applicability of the pertinent Geneva rules and the obligation to punish violations. Other times, the council "forgets" to mention the point.

When Iraq invaded Kuwait in 1990, the Security Council neglected for six weeks to mention the protections the Geneva Conventions guaranteed for civilians in Kuwait. When the council authorized the use of force to liberate Kuwait, the resolution failed to remind States in the coalition of their obligations as combatants under the Geneva Conventions or humanitarian law. In fact, one of the early sanctions resolutions violated the rule that requires free passage for many sorts of humanitarian aid intended for civilians, even

U

civilians of an adversary. Concerning its operation in Bosnia-Herzegovina, as well as that of its recent peacekeeping operation in Cambodia, the Security Council issued no statement on the relevance of humanitarian law to the UN peacekeeping deployment.

Tension over the conventions reflects the different institutional cultures of the UN and the **International Committee of the Red Cross (ICRC)**. The UN's founding charter defined it as a body that would establish world peace—a lofty aim that seemingly precludes it from becoming a combatant or occupying power. The UN opted out of a role in the codification of the laws of war in 1949 with a condescending dismissal of the enterprise. "War having been outlawed, the regulation of its conduct has ceased to be relevant," the UN International Law Commission explained. For this reason, the drafting was undertaken under ICRC auspices in Geneva.

The arm's-length attitude of the UN headquarters has its counterpart in the field. In the absence of a controlling international legal regime, and with

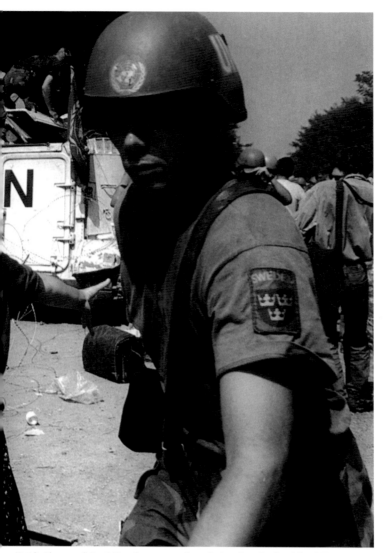

Not in the mandate: A Bosnian woman from Srebrenica pleads with a UN peace-keeper, 1995.

ambiguous mandates that often drift from passive peacekeeping to active peace-enforcing, the military on the ground takes charge. Field commanders, bearing in mind the often-clearer priorities of their own governments, formally answer to a Security Council that is incapable of managing from long distance. Often the commanders pick and choose what they do based on their reading of the mandate. War crimes get short shrift. In Bosnia, UN personnel in mid-1992 visited Sonja's Kon-Tiki, a restaurant-pension outside Sarajevo, on whose grounds, according to the Bosnian government, was a Serb-run concentration camp. UN forces never asked questions, investigated, or protested, explaining that neither the UN command nor their governments had provided them any lists of concentration camps. In Somalia, when Canadian soldiers killed a Somali intruder in cold blood in March 1993, the Canadian commander did not punish the crime but covered it up. (Following

U

an official inquiry, the Airborne Regiment involved was later disbanded.) Later that year, UN forces detained hundreds of Somalis then denied ICRC access to prisoners of war and persisted until the ICRC suspended all operations in protest.

The anomaly troubles many thoughtful UN officials. The Serb-run camp was "so blatant" a violation of international law, said Kofi Annan, now the UN Secretary-General. "They should have seen it and reported. And in fact if they had reported, it is the sort of thing that would have gone public much earlier than it did." As for the UN legal office's view of the conventions, "We have asked them to respect the Geneva Conventions whether we signed it or not." But he also expressed understanding for troops in the absence of explicit Security Council mandates. "Soldiers like to have a clear mandate," he said. "They will not go out of their way" to look for war crimes.

The ICRC's ideal solution, according to a senior official, is to "declare openly that UN troops are bound by international humanitarian law and that everyone under the UN flag will be informed, trained, and monitored." Whether that will occur is unclear. ICRC and UN experts have discussed since 1993 a set of guidelines governing UN forces in combat, and it was still in the drafting stage at the time of writing. A draft in early 1998 required UN troops only to "respect the principles and spirit of international humanitarian law," without binding them legally; a later draft asserted the applicability of the Geneva Conventions by virtue of the fact that UN members are party to the treaties. But both drafts envisioned that a UN soldier who commits a prohibited act could be tried by his own government but not by another State or by a tribunal, thus averting **universal jurisdiction**. "We fought and lost that battle," commented an ICRC legal expert. ICRC officials, asserting that universal jurisdiction applies nevertheless, hope that the establishment of an International Criminal Court will set a new standard that UN peacekeepers will not be able to ignore.

U

Unlawful Confinement

By Ed Vulliamy

The column of prisoners blinked into the sunlight as they emerged from within a dark, capacious hangar and were drilled in a straight line across a yard into a canteen under the watchful eye of a beefy machine gunner, aloft at his post.

In the minute that was permitted, the men devoured their watery bean stew. Their skin was folded over their bones like parchment. They clutched their spoons, their spindly fingers shaking. Their huge, hollow eyes fixed upon us. "I do not want to tell any lies," said one emaciated figure, "but I cannot tell the truth."

This was lunchtime at Omarska, the Serb-run camp for Muslim and Croatian prisoners. Crews from ITN television and I witnessed the scene on August 5, 1992, before we were ignominiously bundled out.

The truth—which emerged only with time—was that Omarska was a hellish **concentration camp** in our lifetime, just down the road from Venice. It was a place where killing, cruelty, and ritual humiliation had become a form of twisted recreation. The guards were often drunk and singing as they tortured, beat, mutilated, and slaughtered prisoners, and there was a particular taste for forced fellatio, forced sex with animals, and sexual mutilation. The UN Commission of Experts called Omarska a *"de facto* death camp."

One prisoner was forced to bite off the testicles of another who, as he died, had a live pigeon stuffed into his mouth to stifle his screams. An eyewitness, testifying later at the United Nations International Criminal Tribunal for the Former Yugoslavia (ICTY) at The Hague described the behavior of the guards during this barbarism as being "like a crowd at a sports match."

At the end of these orgies of violence—usually on the tarmac yard or in two outbuildings, the White House and Red House—the cadavers of the dead would be loaded onto trucks by their friends or with bulldozers. There was a macabre intimacy to this carnage: people knew their torturers; they had been neighbors. Omarska had already been emptied of most of its prisoners before we arrived and was rapidly closed the day after our visit. It was a bitter kernel at the core not just of Bosnia's war, but of our time.

Omarska also provides a textbook case of unlawful confinement, a war crime. The legacy of Omarska was dramatically recalled at the first war crimes trial since Nuremberg, at The Hague in 1996. A part-time guard at the camp, Dusko Tadic, was charged with **war crimes** and **crimes against humanity**.

The laws of war on unlawful confinement vary according to whether a conflict is internal or international; they are intricately detailed for international conflicts but impose minimal standards for internal conflicts.

In an international conflict, unlawful confinement is a grave breach of the Fourth Geneva Convention of 1949. The statute of the ICTY states that (unlawful) imprisonment directed against the civilian population is a crime against humanity. Imprisonment as a form of **persecution** on political, racial, or religious grounds is also a crime against humanity.

Based on his role in the "seizure, collection, segregation, and forced transfer of civilians to camps," the tribunal found Tadic guilty of persecution on political, racial, or religious grounds, a crime against humanity. (In a 2–1

U

split, the judges ruled that the facts of this case did not prove that Bosnia was an international conflict and therefore ruled out all grave breaches.)

Not all confinement of civilians is unlawful. Article 42 of the Fourth Convention allows for a "detaining power" to intern those who pose a security threat, "only if the security of the detaining power makes it absolutely necessary." The descriptions for this are "internment" or "assigned residence." A civilian may also be lawfully interned if he or she commits certain minor offenses against an occupying power or poses a genuine threat.

The International Committee of the Red Cross (ICRC) Commentary on the Conventions calls internment a way of "getting people out of the way, and where supervision is more easily exercised." A civilian in a foreign country at war may be interned "if the security of the detaining power makes it absolutely necessary." A civilian in occupied territory may be interned if it is "necessary, for imperative reasons of security, to take safety measures concerning protected persons." There must have been some clear action threatening the security of the detaining power, such as espionage or sabo-

Bosnian prisoners kept in a cowshed in Manjaca. Bosnia, September 1992.

tage or belonging to "organizations whose object is to cause disturbances" or threaten (the belligerent's) security by other means. Merely being an enemy national is not enough. Civilians may be held or imprisoned as suspects or criminals, so long as they enjoy the rights relating to fair trials.

It is lawful to remove civilians for their own security in an emergency, such as an impending battle, into temporary shelters. Even so, they must be well cared for and returned home as soon as it is safe to do so. Enemy combatants, of course, may be interned as prisoners of war.

Neither the Geneva Conventions nor Additional Protocol II of 1977, which all parties to the Bosnia conflict agreed to follow, codifies the rules as to when civilians may be interned in an internal armed conflict. But the rules stipulate that if the internment is a sentence for a crime, the defendant must be allowed all the rights of a fair trial.

At a briefing inside Omarska the local police chief, Simo Drljaca (later shot dead by British troops in summer 1997 while resisting arrest), insisted

U

that a security threat existed—the Serbs even staged a pathetic mock gun battle to try to convince us. The authorities, he said, were screening inmates in order to find Muslim insurrectionists.

This proved to be a grotesque lie; the overwhelming majority of Drljaca's captives were unarmed civilians. Even if they had been armed or hostile, the law still requires certain standards, beginning with Article 37 of the Fourth Geneva Convention, which stipulates that: "protected persons who are confined pending proceedings or subject to a sentence involving loss of liberty shall, during their confinement, be humanely treated." This stipulation includes prisoners being protected from attack, fed, clothed and otherwise cared for. Similar requirements for humane treatment apply to internal conflicts. Additional Protocol II also requires that they be properly fed, clothed, and sheltered, and "be afforded safeguards as regards health and hygiene."

If the detainees of Omarska had been prisoners of war, they would have been entitled to "not be held in close confinement except where necessary to to safeguard their health"—i.e., the stinking human chicken coop in which they were held was clearly illegal.

Detainees must have sufficient sleeping space and be allowed to hold services in their adopted religion. The detaining power is obliged to provide medical care and an "adequate infirmary"—all provisions for which Omarska was the direct antithesis.

In contrast to the watery bean stew, daily food rations must be of a proper "quantity, quality and variety" to maintain health. The "investigations" which Mr. Drljaca claimed he was carrying out "shall be conducted as rapidly as circumstances permit" and brought to a trial as rapidly as possible. It was unlawful for men to be left festering, whatever the camp conditions.

Internees in an international armed conflict must be able to "retain articles of personal use," and "articles which have above all a personal or sentimental value may not be taken away"—in contrast to the wholesale pillaging of valuables in the Serbian camps. The arbitrary and systematic or widespread imprisonment of large numbers of civilians during conflicts— internal or international—is a crime against humanity.

If the prisoners are noncombatants—as the vast majority of Omarska's victims were—then they are automatically covered by Article 3 common to the four Geneva Conventions. This provision, applying explicitly to noninternational conflicts, states that "persons taking no active part in the hostilities . . . shall in all circumstances be treated humanely, without any adverse distinction founded on race, color, religion or faith, sex, birth or wealth, or any other similar criteria."

It prohibits "violence to life . . . in particular murder of all kinds, mutilation, cruel treatment and torture" and "the passing of sentences and the carrying out of executions without previous judgment pronounced by a regularly constituted court."

Additional Protocol II of 1977 provides a further list of fundamental guarantees and rights for nonmilitary internees in noninternational conflicts: the wounded and sick must be respected and properly treated; internees are to be provided with food and drinking water to the same extent that local civilians have them, and they are to be properly sheltered.

Under the Geneva Conventions, the detaining power is obliged to admit bodies such as the ICRC into its camps in an international armed conflict. But in Bosnia such organizations were kept out for three long, bloody months. They would have been another awkward group that knew the rules, and would recognize how thoroughly they were being torn to shreds.

(See **occupation of territory**.)

Victims, Rights of

By Lindsey Hilsum

Hiding in her house in Kigali, hearing the cries of her neighbors as they were being slaughtered, Monica Uwimana did not know where to turn for help. Gangs of youths were moving from house to house with machetes and nail-studded clubs killing Tutsis like her. She called UN employees. They said they could not help. She called a foreign reporter and asked for advice. The journalist had none.

Many Rwandans believe that UN peacekeepers had an obligation to help them. But the UN Security Council withdrew most of the troops at the height of the Rwanda genocide in April 1994 and did not order a new force in until it was too late.

In theory, civilians can turn to a neutral country and try to make it to a foreign embassy. But even if Monica Uwimana could have gotten past the roadblocks, she might have been turned away, for most embassies take in and protect only victims who have a proven link to their country.

Rwanda is the extreme example of a humanitarian crisis in which the international community and its representatives all but disappeared from the scene when they were most needed. And it encapsulates the predicament for victims of armed conflict, of crimes against humanity, or as in this instance, of genocide. States have the obligation to pay compensation for violating international conventions and are responsible for the misdeeds of their troops. The Hague Convention of 1907 states: "A belligerent party which violates the provisions of the said convention shall, if the case demands, be liable to pay compensation. It shall be responsible for all acts committed by persons forming part of its armed forces." Judicial institutions are trying cases from the wars over the succession to Yugoslavia and the Rwanda genocide, and a new world criminal court is being formed at this writing. Ultimately in these cases there will be accountability. But at the moment of maximum violence, protection is almost nonexistent.

The International Committee of the Red Cross (ICRC) is one of the first places victims turn. Its mandate is based on the Geneva Conventions: to protect the most vulnerable individuals, be they prisoners of war or civilians who come under attack; to trace the missing and reunite them with their families; to supervise repatriation of prisoners; and to remind all sides in a conflict that they are obliged to uphold the conventions. During the Rwanda genocide, its expatriate and local staff expanded their mandate and sheltered as many as nine thousand Rwandans in the ICRC compound. But the ICRC was overwhelmed. Its representatives collected thousands of wounded civilians and brought them to hospital. That did not spell protection, for on one occasion, soldiers entered the hospital after the foreigners had departed and massacred the patients. On another, Tutsis were dragged out of ICRC vehicles and killed. In parts of Rwanda, local staff of the national Red Cross participated in the killing.

The UN High Commissioner for Refugees (UNHCR), by its mandate, attempts to provide protection for those who flee their country because of conflict. The massive growth in the number of **internally displaced** persons (IDPs) has led UNHCR to set up operations in an increasing number of coun-

V

tries to handle them. And an ever growing number of nongovernmental organizations (NGOs) are attempting to help the victims of armed conflict. But few national or international NGOs operate in the midst of the conflict, unless an outside power guarantees their security. And the conflict in Bosnia shows the limits of such protection, for outside military force was deployed to protect convoys of food and medicine attempting to reach UN-declared "safe areas," but did almost nothing to safeguard the civilians or, when they came under attack, the safe areas as well.

In the post–Cold War era, aid organizations increasingly are targeted along with the civilians they are protecting. The head of the ICRC mission in Bosnia was targeted and killed in June of 1992, leading the ICRC to withdraw its entire presence from that country temporarily. It was then that Bosnian Serbs began their full-scale ethnic cleansing campaign. In Burundi, three ICRC delegates were ambushed on a main road and murdered in 1996. And in Chechnya, gunmen broke into an ICRC compound and killed six delegates in 1996. Attacks on those who try to help victims are the most dramatic evidence of the total disregard for the laws of war that marks contemporary conflict.

Under international law, States are obliged to prevent and, that failing, punish massive violations of the laws of war. For reasons of domestic politics, States often prefer to stay out of each others' conflicts; and the judicial instruments to justify intervention have at best weak enforcement mechanisms. The 1948 Genocide Convention, which requires States parties to "prevent and to punish" genocide, contains no mechanism for determining if a genocide is under way. Article 90 of Additional Protocol I of 1977 set up an **International Humanitarian Fact-Finding Commission** to investigate charges of war crimes, but it requires the consent of both parties to function and has been in general disuse. The newest attempt is the UN drive to create an International Criminal Court, whose prosecutor is to be empowered to launch investigations into war crimes and crimes against humanity while crimes are underway.

As for compensation, victims have a right under international and domestic law to sue, but after a genocide such as Rwanda's, there is rarely anyone rich enough left to pay the damages. The victims of the Nazi Holocaust received reparations from successor German governments. But "comfort women," used as sex slaves by Japanese troops during World War II, have yet to receive compensation fifty years later, even though the government admitted in 1993 that Japan's military was responsible for the crime. On April 27, 1998 the Tokyo district court ordered compensation paid to three Korean women, but the government has appealed. The UN Commission on Human Rights has advocated a set of principles to assist victims of human rights violations. The principles include a family's right to know the fate of missing people, the right to reparations, the right to criminal justice, and the principle that governments take steps to prevent recurrences. These principles are only recommendations, however.

By luck, chance, and the grace of God, Monica Uwimana survived. Her five children, who had been staying with grandparents in the countryside, were murdered. She has little faith in international law.

(See **protected persons; Red Cross/Red Crescent emblem; refugees, rights of; transfer of civilians.**)

Wanton Destruction

By Jeremy Bowen

It seemed a little safer on the low hill on the edge of Grozny. We wanted to avoid a repeat of the day before, when we had been caught in a Russian air strike in the center of the city. I had lain in the lee of a small wall, wishing my flak jacket covered my legs as well as my back, waiting for the cluster bombs to stop exploding. About a hundred yards away the bomb fragments killed the four Chechen fighters I had been interviewing a minute or so earlier. None of us in the BBC team had been feeling very lucky before the air strike. Now we felt like marked men, like everybody else in Grozny in the first few days of 1995.

We stood on the hill, filming, at fairly long range, the fires that the Russian bombardment had started. Then, new explosions, fire and smoke started to pour out of central Grozny. Perhaps I was just knocked back by a surge of adrenaline and fear, but my memory tells me that the earth shook and the blast vibrated through my guts. In the next few seconds the line of flame and smoke moved right along the line of the city's main avenue that starts in Minutka Square and ends at the Chechen parliament building. It was a massive, coordinated attack by the heavy artillery and multiple rocket launchers I had seen on the Russian side of the lines. It was hard to believe that anybody could survive the inferno. Grozny disappeared under new clouds of flame and smoke and we got out with our tapes.

I went back into the center of Grozny most days that January. There were many more Russian attacks. Block after block of typical Soviet concrete-and-steel buildings were destroyed. In the few weeks after President Boris Yeltsin ordered his troops to end the Chechen rebellion, the Russians flattened the center of the city. Its destruction was more complete than anything I saw in the former Yugoslavia (including Mostar and Vukovar) and six other wars.

The laws of war state that an attacker must attempt to distinguish between military targets and civilians and their **property**. If he does not, he is guilty of the war crime of **indiscriminate attack**. If the attack also results in extensive, unnecessary, and willful damage then he is also guilty of wanton destruction. **Proportionality** is everything. The laws recognize that a legitimate military operation can kill noncombatants or damage their property. But any damage must not be excessive in comparison to the direct and concrete military advantage anticipated.

Despite the laws' clarity, their application is often clouded by other considerations. At the Nuremburg Trials, Hermann Goering, the German air minister, and all the major war criminals were charged with "the devastation of towns, not justified by **military necessity**, in violation of the laws of war." The charges were not pursued, perhaps because they were accused also of a wide range of other crimes and because the Allies did not want to draw attention to their own bombing campaigns in Germany and Japan.

And in Grozny, Russia could cite the fact that small groups of Chechen fighters were moving around the city almost at will, working their way up to the main confrontation line where they were killing hundreds of Russian conscripts. The shelling I witnessed followed the disastrous failure of a force of

Russian tanks to break into the city center. Moscow might argue that shelling was the best and only way to take on the highly motivated Chechens.

If Grozny itself is an ambiguous case under the laws of war, there were plenty of examples that were crystal clear. The scene was a crossroads on the road into Grozny. Refugees had been flooding out of the city in the face of the Russian attack, and enterprising traders had set up corrugated iron shacks to sell drinks and food to those who had money. You could hear the noise of shelling coming from Grozny. Sometimes Russian warplanes flew overhead on their way to bomb the city. In the middle distance the silvery shape of a Russian helicopter-gunship hovered almost motionless over one of the outlying villages. Every now and then it launched a missile into the village, where the Chechens were putting up stiff resistance.

The war was all around, but the crossroads seemed like a backwater. I

Grozny: A woman stands in the ruins of the Chechen capital after the Russian assault, 1996.

never saw Chechen fighters use it. The closest bridges were three-quarters of a mile away, and the Russian Air Force had blown up one.

But one morning in January 1995, Russian warplanes had attacked the crossroads, bombing and strafing. There were wounded in the hospital and, we were told, about half a dozen dead—all civilians. There were impact craters in the road. All that was left of the food-and-drink stands were a few twisted pieces of corrugated iron. The traders were picking up where they had left off, rebuilding the stands. And the refugees were still moving out of Grozny. The devastation of the crossroads, though on a far smaller scale than the attack on Grozny, was by all available evidence, a pure example of wanton destruction.

(See **civilian immunity**; **immunity**; **legitimate military targets**; **military objectives**; **pillage**.)

W

War Crimes, Categories of

By Steven R. Ratner

The term *war crimes* evokes a litany of horrific images—concentration camps, ethnic cleansing, execution of prisoners, rape, and bombardment of cities. These images correspond in many ways to the legal definitions of the term, but international law draws lines that do not in all ways match our sense of the most awful behavior.

War crimes are those violations of the laws of war—or international humanitarian law (IHL)—that incur individual criminal responsibility. While limitations on the conduct of armed conflict date back at least to the Chinese warrior Sun Tzu (sixth century B.C.E.), the ancient Greeks were among the first to regard such prohibitions as law. The notion of war crimes *per se* appeared more fully in the Hindu code of Manu (circa 200 B.C.E.), and eventually made its way into Roman and European law. The first true trial for war crimes is generally considered to be that of Peter von Hagenbach, who was tried in 1474 in Austria and sentenced to death for wartime atrocities.

By World War I, States had accepted that certain violations of the laws of war—much of which had been codified in the Hague Conventions of 1899 and 1907—were crimes. The 1945 Charter of the International Military Tribunal at Nuremberg defined war crimes as "violations of the laws or customs of war," including murder, ill-treatment, or deportation of civilians in occupied territory; murder or ill-treatment of prisoners of war; killing of hostages; plunder of public or private property; wanton destruction of municipalities; and devastation not militarily necessary.

The 1949 Geneva Conventions, which codified IHL after World War II, also marked the first inclusion in a humanitarian law treaty of a set of war crimes—the grave breaches of the conventions. Each of the four Geneva Conventions (on wounded and sick on land, wounded and sick at sea, prisoners of war, and civilians) contains its own list of grave breaches. The list in its totality is: willful killing; torture or inhuman treatment (including medical experiments); willfully causing great suffering or serious injury to body or health; extensive destruction and appropriation of property not justified by military necessity and carried out unlawfully and wantonly; compelling a prisoner of war or civilian to serve in the forces of the hostile power; willfully depriving a prisoner of war or protected civilian of the rights of a fair and regular trial; unlawful deportation or transfer of a protected civilian; unlawful confinement of a protected civilian; and taking of hostages. Additional Protocol I of 1977 expanded the protections of the Geneva Conventions for international conflicts to include as grave breaches: certain medical experimentation; making civilians and nondefended localities the object or inevitable victims of attack; the perfidious use of the Red Cross or Red Crescent emblem; transfer of an occupying power of parts of its population to occupied territory; unjustifiable delays in repatriation of POWs; apartheid; attack on historic monuments; and depriving protected persons of a fair trial. Under the Geneva Conventions and Additional Protocol I, States must prosecute persons accused of grave breaches or hand them over to a State willing to do so.

W

The grave breaches provisions only apply in international armed conflicts; and they only apply to acts against so-called protected persons or during battlefield activities. Protected persons are, in general, wounded and sick combatants on land and sea, POWs, and civilians who find themselves in the hands of a state of which they are not nationals.

Most violations of the Geneva Conventions and Additional Protocols are not grave breaches. Of those not listed as grave breaches, many are still considered war crimes, although in those cases States do not have the same obligation to extradite or prosecute as they do for grave breaches. Other nongrave breaches are not war crimes, but simply **illegal acts** for which only the violating State is responsible under international law. To give one simple example, if the commander of a POW camp failed to keep a record of all disciplinary punishments (a violation of Article 96 of the Third Geneva Convention), he would likely not be committing a war crime—although some may disagree. Distinguishing among nongrave breaches to determine which are crimes is not an exact science, though it would seem that the more serious nongrave breaches do incur individual responsibility. (The U.S. military maintains that all violations of the laws of war, including those of the Geneva Conventions, are war crimes.)

Wartime atrocities not prohibited under the Geneva Conventions or Additional Protocol I may nonetheless be war crimes under the customary law rubric of "violations of the laws and customs of war" (the same phrase as in the Nuremberg Charter). For interstate conflicts, states agree that such war crimes include certain violations of the 1907 Hague Convention and Regulations, such as use of poisonous weapons, wanton destruction of cities not justified by military necessity, attacks on undefended localities, attacks on religious and cultural institutions, and plunder of public and private property. The Statute of the International Criminal Court (ICC) lists as war crimes for international conflicts not only the grave breaches of the Geneva Conventions, but some twenty-six serious violations of the laws and customs of war, most of which have been considered by States as crimes since at least World War II.

As for **civil wars**, unfortunately, international law today has fewer rules regulating the conduct of internal conflicts, which many States consider part of their domestic jurisdiction and, consequently, there is a shorter list of war crimes. Additional Protocol II of 1977, which contains basic rules for the conduct of internal conflicts, has no criminal liability provisions, and the reach of customary law war crimes is not as clear with respect to such wars as it is for international wars. The Statute of the International Criminal Tribunal for the Former Yugoslavia includes "serious violations of Common Article 3 of the Geneva Conventions" (the one article of the Geneva Conventions that addresses civil wars), as well as other rules to protect victims of armed conflict and basic rules on methods of warfare. The tribunal defined a serious violation as one that has grave consequences for its victims and breaks a rule protecting important values. This would presumably include violence to life or health (murder, ill-treatment, torture, mutilation, corporal punishment, rape, enforced prostitution, indecent assault), summary executions, hostage taking, collective punishment, and pillage. This list, while shorter than the list of grave breaches or other interstate war crimes, nonetheless would cover some of the most horrific acts during recent conflicts. The Statute of the International Criminal Tribunal for Rwanda includes as war crimes serious violations of Common Article 3 as well as serious viola-

W

tions of Additional Protocol II. The Statute of the ICC lists as war crimes for internal conflicts four serious violations of Common Article 3 (violence to life and person, outrages upon personal dignity, hostage taking, and summary executions), as well as twelve serious violations of the laws and customs of war (e.g., attacks on civilians, pillage, rape, or mutilation).

Though perhaps an obvious point, it should be noted that the laws of war only cover atrocities during armed conflict. They exclude many of the worst abuses of this century, such as Stalin's purges and destruction of the Kulaks, most of the Khmer Rouge's terror, and Mao's forced collectivizations. While these atrocities are international crimes—**crimes against humanity**, or, in some cases, **genocide**—they are not war crimes.

Finally, the creation of a body of law criminalizing certain violations of the laws of war does not mean that war criminals will actually be prosecuted. This remains a matter for States and, increasingly, the United Nations and other international organizations. The Geneva Conventions require all parties to search for and either extradite or try all persons suspected of having committed grave breaches. And international law gives all States the legal right to prosecute war criminals under the theory of universal jurisdiction. While States have at times prosecuted war criminals (e.g., the U.S. trial of the My Lai offenders), the more pervasive pattern, despite the obligations of the Geneva Conventions, is either mere administrative punishment or impunity. The ad hoc tribunals for Yugoslavia and Rwanda have jurisdiction over both grave breaches of the Geneva Conventions and other crimes committed in these particular conflicts, and the ICC will, as noted, have jurisdiction over most war crimes.

(See **international vs. internal armed conflict**)

W

Water Supplies and Works, Destruction of

By Emma Daly

The old woman reached into her plastic bucket and pulled out a triangular shard of human bone, still pink and glistening, a gruesome reminder of her daily struggle to find water.

Sarajevans cross the ruined bridge across the Mitjacka River to get water, 1993.

She had been waiting in line for water, at a standpipe protected, she had thought, by the ruins of an old school, when a mortar bomb crashed through a hole in the roof. Seven people were killed and twelve wounded, including the elderly woman herself, who had a slight graze on her forehead and a serious case of shattered nerves.

Collecting water was one of the most dangerous and dispiriting daily tasks in Sarajevo between April 1992 and December 1996. The secessionist Serb forces frequently cut off the city's water supply (and its gas and electricity as well). And even when they permitted the water to flow, they routinely fired on those queuing up for it.

As a general principle, in both internal and international armed conflict it is lawful to attack only **military objectives**. From this derives the rule stated in Article 54 of the first of the two 1977 Additional Protocols to the Geneva Conventions that "**starvation** of civilians as a method of warfare is prohibited." Denying the civilian population water is just as illegal as denying them food. Article 54 states that "it is prohibited to attack, destroy, remove or render useless objects indispensable to the survival of the civilian

W

377

population," and includes not only foodstuffs, livestock, and the like, but "drinking water installations and supplies and irrigation works."

But though the idea would have made little sense to the people of besieged Sarajevo, water supplies do not enjoy absolute protection under international law. If water supplies are being used exclusively by civilians, legally they are supposed to be immune. But if they are being used by both combatants and noncombatants, the picture changes.

The premise of all laws of war is that it is perfectly legal to attack **legitimate military targets.** So when water and waterworks are used exclusively to sustain military forces they can be targeted. Moreover, according to the language of Additional Protocol I, where water and waterworks are used "in direct support of military action" they can be destroyed. For example, if a water installation is being used by soldiers as a firing position or to conceal supplies then it, like other generally protected spaces such as **hospitals,** is not legally protected from attack.

Nonetheless, these exceptions are not as broad as they first appear and contain their own limitations and exceptions. The laws state that any harm to civilians must not be excessive compared to a concrete and direct military advantage. And Additional Protocol I, Article 54 states that "in no event" shall actions against targets such as waterworks be undertaken when they may be "expected to leave the civilian population with such inadequate food or water as to cause its starvation or force its movement." Military necessity alone does not give soldiers license to destroy a water installation if it is indispensable to the survival of the civilian population.

Whether what went on in Sarajevo when the Serbs cut off the water was a war crime is problematic. Often the real crime seems to have been sniping at and shelling the people lined up for water, rather than the cut-off itself. A deliberate and systematic cutting off of water to the civilian population, however, would be a war crime.

Fearing that the Sarajevo experience is the shape of things to come, and convinced that in an increasing number of conflicts the lack of clean water kills more people than bullets or bombs, the International Committee of the Red Cross (ICRC) is campaigning to have a blanket ban on attacking waterworks. It is pressing to have the immunity from attack, of the sort given to medical staff, given in practice to water engineers and other personnel seeking to keep water supplies flowing or to repair water systems. Such personnel are protected under Additional Protocol I because they fall into the category of civil defense personnel. The ICRC position asserts "the absolute imperative" of water for the survival of the civilian population.

W

Weapons

By Burrus Carnahan

The American Civil War saw the first use of many weapons that would revolutionize warfare—armored warships, submarines, land mines, and machine guns to list a few. One Civil War innovation would have a more dubious fate, however, becoming the first weapon specifically outlawed by international treaty. This was a rifle bullet that would explode on impact with a human body. Immediately after the war, the U.S. Army Ordnance Department concluded that exploding rifle bullets were inhumane, and should never be purchased again.

Experience during the Civil War had shown that any soldier hit by an ordinary rifle bullet was likely to be put out of action by that wound alone. In most cases, exploding bullets merely made an already disabling wound worse. The suffering caused by such bullets was therefore militarily unnecessary and inhumane.

The same conclusion had been reached by the Russian government at almost the same time. During the 1860s, the czar's army had also developed an exploding rifle bullet, and similar doubts had arisen about its humanity. Unlike the United States, however, Russia faced a number of potentially hostile land powers, and the czar's government was reluctant to give up any new weapon unless it could be assured that potential enemies would also forgo its use. In 1868, therefore, the Russian government convened an international conference at St. Petersburg to consider this issue. (The United States did not participate—this was an era of isolationism in U.S. foreign policy.)

The resulting treaty, called the St. Petersburg Declaration, banned the use of exploding or incendiary bullets weighing less than four hundred grams. It also stated certain important general principles, as follows: "That the only legitimate object . . . during war is to weaken the military forces of the enemy; "That for this purpose it is sufficient to disable the greatest possible number of men; "That this object would be exceeded by the employment of arms which uselessly aggravate the sufferings of disabled men, or render their death inevitable; and "That the employment of such arms would, therefore, be contrary to the laws of humanity." These principles are now accepted as part of customary international law, binding on all nations, whether or not they are parties to the St. Petersburg Declaration.

International conferences meeting at The Hague in the Netherlands in 1899 and 1907 distilled the St. Petersburg principles into the familiar principle that it is forbidden to use weapons that cause "unnecessary suffering" or "superfluous injury." This principle, which is also part of customary international law, was reaffirmed by a diplomatic conference in Geneva, Switzerland, in 1977.

This rule prohibits, for example, the use of explosive projectiles filled with clear glass. Glass fragments would make a soldier's wounds more difficult to treat, because a surgeon would have trouble seeing them. Once a soldier is being treated in a field hospital, however, he or she is obviously out of combat action. It is therefore militarily unnecessary and superfluous to make the wounds more difficult to treat. For similar reasons, it is forbidden to use explosive projectiles designed to injure with fragments not

W

379

detectable by X-rays. Poisoned bullets and barbed bayonets are also generally regarded as prohibited. The rule against the use of dumdum bullets designed to flatten on impact also reflects the principle against unnecessary suffering and superfluous injury.

In applying the principle against unnecessary suffering and superfluous injury, the military advantages of the weapon must always be weighed against the suffering it causes. After all, the very phrase "unnecessary suffering" implies that there is such a thing as necessary suffering. A weapon cannot be considered forbidden simply because, in the abstract, it produces great suffering; the military side of the equation must always be considered as well. The literature of humanitarian nongovernmental organizations (NGOs) often falls into this error by stressing the inhumane consequences of a weapon's use, and arguing on that basis alone that the weapon causes unnecessary suffering.

It should be noted that a weapon may be unlawful if used for one purpose, and yet lawful if used for another purpose. For example, when combat between airplanes became a reality in World War I, the British armed the machine guns on their warplanes with incendiary bullets. The initial reaction of the German government was to threaten to try captured British airmen as war criminals for violating the St. Petersburg Declaration. Upon reflection, however, the German government backed down. Incendiary bullets in air warfare are intended to destroy enemy aircraft, not cause additional injury to enemy troops, and the St. Petersburg Declaration was intended only to deal with the latter problem. Today, legal experts generally regard the use of incendiary and small caliber explosive bullets as lawful in air warfare, though their use in infantry rifles would still be forbidden.

Customary international law also prohibits the use of **indiscriminate** weapons. An indiscriminate weapon is one that cannot be directed at a legitimate military objective. The V-2 rockets used by Germany in World War II were indiscriminate weapons, in that they could not be directed at any target smaller than an entire city. After the 1991 **Gulf War**, the U.S. Department of Defense reported to Congress that the SCUD missiles used by Iraq (which were not very much more accurate than the V-2) were indiscriminate, and that their use constituted a war crime. Similarly, the balloons carrying incendiary bombs, which the Japanese launched into the jet stream toward the United States in 1945, were indiscriminate weapons. The Japanese government hoped they would cause forest fires in the western United States, but the balloons could not be controlled enough to fulfill even this function.

A weapon is not indiscriminate merely because it is highly destructive. Nuclear weapons, for example, are not indiscriminate in this legal sense. They can be effectively directed against, and destroy, **military objectives**. The legal issues raised by **nuclear weapons** are whether they will cause civilian casualties and environmental damage disproportionate to the value of the military targets they destroy.

(See **biological weapons**; **chemical weapons**; **mines**; **poisonous weapons**.)

W

Willful Killing

By Peter Maass

Slobodan was being a gracious host. Whenever we entered an exposed stretch of territory, he would stop, listen like a terrier for signs of trouble, and then sprint ahead, waving me on when he felt it was safe. It was the winter of 1993, the Bosnian War was in full throttle, and Slobodan was taking me to his place of work, a ransacked apartment in a bombed-out building on the front line around Sarajevo.

A twenty-one-year-old, pony-tailed apprentice sniper takes aim in Karlovac, Croatia, 1991. He is entitled to three cartridges a day.

Slobodan was a Bosnian Serb sniper. Because he was off duty when he showed me around, he was armed only with a pistol. Once we reached his perch, though, he cheerfully pointed it at the Sarajevans running across exposed ground a few hundred yards away. "I can shoot!" he said in excited English. "Look, look, people, pistol, pop-pop!" Then he calmed down and smiled. "No problem, no problem. No shoot people. No, no shoot."

What he actually was saying was that he didn't shoot civilians, only soldiers. This was improbable. I had been in Sarajevo long enough to know that civilians were pretty much the only targets of snipers like Slobodan. I had talked to people who were shot by snipers, I saw a youth get shot near the Holiday Inn near the front line, and I knew, as everyone did, that the cold weather and lack of food in Bosnia's besieged capital were not the worst killers. It was the snipers you worried about the most, because they were the ones firing all those bullets that found their way into so many arms and legs and heads and hearts.

There is no prohibition on sniping at combatants during wartime, but

W

the intentional killing of civilians is a war crime. And it was likely that Slobodan and his sniping pals were guilty of willful killing—the legal term for that crime—many, many times over.

The 1977 Additional Protocol I to the Geneva Conventions makes it clear that civilian deaths that are incidentally, even if foreseeably, caused by justifiable military operations are legal, subject to the principle of proportionality. But if the killing of a civilian, a noncombatant, is intentional or is not justified by **military necessity**, a war crime has been committed. For example, the execution of hostages or prisoners would be such a crime. In an international conflict, the violation could be prosecuted as willful killing under the grave breaches provisions of the Geneva Conventions; in an internal conflict, the crime could be prosecuted as murder under domestic law or under Article 3 common to the Four Geneva Conventions of 1949.

The sorts of people covered under the willful killing and murder rubrics include, among others, not just civilians in the ordinary sense of the word, but prisoners of war, sick or wounded or surrendering soldiers, and medical and religious personnel.

The crime of willful killing is an active component of international law. The International Criminal Tribunal for the Former Yugoslavia is empowered to prosecute acts of willful killing, and several defendants have been charged with the crime. However, in a controversial decision in the case of Dusko Tadic, a Serb prison guard, the tribunal ruled that Tadic could not have committed acts of willful killing because the Bosnian War was not international in character. As a result, Tadic was declared not guilty of the willful killing charges, although the ruling is under appeal.

With the Tadic case in mind, what penalties might a sniper like Slobodan face? If the Bosnian War is ultimately determined to have been an international conflict, he could be charged with willful killing for each protected person he shot. If it is determined to be an internal conflict, he could be charged with murder. But whatever the charge, he would be subject to multiple counts. On the day he served so politely as my tour guide, I asked whether he had shot anyone. "Today, no," he replied. "Yesterday, yes. Pop, pop!"

W

Willfulness

By A. P. V. Rogers

In trials for war crimes or grave breaches, the prosecution must generally prove not only that the accused did the act complained of but also that he intended the consequences of his act. This intent is usually referred to by lawyers as *mens rea*, criminal intent or basic intent.

If, for example, in attacking a military target, a commander causes unintended civilian casualties because of a weapons malfunction or faulty target intelligence, he would not be guilty of an offense because he lacked criminal intent, despite the consequences of his actions.

Even if treaty provisions are silent on the question of intent as in "taking of hostages," basic intent must still be proved. If a soldier is ordered to take civilians from a battlefield village under armed guard to a town well away from the fighting and there hand them over to the garrison commander and it later transpires that they were being held as hostages to protect the military headquarters in that town from attack, his defense might be lack of criminal intent as he was unaware that the civilians were hostages and assumed they were being taken to a place of safety.

Often a grave breach provision of a treaty specifies the intent as willfulness, as in "*willful* killing, torture or inhuman treatment" or "*willfully* . . . making the civilian population or individual civilians the object of attack." Or it may take the form of wantonness, as in "extensive destruction . . . of property, not justified by military necessity and carried out unlawfully and *wantonly*."

The terms *willful* and *wanton* include intentional or deliberate acts and also cases of recklessness. Criminal liability is not limited to positive acts. It can arise in the event of a failure to act when there is a duty to do so and the failure is either with intent that the consequences should follow or is due to recklessness about those consequences.

In the International Committee for the Red Cross (ICRC) Commentary on the Additional Protocols, willfulness is explained thus: the accused must have acted consciously and with intent, i.e., with his mind on the act and its consequences and willing them . . . : this encompasses the concepts of "wrongful intent" or "recklessness," viz., the attitude of an agent who, without being certain of a particular result, accepts the possibility of it happening; on the other hand, ordinary negligence or lack of foresight is not covered, i.e., when a man acts without having his mind on the act or its consequences. However, negligence may suffice for disciplinary action under national law.

The statute of the International Criminal Court specifies that an accused person is only to be convicted if his offense was committed "with intent and knowledge." An accused has intent if, in relation to conduct, he "means to engage in the conduct" and, in relation to a consequence, he "means to cause that consequence or is aware that it will occur in the ordinary course of events." Knowledge means "awareness that a circumstance exists or a consequence will occur in the ordinary course of events."
(See **due process; wanton destruction; war crimes; willful killing.**)

W

AFTERWORD

By Kenneth Anderson, legal editor

A Note on the Legal Standards Applied in This Book

International humanitarian law (IHL) must always balance between two poles. On the one hand is the lawyerly desire to be legally precise, to be technically accurate about frequently difficult concepts and distinctions of law. On the other is the desire to codify a law to which ordinary soldiers and their officers will have allegiance because they understand it and its underlying humanitarian rationale.

Equally important is the perception of the general public. In order to bring this topic before the broadest possible audience, the intent behind this book is to combine technical accuracy and readability.

As legal editor, I accept the responsibility for the legal analysis and rules of IHL promulgated in this volume. Individual authors have retained their independent voices as to the facts and phenomena that, frequently, they have witnessed. Independent authorial analysis is more pronounced in the longer country and conflict articles, such as those covering the Arab-Israeli wars, Cambodia, and the Gulf War. The editors have generally let authors develop their own statements of the circumstances, and social and political causes of the conflicts. Still, insofar as is possible, I have sought to draw my best estimation of their legal significance and status under the terms of IHL. In our quest for accuracy and fairness we have had the benefit of unstinting advice from many prominent legal authorities. (See **acknowledgements**.) In the case of articles written by prominent legal experts in IHL, we have given them latitude to express individual judgements on difficult or unsettled matters, while recognizing that not all issues are settled. However, any errors of legal analysis or judgment are mine alone.

Technical accuracy versus simplification is not the only tension that faces a book such as this. There is always the risk that for the sake of clarity one suggests that there are always determinate rules in IHL that yield plain and unwavering answers to any question of application. IHL, like other bodies of law, contains important matters whose scope and interpretation are susceptible to considerably different readings. In short, what various sources urge as applicable law is not always uniform, and it would in fact be surprising if it were so. Of the differences that can arise, perhaps the most important is between the aspirations of those who would like to see the rules of armed conflict extended in one way or another and the defenders of actual and traditional practices of States and their militaries.

In the past, it would perhaps be fair to say, Western and U.S. journalists tended to accept the characterization of law given by their own militaries, or worse, never questioned the legality of military actions. Today the world is filled with international nongovernmental organizations, legal scholars, and many others seeking to influence international public opinion and happy to offer their views on international law. Often their views are presented (and often accepted) uncritically as objective statements of law without consideration of contrary opinions. This book does not attempt to resolve the issues and debates between those with activist briefs and those closer to the status quo.

Where the law or its interpretation is unsettled or contested, we seek to identify the controversy and not act as though it does not exist.

The status of Additional Protocol I of 1977 requires a special note. Protocol I has been very broadly accepted by States although the United States and other significant military powers, including, for example, Israel and Turkey, have not ratified. It is often relevant to note which countries have taken on actual treaty obligations and which have not. Additionally, ratifying States have also expressed reservations and these, too, define a country's treaty obligations. Some commentators and international activist organizations tend to be impatient with questions of which countries have bound themselves to the terms of Protocol I and which have not. Their view is that a treaty that has achieved such wide acceptance must perforce constitute customary international law, which as Professor Theodor Meron explains in his article on customary law, binds even those States that have not ratified it. Again, the intent of this book is to clarify rather than resolve the issue.

It is important to realize, however, that the United States, a State whose practices matter significantly, has accepted large portions of Protocol I as declaratory of customary international law on some of the critical substantive matters of IHL including, for example, the prohibitions on direct attack against civilians and indiscriminate attack involving civilians.

Another unsettled debate is over the weight to attach to the future of the newly established International Criminal Court (ICC). Although this book indicates how various IHL issues may be affected by the existence of the ICC, by its Statute, adopted in Rome in 1998, and by the international criminal tribunals for the former Yugoslavia and Rwanda, the fact that the United States has chosen to remain outside the ICC cannot be ignored. Whether the United States will eventually join, or whether the world will move toward some two-tier system in which most States at least nominally adhere to an international adjudication system while the world's leading military power and political guarantor of international stability stands apart, is not known at this point. In the last analysis, however, State practices still matter.

The Rome Statute of the ICC is the most important revision of IHL since the Additional Protocols of 1977. IHL is therefore on the cutting edge of movements of profoundly larger import than simply conduct upon the battlefield; those who say that the concept of sovereignty is at issue in the proper role and scope of IHL are wholly correct. This book aims to make accessible to the public, and to the journalists who write about these matters for the public, the body of law that stands at this cutting edge.

Note on the Law and Legal Terms

By Alan Dorsey

The terms *international humanitarian law* or *IHL*, *laws of war*, *laws of armed conflict*, *rules of war*, etc., are, generally speaking, synonymous and interchangeable. Lawyers, human rights groups, relief organizations, the ICRC, and most States favor *international humanitarian law*, whereas militaries typically prefer the term *laws of war*, or some variation. In this book, we tend toward international humanitarian law, or IHL, except where an author has explicitly chosen a different usage.

International law is a complex mix of multilateral treaties, customary law, State practice, UN Security Council resolutions, judicial decisions, the work of advisory commissions and legal experts, and "general principles of law." In the simplest formulation, it might be said that the four Geneva Conventions of August 12, 1949, and the two Additional Protocols of June 8, 1977, form the heart of IHL and are the most frequently cited sources.

The short forms for the names of the various treaties and conventions used in this book have been adapted from widely accepted legal references. Short forms are given for those treaties mentioned in the book and/or for reference. This list is not exhaustive and not every treaty mentioned in the book is in this list as some (the International Labor Organization Conventions, for example) are not considered to be part of IHL proper.

Major International Humanitarian Law

Statements and treaties, in chronological order:
Title, place of promulgation or deposit, date, short form in italics.

Instructions for the Government of Armies of the United States in the Field. April 24, 1863. *Lieber Code*

Convention for the Amelioration of the Condition of the Wounded in Armies in the Field. Geneva, August 22, 1864. *1864 Geneva Convention*

Declaration Renouncing the Use, in Time of War, of Certain Explosive Projectiles. St. Petersburg, November 29 - December 11, 1868.
St. Petersburg Declaration of 1868

Convention II with Respect to the Laws and Customs of War on Land and its annex: Regulation concerning the Laws and Customs of War on Land.
The Hague, July 29, 1899. *1899 Hague Convention* or *1899 Hague Regulations*

Convention for the Amelioration of the Condition of the Wounded and Sick in Armies in the Field. Geneva, July 6, 1906. *1906 Geneva Convention*

Convention IV respecting the Laws and Customs of War on Land and its annex: Regulations concerning the Laws and Customs of War on Land. The Hague, October 18, 1907. *1907 Hague Conventions* or *1907 Hague Regulations*

Protocol for the Prohibition of the Use of Asphyxiating, Poisonous or Other Gases, and of Bacteriological Methods of Warfare. Geneva, June 17, 1925.
1925 Geneva Protocol

Convention for the Amelioration of the Condition of the Wounded and Sick in Armies in the Field. Geneva, July 27, 1929. *1929 Geneva Convention*

Agreement for the Prosecution and Punishment of the Major War Criminals of the European Axis, and Charter of the International Military Tribunal. London, August 8, 1945. *Nuremberg Charter*

Convention on the Prevention and Punishment of the Crime of Genocide. United Nations, December 9, 1948. *Genocide Convention*

Convention I for the Amelioration of the Condition of the Wounded and Sick in Armed Forces in the Field. Geneva, August 12, 1949.
First Geneva Convention (of 1949) or GCI

Convention II for the Amelioration of the Conditions of Wounded, Sick, and Shipwrecked Members of Armed Forces at Sea. Geneva, August 12, 1949.
Second Geneva Convention (of 1949) or GCII

Convention III Relative to the Treatment of Prisoners of War. Geneva, August 12, 1949.
Third Geneva Convention (of 1949) or GCIII

Convention IV Relative to the Protection of Civilian Persons in Time of War. Geneva, August 12, 1949. *Fourth Geneva Convention (of 1949) or GCIV*

Hague Convention on the Protection of Cultural Property in the Event of Armed Conflict. The Hague, May 14, 1954.
1954 Convention on Cultural Property

Convention on the Prohibition of the Development, Production and Stockpiling of Bacteriological Biological and Toxic Weapons and on their Destruction. Opened for Signature at London, Moscow, and Washington. April 10, 1972.
Biological Weapons Convention or BWC

Protocol I Additional to the Geneva Conventions of August 12, 1949, and Relating to the Protection of Victims of International Armed Conflicts. Geneva, June 8, 1977.
Additional Protocol I or API

Protocol II Additional to the Geneva Conventions of August 12, 1949, and Relating to the Protection of Victims of Non-International Armed Conflicts. Geneva, June 8, 1977.
Additional Protocol II or APII

1980 Convention on Prohibitions or Restrictions on the Use of Certain Conventional Weapons That May Be Deemed to Be Excessively Injurious or to Have Indiscriminate Effects. United Nations, October 10, 1980.
1980 Conventional Weapons Convention or CCW

Convention on the Prohibition of the Development, Production, Stockpiling and Use of Chemical Weapons and on Their Destruction. Paris, January 13, 1993.
1993 Chemical Weapons Convention

Statute of the International Tribunal for the Prosecution of Persons Responsible for Serious Violations of International Humanitarian Law Committed in the Territory of the Former Yugoslavia Since 1991. United Nations, May 25, 1993.
Yugoslavia Tribunal Statute or ICTY

Statute of the International Criminal Tribunal for the Prosecution of Persons Responsible for Genocide and Other Serious Violations of International Humanitarian Law Committed in the Territory of Rwanda and Rwandan Citizens Responsible for Genocide and Other Such Violations Committed in the Territory of Neighboring States

between January 1, 1994 and December 31, 1994. United Nations, November 8, 1994.
Rwanda Tribunal Statute or ICTR

Protocol on Prohibitions or Restrictions on the Use of Mines, Booby-Traps and Other
Devices. United Nations, as amended May 3, 1996.
Protocol II of the 1980 Conventional Weapons Convention

Convention on the Prohibition of the Use, Stockpiling, Production and Transfer of Anti-
Personnel Mines and on Their Destruction. United Nations, September 18, 1997.
Ottawa Treaty

Rome Statute of the International Criminal Court. United Nations, July 17, 1998.
Rome Statute or ICC Statute

Some Titles for Further Reading

War Crimes: Brutality, Genocide, Terror, and the Struggle for Justice
by Aryeh Neier
Times Books,1998

*Accountability for Human Rights Atrocities in International Law: Beyond the
Nuremberg Legacy*
by Stephen R. Ratner and Jason S. Abrams
Oxford University Press, 1997

Documents on the Laws of War
Edited by Adam Roberts and Richard Guelff
Oxford University Press, 1989

Law on the Battlefield (Melland Schill Studies in International Law)
by A. P. V. Rogers
Manchester University Press, June 1996

The Anatomy of the Nuremberg Trials : A Personal Memoir
by Telford Taylor
Little Brown & Company, 1993

Selected Legal Resources On-Line

http://www.icrc.org
International Committee of the Red Cross (ICRC)
The full texts of international humanitarian law treaties and commentaries are avail-
able at the ICRC web site. The ICRC also publishes the Geneva Conventions and the
Additional Protocols, which can be ordered from their headquarters in Geneva.

http://www.un.org/law
United Nations
This site contains the texts of international law treaties and information about the
International Court of Justice, the International Criminal Court, and the former
Yugoslavia and Rwanda Tribunals.

http://www.crimesofwar.org
Crimes of War Project
Under construction, this site will develop themes in this book.

Contributors

Eddie Adams is a photojournalist for AP/Wide World Photos. He won the Pulitzer Prize in 1969 for his photo of a street execution in Vietnam.

Ewen Allison is an attorney in Washington, D.C., and is the senior legal researcher for the Crimes of War Project at American University.

Christiane Amanpour is the chief international correspondent for CNN and contributing correspondent for CBS's 60 Minutes. She has won two Columbia DuPont Awards, two Emmys, two Polks, a Peabody, a Sigma Delta Chi Award, a Livingston Award, and a Breakthrough Award.

Jon Lee Anderson, a freelance writer, is the author of Che Guevera: A Revolutionary Life (Grove Press, 1997), and Guerrillas: The Men and Women Fighting Today's Wars (Harper Collins, 1993).

Kenneth Anderson is associate professor of law at Washington College of Law, American University. He was previously general counsel of the Open Society Institute, director of the Human Rights Watch Arms Division, and John Harvey Gregory Lecturer on World Organization at Harvard Law School.

Dmitri Baltermants was a correspondent for Izvestia and photographed the battles of Moscow and Stalingrad and the liberation of Poland. He won recognition abroad only after a 1965 traveling exhibition of his work.

Micha Bar-Am, a photojournalist with Magnum Photos, has covered Israel and international issues since 1956, and has worked as Curator of Photography at the Museum of Tel Aviv since 1977. He has published a retrospective, Israel—A Photobiography (Simon & Schuster, 1998).

Nomi Bar-Yaacov is a correspondent with Agence France-Presse Jerusalem and author of Human Rights in States of Emergency Under the European Convention of Human Rights (Council of Europe, 1990).

M. Cherif Bassiouni is a professor of law and director of the International Criminal Justice and Weapons Control Center at DePaul University in Chicago. He chaired the UN Commission of Experts on the former Yugoslavia, and is the author of Crimes Against Humanity in International Criminal Law (Martinus Nijhoff, 1998).

Maud S. Beelman is currently director of the International Consortium of Investigative Journalists at the Center for Public Integrity. She covered the recent conflicts in the former Yugoslavia for the Associated Press.

Nina Berman is a photographer with Sipa Press. In January of 1993, she traveled to Croatia and Bosnia to document the rape of Muslim women for Newsweek. She has received two 1994 Picture of the Year Awards.

Robert Block is Africa correspondent for The Wall Street Journal. He has won numerous awards for his reporting including the 1996 Amnesty International Press Award.

Alexandra Boulat is a photographer with Sipa Press.

Jeremy Bowen is Middle East correspondent for the BBC and has covered most major international stories since 1980, reporting from some 70 countries. He was awarded the Silver Nymph at the Monte Carlo TV Festival for his coverage of the siege of Mostar in 1993.

Colette Braeckman is the Africa editor for Le Soir (Brussels). She is the author of Terreur Africaina (Fayard, 1996), Histoire d'un Genocide (Fayard, 1994), and Le Dinosaure: le Zaire Mobutu (Fayard, 1991).

Didier Bregnard is a photographer with the International Committee of the Red Cross (ICRC).

Victoria Brittain is the deputy foreign editor for The Guardian (London) and the author of Death of Dignity: Angola's Civil War (Pluto, 1998).

David Burnett is a photographer and cofounder of Contact Press Images. He has covered conflicts including the Vietnam war, the aftermath of the Chilean Coup, and Cambodian refugees. He won the Robert Capa Gold Medal in 1973.

John Burns is a foreign correspondent for The New York Times. He twice won the Pulitzer Prize for international reporting, in 1993 for coverage of Bosnia, and in 1997 for reports on the Taliban regime in Afghanistan. He won the George Polk awards in 1979 and 1997.

Robert Capa was a renowned war photographer who co-founded Magnum Photos in 1947. Famous for his coverage of the Spanish Civil War and WWII, he was killed in 1954 by a landmine while covering Vietnam.

Burrus M. Carnahan is a retired USAF lieutenant colonel. A professorial lecturer in Law at George Washington University, Washington D.C., he was a member of the U.S. delegation to the UN Conventional Weapons Convention conference.

Gilles Caron, a photojournalist, covered the Six-Day War, Vietnam, Biafra, and Northern Ireland in five short years of an examplary career. Caron disappeared in 1970 while covering the Cambodia–Vietnam border at the age of thirty.

Anna Cataldi is a freelance journalist and editor of Letters from Sarajevo (Element, U.K., 1994), Bambini di Guerra (Valle D'Aosta, Italy), and Fifty Years Later (Mondadori, Italy, 1998). In 1998, she was named "Peace Messenger" by the Secretary-General of the UN.

Roger Cohen is Berlin bureau chief of The New York Times and author of Hearts Grown Brutal: Sagas of Sarajevo (Random House, 1998). He shared the Oversees Press Club's Burger Human Rights Award for his reporting on a Bosnian Serb-run concentration camp.

Ernest Cole documented apartheid in South Africa, culminating in the highly acclaimed book House of Bondage (Random House, 1967). A documentary film on his life is currently being produced.

Karim Daher is a photographer with Gamma Liaison. He has covered various conflicts including the war in Lebanon, Liberia, and the former Yugoslavia.

Emma Daly is a freelance journalist who writes for The Observer (London) and the Christian Science Monitor. She has covered conflicts in Europe, Central America, and Africa for The Independent (London) and Reuters.

Manoocher Deghati, a photojournalist, has covered conflicts for ten years for Sipa Press and AFP, specializing in the Middle East.

Reza Deghati is a photojournalist who has worked for Newsweek in Iran, and for Time in the Middle East.

Raymond Depardon is a photojournalist with Magnum Photos and has worked in various countries including Chile, Chad, and Afghanistan. He was awarded the Grand Prix National de la Photographie in 1991. His books include En Afrique (Seuil, 1996) and Return to Vietnam (Verso, 1994).

Hamilton DeSaussure is emeritus professor of law at the University of Akron, Ohio. He held the Stockton Chair in International Law at the Naval War College from 1979 to 1980.

Alan Dorsey is deputy project manager for the Crimes of War Project, and formerly a staff member of the ICRC Delegation to the United Nations in New York.

Corinne Dufka is a photographer with Reuters based in Nairobi, Kenya. She has received a Robert Capa Gold Medal, a World Press Photo Award, a Pictures of the Year award, and the International Women's Media Foundation Courage in Journalism Award.

H. Wayne Elliott is a retired lieutenant colonel for the United States Army. He is a former chief of the international law division at the Judge Advocate General's School, U.S. Army.

Douglas Farah is an investigative reporter for The Washington Post. He won the Sigma Delta Chi award for international reporting in 1988, and the Maria Moor Cabot award for his Latin American reporting in 1995.

Dr. Horst Fischer is academic director of the Institute for International Law of Peace and Armed Conflict at the Ruhr-Universität in Germany, and professor of IHL at Leiden University in the Netherlands. He is also the legal advisor for international affairs for the German Red Cross and is editor of the Yearbook of International Humanitarian Law.

Leonard Freed is a freelance photographer who has covered, among other issues, the Arab-Israeli wars, and post-war Iraq.

Paul Fusco is a photojournalist with Magnum

Photos. He worked as a staff photographer for Look magazine until 1971.

Jean Gaumy, a French photographer with Magnum Photos, has traveled and worked in Europe, Africa, Central America, the Middle East, and Iran.

Tom Gjelten is diplomatic correspondent for National Public Radio and author of Sarajevo Daily: A City and Its Newspaper Under Siege (Harper Collins, 1995). He won the George Polk Award and the Robert F. Kennedy Journalism Award for his reporting on Bosnia.

Robert Kogod Goldman is a professor of law and co-director of the Center for Human Rights and Humanitarian Law at the Washington College of Law, American University. He is first vice president of the Inter-American Commission on Human Rights.

Richard Goldstone is a justice on South Africa's Constitutional Court. He was the first Prosecutor at the International Tribunals for the Former Yugoslavia and Rwanda. He chaired the "Goldstone Commission," which investigated political violence in South Africa.

Thomas Goltz is a journalist and lecturer on post-Soviet and Turkish affairs. He is the author of Azerbaijan Diary (M.E. Sharpe, 1998) and Requiem for a Would-Be Republic: The Rise and Demise of the Former Soviet Republic of Azerbaijan (Isis, Istanbul, 1994).

Christopher Greenwood is a professor at the London School of Economics. He is the author of Command and the Law of Armed Conflict (H.M. Stationery Office, London, 1993).

Joel Greenberg is a reporter in the Jerusalem bureau of The New York Times. He covered the Palestinian uprising for The Jerusalem Post and has also contributed to The New Republic and the Christian Science Monitor.

Philip Jones Griffiths is a photographer with Magnum Photos. He covered the war in Vietnam and his book Vietnam, Inc. (Macmillan, 1971) is considered by many as the most important photographic work about the war. He has also compiled a collection of his photographs into a book entitled Dark Odyssey (Aperture, 1996).

Roy Gutman, director of the Crimes of War Project, and co-editor of this book, covers foreign affairs in the Newsday Washington bureau. He won the 1993 Pulitzer Prize for international reporting for his revelations of concentration camps and other practices of ethnic cleansing in Bosnia, as well as the Polk Award, the Hal Boyle award of the Overseas Press Club, and the Selden Ring Award for investigative reporting. He is the author of Banana Diplomacy (Simon & Schuster, 1987) and A Witness to Genocide (Macmillan, 1993).

Ron Haeberle is a photographer for Time/Life. As a U.S. Army photographer in Vietnam, he documented the My Lai massacre in 1969.

Françoise J. Hampson is a professor at the University of Essex (U.K.) and co-director of its Children and Armed Conflict Unit. She is a member of the UN Sub-Commission on the Prevention of Discrimination and Protection of Minorities, the ICRC expert committee on customary law, and governor of the British Institute of Human Rights.

Sheldon H. Harris, professor of American history emeritus at the California State University, Northridge, is the author of Factories of Death: Japanese Biological Warfare and the American Cover-Up (Routledge, 1994), which has won two scholarly awards.

Florence Hartmann, a journalist with Le Monde in Paris, was their permanent correspondent in the former Yugoslavia from 1989 to 1994. She has a forthcoming book on Slobodan Milosevic and the Yugoslav crisis.

Amira Hass is an Israeli journalist for Ha'aretz in the West Bank and Gaza. She is the author of Drinking the Sea at Gaza: Days and Nights in a Land under Siege (Metropolitan, 1999).

Ron Haviv, associated with Saba Press Photos, has photographed conflicts in Panama, the Persian Gulf, South Africa, and Haiti. His awards include The Leica Medal of Excellence, and the World Press Photo Award in 1992 for his work in the Balkans.

Brooke Hellewell is a graphic designer based in New York City.

Lindsey Hilsum is the diplomatic correspondent for Channel Four News (London), a contributor to the Times Literary Supplement and The New

Statesman, and has made several documentaries. She won the 1996 Amnesty International Human Rights Journalist of the Year Award for her reporting on Rwanda.

Michael H. Hoffman, an attorney, is officer for international humanitarian law for the American Red Cross and a retired lieutenant colonel in the U.S. Army Reserve. He is a faculty member at the International Institute of Humanitarian Law in San Remo, Italy.

Mark Huband, Cairo correspondent for the Financial Times (London), won the U.K. Foreign Correspondent of the Year award, 1991. He is the author of The Liberian Civil War (Cass, 1998) and Warriors of the Prophet: The Struggle for Islam (Westview, 1998).

Henri Huet, a French combat photographer, covered Vietnam and later worked for UPI and the AP. Huet was killed when his helicopter was shot down in Laos in 1971.

Michael Ignatieff, a writer and historian, is the author of Blood and Belonging: Journeys into the New Nationalism (Noonday, 1993), and The Warrior's Honor: Ethnic War and the Modern Conscience (Henry Holt, 1998).

Rikio Imajo is a photographer with the Associated Press based in Tokyo.

Kenneth Jarecke is a photojournalist with Contact Press Images. He was in Beijing, China, during the 1989 Tiananmen events, and also covered Desert Storm during the Gulf War in 1991.

Christian Jennings, a freelance journalist, covered the Rwandan genocide for Reuters and is author of the forthcoming Across the Red River: Four Years of Genocide in Rwanda and Burundi (Victor Gollancz, 1999).

William E. Jones served as an aerial photographer in the Army Air Corps during WWII. During the occupation of Japan, he took low altitude atomic bomb damage photographs of both Hiroshima and Nagasaki. These images are in The National Atomic Museum as well as in the book Picturing the Bomb (Harry N. Abrams, Inc., 1995).

Andree Kaiser, a German photographer with Sipa Press, has covered social and political issues in

Eastern Europe for Reuters, Der Spiegel and Stern magazine. His reportage on the Balkan conflict has been published in Newsday, Newsweek, Epoca, and Paris Match.

Frits Kalshoven is president of the International Fact-Finding Commission. He is a retired professor at Leiden University, served on the Netherlands delegation at the drafting of the 1977 Additional Protocols, and chaired the UN Commission of Experts on the former Yugoslavia. He is the author of Constraints on the Waging of War (Martinus Nijhoff, 1987).

Yunghi Kim is a photographer with Contact Press Images. Her coverage of Rwandan refugees earned her the Overseas Press Club Award and a first prize from the World Press Photo Foundation and has covered the aftermath of the "Comfort Women".

Joseph Koudelka, a photographer with Magnum Photos, won the Robert Capa Gold Medal in 1969 for his coverage of the Russian invasion of Prague. Other awards include the Prix Nadar (1978) and the Grand Prix International Henri Cartier-Bresson (1991).

Daoud Kuttab is director of modern media, Al Quds University, Jerusalem, and co-director of Internews Middle East. In 1997 he received the Committee to Protect Journalists International Press Freedom Award.

Peggy Lampl is project director for the Crimes of War Project. She has been involved in a range of public policy issues and has served as a Deputy Assistant Secretary of State (U.S.) and as executive director of The Children's Defense Fund and the League of Women Voters.

Charles Lane is the editor of The New Republic. He is a former general editor of Newsweek and has served as its Berlin bureau chief. He received a Citation for Excellence from the Overseas Press Club for his coverage of the former Yugoslavia.

Annie Leibovitz is a photographer with Contact Press Images. Known for her portrait photography in Rolling Stone and Vanity Fair, she went on several personal assignments to photograph Sarajevo and Rwanda from 1993 to 1994.

Alex Levac is staff photographer at Ha'aretz (Jerusalem). He received the 1993 Rita Poretzky

Award for Photography from the Tel Aviv Museum of Art and is author of An Eye to Zion (Am Oved, 1996).

Howard S. Levie is an adjunct professor of International Law at the Naval War College and professor emeritus of law at the St. Louis University Law School. He drafted the Korean Armistice Agreement and served as chief of the International Affairs Division, Office of The Judge Advocate General. He is the author of Terrorism in War: The Law of War Crimes (Oceania, 1993) and Levie on the Law of War (Naval War College, 1998).

Gideon Levy, a columnist for Ha'aretz (Tel Aviv), served as press aide to Israeli Prime Minister Shimon Peres from 1978 to 1982. He won the Israeli Human Rights Award from the Association for Civil Rights in Israel in 1996.

Lee Lockwood is a photojournalist with Black Star photo agency and has contributed to Life magazine and other publications. He is the author of Castro's Cuba, Cuba's Fidel (Westview, 1980).

Paul Lowe, an English freelance photographer with Magnum Photos, has covered international events in eastern Europe and the Middle East. His awards include World Press Photo Foundation Photographer of the Year in 1992, as well as the 1996 Global News Picture Award.

Peter Maass, a freelance writer, reported from the former Yugoslavia for The Washington Post. He is the author of Love Thy Neighbor, A Story of War (Knopf, 1996), which won the 1996 Los Angeles Times Book Prize and the 1996 Overseas Press Club Book Prize.

Sean Maguire is chief correspondent in Warsaw for Reuters News Agency, and covers Kosovo and other eastern European issues. He has reported on the Gulf War and the conflicts in the former Yugoslavia for Reuters Television and News Service.

Steve McCurry, a photographer with Magnum Photos, has covered conflicts in Asia, Afghanistan, and the Middle East. He won the Robert Capa Gold Medal in 1980 and has worked for National Geographic. He is the photographer of The Imperial Way (Houghton Mifflin, 1985).

Don McCullin is a photographer with Contact Press Images. His Sleeping With Ghosts (Aperture, 1998) is a collection of his photographs spanning thirty years of coverage of armed conflicts around the world.

Susan Meiselas is a photographer with Magnum Photos who covered Latin America in the 1980s. She is the author of Kurdistan: In the Shadow of History (Random House, 1997). Her awards include the Robert Capa Gold Medal in 1979 and the Leica Award for Excellence in 1982.

Sheryl A. Mendez is the photo editor/researcher for the Crimes of War project. Between 1989 and 1998, she worked for Magnum Photos developing and researching editorial stories and projects. Currently, she is a freelance journalist/photographer working on documentary projects mainly in the Middle East.

Theodor Meron is the Charles L. Denison Professor at the New York University Law School, a member of the ICRC committee of experts on customary law, and served on the U.S. delegation to the Rome conference for an international criminal court. He is the author of Human Rights and Humanitarian Norms As Customary Law (Oxford University Press, 1991) and Bloody Constraint: War and Chivalry in Shakespeare (Oxford University Press, 1998)

Ed Miles is an associate director of the Vietnam Veterans of America Foundation (VVAF). He was project director for the VVAF's Cambodian Prosthetics Project, has worked in the former Yugoslavia on democracy building programs, and on the International Campaign to Ban Landmines for which VVAF shared the 1997 Nobel Peace Prize.

Rich Mkhondo is a correspondent in Washington, D.C. for Independence Newspapers in South Africa. He is the author of Reporting South Africa (Heinemann, 1993) and a forthcoming book on post-apartheid life in South Africa.

Etienne Montes is a photographer who has covered conflicts in Spain, El Salvador, Nicaragua, Guatemala, Honduras, Cuba, Chilé, Peru, South Africa, Lebanon, and Ireland.

Benny Morris is a professor of history at Ben-Gurion University, Beersheba, Israel. He is author of Israel's Border Wars, 1949-1956: Arab Infiltration, Israeli Retaliation, and the

Countdown to the Suez War *(Oxford University Press, 1997) and the forthcoming* Righteous Victims: A History of the Arab-Zionist Conflict *(Knopf, 1999).*

Caryle Murphy *is a reporter for* The Washington Post. *She won the Pulitzer Prize for international reporting and a George Polk Award for coverage of the Iraqi occupation of Kuwait in 1991.*

Karma Nabulsi *is a lecturer and research fellow at Oxford University. She is the author of* Traditions of War: Occupation, Resistance and the Law *(Oxford University Press, 1999) and "An Ideology of War not Peace: Jus in Bello and the Grotian Tradition of War" (Journal of Political Ideologies, 1999).*

James Nachtwey, *a photojournalist, won the World Press Photo Award in 1992 and 1994, the Magazine Photographer of the Year Award six times, and the Robert Capa Gold Medal in 1983, 1984, 1986, and 1994. His work is published in the retrospective* Deeds of War *(Thames & Hudson, 1989).*

Nanzer *is a photographer with Sipa Press.*

Elizabeth Neuffer *served as European bureau chief for the* Boston Globe. *She is Edward R. Murrow Press Fellow at the Council on Foreign Relations and is working on a book on post-war justice issues in Bosnia and Rwanda.*

Don Oberdorfer *is journalist in residence at the Johns Hopkins University's Nitze School of Advanced International Studies. He is the author of* The Two Koreas *(Addison Wesley, 1997) and* Tet: A History of the 1968 Tet Offensive in Vietnam *(Da Capo, 1984).*

Diane F. Orentlicher *is a professor of law and Director of the War Crimes Research Office at the Washington College of Law, American University. She is the author of "Settling Accounts: The Duty to Prosecute Human Rights Violations of a Prior Regime" (Yale University Law Review, 1991).*

Emmanuel Ortiz *is a freelance photographer who has covered conflicts in Peru, Chile, Bolivia, Argentina, Croatia, Bosnia and Macedonia. He is the author of* Ex-Yougoslavie *(Florent-Massot, 1996).*

William A. Orme, Jr. *is a reporter for* The New York Times *in Jerusalem. He served as executive director of the Committee to Protect Journalists from 1993 to 1998. He is the author of* A Culture of Collusion: An Inside Look at the Mexican Press *(University of Miami North-South Press, 1997), and won the First Amendment Award from the Society of Professional Journalists in 1998.*

Ramazan Ozturk *works as a freelance photographer for* Time *magazine and for the daily* Sabah *(Turkey). He has covered the Iran-Iraq War, the Halabja gas attack, the wars in Bosnia, and many important events in Turkey since 1974.*

Gilles Peress *is a photographer for Magnum Photos who has covered conflicts in Northern Ireland, Iran, Turkish immigrant workers in Germany, and more recently, Bosnia and Rwanda. His books include* Telex Persan *(Scalo, 1994/ 1998),* Farewell to Bosnia *(Scalo, 1994), and* The Silence *(Scalo, 1995).*

Mark Perry *is an associate director at the Vietnam Veterans of America Foundation, which shared the 1997 Nobel Peace Prize. He is the author of* A Fire in Zion *(William Morrow, 1994), and* Conceived in Liberty *(Viking, 1997).*

Photo Archive Group, *headed by Chris Riley and Doug Niven, was established as a non-profit organization to preserve the documentary materials found at the S-21 secret prison operated by the Pol Pot regime in Phnom Penh from mid-1975 through the end of 1978. S-21 was later transformed into the Tuol Sleng Museum of Genocide. Negatives were selected and compiled in the book* The Killing Fields *(Twin Palms, 1996).*

Nicole Pope *is a correspondent based in Turkey for* Le Monde *(France). She is is the co-author of* Turkey Unveiled: Ataturk and After *(Overlook, 1998), and* History of Modern Turkey *(Overlook, 1999). She worked for the ICRC in Iraq during the Iran-Iraq War and in Lebanon after the 1982 Israeli invasion.*

Peter Pringle *is a correspondent for The* Independent *(U.K.) and served as bureau chief for its Washington, New York and Moscow bureaus. He is author of* Chernobyl: The End of the Nuclear Dream *(Pan, London, 1986) and* Cornered: Big Tobacco at the Bar of Justice *(Henry Holt, 1998).*

Gaby Rado is the foreign affairs correspondent for ITN's Channel Four News in the U.K. He received a 1998 Amnesty International Award, and shared Amnesty's 1996 award for coverage of Srebrenica.

Jonathan C. Randal was a foreign correspondent for The Washington Post from 1969 to 1998. He is the author of After Such Knowledge, What Forgiveness? My Encounters in Kurdistan (Farrar, Straus, Giroux 1997).

Steven R. Ratner is a professor of law at the University of Texas and a Fulbright Senior Scholar and Asser Research fellow at the T.M.C. Asser Institute in The Hague. He is coauthor of Accountability for Human Rights Atrocities in International Law: Beyond the Nuremberg Legacy (Oxford University Press, 1997), and a member of the UN's expert group investigating potential prosecution of Khmer Rouge officials for their atrocities in Cambodia.

Erich Rathfelder is a German journalist for Die Tageszeitung (Berlin) who has reported extensively on the conflict in Yugoslavia. He is the author of Sarajevo und Danach (Beck-Verlag, 1998) and Krieg in Europa (Reinbek, 1992).

Barry Renfrew is Moscow bureau chief for the Associated Press. He covered the Soviet intervention in Afghanistan and conflicts in New Caledonia, Pakistan, southern Africa and Russia. He won three awards from the Associated Press Managing Editors Association for his work in Afghanistan, South Korea and Chechnya.

Pierre Richard covers the Montreal city desk for the Journal De Montreal in Canada and served as the Journal's Moscow correspondent. He won the 1997 Bourse de l'éditeur prize for his documentary on the Sudanese slave market.

David Rieff, coeditor of this book, is a freelance author who has contributed to Foreign Affairs, Harper's, The New Republic, New York Review of Books, The Times Literary Supplement, The New Yorker, and other publications. He is the author of Slaughterhouse: Bosnia and the Failure of the West (Simon & Schuster, 1995).

Patrick Robert is a freelance photographer with Sygma Photo Agency who has covered the Palestinian uprising in the Israeli occupied territories, the war in Afghanistan, the revolution in

Romania, the Soviet Union, and wars in Somalia, Libya, Bosnia, Georgia, Rwanda and Liberia.

Adam Roberts is the Montague Burton Professor of International Relations at Oxford University. He is author of United Nations, Divided World: The UN's Roles in International Relations (Oxford University Press, 1994) and is the coeditor of Documents on the Laws of War (Oxford University Press, 1999).

Gwynne Roberts, independent film director, produces documentaries for Channel Four News, the BBC, CBS's 60 Minutes, and others. In 1998 he released Saddam's Killing Fields, a documentary on the condition of the Kurds in Iraq. In 1992 he received an Overseas Press Club Award for Wings of Death, a landmark documentary establishing the gassing of the Iraqi Kurds .

Arturo Robles is a photographer who arrived in El Salvador in 1980 as a stringer for Associated Press. He has covered conflicts in Nicaragua, the military invasion of Panama, and now works in Colombia.

George Rodrigue is managing editor of the Press-Enterprise (Riverside, California). A former Washington correspondent and European bureau chief for The Dallas Morning News, he shared the 1994 Pulitzer Prize for international reporting.

A. P. V. Rogers, OBE, is a retired major general in the British Army and a recognized expert on the laws of war. He received the 1997 Paul Reuter prize for Law on the Battlefield (Manchester University Press, 1996).

David Rohde is a reporter for The New York Times and author of Endgame: The Betrayal and Fall of Srebrenica (Farrar, Strauss, Giroux, 1998). His investigation of mass graves at Srebrenica for the Christian Science Monitor won the 1996 Pulitzer Prize for international reporting as well as the Sigma Delta Chi and Overseas Press Club Awards.

Tim Ross, a photographer, is a 1999 Soros Foundation grant recipient documenting issues of heroin use in Colombia and actively works with street children there. He has covered numerous conflicts including the Falklands, Panama, Grenada, Nicaragua, and El Salvador.

Peter Rowe is a professor in the Department of

Law, the University of Lancaster in England. He is the editor of The Gulf War 1990-91 in International and English Law (Routledge, 1993).

Elizabeth Rubin is a contributing editor to The Forward (Manhattan) and Harper's magazine. She has also contributed to The New Yorker and The New York Times Magazine. She received an Overseas Press Club Citation for Excellence for reporting on mercenaries for Harper's.

John Ryle is a columnist for The Guardian (London) and consultant to the UN, EU, and nongovernmental organizations in Africa.

Sebastião Salgado is a photographer for Contact Press Images. His work has covered various documentary subjects and he has published various books including Other Americans (Pantheon, 1986), Sahel: L'Homme en Detresse (Prims Presse, 1986), An Uncertain Grace (Aperture, 1990) and Workers (Aperture, 1993).

Kyoichi Sawada was a photojournalist best known for his photos of Southeast Asia. He won the Pulitzer Prize in 1966, a World Press Photo contest Grand prize, and the Overseas Press Club Award. After his death in Cambodia in 1970, he was awarded the Robert Capa Gold Medal.

Sydney H. Schanberg won the 1976 Pulitzer Prize for his New York Times reporting on the fall of Cambodia. He also won two Overseas Press Club Awards, two George Polk Memorial Awards, two Newspaper Guild Front Page Awards, and the Sigma Delta Chi Award for distinguished journalism. He is the author of The Death and Life of Dith Pran (Viking, 1985), the basis for the film The Killing Fields.

Serge Schmemann is on special assignment to The New York Times and has served as its bureau chief in Moscow, Bonn, and Jerusalem. He wrote Echoes of a Native Land: Two Centuries of a Russian Village (Knopf, 1997). He won the 1991 Pulitzer Prize for international reporting for his coverage of the reunification of Germany, and two awards from the Overseas Press Club for his stories on the Soviet Union and Germany.

Kurt Schork is a war correspondent for Reuters News Agency, and has covered conflicts in Afghanistan, Albania, Bosnia, Cambodia, Chechnya, Iraq, Kashmir, Kosovo, South Africa, Sri Lanka, and Turkey.

David "Chim" Seymour was one of the founding members of Magnum Photos in 1947. His work covered political events in Europe, especially the Spanish Civil War. He was killed in 1956 by Egyptian machine-gun fire.

Thom Shanker is the assistant Washington editor for The New York Times. At The Chicago Tribune, he was foreign editor, Moscow bureau chief, and, while Senior European correspondent covered the war in Bosnia from 1992 to 1994.

William Shawcross is a freelance journalist who has covered Eastern Europe and Southeast Asia. He is author of The Quality of Mercy: Cambodia, The Holocaust, and Modern Conscience (Simon & Schuster, 1984), and Sideshow: Kissinger, Nixon, and the Destruction of Cambodia (Simon & Schuster, 1987).

Jean-Marie Simon is an attorney in Washington, D.C., and serves on the Advisory Committee for Human Rights Watch/Americas Division. She is the author of Guatemala: Eternal Spring, Eternal Tyranny (W.W. Norton, 1988).

Lewis M. Simons is a freelance writer for National Geographic and other publications. He shared the 1986 Pulitzer Prize for international reporting, and has won a George Polk Award, three Overseas Press Club Awards, and an Edward R. Murrow Award.

Patrick J. Sloyan is the senior correspondent for Newsday's Washington bureau. He received the 1992 Pulitzer Prize for international reporting, and has won the American Society of Newspaper Editors', the George Polk, and Raymond Clapper Awards for outstanding journalism.

Frank Smyth is a freelance journalist who covered the El Salvador conflict for CBS News Radio, and The Economist. He has served as an investigative consultant to Human Rights Watch and Amnesty International.

Cpl. Graham Spark was a photographer in the British Royal Air Force for fifteen years. He was stationed in Sarajevo in 1997 to document the work of multinational soldiers traveling through Bosnia. He is currently working on a retrospective.

Dr. Heike Spieker is an associate professor at the Institute for International Law of Peace and Armed Conflict in Bochum, Germany. She is author of The Customary Law Protection of the Natural Environment in Times of International Armed Conflict (UVB-Universitätsverlag, Bochum, 1992).

Chris Steele-Perkins is a photographer with Magnum Photos covering conflict and relief issues. He has received the Tom Hopkinson Prize for British Photojournalism, the Oscar Barnack Prize, and the Robert Capa Gold Medal.

Alexandra Stiglmayer was a writer for Time magazine and is the author of Mass Rape: The War Against Women in Bosnia-Herzegovina (University of Nebraska Press, 1994.) She is currently the spokesperson for the Office of the High Representative in Sarajevo.

Tom Stoddart is a photographer with IPG and Matrix who has covered events including the Israeli invasion of Beirut, the fall of the Berlin Wall, and the refugee crisis in Rwanda. He has won the Nikon Press Photographer of the Year Award in 1990 and 1991.

Eric Stover is the director of the Human Rights Center and an adjunct professor of public health at the University of California at Berkeley, and served as executive director of Physicians for Human Rights. He is the coauthor (with Gilles Peress) of The Graves: Srebrenica and Vukovar (Scalo, 1998).

Jeff Streeper has designed Vietnam: The Land We Never Knew by Geoffrey Clifford (Chronicle Books, 1989), Annie Leibovitz 1970-1990 by Annie Leibovitz (Harper Perennial, 1991) and A Simpler Way by Margaret J. Wheatley and Myron Kellner-Rogers (Berrett-Koehler, 1996).

Anthony Suau has been a Time contract photographer since 1990. His coverage of famine in Ethiopia earned him the Pulitzer Prize in 1984. Other awards include the World Press Photo Foundation Photo of the Year, and Magazine Photographer of the Year in 1994.

Terence Taylor is the assistant director for the International Institute for Strategic Studies in London. He is the author of Escaping the Prison of the Past: Rethinking Arms Control and Non-proliferation Measures (Stanford University,

1996). He served as the United Kingdom's commissioner on the UN Special Commission on Iraq.

Larry Towell, is a photographer represented by Magnum Photos. His honors include the World Press Photo Award, the Canon Photoessayist Prize, the W. Eugene Smith Prize and the Oscar Barnack Prize. Recent books include El Salvador (DoubleTake/Norton, 1997) and Then Palestine (Marval, 1998; Aperture, 1999).

David C. Turnley is a photographer with The Detroit Free Press. He has covered conflicts in Armenia, Tiananmen Square, and the Gulf War. His books include In Times of War and Peace (Abbeville, 1997). He received the Overseas Press Club Robert Capa Gold Medal for his photographs of Bosnian refugees.

David Turns is a barrister and lecturer in law at the University of Liverpool in England. He is the editor of International Law and Espionage (Martinus Nijhoff, 1995, begun by the late Dr. J. Kish).

Lawrence Weschler is a staff writer for The New Yorker. He is a two-time winner of the George Polk Award and 1998 winner of the Lannan Literary Award. He is the author of A Miracle, A Universe: Settling Accounts with Torturers (University of Chicago Press, 1998), Calamities of Exile (University of Chicago Press, 1998), and the forthcoming Vermeer in Bosnia (Pantheon, 1999).

Marita Vihervuori is a Finnish journalist with the Austrian Press Agency. She has written eight books on Iran and Libya, including Iran: Maa Mullahin Varjossa Allahin Nimeen (Otava, Helsinki, 1989). Her next book is on the fall of Yugoslavia.

Ed Vulliamy is a U.S. and international correspondent for The Observer (London). His prizes include: British Press Awards, International Reporter of the Year (1992 and 1996); Amnesty International Award for newspaper journalism (1992); James Cameron Memorial Award (1994), and "What the Papers Say" Foreign Correspondent of the Year (1992). He wrote Seasons in Hell: Understanding Bosnia's War (Simon & Schuster, 1994).

Shi Young, along with James Yin, is the author of The Rape of Nanking: An Undeniable History in Photographs (Triumph, 1997).

Acknowledgments

This book is that rarest of works, breathed into being by an enormous number of people who agreed it was urgently needed. For our editors, legal advisers, expert readers, and, most of all, our writers, who worked for a pittance and suffered through double editing and repeated requests for rewrites, it was clearly a labor of love, and there is no way to thank them adequately. At the same time, we are deeply grateful to the individuals and institutions who provided the funding and facilities to do the job.

Herbert and Marion Sandler and The Sandler Family Supporting Foundation quickly saw the potential and stepped forward with the funds that enabled us to launch the project. The Ford Foundation, through the efforts of Larry Cox, our program officer, provided the rest of the budget, permitting completion in the shortest possible time.

Sanford J. Ungar, dean of the American University School of Communication, graciously provided an office and every possible form of administrative support with the help of assistant dean, Patrick Martin. Claudio Grossman, dean of AU's Washington College of Law, enthusiastically supported the involvement by WCL's unique faculty. Professor Diane Orentlicher threw herself behind the project and, aided by the WCL War Crimes Research Office and a grant from the Open Society Institute, organized a conference in October 1996 that helped determine our agenda; she suggested authors, critiqued plans, and closely supervised a large portion of the articles. WCL Professor Kenneth Anderson took on the enormous task of legal editing, and Professor Robert Kogod Goldman was a source of solid advice throughout. The War Crimes office with OSI funding sponsored the legal research by Ewen Allison, an indefatigable WCL graduate who put himself on call around the clock and had the assistance of Deans' Fellows, Mair McCafferty and C. Jeffrey Tibbels.

Eric Stover, former executive director of Physicians for Human Rights, organized a critical second conference in April 1997 at the Human Rights Center he heads at Berkeley. He brought clarity of purpose to every strategic moment and played a central role in obtaining funding. Aryeh Neier, President of the Open Society Institute gave wise counsel at both conferences, offered moral support when it was most needed, and also critiqued a number of articles. Anna Cataldi, the Italian writer, assembled the journalists, photographers, and legal scholars for our first brainstorming session and prodded and promoted our efforts from beginning to end.

It was essential in a book combining law and journalism that we strive to meet the standards of both professions. Maj. Gen. (ret.) A. P. V. Rogers of the British Army, our consultant on military law, undertook a detailed legal review. Louise Doswald-Beck, Urs Boegli, and Jean-Francois Berger of the International Committee of the Red Cross read the text and made useful suggestions. Lt. Col. Scott Morris of the U.S. Judge Advocate-General corps and Lt. Col. (ret.) H. Wayne Elliott, a former chief of the JAG international law division, gave us valuable criticism and encouragement. Jim Toedtman, *Newsday's* Washington bureau chief, made numerous helpful suggestions. Thom Shanker of *The New York Times* edited the three articles on sexual violence and read the final text. Views expressed in the articles are those of the authors and do not represent the position of any government, institution, or organization, nor our expert readers. Editorial judgments are the responsibility of the writers and editors.

Tremendous energy and time went into photo-editing and design. Sheryl Mendez broke off work on two projects in the Middle East to join the project as photo editor and researcher, a task to which she brought visual and political astuteness, moral commitment, and astonishing drive. Brooke Hellewell, our unflappable deputy design editor, was a key player, whose formidable design and organizational skills were matched by her stamina.

Peggy Lampl, our long-suffering project manager, defused every crisis, and played a key role in editing. One of our luckiest breaks was the appearance of Alan Dorsey, former librarian for the ICRC in New York, who had begun graduate studies at AU. Serving as deputy project manager, he brought invaluable experience and knowledge of IHL, and imposed order on the project and our office.

Ron Goldfarb, our devoted literary agent, stayed on as general counsel in future project activities. Tabitha Griffin, our editor at W. W. Norton, gave us constructive criticism and enthusiastic support. Carole Kismaric advised us at crucial early moments on budget and organization. Professor Brad Blitz of Lewis & Clark College, Pat Watson, Evelyn Leopold of Reuters, Ian Williams of *The Nation*, Chuck Lane of *The New Republic*, Tom Gjelten of National Public Radio, and Michael Muskal and Jim Dooley of *Newsday*, provided wise guidance. W. Hays Parks, Special Assistant to the Judge Advocate General, and Professor Steve Ratner, of the University of Texas at Austin, gave us welcome moral support and timely legal guidance.

Newsday editor Anthony Marro, A.M.E. Les Payne, foreign editor Tim Phelps, and Washington news editor Anne Hoy enthusiastically backed the book and tolerated my absences. And on a personal note, truly special thanks go to my patient wife, Betsy, and daughter, Caroline, who let me give up practically every evening, weekend, and vacation day for eighteen months.

Every participant and every outside supporter made a difference. I hope each will look on the finished product with pride, bearing in mind that the educational effort to be built around the book is still a work in progress.

—*Roy Gutman*

Crimes of war : what the
public should know / Roy
Gutman and David Rieff,
editors.